Created and Directed by Hans Höfer

INSIGHT GUIDES
Java

Original text by Peter Hutton
Revised by Jeremy Allan
Photography by Luca Invernizzi Tettoni and others

Editorial Director: Geoffrey Eu

HOUGHTON MIFFLIN COMPANY

APA PUBLICATIONS

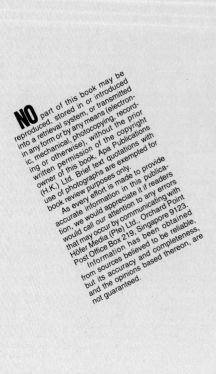
Java

First Edition (Reprint)
© **1993 APA PUBLICATIONS (HK) LTD**
All Rights Reserved
Printed in Singapore by Höfer Press Pte. Ltd

Distributed in the United States by:	Distributed in Canada by:	Distributed in the UK & Ireland by:	Worldwide distribution enquiries:
Houghton Mifflin Company	**Thomas Allen & Son**	**GeoCenter International UK Ltd**	**Höfer Communications Pte Ltd**
2 Park Street	390 Steelcase Road East	The Viables Center, Harrow Way	38 Joo Koon Road
Boston, Massachusetts 02108	Markham, Ontario L3R 1G2	Basingstoke, Hampshire RG22 4BJ	Singapore 2262
ISSN: 1064-7902	ISSN: 1064-7902		
ISBN: 0-395-65771-7	ISBN: 0-395-65771-7	ISBN: 9-62421-174-4	ISBN: 9-62421-174-4

Dear Reader,

I f the Indonesian archipelago is like a string of pearls strewn across the tropical seas, then Java is the clasp that holds the string together. Here is the home to over 100 million people and also to Java Man, one of the world's earliest keys to the evolution of the human species. Here too, is a land of captivating physical beauty, possessing a deep cultural heritage. Java's dance and textile traditions are famous throughout the world, as are her ancient temples and royal palaces. In Java, the elements of the past are so gloriously intertwined with the present that any visitor who values the history and culture of a place cannot but lick his lips at the prospect of a richly satisfying experience.

Insight Guide: Java is unique for several reasons. The original _Java_ was the second in a series that now spans over 170 titles. It was first published in 1974, close on the heels of our groundbreaking _Guide to Bali_, which proved that there was a vast, untapped market for thought-provoking guide books that educated, informed and entertained – and featured great photography to boot. _Java_ was conceived as a companion to the Bali guide and together, they formed the basis for the trademark _Insight Guides_ style of "covering" a destination from top to toe, from the main roads to the back roads, and in many cases, going to places where there were no roads at all. As a consequence of this commitment to a concept, readers of our books have certain expectations about a place, and we at Apa take great pleasure in both creating and meeting those expectations.

Hutton journeying in Java.

It has been more than two decades since I made a comprehensive journey of discovery to Java together with the late **Peter Hutton**, a multi-faceted talent who went through various careers as cook, stockman, film extra and advertising man before his metamorphosis into a writer of incomparable grace, style and sensitivity. Eighteen months and 17,500 kilometres later (in an island only 1,100 kilometres long), the first edition of _Java_ rolled off the presses. The book was an immediate success and was adopted by the Indonesian government as the official guide to Java. It took a detailed and revealing look at what was then a little-known and diversely intricate island. _Java_ was not, of course, just a two-man show. The voyage through Java became an enduring love affair with a unique and extraordinarily resilient culture. In the course of our extensive and intensive travels, we must have met half of Java's population.

Since that first trip, Apa has revisited Java many times, revising the guide and publishing more titles on Indonesia in the process. In that time, the forces of change have left their indelible mark on the island, but the Java of the 1990s still holds the same exotic fascination for a new generation of travellers.

Tettoni in focus.

This completely revamped edition marks *Java's* return to the bookstands after an absence of several years. Its appearance has been long overdue. In many ways, it is a tribute to its author. Peter Hutton's inspired original text had an elegant, almost poetic quality to it. His fluid, descriptive style has lost little of its relevance and certainly none of its appeal. Jakarta-based journalist **Jeremy Allan** was given the delicate task of placing a 1990s perspective to the text. Allan and well-known travel photographer **Luca Invernizzi Tettoni** journeyed across Java to ensure a visually representative and factually accurate book. Several Apa regulars also made important pictorial contributions to *Java*, including **Gorazd Vilhar**, **Kal Muller**, **Lyle Lawson** and **Jill Gocher**.

More and more people are discovering the joys of travelling to Java. The numbers have increased progressively over the years, albeit not in proportion to those visiting neighbouring Bali, which – not surprisingly – remains the most popular destination in Indonesia. Bali is indeed magical, while Java's charms are more subtle. Java is a place that appeals to people who thrive on strong human involvement and who understand that here, the dimension of time has no meaning without a basic appreciation of history and culture. Java is a special place for special people. It *is* Indonesia.

Hans Höfer
Publisher

REKLAME
ANTARA

JL. KRAMAT BARU DEPAN CTC.

Mengerjakan :
- STEMPEL
- BADGE-VANDEL
- LENCANA
- SLIDE-PLAKAT

Leter: PLASTIK, KUNINGAN

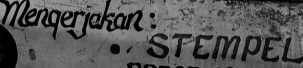

CONTENTS

History

People & Culture

Places

Maps

TRAVEL TIPS

**For detailed Information
See Page 287**

rahayu *Republik Indonesia*

JOKOTOLE-KMP. TRUNOJ

A Chance To Be Personal

If the soul of Java could be captured in oils, the result would be subtle and great: a balance of light and shade, nuances of warmth and softness amid brush-strokes with an edge of honed steel; there would be highlights of diamond brilliance, green flowing into burning gold, and ruby fire touching fathomless azure.

But to begin with there is a clean canvas and a preliminary sketch of a restless, contradictory subject.

The sketch is of an island lying 6 to 9 degrees below the equator, more than 12,000 km from London, 17,000 km from New York, and 7,300 km from Tokyo. An island which is the fifth largest in the Indonesian archipelago after Kalimantan, Sumatra, Irian Jaya and Sulawesi. Overlaid on a map of Europe the archipelago stretches from the west coast of Eire to the Ukraine and Sevastopol in the east, from Berlin in the north to Belgrade and Bucharest in the south, covering an area of more than 10 million sq km…and even though much of the archipelago is warm sea and ocean, the total land mass is the size of Mexico, and Java the size of Greece.

That is the bird's-eye view. As you draw closer, as the outline of Java assumes a palpable third dimension, the quirks and delights of a beautiful island make themselves apparent and reveal its panorama, through time and space, of history, culture and people.

Java is people. Including the island of Madura there are more than 115 million of them in an area of 133,000 sq km (the size of England), representing an average density of roughly 850 per sq km, or more than twice that of Holland or Japan. There are more than 9 million official residents in Jakarta, with an undetermined number of unregistered inhabitants, and over 2 million in Bandung and an estimated 4 million in Surabaya, but fewer than 25 other cities in Java have more than 100,000 inhabitants. About 85 percent of the population live in rural and semi-rural areas, with 60 percent of the work force engaged in agriculture.

Not everyone is "Javanese." In the uplands of West Java the majority of the population is Sundanese; the Javanese proper come from Central Java and a part of East Java; and the Madurese come from the island of Madura, though many now live in East Java. Each group has a different heritage in customs, culture and language; although Bahasa Indonesia, the Indonesian language, is the lingua franca throughout the island, in many small towns and villages day to day communication is still carried out in Sundanese, Javanese and Madurese.

Coming to terms with Java means coming to terms with people, and in Java, perhaps more than in any place else in the world, the

Preceding pages: Hamengkubuwono X, present Sultan of Yogyakarta, poses with his wife; Candi Sewu is part of the spectacular temple complex at Prambanan; circumcision ceremony at Cirebon; hawking wares in Surabaya. **Left**, watchful in Yogya.

travel experience offers the chance to be personal.

Java is like a hot bath. You can jump in and scald yourself, and shriek. Or you can ease in adjusting to the warmth, until there is nothing to do but luxuriate and let the world go by.

The people of Java do things with a "we" consciousness. There is a strong sense of community, of sharing, of warm involvement with the lives of others. The notion of "an Englishman's home is his castle," or the Western obsession with privacy, are foreign to Java. The average Westerner, enmeshed in a private world, also shrinks from physical contact. The Javanese do not. A seat meant for two will always take three, buttock to thigh. It doesn't matter. Proximity means friendliness and warmth; people are people.

Outside of the larger towns, personal contact becomes even more vital and apparent in its expression. The arrival of a foreigner is an entertainment, an event which adds spice and flavour to an ordinary day. It is something else to talk about. You'll be greeted with shrill cries of "Belanda! Belanda!" (which originally meant "Hollander," and now applies to any paleface); half a hundred children envelop your car; dozens of eyes fix on you as you tuck into a plate of *nasi goreng* (fried rice) at a food stall. Giggles, cheekiness and laughter. Sometimes, tired and fretful after the rigours of a journey, you may feel like screaming. Having withstood the noisy overtures, you will find it easy to slip into the life of the community and find warmth, generosity and friendship in the most unexpected circumstances. Java is people.

Java is also a wonderful place for the tourist, the traveller and the explorer. Exploration, in fact, is another aspect of the island's charm, another segment of the chance it offers to be self-indulgently personal, for there are discoveries to be made which will titillate the palate of even the most jaded, world-weary voyager.

An island of great and varied beauty, a treasure of historic and outstanding temples, a casket of cultural gems, Java is full of surprises, not the least of which is the realisation that the outside world knows little about what it has to offer. There are dozens of ancient temples and monuments, there are heavy jungles and savannah, boisterous coastlines and manicured *padi*-fields, majestic stands of bamboo and groves of coconut palms, mangrove swamps and high plateaux on which the temperatures can plummet to freezing-point, and a long line of mountain peaks, crater lakes and smouldering volcanoes.

Culturally, Java is a giant *pot-pourri*. There is a repertoire of dance, drama and comedy which draws its inspiration from Hindu epics thousands of years old, from the exploits of Islamic warriors, and from tales of ancient Javanese heroes; there are trance rituals whose origins are as misty as mankind's own beginnings; there are puppets in leather and wood who entrance local audiences through all-night performances; and there is a music of gongs and chimes

Gamelan **music is an integral part of Javanese culture.**

which is as glistening and fluid as quicksilver, yet as textured as the face of the land.

It is not a forced culture. Older than Java's memory, it is as relevant now, in the continuum of living, as it was yesterday or a thousand years ago. This sense of immediacy and timelessness also animates the work of Java's artisans and craftsmen: the woodcarvers, the waxers and dyers of *batik* cloth, the potters and silversmiths, and even the journeyman painters who decorate the island's three-wheeled pedicabs The survival of these traditions (not merely intact, but aglow with vitality) through the turbulent years of this century says much about the strength of Java's spirit.

Java's ability to absorb outside influences, and to reshape them for use within the context of its own needs and tastes, is as old as the island's recorded history. New arts and interests of Western origin are increasingly evident, and many have already assumed a Java-nese veneer and have taken their place alongside the older forms with little or no conflict.

An island of such depth and complexity as Java naturally has a darker side to its personality. No country in the world, after hundreds of years of domination by a foreign power, has ever been able to achieve social and economic perfection in a mere 45 years. And, it would be dishonest to suggest that over-populated Java is without problems. The distance between the privileged and the poor is obvious; there is a need for more educational and medical facilities; there are signs of youthful alienation coupled with an overt rejection of older communal and cultural values.

Yet one of the joys of Java is the sensation that Java will pull through. Despite certain social and economic problems, there is an underlying current of hopefulness, not of self-destructive resignation. Life may not be entirely a bed of roses, but there are flowers. And they bloom. Desperate people cannot laugh with the spontaneity of the Javanese; nor can they find real pleasure in simple things; and least of all can they be as generous in action and in spirit as the people of Java.

The great canvas of Java is perhaps best looked at as a mosaic of small portraits, an assembly of beautifully executed miniatures, each one delineating and capturing the essence of a mood, a place, a time. Individually, the portraits are fascinating. Seen together, they illuminate the complex interrelationships within the island, imbuing them with an aura of strangely compelling magic.

Java offers a unique chance to be personal. Take the chance. You will find yourself engulfed in a world of extraordinary variety and vitality, of compassion, subtlety and drama; you will find it impos-sible not to become involved; and the least of your rewards will be an appreciation and an understanding of a remarkable island. You may also become the happy victim of a great and enduring passion.

Picking tea leaves at Puncak.

There is plenty of visible history in Java. Most of it is easily and pleasurably accessible, and is a fine excuse (if an excuse is needed) for walking and exploring.

Everywhere there are elements of the past. At an obvious level there are splendid monuments in stone, temples like Borobudur, Prambanan and Penataran. But Java's awareness of its past is not limited to the adulation of piles of stone: it also celebrates the names and deeds of its outstanding sons, ancient and modern. Roads and streets throughout the island record nationalist leaders and thinkers like Haji Agus Salim and Husni Thamrin; military heroes like General Sudirman who, wasted by tuberculosis, often led his guerrilla forces from a litter, and whose likeness adorned the older series of Indonesian banknotes; popular heroes like Prince Diponegoro, leader of the bloody but futile rebellion of 1826–30; Hayam Wuruk, the greatest king of the Majapahit dynasty; Gajah Mada, the amazing *patih* (prime minister) who was largely responsible for Majapahit's most glorious period of power and influence; Falatehan (or Fatahillah), the Islamic warrior-missionary who in 1527 flung the Portuguese back from Sunda Kelapa, today's Jakarta.

Even older memories are kept alive at the highest levels of the nation. Indonesia's motto, *Bhinneka Tunggal Ika*, "They are many; they are one" (more commonly translated as "Unity in Diversity") is a Sanskrit phrase; so too is the word *pancasila*, the "Five Principles" on which the Republic is based; the "supporter" of the Indonesian coat-of-arms is the *garuda*, the mythical sun-bird which has played an important role in Javanese legend and which earlier still occurs in Hindu mythology as the "vehicle" of the god Visnu.

In 2,000 years Java has been influenced by, and had thrust upon it, a variety of religious, social, political and commercial forces. All of them have in some way left their mark:

one has only to peel back the layers of modern Java to find an astonishing array of customs and beliefs that have maintained themselves through the centuries, no matter how many times or in how many different ways they have been overlaid with a new influence. Java is famous for this "syncretism," about which so much has been written…the ability to absorb and adapt external influences without necessarily discarding older beliefs, practices and values. What is obvious is a mere fraction of what it is.

Any history of Java is also, to a large degree, a history of Indonesia. Although much smaller than its neighbours Sumatra and Kalimantan (Indonesian Borneo), Java was (and still is) agriculturally richer, and easily maintained a larger population; it controlled the trade route east to the fabled "Spice Islands" of Ternate, Tidore, Banda and Ambon, all of which traded with Java for rice; it exerted a powerful influence on the important north and northeast sea-lanes to Indo-China and the Chinese mainland, a source of silk and porcelain; and it had a say in the trade that moved northwest through the Straits of Malacca to Burma and farther on to India. Whether a muddle of competing kingdoms, a reluctant colonial vassal, or a trio of provinces in an independent republic, Java has never, in two thousand years, relinquished its joint roles of political linchpin and entrepot centre for the Indonesian archipelago.

Indonesia's controversial prehistory: Recent excavations at two sites in northern Thailand have revealed that a metal-age culture was underway there in the 4th millennium BC – much earlier than in either China or India. This discovery has already overturned the conception of Southeast Asia as a prehistoric backwater, and some scholars are now speculating that this region was in fact one of the great prehistoric cradles of human cultural development.

Such speculation is somewhat premature in the case of Indonesia, where relatively few Neolithic sites have been excavated and dated with precision. But numerous excavations being undertaken here are expected to turn up new and exciting discoveries. Indonesian

Preceding pages, the refined lifestyle of the early Javanese kings is realistically portrayed in the reliefs of Borobudur. **Left**, the serene beauty of a Bodhisattva at Candi Sari. **(9th century)**

archaeological findings have contributed more than their share of controversy in the past. In 1890, a Dutch military physician by the name of Eugene Dubois discovered a fossilised primate jawbone in Central Java that possessed distinctively human characteristics. The jawbone was found in association with fossils of mammalian species thought to have died out several hundred thousand years ago, and was at first discounted by Dubois as belongings to an extinct species of apes. But when, in the following year, he discovered two more hominoid fossils in similar circumstances, he became convinced that he had unearthed the world's first evidence of Darwin's long-

sought "missing link." He named his discovery *pithecanthropus erectus* (upright ape-man), and published his findings in 1894.

Unfortunately for Dubois, Darwin's evolutionary theories were still being hotly disputed at this time, and his discovery, dubbed "Java Man," was vehemently denounced by religious groups. Crushed, Dubois withdrew his specimens and thereafter ceased to work in the field of paleoanthropology. It was not until more than two decades later, with the discovery of similar fossils outside Peking in 1921, that he was eventually vindicated.

"Java Man" and "Peking Man" are now recognised as members of the species *Homo*

erectus, a direct ancestor of man who inhabited the Old World from about 1.7 million until 250,000 years ago. The body skeleton of *Homo erectus* was essentially modern, but his skull was thick, long and low and he possessed a massive face with strongly protruding brow ridges. Many fossils of this type have been discovered in central Java since Dubois' time, some of which are more than a million years old. Replicas are on display at the Geological Museum in Bandung and the Sangiran site museum, outside Surakarta.

Recent research has shown that *Homo erectus* probably could not speak, but that he could utter sounds with which to communicate. He was an omnivore and a food gatherer who lived in caves as well as in open camp sites and was apparently the first creature to know the use of fire. He also produced an extensive stone tool kit that included flaked choppers, axes and hand-adzes. Thousands of stone tools dating from between 500,000 and 250,000 years ago have been collected from the bed of the Baksoka River near Pacitan, in south-central Java. Similar tools have also been found in Flores and Timor, which raises the intriguing possibility that *Homo erectus* may have spread to the eastern islands. Unfortunately these tools cannot be accurately dated.

This classification of more recent hominoid fossils is still very much in doubt, particularly for the transitional species between *Homo erectus* and modern man. Central to the problem of classification is the question of whether modern man evolved in a single place (thought by some to be sub-Saharan Africa) and then spread to other areas, or whether parallel evolutions occurred in various places and at different rates.

Fossil records can be interpreted to support both views. In the Indonesian sphere, the controversy is centered around the dating and classification of the so-called "Solo Man" fossils discovered between 1931 and 1933 next to the Solo River at Ngandong, in central Java. Some scholars classify "Solo Man" as an intermediate species dating from perhaps 250,000 years ago, and claim him as evidence of a distinct Southeast-Asian evolutionary descent from *Homo erectus* to modern man. Others insist that "Solo Man" was simply an advanced *Homo erectus* species who survived in isolation and then died out completely. More accurately dated discoveries will be needed to resolve the issue.

Fossil records of modern man (*Homo sapiens*) dating from as early as 60,000 years ago have been found in China and mainland Southeast Asia, and this compares favourably with the appearance of *Homo sapiens* in other parts of the world, though two imprecisely dated African fossils are said to be more than 90,000 years old. Modern man also inhabited Indonesia, New Guinea and Australia by about 40,000 years ago and perhaps even earlier.

All Southeast Asian *Homo sapiens* fossils prior to about 5,000 BC have been identified as members of the Australoid group of Australoid genetic contribution that becomes increasingly marked as one moves eastward in the archipelago.

From the little evidence we have it appears that early *Homo sapiens* continued and refined the flaked-stone tool-making industries of *Homo erectus*, also fashioning instruments of bone, shell and bamboo. They gathered and hunted, eating a great variety of fruits, plants, molluscs and animals, including tapirs, elephants, deer and rhinoceri. It seems that they were also cannibals, because crushed human bones have been found alongside discarded shells and animal debris. Beginning about 20,000 years ago, there is evidence of human burials and partial cre-

peoples who survive in isolated pockets in Malaya and the Philippines today as the black-skinned, wiry-haired *negritos*. It is thought therefore that Australoid peoples were the original inhabitants of the entire region, and then were absorbed, driven to the uplands or pushed eastward by subsequent "waves" of Mongolian migration. According to the view, Australoid physical traits found today among the predominantly Mongolian populations of Indonesia, such as curly hair and dark skin, are evidence of an

Left, reconstructed skull of Java Man. **Above**, Central Javanese neolithic stone tools.

mations; several cave paintings (mainly hand stencils but also human and animal figures) found in southwestern Sulawesi and New Guinea may be 10,000 or more years old.

The Neolithic or New Stone Age is characterised here as elsewhere by the advent of village settlements, domesticated animals, polished stone tools, pottery and food cultivation. Its first appearance is everywhere being pushed back in time by new archaeological findings, but worldwide it appears to have begun soon after the end of the last ice age around 10,000 BC. In northern Thailand, one recently discovered Neolithic site has been reliably placed in the 7th millennium

BC. For Indonesia, however, there is no evidence prior to the 3rd millennium BC and most sites are of a more recent date. This situation is likely to change as new discoveries are made, but it must be remembered too that cultural development in such a geographically fragmented area was highly uneven, and that remote tribes in New Guinea were still living in the Stone Age well into this century.

The first agriculturalists in Indonesia must have grown taro before the introduction of rice. In fact rice came to much of Indonesia only in recent centuries, and taro is still a staple crop on many eastern islands, together with bananas, yams, breadfruits, coconuts

former have been found in south Sumatra and Java.

Neolithic Indonesians were undoubtedly seafarers, like their Polynesian cousins who spread across the Pacific at this time. Nautical terms bear significant similarity throughout the Austronesian family of languages, and stylised boat motifs are depicted on early pottery and in early bronze reliefs, as well as on the houses and sacred textiles of primitive tribes. Today the outrigger is found throughout Indonesia and Oceania.

The _Dong-son_ bronze culture: It was once thought that Southeast Asia's Bronze Age began with the Chinese-influenced _Dong-son_ bronze culture of North Vietnam in the 1st

and sugarcane. The dog, goat, buffalo, chicken and pig were all domesticated by the 1st millennium BC, and most animals were probably slaughtered only for ritual sacrifies and communal feasts. Chicken entrails were employed for the art of augury, examined by a priest or shaman to determine auspicious dates for important undertakings such as a hunt or a marriage. Barkcloth clothing was produced with stone beaters, and pottery was shaped with the aid of a wooden paddle and a stone anvil tapper.

Two major categories of stone axes were known: quadrangular and round, and the remains of early workshops producing the

millennium BC, however the discovery of 5,000-years-old copper and bronze tools at Ban Chiang and Non Nok Tha in northern Thailand has raised the possibility of developments elsewhere in the region. Nevertheless, all early Indonesian bronzes known to date are clearly of the _Dong-son_ type and probably date from between 500 BC and 500 AD.

The finest _Dong-son_ ceremonial bronze drums and axes are distinctively decorated with engraved geometric, animal and human motifs. This decorative style was highly influential in many fields of Indonesian art, and seems to have spread together with the bronze casting technique, as old stone moulds have been found at various sites in Indonesia. The sophisticated "lost wax" technique of bronze casting was employed, and bronzes of this type have been recovered as far east as New Guinea and Roti.

Who were the Indonesian producers of *Dong-son* type bronzes? It is difficult to say for sure, but it seems that small kingdoms based on wet-rice agriculture and foreign trade flourished already in the archipelago during this period. Articles of Indian manufacture have been found at several prehistoric sites in Indonesia, and, it is certain that by the 2nd century BC (if not earlier), trade was widespread throughout the archipelago.

have now been visited by millions. Yet their creators remain largely an enigma. Who built these Indian monuments and how is it that Southeast Asians came to have such a profound knowledge of Indian culture in ancient times?

Part of our bewilderment is undoubtedly the product of a longstanding and erroneous conception of Southeast Asia as a prehistoric backwater. This view forced many earlier scholars to conclude that nothing short of massive Indian invasions and migrations to the region could have effected the sort of changes necessary for Indianised kingdoms to flourish as they did. The problem with this hypothesis is that there is absolutely no evi-

The Indianisation of the Archipelago: Beginning in the 2nd century AD, a number of highly sophisticated civilisations emerged in Southeast Asia – civilisations whose cosmology, literature, architecture and political organisation were all closely patterned on Indian models. These kingdoms are best known for the wonderful monuments which they created: Borobudur, Prambanan, Angkor, Pagan and others, many of which were "rediscovered" in the 19th century, and

<u>Left</u>, *Dong-son* bronze-age ceremonial drum. <u>Above</u>, 5th century inscription of a Hindu ruler of West Java, King Purnavarman.

dence to support it. Southeast Asia was actually a thriving trade and cultural centre in prehistoric times.

While the reality of the Indianisation process as far more complex than will probably ever be known, the most recent and most plausible theory is that Southeast-Asian rulers Indianised their own kingdoms, either by employing Indian Brahmans or by sending their own people to India to acquire the necessary knowledge. The motivation for doing this is clear – Sanskrit writing and texts, along with sophisticated Indian ritual and architectural techniques, afforded a ruler greater organisational control, wealth and social status. It also enabled him to participate in an expanding Indian trading network.

Support for this hypothesis has come from detailed studies of Hindu period temples, which show that they not only employ many diverse Indian architectural and artistic styles in an eclectic fashion unknown in India, but that they also incorporate pre-Hindu indigenous design elements.

It seems that Java was known by Indian chroniclers as early as 600 BC. The earliest plausible reference to Java in the Christian era occurs in Chinese annals of the Han dynasty, recording the visit in 132 AD of an embassy from "Yavadvipa." A little later, about 160 AD, the Alexandrian geographer

mountain, the Mahameru, which is the abode of the Hindu gods. Beneath the otherwise severe, unornamented throne of the Susuhunan of Surakarta, a titular Muslim prince, is a tiger skin symbolising his role as the embodiment of Siva. In a *ketoprak* play retelling the Christmas story, *Kelahiran Jesus Kristus*, Mary and Joseph wear traditional Javanese dress, the Three Kings wear court clothing…and Joseph approaches his father-in-law with the stifling obsequiousness that still dominates Javanese social contacts between inferiors and superiors.

Under the northern Gupta dynasty (300–600 AD) India enjoyed one of its "golden ages." Buddhism, that gentle, contemplative

Ptolemy mentions the East Indian islands, and while it is doubtful that Roman traders ever reached the archipelago, Roman beads have been found in Borneo, presumably carried by Indian merchants.

India was to have a profound influence on Java. The great Indian poet Rabindranath Tagore, visiting Java, said "I see India everywhere, but I do not recognise it."

At the celebration of Idul Fitri, the feast-day marking the end of the Muslim fasting month, immense conical mounds of rice are carried to the Masjid Besar, the Great Mosque, in Yogyakarta…mounds known as *gunungan* or mountains, a direct reference to the sacred

offshoot of Hinduism, penetrated China, and many Chinese Buddhist pilgrims chose to take the sea voyage through Southeast Asia to India rather than face the perils of the mountainous overland route. This sea voyage sometimes led to Java, and always to Sumatra.

One such pilgrim, Fa-hsien, observed in 414 AD that Hinduism was practised in both islands. The oldest inscription in Java, found near modern Bogor, dates from the same time, and records in Sanskrit the name of King Purnavarman of Taruma…but virtually nothing is known about his kingdom.

Another pilgrim, I-tsing, travelled from

671 to 695 and spent 10 years at a Buddhist monastery school in Sumatra: "If a Chinese priest wishes to go to the west (India) in order to hear and read he had better stay here one or two years and practise the proper rules and (then) proceed to Central India."

The Mataram Empire: I-tsing's monastery may have been a part of the great thalassic empire, Srivijaya, then rising in Sumatra. While the Buddhist kings of Srivijaya were building their maritime domination throughout the Straits of Malacca, Sanjaya, a Hindu king, was consolidating his power over villages in the rich alluvial plain between the Progo and Opak rivers to found what would later be called the Mataram Empire.

tance of religion in building these empires. In the fertile, underpopulated Java of the time, the village was the basic organisation of Javanese society. For a king to impose a greater political power he needed to supply something in return.

Imported religion served this purpose admirably. Javanese pilgrims are known to have visited India in the 9th century, and its seems likely that wandering Indian monks hopped on the frequent trading ships sailing between India and Java. These peripatetic religious scholars brought India's intellectual and cultural sophistication to a land as ready to embrace and expand on philosophical ideas as the Javanese earth receives and

Unlike the previous kingdoms on the North Coast and in Sumatra, which depended on trade, Mataram was a inward-looking, agrarian-based Javanese empire. With an economic self-sufficiency granted by the land's incredible fertility, Sanjaya was able to gather together the separate village units under the banner of imported Indian religion.

The great stone temples scattered throughout Central and East Java attest not only to the wealth of resources in Java but the impor-

Left, Candi Plaosan, a Buddhist sanctuary built in the 9th century. **Above**, the Bull Nandi in the complex of Lara Jonggrang Temple.

nurtures rice seedlings.

Under Hinduism and Buddhist as practised in ancient Java, the king was a semi-divine link between heaven and earth. To secure this status for eternity, and to involve the populace in a massive communal effort, the kings embarked on a centuries-long program of constructing the monuments that still rise from the Javanese farmland.

The first and greatest is Borobudur. This enormous edifice, was begun in 775 AD and most probably was intended to be a Hindu temple or a stepped pyramid dedicated to some indigenous cult. Ten years later, when Sanjaya was overthrown by the Sailendra dynasty, only the first two tiers had been completed.

The Buddhist Sailendra also saw the value of this glorious construction program, but could hardly accept a huge Hindu monument in their midst. They set about converting the monument to reflect Buddhism, and during the next half century completed the five-tiered structure.

Borobudur has hardly been completed when Rakai Pakitan, a descendent of Sanjaya ruling the fringes of Mataram as a vassal to the king, married into the ruling clan and took power for himself. The Sailendras fled to the co-religionist Srivijaya empire, where they harrassed Javanese shipping for a cen-

was also the beginnings of the great Javanese tradition of syncretism as the line between Hinduism and Buddhism became increasingly blurred.

The East Javanese Kingdoms: Around 930 AD, the first Mataram Empire came to an abrupt end as the capital was transferred to East Java. The likeliest explanation was a devastating eruption of Mount Merpati which covered the farmlands and closed roads to the ports on the North Coast.

Unlike modern Java, the most densely-populated rural area on earth, ancient Java was largely empty. It is conceivable the entire population simply packed up and moved to more hospitable lands.

tury. Rakai Pakitan consolidated his position with a temple construction programme of his own.

The temple complex at Prambanan was probably intended as a Hindu counterpart to Borobudur, as the new king could do nothing about the gigantic monument to a rival religion in his kingdom. Although the Hindu king made some cosmetic changes to the structure, he left Borobudur largely alone. He even built a new Buddhist temple, Candi Sewu, about 2 km from Prambanan.

This may have been political prudence, as most of the populace including his wife seems to have adopted Buddhism, but this

Eastern Java prospered until a seaborne attack by the rival Srivijaya kingdom splintered it into numerous petty states. The empire was rebuilt by the most famous of the early Javanese kings, Airlangga, who ruled somewhere to the south of Surabaya from 1019 to 1049.

Before claiming the throne and uniting East Java, Airlangga spent years as a hermit, accumulating wisdom and magical powers through fasting and meditation. Significantly, it was during his reign that the ancient Hindu story of Arjuna's ascesis and temptation, the famous *Arjuna Wiwaha* , was first translated into Old Javanese.

Airlangga was followed by the Kediri dynasty (1049–1222), during which another Hindu epic, the *Bharatayuddha* or "War of the Bharatas," was translated; these were important, for these popular tales are an integral part of Java's modern cultural tradition. For the rest, Kediri's fame is essentially negative, since in later dynastic chronicles it invariably appears as the force opposing the establishment of a new regime.

The next dynasty, Singosari, which lasted a mere 70 years, was engulfed in a welter of gore, with all the elements of a Shakespearean tragedy: successive rulers vainly tried to thwart a curse that seven kings and princes should die by a sword fashioned for the

duism, always slender in Java, had evolved into a form of Tantric Syncretism, heavily imbued with overtones of magical and arcane practices that had originated in Tibet and spread down towards and into the archipelago under the influence of India and of the Mongol ruler Kublai Khan. The last Singosari ruler, Kertonegoro, refused to pay obeisance to the Great Khan. This shocking effrontery was set to rights by a military expedition of 20,000 men who invaded Java, achieved minor victories, and were then surprisingly thrashed by Kertonegoro's son. However, since Kertonegoro was dead (he died before the arrival of the Khan's forces), the Chinese troops felt that honour had been satisfied,

dynasty's usurping founder, Ken Angrok, who tested his new weapon by murdering the smith who forged it. Singosari also saw the building of some of East Java's more striking temples, and the introduction of a unique sculptural style that owed little or nothing to original Indian models, with figures in a flat, two-dimensional style derived from the *wayang kulit* theatre.

Distinctions between Buddhism and Hin-

Far left, the image of Durga in the main chamber of the Hindu temple at Prambanan. **Left**, King Airlangga as Visnu on garuda. **Above**, a relief at Candi Penataran (14th century).

and the new king was enthroned. The year was 1293 and Majapahit, Java's greatest dynasty, was on its way.

In the previous year, 1292, Marco Polo had passed by though not landed in Java. He was not the first European in the area, but his informative memoirs survived, and his notes on Java (although second-hand) are interesting: "(Java) is the biggest island in the world having a circumference of more than 3,000 miles. The people are idolators ruled by a powerful monarch and paying no tribute to anyone on earth. It is a very rich island, producing pepper, nutmegs, spikenard, galingale, cubebs and cloves…. It is visited by great numbers of ships and merchants who buy a great range of merchandise, reaping handsome profits and rich returns. The quantity, of treasure in the island is beyond all computation."

His estimates of Java's riches were indeed correct, though the size of the island was greatly exaggerated, and nutmeg and cloves never grew there. Nevertheless, knowledge of such wealth was shortly to inflame the cupidity of Europe, and within three centuries Java was brutally wrenched into the orbit of Western influence. Another of Polo's observations (this time first-hand) was equally important to the future of Java:

"You must know that the people of Ferlec [modern Peureulak, on the far northeast coast of Sumatra] used all to be idolators, but owing to contact with Saracen merchants, who continually resort here in their ships, they have all been converted to the law of Mahomet."

Islam had planted its first, and irreversible, step in Indonesia. Marco Polo's "Saracens" were almost certainly Gujeratis (themselves only recently converted) making the long voyage from Cambay, north of modern Bombay. The progress of Islam from northern Sumatra to Java was slow, but considerable, for it set in motion a power struggle between the lords of the coastal ports and the kings of the agrarian, inland states for whom rivers like the Solo and the Brantas were the only means of contact with the outside world.

Majapahit's wealth lay principally in the rice it grew on rich alluvial plains and on terraced *padi*-fields. In its heyday, when it controlled or at least received tribute from most of today's Indonesia, there was no problem finding coastal merchants who were happy to trade imported cloths and luxury goods for Java's rice. But Majapahit was never a maritime power in its own right, for its rulers, like "proper" Victorian families, disdained to soil their hands with trade, and relied on more enterprising, business-oriented souls to "do the dirty work." This lapse, though understandable in the context of a rigidly structured society, was to prove fatal.

The now famous dynasty got off to a promising start under Wijaya, who had beset the fearsome troops of Kublai Khan and established his *kraton* (palace) some 60 km southwest of Surabaya where the little town of

Trowulan now stands. For almost 40 years it ambled along, sometimes bumpily, without seeming to anticipate its greatness. Other minor kings and princes nibbled at its borders. Java was anything but unified. Then, towards the end of the 1320s, the miracle occurred. A lowly officer in the palace guard put down an anti-royalist revolt and was rewarded with the title of *patih* or prime minister. Shortly afterwards he quelled another uprising, and thereupon vowed to devote himself to the reunification of Java. He was almost laughed out of court, but his time came, and eventually it was Gajah Mada who had the last laugh.

During the regency of Queen Tribhuvana, and through the first 14 years of the long

reign of Hayam Wuruk (who ruled from 1350–89), Gajah Mada skillfully expanded and consolidated Majapahit's territories, reorganised its administrative structure and brought peace to a troubled land. How much was achieved by conquest, and how much was simply the acknowledgement by weaker rulers of Majapahit's strength, will probably never be known, but the extent of the kingdom is said to have stretched from Sumatra and part of Malaya through Borneo and east to the Moluccas.

Gajah Mada died in 1364, Hayam Wuruk in 1389. Neither prime minister nor king left a worthy successor, and Majapahit's brilliant but brief flame was reduced to a mere flicker within a generation. By the time Cristoforo Colombo had discovered the West Indies in 1492 while looking for a route to the East Indies, and Vasco da Gama had rounded the Cape of Good Hope and reached India in 1498, Majapahit was snuffed out forever. With it died the last of the great Hindu-Javanese kingdoms, for Islam was now firmly established along the north coast of Java.

Majapahit, and the other Hindu kingdoms that preceded it, have left their mark on modern Java: their heroes are also today's heroes, the tales and stories-within-stories they introduced are still highpoints in the Javanese cultural tradition, their beliefs are

the bedrock of many current attitudes and social observances. But the decline and fall of Majapahit was hastened by the advent of one of the two great forces that helped mould Java as it exists today: Islam.

Islam and the spice trade: Shortly after Majapahit's fall the strongest power in the area was Malacca, initially a modest trading centre on Malaya's west coast. Under the leadership of Iskandar Shah, a Sumatran from Palembang who became a Muslim

Left, Majapahit Palace Gate. Above, a Majapahit king portrayed as Visnu, now in the museum of Jakarta.

around the year 1420, Malacca set forth on a path of glory that was to last, under Muslim, Portuguese, Dutch and English rulers, for more than 300 years. Strategically placed on the eastern shore of the Straits of Malacca, the new city controlled the trade route linking, in the east, China, Indo-China and the Moluccas, with the great Indian and Arabic ports to the west.

A century later an ill-fated Portuguese "ambassador," Tome Pires, destined to die in a Chinese prison at Canton, reported that many foreign merchants had settled in Java's north coast ports. They were no doubt Gujerati Muslims from Cambay, with a leavening of Omanis and Persians, whose predecessors had slowly ranged eastwards from Aceh to Surabaya, bringing with them trade goods, the Qur'an, the Hadith and an inseparable proselytising fervour.

By 1500 every major port, from Aceh through Palembang, Malacca, the Javanese north coast (Banten, Cirebon, Demak, Tuban, Gresik) and across to the Spice Islands, was in Muslim hands. The cloves, nutmeg and mace from the Moluccas and Amboina, the pepper from Sumatra and West Java, were moved on Muslim ships through Muslim traders to Muslim middlemen who sent the treasures through more Muslim ships to Muslim merchants in the Gujerati ports of India. "Because of the expansive, missionary nature of Islam," said Jacob van Leur (a brilliant Dutch historian killed at the age of 34 in the Battle of the Java Sea), "every Muslim is a propagandist of the faith. That is why the trader from the Muslim world was the most common 'missionary' figure in foreign regions. That is why…the faith was certain to follow the routes of trade."

Dominating the seaways, the Muslim sailors and traders effectively stifled (or absorbed) the commercial advantages of inland Majapahit. Power at sea, during the 15th century, was the key to success. If Islamisation at first occurred peacefully in the coastal kingdoms of Java, a turning point was reached sometime in the early 16th century when the newly founded Islamic kingdom of Demak (on the north central coast) attacked and conquered the last great Hindu-Buddhist kingdom of Java. They drove the Hindu rulers to the east and annexed the agriculturally rich Javanese hinterlands. Demak then consolidated its control over the entire north coast by subduing Tuban, Gresik, Madura, Surabaya, Cirebon, Banten and Jayakarta – emerging as the master of Java by the 16th century.

The traditional account of the Islamisation of Java is quite different, but equally interesting. According to Javanese chronicles, nine Islamic saints – the so-called *wali sanga*, propagated Islam through the Javanese shadow play (*wayang kulit*) and *gamelan* music. They introduced the *kalimat shahadat* or Islamic confession of faith and the reading of Koranic prayers to performances of the Ramayana and Mahabarata epics. No better explanation could be given for the origins of Islamic syncretism in Java.

Islam in this period, was the faith of traders and urban dwellers, firmly entrenched in the maritime centres of the archipelago. Many of these towns were quite substantial; Malacca is estimated to have had a populaion of at least 100,000 in the 16th century – as large as Paris, Venice and Naples but dwarfed by Peking and Edo (Tokyo) which then had roughly 1 million inhabitants each. Other cities in Indonesia were comparably large: Semarang had 2,000 houses; Jayakarta had an army of 4,000 men; Tuban was then a walled city with 30,000 inhabitants. Such statistics indicate that the urban population of Indonesia in the 16th century at least equalled the agrarian population. Thus the typical Indonesian of that period was not a peasant as he is today but a town dweller engaged as an artisan, sailor or a trader.

Indonesian cities were also physically different from cities in Europe, the Middle East, India or China. Built without walls for the most part, Indonesian cities were located at river mouths or on wide plains, and relied on surrounding villages for their defence. Javanese cities were also very green. Coconut, banana and other fruit trees were everywhere, and most of the widely spaced wooden or bamboo houses had vegetable gardens. With no more than perhaps 5 million people in the entire archipelago, land had no intrinsic values. Thus in 1613 when the English wanted some land to build a fortress in Makassar, they compensated the resident, not for the space but for the coconut trees growing there.

A 19th century rendering of the mosque of Banten (Bantam).

1. *Marché à Bantam.* 2. *Douane.* 3. *Chinois, habitans de Java, etc. avec toutes sortes de marchandises*
10. *Tour où l'on fait sentinelle.* 11. *Châtea*

1. *Marckt tot Bantam.* 2. *Tol huys.* 3. *Chineesen, Iavanen etc. met allerley Koopmanschapp*
Vol Kraemen. 9. *Mosquée* 10. *Wacht tooren.* 11.

Commerce et Marcha
KOOPHANDEL

à Leide Chez Pierre van der Aa.

Pois.5.Epiceries.6.Fruits.7.Meubles.8.Rue de la Cour pleine de boutiques.9.Mosquée.
Ville.12.Le Port.

Hun gewicht. 5.Specerijen. 6. Fruijten.7.Huijs raeden.8 de Hof straet
.12.de Stad.13.de Haven.

a Bantam.
AEREN.

The arrival of the Portuguese: Spices were available in Europe, but were exorbitantly expensive by the time they had been carried overland from the Far East to Constantinople and through the clearing houses of Venice. The answer, with its promise of great profit, was to find a sea-route to Southeast Asia and then to control it.

In 1498 Vasco da Gama established a base at Calicut on the west coast of India. In 1508 a hard-hitting Portuguese fleet demolished a combined Egyptian and Indian force off Diu, at the mouth of the Gulf of Cambay, and thus made the Indian Ocean safe for Portuguese merchant shipping. In 1510 the irrepressible Afonso d'Albuquerque established what was to be a long-lasting enclave at Goa, and the following year took the powerful trading city of Malacca by storm. By 1512 the Portuguese had reached the Spice Islands, and in 1522 they founded a trading post in the town of Sunda Kelapa, then controlled by the Hindu state of Pajajaran in West Java; their *padrao* or commemorative stone can still be seen in the Central Museum in Jakarta (as Sunda Kelapa is now called). The Portuguese were thrown out of Sunda Kelapa in I527, but they virtually monopolised the spice trade for a century until the Dutch captured Malacca in 1641.

The 15th century saw Islam's penetration and expansion, the 16th century its consolidation in Java. Wealthy trading ports like Demak and Surabaya flourished, and feuded with the Portuguese; Jepara rose for a brief moment of glory, and under a war-like queen despatched two fleets against Malacca. At the end of the century, two important events took place. The first was the rise of the last great central Javanese kingdom, another Mataram founded by Senopati, expanded by the conquests of Sultan Agung. The second was the arrival of the Dutch, who were eventually to control the archipelago.

Enter the Dutch: The Dutch, religious and trade rivals of the Catholic Portuguese, were

Previous pages, Bantam in its heydays in a Dutch engraving. Left, Sultan Hamengkubwono VIII of Yogyakarta with the Dutch Resident. Right, Jan Pieterszoon Coen.

initially interested only in trade and not in territorial aggrandisement. Their first exploratory fleet of four ships anchored off Banten in 1596 and bought a cargo of pepper. Other fleets followed. Appalling shipboard conditions, a high mortality rate, and the dangers of shipwreck and foundering were regarded as a trivial price to pay for profits that could (with luck) run to as high as a thousand percent .

Indeed, so keen was the interest in direct trade with the Indies, that all Dutch traders

soon came to recognise the need for cooperation – to minimise competition and maximise profits. In 1602, therefore, they formed the United Dutch East India Company (known by its Dutch initials – VOC), one of the first joint-stock corporations in history. It was capitalised at more than 6 million guilders and empowered by the states-general to negotiate treaties, raise armies, build fortresses and wages war on behalf of the Netherlands in Asia.

The VOC's whole purpose and philosophy can be summed up in a single word – monopoly. Like the Portuguese before them, the Dutch dreamed of securing absolute control of the East Indies spice trade, which traditionally had passed through many Muslim and Mediterranean hands.

In its early years the VOC met with only limited success. Several trading posts were opened, and Ambon was taken from the Portuguese (in 1605), but Spanish and English, not to mention Muslim, competition kept spice prices high in Indonesia and low in Europe. Then in 1614, a young accountant by the name of Jan Pieterszoon Coen convinced the directors that only a more forceful policy would make the company profitable. Coen was given command of VOC operations, and promptly embarked on a series of military adventures that were to set the pat-

a recently arrived English fleet joined the Jayakartans. Coen was not so easily beaten, however (his motto: "Never Despair!"), and escaped to Ambon leaving a handful of his men in defence of the fort and its valuable contents.

Five months later, Coen returned to discover his men still in possession of their post. Though outnumbered 30-to-1 they had rather unwittingly played one foe against another by acceding to any and all demands, but were never actually required to surrender their position due to the mutual suspicion and timidity of the three attacking parties, Coen set his adversaries to flight in a series of dramatic attacks, undertaken with a small

tern for Dutch behaviour in the region.

Coen's first step was to establish a permanent headquarters at Jayakarta on the northwestern coast of Java, close to the pepper-producing areas of Sumatra and the strategic Sunda Straits. In 1618, he sought and received permission from Prince Wijayakrama of Jayakarta to expand the existing Dutch post, and proceeded to throw up a stone barricade mounted with cannon. The prince protested that fortifications were not provided for in their agreement and Coen responded by bombarding the palace and reducing it to rubble. A siege of the fledgling Dutch fortress ensured, in which the powerful Bantenese and

force of 1,000 men that included several score fearsome Japanese mercenaries. The town of Jayakarta was razed to the ground and construction of a new Dutch town begun, eventually to include canals, draw-bridges, docks, warehouses, barracks, a central square, a city hall and a church – all protected by a high stone wall and a moat – a copy, in short, of Amsterdam itself. The new city was renamed Batavia.

Coen's next step was to secure control of the five tiny nutmeg and mace-producing Banda Islands. In 1621, he led an expeditionary force there, and within a few weeks, rounded up and killed most of the 15,000 inhabitants in the islands. Three of the islands were then transformed into spice plantations managed by Dutch colonists and worked by slaves.

By such nefarious means the Dutch achieved effective control of the eastern archipelago and its lucrative spice trade by the end of the 17th century. In the western half of the archipelago, however, they became increasingly embroiled in fruitless intrigues and wars, particularly on Java. Ths came about largely because the Dutch presence at Batavia disturbed a delicate balance of power.

As early as 1628, Batavia came under Javanese attack. Sultan Agung (1613–46), third and greatest ruler of the Mataram kingdom, was then aggressively expanding his domain and had recently concluded a successful 5-year siege of Surabaya. He now controlled all of central and eastern Java, and next, he intended to take western Java by pushing the Dutch into the sea and then conquering Banten.

He nearly succeeded. A large Javanese expeditionary force momentarily breached Batavia's defences, but was then driven back outside the walls in a last-ditch effort led by Governor-General Coen. The Javanese were not prepared for such resistance and withdrew for lack of provisions. A year later, in 1629, Sultan Agung sent an even larger force, estimated at 10,000 men, and prepared huge stockpiles of rice for what threatened to be protracted siege, Coen, however, learned of the locations of the rice stockpiles and captured or destroyed them before the Javanese even arrived. Poorly led, starving and stricken by disease, the Javanese troops died by the thousands outside of Batavia, and never again did Mataram pose a threat to the city.

Relations between the Dutch and the Javanese improved during the despotic reign of Amangkurat I (1646–77), one reason being that they had common enemies – the *pasisir* trading kingdoms of the north Java coast.

It was ironic, then, that the Dutch conquest of Makassar later resulted, albeit indirectly, in the demise of Amangkurat I. The Makassar wars of 1666–69, and their aftermath, created a diaspora of Makassarese and Buginese refugees. Many of them fled to eastern Java, where they united under the leadership of a

Madurese prince, Trunajaya. Aided and abetted by none other then the Mataram crown prince, Trunajaya successfully stormed through Central Java and plundered the Mataram capital in 1676–77. Amangkurat I died fleeing the enemy forces.

Once in control of Java. Trunajaya renounced his alliance with the young Mataram prince and declared himself king. Having no one else to turn to the crown prince pleaded for Dutch support, promising to reimburse all military expenses and to award the Dutch valuable trade concessions. The bait was swallowed, and a costly campaign was promptly mounted to capture Trunajaya. This ended, in 1680, with the restoration of the

crown prince, now styling himself Amangkurat II, to the throne.

But the new king was then in no position to fulfil his end of the bargain with the Dutch – his treasury had been looted and his kingdom was in ruin. All he had to offer was territory, and although he ceded much of western Java to the VOC, they still suffered a heavy financial loss.

On December 31, 1799, Dutch financiers received stunning news – the VOC was bankrupt! During the 18th century, the spice trade had become less profitable, while the military involvement in Java had grown increasingly costly – this at least is the broad outline

Left, a Dutch fleet fights the Bantamese. **Right**, a Dutch trader assaulted by the natives.

of events leading to one of the largest commercial collapses in history.

It was a great war in Java (1740–55), however, which dealt the death blow to delicate Dutch finances. And once again, through a complex chain of events, it was the Dutch themselves who inadvertently precipitated the conflict. The details of the struggle are too convoluted to follow here, but it began in 1740 with the massacre of the Chinese residents of Batavia, and ended 15 years later, only after many bloody battles, broken alliances and kaleidoscopic shifts of fortune had exhausted (or killed) almost everyone on the island. Indeed Java was never the same again, for by the 1755 Treaty of Giyanti,

in the Indies. In 1800, the Netherlands government assumed control of all former VOC possessions, now renamed Netherlands India, but for many years no one could figure out how to make them profitable. A number of factors, notably the Napoleonic Wars, compounded the confusion.

A new beginning of sorts was finally made under the iron rule of Governor-General Marshall Daendels (1808–11), a follower of Napoleon who wrought numerous administrative reforms, rebuilt Batavia, and constructed a post road the length of Java.

The English interregnum – a brief period of English rule under Thomas Stamford Raffles (1811–16) – followed. Raffles was an

Mataram had been cleft in two, with rival rulers occupying neighbouring capitals in Yogyakarta and Surakarta. Nor did the VOC ever recover from this drain on its resources, even though it emerged at this time as the pre-eminent power to Java.

It is one of the great ironies of colonial history that to fully exploit their colony, the Dutch had to first lose their shirts. The domination of Java – achieved at the expense of VOC bankruptcy – profited the Dutch handsomely in the 19th century.

In the traumatic aftermath of the VOC bankruptcy, there was great indecision in Holland as to the course that should be steered

extraordinary man: a brilliant scholar, naturalist, linguist, diplomat and strategist, "discoverer" of Borobudur and author of the monumental *History of Java.* In 1811, he planned and led the successful English invasion of Java, and was then placed in charge of its government at the tender age of 32. His active mind and freetrade philosophy led him to promulgate reforms almost daily. Essentially, Raffles wanted to replace the old mercantilist system (from which the colonial government derived its income through a monopoly on trade), by one in which income was derived from taxes, and trade was unrestrained. This enormous task was barely begun when the order came from London, following Napoleon's defeat at Waterloo, to restore the Indies to the Dutch.

Java becomes a Dutch colony: So numerous were the abuses leading to the Java War, and so great were the atrocities committed by the Dutch during it, that the Javanese leader, Pangeran Diponegoro (1785–1855), has been proclaimed a great hero even by Dutch historians. He was indeed a charismatic figure – crown prince, Muslim mystic and man of the people – who led a series of uprisings against the Dutch and his own ruling family. His guerilla rebellion might have succeeded but for a Dutch trick; lured to negotiate, Diponegoro was captured and exiled to Sulawesi.

The cost of the conflict in human terms was staggering – 200,000 Javanese and 8,000 Europeans lost their lives, many more from starvation and cholera than on the battlefield. At the end of the war 90 percent of island was under direct Dutch rule.

By this time however, the Dutch were in desperate economic straits. All efforts at reform had ended in disaster, and the government debt had reached 30 million guilders. New ideas were sought, and in 1829, Johannes

Left, one of many battles between the Dutch army and Indonesian forces. **Above left**, Prince Diponegoro and **right**, a Javanese soldier.

van den Bosch submitted a proposal to the crown for what he called a *Cultuurstelsel* or "Cultivation System" of fiscal administration in the colonies. His unoriginal notion was to levy a tax of 20 percent (later raised to 33 percent) on all land in Java, but to demand payment not in rice, but in labour or use of the land. This, he pointed out, would permit the Dutch to grow crops that they could sell in Europe.

Van den Bosch soon assumed control of Netherlands India, and in the estimation of many, his Cultivation System was an immediate, unqualified success. In the very first year, 1831, it produced a profit of 3 million guilders and within a decade, more than 22 million guilders were flowing annually into Dutch coffers, largely from the sale of coffee, but also from tea, sugar, indigo, quinine, copra, palm oil and rubber.

With the windfall profits received from the sale of Indonesian products during the rest of the 19th century, almost a billion guilders in all, the Dutch not only retired their debt, but built new waterways, dikes, roads and a national railway system. Indeed, observers like Englishman J. B. Money, whose book *Java, Or How To Manage A Colony* (1861) was received in Holland with a great fanfare, concluded that the system provided a panacea for all colonial woes.

In reality, of course, the pernicious effects of the Cultivation System were apparent from the beginning. While in theory the system called for peasants to surrender only a portion of their land and labour, in practice certain lands were worked exclusively for the Dutch by forced labour. The island of Java, one of the richest pieces of real estate on earth, was thus transformed into a huge Dutch plantation. As noted by a succession of writers, beginning with Maultatuli (*nom de plume* of a disillusioned Dutch colonial administrator, Douwes Dekker) and his celebrated novel *Max Havelaar* (1860), the system imposed unimaginable hardships and injustices upon the Javanese.

system, Javanese agricultural development only encouraged more agriculture, due to Dutch intervention. This eventually created a two-tier colonial economy in which the towns developed apart from the vast majority of rural peasants.

The road to independence: At the beginning of the 20th century, signs of change were everywhere in the Indies. Dutch military expeditions and private enterprises were making inroads into the hinterlands of Sumatra and the eastern islands. Steam shipping and the Suez Canal (opened in 1869) had brought Europe closer, and the European presence in Java was growing steadily. Gracious new shops, clubs, hotels and homes

The long-range effects of the Cultivation System were equally insidious and are still being felt today. The opening up of new lands to cultivation and the ever-increasing Dutch demand for labour resulted in a population explosion on Java. From an estimated total of between 3 and 5 million in 1800 (a figure kept low, it is true, by frequent wars and famines), the population of Java grew to 26 million by 1900.

Another effect is what anthropologist Clifford Geertz has termed the "involution" of Javanese agriculture. Instead of encouraging the growth of an urban economy, as should have occured under a free-market

added an air of cosmopolitan elegance to the towns, while newspapers, factories, gas lighting, trains, tramways, electricity and automobiles imparted a distinct feeling of modernity. Indeed, thousands of newly arrived Dutch immigrants were moved to remark on the extremely tolerable conditions that greeted them in the colonies – that is to say, it was just like home or even better.

But if Netherlands India was becoming increasingly Europeanised, elsewhere in Asia turn-of-the-century modernisation was bringing with it a new spirit of nationalism – reflected in the Meiji Restoration and the Japanese victory over Russia (1898), the revolution in China (1911) and the Chulalongkorn reforms in Thailand.

In the Indies, nationalism was slow in developing, but just as inevitable. Humanitarian elements in Dutch society pushed for a dismantling of the cultivation system and efforts to educate the Indonesians.

The "Ethical Policy" adopted by the Dutch government reflected the realisation that the burgeoning population of Java would be a better market for Dutch goods than as a source of cheap plantation labour. The Dutch now sought to raise Javanese living standards through education and better health care. The Cultivation System was abolished by stages, with unprofitable pepper planta-

In 1908, a local doctor founded Budi Utama, "Noble Endeavour," a cultural organisation that became a backbone of the independence movement. At the same time, some Muslim small traders banded together to form the Sarekat Islam. Working patiently, gently testing the limits of official Dutch tolerance, these and other groups began the long, slow process of creating a national consciousness in late colonial Java.

From 1927 to the early 1940s, while the Dutch increasingly clamped down on independence protest activities, a brilliant generation of activitists and theoreticians rose to prominence. Shuttling in and out of jail or exile during the 1930s, Sukarno, Hatta, Sutan

tions quickly sold off while some literal money trees such as West Java coffee plantations remained under the system until World War I.

The movement to provide education would be the undoing of Dutch colonialism. Though enrollment in native schools was initially restricted to the wealthy, under a series of reform-minded administrations large numbers of Indonesians eventually had access to some form of education.

Left, Dutch officials inspect a plantation. **Above**, Javanese aristocracy and Dutch administrators at a formal reception in Solo, 1930 ca.

Sharir and others gave a much-needed focus to national consciousness. Through his flamboyant personality and oratorical gifts – he could hold an audience of many thousands spellbound for hours in the rain or burning tropical sun – Sukarno became the most visible leader of the movement.

Dutch efforts to crush the movement were ultimately in vain. In 1942, with embarrassing ease, the Japanese army swept down through the Malay Peninsula and into Java. Though initially greeted as liberators, Japanese brutality and systematic exploitation of Java's resources made it clear they were just another opressive colonial power.

With Dutch colonial officers having having fled to Australia or been killed or interned, the Japanese turned to the Indonesians to operate the bureaucracy. When the Japanese military advance was halted soon after the invasion of Southeast Asia, Tokyo placed high priority on organising populations in the occupied territories into militias to form a first line of defense against an allied counter attack. The Indonesians, finally placed in positions of middle-management responsibility, began acquiring the skills, experience and self-confidence to realise their dream of independence.

In 1944, when the Japanese privately acknowledged they were losing the war, they

On 17 August 1945, after 2 days of indecision and prompted by enthusiastic persuasion from youth groups, Sukarno read a brief declaration of independence to a small crowd outside of his house. The Republic of Indonesia was born.

While the Indonesians were consolidating their new nation, the Dutch, wholly ignorant of events in their former colony, made plans to restore the colonial regime. With forces in the region, the British were asked to accept the Japanese surrender and administer Indonesia until the Dutch could arrive in sufficient numbers to take back their colony.

The British soon realised they had been parachuted into another war. Tensions be-

started openly supporting the concept of Indonesian independence, hoping this would rally a grateful nation to their side. The prewar independence leaders once again adopted a high profile, and began organising for their new nation. On 9 August 1945, three leaders, Sukarno, Hatta and Radjiman, flew to Saigon to meet Field Marshall Terauchi Hisaichi, Commander of the Southern Area. The Japanese promised to grant Indonesia independence, and appointed Sukarno and Hatta to lead a preparatory committee.

But events outpaced all participants. The day after the Indonesian delegation arrived back in Jakarta, the Japanese surrendered.

tween the British and Japanese troops and the Indonesians flared up in October, culminating in the murder of British General Mallaby and subsequent massacre of thousands of Indonesians in Surabaya.

After the British turned over administration to the Dutch, the former colonials acted quickly to crush the Republican administration. A major military campaign forced the Republicans out of the plantations of West Java and the seaports of the North Coast into overcrowded Central Java. After a second "police action" in December 1948, the Dutch gained control of all major cities in Java, and the Republicans retreated to the mountains to continue an effective campaign of guerilla harrassment, including a brief reoccupation of Republican capital Yogyakarta.

But the ragtag Indonesian army had powerful friends. The United States, now saw the Republican Indonesia as potential, highly-strategic ally against the communist bloc. Always eager to rush to the defense of oppressed peoples whenever it suits their interest, the Americans withdrew Marshall Plan aid to the Netherlands and supported United Nations' moves to end the conflict.

Facing unceasing guerilla fighting and civilian non-cooperation in the occupied areas, and equally fierce diplomatic pressure in faraway New York, the Dutch caved in.

struct a modern democratic state with a population who had only known 350 years of colonialism and indigenous paternalism.

They failed, and it is highly unlikely that any group could have succeeded under those conditions. Sukarno, with his energy, charisma and nationalist zeal, was often described as the best-qualified person on earth to create an independent nation and the worst-qualified to run one. Though Sukarno was actually only one of several Fathers of Independence, his high profile and prestige enabled him to to assume increasingly wide powers as the political and economic situation deteriorated.

As the mismanaged economy fall com-

On 27 December 1949 the Dutch formally transferred sovereignty of the Netherlands Indies to the Republican government.

While independent Indonesia proudly took its place in the family of nations, in reality the country was little more than a shell. Virtually all of the infrastructure, plantations and industrial capability had been badly damaged by the Japanese occupation and 4 years of revolution. With a steadily increasing population, the new Indonesian leaders had to both rebuild a ravaged economy and con-

A Rijstafel as served in the Dutch colonies in the '30s.

pletely apart and political representation degenerated in petty squabbling along class, ethnic and religious lines, several groups mounted abortive rebellions. These were crushed by the Army. In 1956, Sukarno used these events to introduce his concept of "Guided Democracy," which reduced parliament to the status of a high school student's council where the principal has the final say.

Sukarno continued to apply his revolutionary techniques of soul-stirring oratory and flamboyant gesture perfectly valid when leading a populace who must fight a modern mechanised army with antiquated rifles and sharp sticks to the wildly inappropriate situation of nation-building. Scarce resources were directed into kitchy monuments and grand palaces, while Sukarno alienated foreign aid donor nations with his "to hell with all of you" foreign policy.

The millions of peasants driven into desperate poverty by the country's economic chaos proved a fertile recruiting ground for the PKI. By the mid 1960s, the Party listed over 20 million members and were making inroads into the Army and Civil Service.

Sukarno cautiously allied himself with the PKI internally and directed his foreign policy toward China and the Soviet Union. On 30 September 1965, the powerkeg finally ex-

ploded when a group of rebel Army officers kidnapped and brutally murdered five generals. Exactly what happened that night is fodder for action films or novels, which as history are probably as valid as the dozens of mutually-contradictory scholarly articles and books that have tried to explain the events. However, it is clear that a previously-obscure general named Suharto, then head of the Army Strategic Reserve, seized the initiative and took command of the Army.

By the next evening, the attempted coup was over, and Indonesia sunk to its lowest period in its history. While Suharto and the Army maneuvered to oust Sukarno from power,

a horrific cycle of mass killings began as Indonesians sought to settle old scores by ostensibly eliminating the PKI.

Sukarno formally retired from the Presidency in March 1968, and Suharto, outwardly the exact opposite of Sukarno but possessing the same iron determination to create a proud and independent nation, set about to put Indonesia back on its feet. With the Army now playing a major role in political life, Indonesia entered a much-needed period of stability. The new government quickly re-established diplomatic relations with Western nations, instituted favourable foreign investment regulations, and started the long process of building a development infrastructure.

Indonesia during the "New Order" years has been characterised by rock-solid political stabilty punctuated by a infrequent outbursts of localised unrest, quickly stamped out by the Army or Police. The mass media is firmly under government supervision, and all political groups have been amalgamated into government-organised "parties." But if civil liberties are at a low ebb in Indonesia, (although most Indonesians, especially the Javanese, have been under some sort of authoritarian government during their entire history) so is infant mortality, population growth and poverty in absolute terms. All have dropped dramatically.

The fortuitous oil boom of the mid 1970s and early 1980s provided the cash to finance development programs, while an equally providential oil glut in the mid 1980s began the process of weaning the economy away from dependence on oil.

In 1985, the government began to systematically dismantling the thousands of monopolistic controls and regulations that had hamstrung the country's trade and industry. Almost overnight, Indonesia's economy kicked into high gear. Investors have flocked to Indonesia, drawn by the cheap, qualified labour and abundant resources.

Java, especially, has benefitted from this economic growth. Many Javanese cities and towns have changed from sleepy backwaters to bustling commercial centers, and new sedans battle with long-haul trucks for space on the crowded highways.

Left, Sukarno and Suharto. **Right**, President Suharto.

In rural Java, from west to east the cyclic pattern of village life continues much as it has for centuries. Here it is difficult to imagine the presence of foreigners or the *Belanda*, the Hollander, for at this level vestiges of colonial rule are as good as non-existent. The following words turn back the clock 200 years, to 1768, but in many ways the description still applies:

Rice is the principal grain that grows here. They have also plantations of sugar, tobacco, and coffee: their kitchen gardens are well replenished with cabbages, purslain, lettuce, parsley, fennel, melons, pompions, potatoes, cucumbers, and radishes. Here are also all manner of Indian fruits, such as plantains, bananas, cocoas, pineapples, mangoes, mangosteens, durians, oranges of several sorts, limes, lemons, the betel and arek nut, gums of several kinds, particularly benzoin: in March they plant rice, and their harvest is in July. In October they have the greatest plenty of fruit, but they have some all the year. They have good timber, cotton (kapok), other trees proper to the climate, besides cedar, and several kinds of red wood. The coconut is very common, which is of universal use, affording them meat, drink, oil and vinegar; and of the fibres of the bark they make them cordage; the branches cover their houses, and they write on the leaves with a steel stile, and with the tree, and the great bamboo cane, they build their houses, boats and other vessels. Here are buffaloes and some oxen, and a small breed of horses. The few sheep we find here have hair, rather than wool, and their flesh is dry. Their hogs, wild and tame, are the best meat we find there, or in any other countries between the tropics, and their venison is good; here are also tigers and other wild beasts, crocodiles, and monkeys.

The palm-thatched houses are now tiled, the lontar scroll has given way to pen-and-paper, there are hardly a handful of tigers left, there are immense rubber plantations,

there are two and sometimes three rice crops a year…yet that 200-year-old picture of rural Java is still essentially accurate. The incursions of foreign powers, and the "Cultivation System," created great hardship for many peasants, but the nature of Javanese life, the cycle of events within a small village community, remained largely untouched by the outside world. *Adat* continues to be observed; balance and harmony are still virtues, for the Javanese abhor excess, and an obsession with deadlines is not an indigenous trait.

Trains and planes may depart and arrive on schedule. Most other things can wait. It is not quite the *mañana* syndrome, for things do get done but they happen in their own sweet time. A favourite phrase is *jam karet*, which translates literally as "rubber time." Rarely must a social event or a meeting start at the appointed hour; time can be stretched to suit the occasion.

The notion of balance and harmony is also important in personal contacts. Great respect and deference are shown to superiors and elders, and there are distinct speech levels that are used according to the status of the person being spoken to. These fine social

Preceding pages, Muslims at prayer. **Left**, a market in Central Java. **Right**, Javanese women enjoy a freedom unknown in other Muslim countries.

divisions may hark back to the Hindu caste system as yet another example of Java's heritage. To lose face, to be made ashamed (*malu*) is something to be avoided, and many Javanese will suggest that something can be done when they know perfectly well it cannot…but in this way they do not give offence, and the listener knows as well as the speaker that the answer has in fact been a polite; graceful "no." *Halus* or refined behaviour is also infinitely preferred to *kasar* or coarse deeds and actions.

Sometimes this carefully controlled bottling up of emotion (at least on the surface) tells only half the story. Occasionally something goes snap and repressions flood out:

coastal parts of East Java there are faces that seem to have come straight from the souks of Arabia. Generations ago, they probably did. Inland, around Surakarta and Yogyakarta where the Mataram dynasty slowly withered, there are gentle, aristocratic old men with long, thin, epicene faces; and many of the daughters of the ancient noble houses can be recognised not only by their almost ethereal prettiness but also by heavy-lidded eyes that seem almost about to pop. Different again are the broad, snub-nosed faces of the peasants.

Over 200 years ago the women of Java were described as being "much fairer than the men, with good features a soft air,

the state of amuk, running amok, when pressures can no longer be borne, or when there is no communally agreed response to or precedent for a totally new and emotionally jarring experience. It seldom happens…but it should be remembered that the Javanese often fought with great savagery during the battles for independence.

"Javanese" is useful but inaccurate shorthand when speaking about the people of Java as a whole, for the Sundanese in the west and the Madurese in the east must both be reckoned with. Their languages are different (though related) and in parts of the island there are obvious physical differences. In the

sprightly eyes, a most agreeable laugh, and bewitching mien, especially in dancing…." One could hardly disagree, especially when watching the exquisitely-composed features of a court dancer, eyes downcast, her slender body moving as fluidly as the notes of a *gamelan*, through poses as rigid as Hindu temple carvings, fingers shivering as gently as falling rose petals. And there's the other side of the coin, the rough peasant woman, her remaining teeth stained red through chewing great black wads of tobacco, a swatch of green paste stuck to her forehead to ward off ills, her bare feet planted firmly on the ground. There is the corseted middle class woman with her bosom thrust high, her movements hampered by a tightly wrapped sarong and teetering high-heeled sandals, her hair rolled in a huge black bun padded out with green wool, the whole effect a caricature of the other Javanese woman – the natural beauty like the brown-eyed, golden-skinned *padi*-field worker or the T-shirted young student with glossy black hair flowing freely over her shoulders.

Benedict Anderson, in his *Mythology and the Tolerance of the Javanese*, pointed out two obvious stereotypes of Javanese women, Sumbadra and Srikandi. Both are wives of the *Mahabharata* hero Arjuna, but that is all they have in common. Sumbadra is the aris-

tant role in the family and in the society around her. The Srikandis may be the women who run the great markets, bringing in their produce for sale, haggling with other fish-wives, gossiping with ribaldry as they sell their tortoise-shell hairpins, prawn paste, meat and mangoes; or they may be the *padi* workers who (after the men have done the ploughing) transplant the young rice shoots and who later harvest every head of rice by hand; and they can be found in offices, shops, schools, hospitals, universities, lawcourts, the armed forces – in fact, everywhere that men work.

Talk is one of the joys of life for the women and the men of Java. The theatricality of an

tocratic ideal, meek and ladylike, devoted to her husband, and unquestioningly loyal; Srikandi is lively and independent, strong-willed and warm-hearted, sufficiently courageous (or foolhardy) to take on a passing knight in battle, quick-witted enough to indulge in philosophical debate.

The visitor, thinking that Java is ostensibly Muslim, may be surprised to find Srikandi. But she is everywhere, has never worn a veil, and has always enjoyed an active and impor-

Far left, a Javanese aristocrat in court dress. **Left**, a Javanese lady. **Above**, a peddler of pottery in Yogyakarta.

evening gathering of "the boys" is a delight, for it is a form of entertainment, and everyone is a storyteller who has his say without interruption. Each performance is a masterpiece of the orator's art. The scene is set with a droning preamble. Soon come the dramatic gestures and pregnant pauses, the voice rising to an appropriately high pitch of indignation before dropping to a conspiratorial basso profundo; then a staccato *entre-acte* before the next set piece, the seemingly interminable monologue occasionally punctuated by passive grunts from the rapt audience – which waits, with indefatigable patience, for its turn will come.

The people of Java have an extraordinary capacity to find pleasure in simple things: watching the flight of a bird, smoking a cigarette, or playing endless games of dominoes (with cards, not chips) in the coffee stall of a small market. Often, of course, there is not the money for anything more diverting that what one can see in the trees and fields; no television, no magazines, nothing that can be done without. Children display incredible ingenuity in making toys out of improbable materials, and a rudimentary truck with wooden wheels, pushed along at the end of a length of fine bamboo, will provide entertainment for weeks. Village life can be difficult and even monotonous. Yet because the

ber. It is not unusual for a little girl of five to care during the day for younger brothers and sisters while her parents work in the fields, an assumption of responsibility that often seems astounding to foreigners. There is no child beating, no cruelty. Their lives are often poor, but in these respects rich.

Children, loved as they are, represent one of Java's major problems. The island is grossly overpopulated, and has long ceased to be agriculturally self-sufficient. Family planning units get close to their targets each year, but the targets are modest to the point of being ineffectual. There are too few teachers, and too few schools, and at the beginning of each school year several million

villagers can accept and enjoy the presence of a butterfly or an insect, or even the fleeting relevance of ephemeral things, there is always something about which to small-talk or in which to be involved.

The children of Java are a delight. Cheeky, mischievous, wide-eyed, laughing, they are visible everywhere. They are also extraordinarily self-possessed little bodies. Never ignored, always loved, and yet firmly controlled by an invisible discipline (they are never chastised in public, for they rarely misbehave), they are part of the family and community group from birth; not just a cipher, but an active and quickly contributing mem-

school-age children have no place to go; they cannot be taught at home, for many of their parents are themselves illiterate. The gap between the haves and the have-nots is enormous.

The people of Java, before the arrival of the Buddhist and Hindu faiths over a thousand years earlier, had been animists and ancestor worshippers. Even now it is hard to imagine a land more likely to enhance a belief in the reality of supernatural forces and spirits, for along the island's rugged, mountainous backbone there lie more than a hundred volcanic cones and craters: 35 of them are active and seven are under constant supervision by volcanologists (running west to east, they are Tangkuban Prahu, Papandayan, Merapi, Kelud, Mahameru or Semeru, Lamongan and Ijen; Kelud, with its hot crater lake, was on the "very dangerous" list in 1973, and Merapi sends frequent flows of mud and lava down its western flank).

Volcanoes ravage. They also replenish. It was on the island's richly productive soil, much of it the residue of old eruptions, that the early Javanese established their crops. Today, about 63 percent of Java's land area is cultivated (exclude the mountain peaks and urban concentrations, and the percentage is getting close to saturation point), and of that area more than a third is irrigated. The

nut palms and banana trees that mark the site of a village.

Rice, of course, had its spirit or soul. To do it the least possible injury the heavy heads of grain were delicately cut with a small wood-mounted blade tucked into the palm of the hand, and no more than three or four stalks were severed at a single stroke…a method of reaping still widely used. Since Hindu times the rice spirit has been identified with the goddess Dewi Sri, and offerings are still made to her before a crop is harvested.

Pre-Hindu Java, with its animistic and ancestor-worshipping beliefs, seems to have had two classes of society: those who owned or controlled the land, and those who worked

most familiar form of irrigation, the flooded *padi*-field known as *sawah*, is hardly a newcomer: some of the terraces, especially those in West Java, are probably 2,000 years old, and appear to have been built by people who combined a doctorate in civil and hydraulic engineering with a lifetime of mountaineering experience. On the plains *padi*-fields dominate the landscape in many areas, with silvery sheets of water or the brilliant greens of young growth or the gold of a ripened crop surrounding small islands of bamboo, coco-

Left, Central Javanese farmers from Dieng Plateau. Above, coming home from the market.

it. At the top, the king. At the bottom, the peasant. The advent of Hindu Brahmanism introduced a different but nonetheless compatible concept of the god-king, the divine ruler, a concept that helped to consolidate the position of the Javanese rulers. The older two-level class division was also modified by the influence of the Brahmanistic caste system, with its pecking order of brahmans (priests and teachers), satriyas (warriors, kings and courtiers), vaisias (traders), sudras (peasants and artisans), and pariahs (outcasts or beggars).

The rural village or *desa*, wedded to its surrounding rice-fields and plantations, was the hub of the economy and the source of the kingdom's wealth. The harmony and welfare of such communities was, and still is to a large degree, dictated by the observance of *adat* or customary law. The most striking element in *adat*, at least to Western minds, is the way in which problems and disputes are resolved through discussion (*musyawarah*) and a consensus of opinion (*mufakat*): the issue is debated and analysed, opinions shift, subtle compromises are made, until there is unanimous agreement on a fair and just decision. The so-called "democratic" mechanism which perversely allows 51 percent to overrule a dissenting 49 percent is a foreign concept in the tight village communities of

Java, for majority rule is considered divisive and unequitable because it leaves an often sizeable minority unsatisfied.

The villager and the agricultural worker, far removed from the direct influence of the courts, retained many of their animistic beliefs, and even the missionary spirit of Islam has never succeeded in eradicating all vestiges of the old practices. Some 90 percent of Java's people are classified as Muslims, but with few exceptions (principally along the north coast from Banten through to Surabaya) the Javanese version of Islam would scarcely satisfy an orthodox *mullah* (teacher) from the Middle East.

Clifford Geertz, in his *The Religion of Java*, distinguished three observable types of religious practice and the social role or status of the people who practised them. The divisions tend to overlap, for an individual may observe several types of practice simultaneously, but the distinctions are useful.

The first group, the *abangan*, are mostly peasants in whom the animistic strain is dominant. The second, the *priyayi*, are broadly the upper middle class and are in some ways the successors of the old Hindu *satriya* caste (as are the heroes of the dance dramas and puppet plays); their religious observances are flexible and eclectic, and the *priyayi* tend to be found in bureaucratic or white-collar positions. The third, the *santri*, are defined as the more-or-less orthodox Muslims who, not surprisingly in the perspective of history, are generally traders and merchants.

The *selamatan* or ceremonial meal is the most common of the *abangan* ceremonies. It may celebrate such important events as a wedding or a birth; it may acknowledge a death or a ritual circumcision; and it may be occasioned by a hundred smaller and different events such as moving into a new house, a bad or ominous dream, a decision to make a long trip, or the return of a prodigal son. Although one person or one family is usually the originator of the *selamatan* it is invariably a communal affair. It may be extremely simple and modest; it may be restricted entirely to men; it may be lavish.

Every *selamatan* includes "rice mountains" (*gunungan*) which, even if the size of a cupcake, are an important part of the ritual meal. In addition to the meal there is often a performance of puppet plays or of mask dances (*wayang topeng*). The name of the ceremony comes from the word *selamat*, which variously means safe or happy, welfare, prosperity, congratulations or good luck, and the *selamatan* ritual meal, with its religious overtones, is designed to bring about and enhance *keadaan selamat*, the "state of *selamat*." However celebrated, or wherever seen, the *selamatan* is still a lively and involving aspect of Javanese life.

Left, **Islamic stories figure prominently in contemporary theatre and dance. Right, a *santri* reads the Koran in a Muslim cemetery.**

Novelty, and the idea of change for the sake of change, are the antithesis of cultural life in Java. Rather, Javanese culture finds its roots and its strength in a continuing statement of the validity and relevance of ancient forms.

The variety of Java's cultural offerings does not begin and end with the "fine arts," for there is no arbitrary division between the sublime and the vulgar, the culture of the courts and that of the market place. The expressions, and the degree of refinement, may be different, but they are also linked by their relevance to daily living and entertainment. The people of Java enjoy spectacle; they love colour and form; they revel in both simple and complex beauty. Plastic roses and crystal chandeliers are part of the same continuum. The brilliant colours of cordial drinks (the soft white meat of young coconut afloat in a sea of crimson syrup), multi-layered rice cakes in pink and green, and hectically ornamented bullock carts and *becaks* are as much a part of the cultural fabric as the magnificent gold-and-glitter costumes of dance heroes and heroines, complementing the view of the art historian A.K. Coomaraswamy: "The basic error in what we have called the illusion of culture is the assumption that art is something to be done by a special kind of man, and particularly that kind of man whom we call a genius. In direct opposition to this is the normal and humane view that art is simply the right way of making things."

The West, always self-conscious, was amazed at its own audacity in producing a mini-cult of "Pop Art." A can of Campbell's soup, said Andy Warhol, is a work of art. The people of Java have known that for centuries: they accept functional beauty, and don't expect to have it pointed out to them because they know it is there. It is there in superbly-woven rice baskets, in the cleanly simple lines of village pottery, in the gaudily-painted hats of south-central Java; it can be found in the sun-ray patterns on horse-carts near Jepara and in the harnesses of Garut; and it is visible

everywhere in endless varieties of designs, colours and patterns.

Repeated expressions and manifestations of well-known traditional themes were, and in many cases still are, the core of Javanese culture. Ancient beliefs were continually reaffirmed through repetition which, far from dulling the senses, actually amplified the experience and confirmed the rightness of a dance movement, of a sculptural form, of a puppet's visual characteristics.

Two strong cultural influences in Java's history have been the great Hindu epics *Ramayana* and *Mahabharata*, which established ethical and aesthetic codes that are still followed in many respects. There are obvious parallels between the impact of these immortal sagas on the life of Java and the impact of Old Testament heroes and villains on the life of medieval Europe. The difference, now, is that while in the West such characters as Lot, Job, Joshua, Goliath and David have become little more than ill-remembered names, the inhabitants of the Hindu epics still strut upon the stage in Java. They have done so for more than a thousand years, and they are unlikely to fall from favour in the next thousand. The West celebrates change. Java celebrates tradition.

Tradition, reinforced by religious, moral and social pressures, naturally imposed limitations which inhibited originality. As in many parts of Asia, in Java the maxim "hasten slowly" was scrupulously observed: "Achieve perfection within limits you understand, do not attempt to surpass your masters for the sake of surpassing." This was the philosophy of Middle Eastern, Indian, Chinese and Japanese artistic masters for centuries, just as it was during the great flowering of Western religious art from the 5th to the 15th centuries.

But in Java, as in medieval Europe, the following of established precepts, the imitation, the repetition, did not mean that artistic expression became static or moribund. In time, however gradually, changes did occur, and Java's culture assumed a distinctive personality; influenced by Indian artistic tenets, it nevertheless put its own mark on a rich and complex heritage: "I see India everywhere, but I do not recognise it." The

Preceding pages, crowding round the *gamelan* orchestra at a *wayang kulit* performance. **Left**, pretty in Prambanan – a traditional greeting.

panakawan (clowns, servants and heroes) were a peculiarly Javanese addition to the Hindu epics, *wayang kulit*, the theatre of shadows, influenced sculptors and masons in a way not seen anywhere else in Asia. The traditional arts which survived for so long survived because they continue to answer spiritual and emotional needs. The concept of a secular culture is largely foreign to Java.

The pressures of modern life, of commercial competition, are naturally being felt, but their influence on traditional cultural forms has so far been small. The movies, television, rock groups and "modern art" have taken space on the Javanese cultural stage, but have merely expanded the options rather

ern counterparts will be with the Old Testament, Chaucer or Shakespeare.

In rural Java conservatism is still strong, and there are reminders of the life-style in towns and hamlets in old Europe: annual harvest festivals, Maypole and Morris dances, celebrations of Midsummer's Night, the feeling of being part of a tightknit, harmonious community. At this level Europe absorbed the new spirit of Christianity, yet kept alive (symbolically at least) the old pagan rituals of the Christmas tree, the mistletoe, the holly leaves and berries. In the same way, and beginning about the same time, animistic, ancestor-worshipping Java accepted Buddhist and Hindu beliefs, and then Islam,

than destroyed the old heritage.

Many young Indonesians do flock to the cinema. Lust and gore are high on the list of movie preferences, which is hardly surprising: there is a tradition of overt violence in all of the ancient epics. The same youngsters, almost without exception, will be enthralled by a performance of *wayang kulit*. Although there those who are more likely to pluck the strings of an electric guitar than to wield a hammer in a *gamelan* orchestra, even those with the long hair and elaborate jewellery who eulogise the rock music icons of the day will generally be more familiar with the intricacies of the *Ramayana* than their West-

and elements of every faith and belief can still be found in Java's traditional cultural expressions.

It is not only at the village level that a sense of timelessness pertains. The courts of Yogyakarta and Surakarta maintain *gamelan* orchestras that were old when Bach was a young organist seeking royal favour. The refined art of classical Javanese dance is taught within the walls of the old palaces. The profession of *dalang* or puppet-master is still honourable and necessary.

If half the population of Java were suddenly swept off the land and into factories, the role and nature of this cultural continuity would undoubtedly change. But it is unlikely that it would change radically, for Java's folk heroes animate much of daily life, far beyond the confines of a stage or a single night-long performance. The Javanese still describe another person's strengths or foibles through epic characters: he's a Bima, she's a Sumbadra, he's a Rama, she's a Srikandi. Countless shops and *warungs* throughout the island are named after the same heroes and heroines. *Becaks* are gaily adorned with scenes of volcanoes, the Apollo moon-landings, pretty landscapes and events and characters from the *Ramayana* and the *Mahabharata*; there are hundreds of household products, from cigarette papers to noodles, named

iconographic principles were accepted and subtly modified in their application to temple architecture, bas-reliefs, free-standing sculpture and bronze-casting. Elements of Chinese design added a distinctive touch to the crafts of woodcarving and furniture-making. Furniture makers borrowed freely from imported styles, producing "Dutch" chairs and tables and magnificent "Chinese" wedding beds (often decorated with scenes from Hindu mythology), "Chinese" chests and herbal cabinets.

Painting on canvas has come late on the Javanese scene. Although there are written records of portrait painting more than 400 years ago, nothing has survived. By the be-

after characters from the *Ramayana* and the *Mahabharata*; and panels of woodcarving, paintings and comic strips portray episodes from these epics because the epics still impinge upon daily life.

The apparent timelessness of many of Java's arts and crafts has not meant stagnation or a refusal to change, for tradition and repetition have in fact reinforced the vitality and relevance of expression. Many outside influences have been absorbed and utilised in the last 1,500 years. Hindu and Buddhist

Local offerings: Western-style stick-ons (left) and an enticing movie poster (above).

ginning of the 19th century the art had so declined that Raffles was able to write that the Javanese "have a tradition, that the art of painting was once successfully cultivated among them, and a period is even assigned to the loss of it; but the tradition does not seem entitled to much credit." A certain amount of illustrative work, in a crude "comic-strip" style, continued to be done on calendars and astrological charts, but it could hardly be called painting. Much finer was the highly stylised artistry of the old *wayang beber* narrative scrolls which are still being reproduced (though not originated) by artists in Surakarta.

The first modern painter of note was Raden Saleh (1816–80). He spent twenty years in the salons and courts of Europe, and later painted some memorable portraits of the royal families of Central Java, but after his death there was a gap of 50 years before a number of schools of modern art surfaced.

Ironically, the Dutch colony should have provided the most fertile environment for serious art. Whereas Southeast Asia's other colonialists, the French and British, would set up, respectively, bars and racetracks for entertainment, the puritanical Dutch established art galleries in their social societies. Travelling exhibitions of the best European art would arrive monthly at the Harmoni in

Of this group, the Affandi was destined for greatest commercial success, while Hendra's works will are beginning to flourish on world art markets.

The generation who came of age after the Independence largely retreated into European abstractism, and has produced little of consequence. Nyoman Gunarsa is the notable exception. This Balinese who settled in Yogyakarta in the mid 1960s, Nyoman's large, dappled canvases are among the first to explore Indonesian themes in a non-traditional, though uniquely Indonesian manner.

Soekamto, on the other hand, is the truest to Javanese cultural roots, producing images in the traditional Javanese style with flat

Jakarta or Societat Concordia in Bandung. But few local painters progressed beyond the *Moie Indie* decorative style of lush ricefields and dusky maidens.

In later years, Yogya and Bandung became the two crucibles of Indonesian painting, and many accomplished artists appeared. Their work was invariably modelled on Western norms, and whilst Hendra Gunawan, Suromo, Rusli, Yudhokusumo, Lee Man Fong, Affandi and others developed highly personal and often compelling styles (subtle, boisterous, "primitive") there was nothing apart from the subject matter to make their works specifically Indonesian.

perspective and incredibly fine detail.

The cream of the new generation of Yogyakarta Art School graduates are exploring a form of expression close to the Javanese heart: surrealism. With their mythic traditions and many aspects of modern life surrealistic in nature, the new generation has embraced this European art form with a flourish, employ surrealist technique to reflect modern Java with all the fluid flexibility of Dali's melting watches on the beach. The leading light is Iwan Sagito, a 33-year old who plumbs the depth of the Javanese psyche to produce compelling and often disturbing images.

Batik has long been one of Java's foremost arts, and can be seen in multitudinous colours and patterns all over the island: severely classical brown-and-cream designs in the courts of Central Java, faded floral ones in the rice-fields, gay ones worn as shirts, more subdued patterns worn as school uniforms; there are millions of sarongs in new and old designs, there are precious ones of soft old silk, and there's a thriving industry churning out – patterned shoes, bags, hats, table-cloths, napkins, place-mats and anything else that can use a printed cloth in a functional or decorative manner. For the visitor, is probably the most vivid visual memory of all.

not to be coloured in the first dyeing are then filled in with wax. Both sides of the cloth are treated in this way. The cloth is then steeped in the dye, and once,the desired colour has been achieved the wax is removed by boiling or scraping. This procedure starts again – wax is applied to those areas on which the second colour is not required, and the process is repeated as many as four or five or even more times according to the number of colours needed for the finished design.

Both men and women are involved in making *batik*. and can be seen at work in tiny home workshops or in large co-operative groups that are virtually factories. Apart from

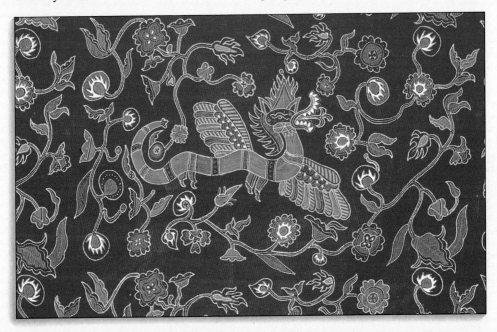

The word *batik* means a length of cloth printed with a wax-and-dye process, though recently it has included machine-printed fabrics with designs based on the traditional patterns.

Genuine *batik* is normally printed on fine cotton or linen, and more rarely on silk. Molten beeswax, impervious to dyes, is applied to those areas of the cloth on which a colour is not required. The basic pattern is first finely outlined in wax, and the areas

the machine-printing of *batik* designs (which is not strictly *batik* at all) carried out on a large scale, the size of a *batik* workshop has no bearing on whether the design is hand-drawn or stamped. Women normally do the designing and the waxing, men normally look after the dyeing, but there is no hard and fast rule, and men often do the waxing of stamped designs.

It is comparatively easy to make crude *batik* but the finest hand-worked materials can take up to 9 months to make, and require the eye of a hawk, the patience of Job, and the combined skills of a chemist and a magician. In the hands of a skilled artisan, *batik* is much

Left, painting in the traditional Javanese style of *wayang beber*. **Above**, a *batik* from the North Coast.

more than a craft. In delicacy and subtlety it can touch sublime heights. It can be bold, subdued, as richly coloured as a full spectrum, or monochromatic. There are motifs 3,000 years old whose origins can be traced back to Assyrian times; there are others that date from the neolithic period of Southeast Asia.

The origins of *batik* are obscure, though it probably developed in Java. Iwan Tirta, a modern authority, suggests that "*batik* may have begun as a kind of painting" and that later, when Islamic influence led to stylisation and abstraction, "this stylisation in painting made it more easily adapted for clothing and dress material, and…slowly a marriage

and helped popularise *batik* but being semi-mechanical it lacks the individual touch and imagination of the canting…nevertheless, it almost put the *batik tulis* artisans out of business, but happily the hand-drawn product is now in increasing demand.

The third influence was the introduction of chemical dyes. New colours and colour combinations developed, especially in the north coast *batik* centres, and even some of the traditional patterns of Central Java (long restricted to indigo, brown and cream or white) are now being produced in brighter colours.

In the last decade the old wax-and-dye process has been applied to an increasingly

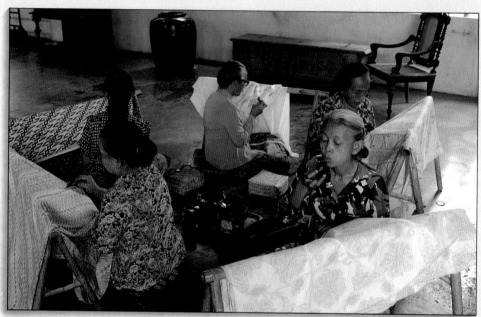

of painting and textile design took place and may well have produced the art of *batik* as we know it today."

There have been three major influences on the development of *batik* printing since the 17th century. The first was the introduction of the *canting*, a short piece of bamboo with a brass or copper reservoir at one end; the reservoir holds the molten wax, which runs onto the cloth through one, two or even three spouts of varying thickness. The *canting* is the pen for hand-drawn or *tulisan* work.

The second influence was the *cap*, a copper stamp introduced about a hundred years ago. It greatly speeded up *batik* production

varied range of modern designs. Some are combinations of motifs from Central Java and the north coast, others have been inspired by modern abstract designs and by Western motifs, whilst others still have modernised ancient stylised motifs with considerable success.

Machine-printed cloths can generally be detected easily because the colour strength on one side will be much stronger than the colour on the other side; only true wax-and-dye *batik* has equal colour density on both sides.

The **Kris**, perhaps more than any other weapon in the world, has been endowed with an aura of myth and mysticism. There are *kris* which, legend has it, removed from their scabbards, refuse to return until they have drawn blood; others are credited with the power of flight; others can reject or even turn on an unworthy owner. One of the strongest and most popular beliefs is that the blade of the *kris* contains the soul of its first or most valiant owner.

The *kris* has probably existed in something like its present form for a thousand years. The earliest dated *kris* was made in Java in 1342, but earlier examples exist. Francis Drake, visiting Java in 1580, noted that the people were warlike, "well armed with swords, targets (shields) and daggers,

number). Although hilts and scabbards have often been elaborately decorated in ivory, gold, silver, rare woods, precious stones, and chiselled and *repousse* work, the sacred blade has always been the most important part of the weapon.

The finest blades were forged from at least two kinds of iron, one of which was generally meteoric iron with a high nickel content (in fact a form of steel). Bars of the different metals were hot-forged together, cut, rolled, hammered…and re-worked again and again until the resulting blade contained layer upon layer of varying grades of iron and steel. Immersed in an arsenic solution, the impure iron turned black, the nickelous iron turned

forged by themselves and exquisitely wrought." Some of the finest *kris* were made during the Majapahit and Mataram dynasties, and as late as the early years of this century talented smiths were still employed by the Susuhunan of Surakarta.

The *kris* is essentially a thrusting weapon, held not like a dagger but with a "pistol grip." The double-edged blade may be 30 to 45 centimetres long, and is either straight-edged or wary; including both edges the number of waves varies from 7 to 25 (always an odd

silver-white, revealing an astonishing range of patterns. These patterns are known as *pamor*, and are highly prized as a sign of craftsmanship. An ability to anticipate the final pattern was an inherent part of the mpu's artistry, and it is easy to understand why an mpu armourer was often credited with magical powers.

Many blades were valued on the originality of their *pamor* work. Others were further embellished with raised gold inlay of superb workmanship. Floral motifs were popular, especially on straight blades, whilst on wavy blades a sacred serpent (*naga*) would weave from the haft almost to the point. *Kris* hilts in

Left, *batik* **pattern-making requires plenty of skill and patience.** <u>**Above**</u>**, the finished product.**

Java were often fashioned in the form of a guardian demon, variously a raksasa or a stylised half-man, half-bird figure (possibly an anthropomorphic garuda). Later, perhaps as a result of Muslim influence, the hilt figure lost its representational form, and most Javanese hilts now show only the faintest hint of a demon on the inside curve of the carved wooden hilt.

In the course of centuries, and even of decades, outstanding blades received new hilts and new scabbards, though the blade itself remain inviolated. Today, the finest *kris*es, whether *pusakas* (sacred heirlooms) or not, are reverently enveloped in "gloves" of velvet. They are treasured for their beauty

magnificent series of temples which still dot the island from the Dieng Plateau in Central Java to the Brantas River in East Java. Many of those erected in Central Java between 750 and 900 AD were inspired by the ideals of Buddhism:

Borobudur (one of the world's greatest Buddhist masterpieces), Mendut, Kalasan, Sewu, Plaosan. Others were built at the same time in honour of the Hindu pantheon: the temples on the Dieng Plateau and the Gedung Songo group above Ambarawa, and the magnificent soaring pinnacle of the Siva temple (*Loro Jonggrang*) at Prambanan.

After the centre of Java's kingly power shifted to the eastern end of the island during

and for their history. *Kris* are still worn with ceremonial court dress and on formal occasions in Central Java, when they can be seen tucked into the back of the colourful waistbands of courtiers, aristocrats and gentry. The *kris* among the royal *pusakas* are the most valued and revered possessions in the old courts, and regular offerings of melati flowers and fragant incense are still made to them.

Temples are the most striking archaeological remains in Java. For more than 750 years, from about 732 AD to the middle of the 15th century, kings, emperors and conquerors ransacked their treasuries to build a

the 10th and 11th centuries, a second spate of temple building activity occurred to the south and southwest of Surabaya. The majority were dedicated to Siva, though some represented a blending of Hindu and Buddhist principles (never far removed in any case) in which Buddha was seen as the elder brother of Siva, Buddha being the spiritual superior while Siva held the temporal reins. Major sites where impressive remains can be seen include Kidal, Jago, Singosari and the huge sprawling complex of Penataran. Unique amongst Java's temples are the sites at Sukuh and Ceta, on the western shoulder of Gunung Lawu on the border of Central and East Java, where in the middle of the 15th century a so-called "Bima cult" based on a puzzling mixture of Hindu and animistic beliefs practised fertility rites. These strange, forbidding temples were the last to be built in Java, for Islam had forced a strong beach-head along the north coast, and the power of the Majapahit kingdom was crumbling fast.

A temple is generally known as a *candi*. Strictly, *candi* means a sepulchral monument housing some of the ashes of a dead monarch, but it has come to refer to any religious edifice.

Borobudur, discussed in more detail in Part Two, is exceptional amongst Java's temples for its size (it is the world's largest *stupa*), shape and overt religious statement. Most other temples adhere to a plan which, although fairly rigid at its core, is nevertheless flexible in detail: a square platform (also an ambulatory) surmounted by a straight-walled temple body which is in turn crowned by a high pyramidal roof; the body of the temple contained an inner chamber or cella in which stood a statue of the deity to whom the temple, was dedicated. In more ambitious projects there were sometimes smaller cellar entered from the remaining three sides of the temple structure, and perhaps an intervening "base" between the platform and the body of the main temple. Buildings which appear to have combined the function of both temple and monastery were rare, but there are fine two-storeyed, three-celled examples at Candi Sari and Candi Plaosan in Central Java.

In the early years of Java's temple-building period sculptural ornament was sparing and essentially simple. The shrines on the Dieng Plateau carry little carving apart from figures of deities and fierce guardian kala heads above the lintels of doorways. A little later reliefs were used on the walls and balustrades of immense undertakings like Borobudur and Prambanan, but even then many temples were simply decorated. It was not until the East Javanese period that ornamentation came into its own with an exuberant and obviously Javanese flavour.

Borobudur's relief panels, fascinating for their domestic, pictorial and narrative detail, are formal and sometimes static; at Prambanan there is a stronger sense of freedom and movement. Three to four hundred years later at Candi Jago and the Penataran complex the relaxed naturalism of Prambanan's panels had almost disappeared, replaced by a strikingly different sculptural style in which figures and animals were carved in a two-dimensional *wayang kulit* manner, surrounded by lush intertwinings of foliage, clouds and rocks where demonic raksasa faces and threatening wraiths can be discerned or imagined; every square centimetre of a panel is filled with voluptuous, sinuous forms.

It is believed that some of the later East

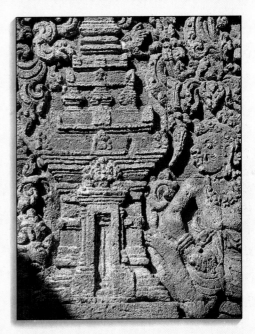

Javanese temples were roofed with wood and thatch above the body of the temple, in much the same way as the multi-tiered Balinese *meru* roofs are constructed today.

Temple building had ceased by the end of the 15th century, and the *masjid* (mosque) became the new place of worship. In Java the rapid rise of Islam was not accompanied, as it had been in India and Iran, by a flowering of art and architecture: there are no tiled glories like the great mosques of Isfahan and Shiraz, and only at Sendangduwur (near Bojonegoro) and Mantingan did Islam leave a legacy of fine ornament in brick, stone and plaster.

Far left, the *kris* is always worn at the back. **Left**, beautifully crafted *kris* hilts. **Above**, an East Javanese *candi*, depicted in the reliefs of the temple of Penataran.

The Performing Arts, of all Java's cultural achievements, are at once the most deeply rooted in the past and the most dramatically evident in the present. There are instruments in the *gamelan* orchestra of Java that have links with the Bronze Age cultures of Central Asia. There are shadow puppets whose origins can be traced back to animistic beliefs that shadows are the manifestations of ancestral spirits. There are masks that once helped village communities protect themselves against demons, and which are still

troupes who work in one place, others who wander through a district or subdistrict like touring repertory companies, always ready for a *selamatan* or for a series of one-night stands.

It is a rich, vibrant tapestry of colour, dance, sound, movement and charm, a finely interwoven mixture of religion, story-telling and entertainment. There has been a constant cross-fertilisation: court dances have become part of the farmer's heritage, the shadow plays of village rituals have developed into

used as aids in exorcism rites. There are dances that were once seen only within the sacred precincts of royal courts. There are trance-inducing dances harking back to ancient beliefs and tribal myths. There are tales and stories based on Hindu, Islamic and indigenous Javanese legends.

Java's performing arts are found everywhere, in much the same way that morality and mystery plays were almost the bread of daily life in medieval Europe, that Punch and Judy puppet shows were regularly performed at fairs and on village greens until recent times. Java still has its strolling minstrels and its mobile theatrical groups; it has famous

one of the island's most consummately sophisticated art forms.

Inevitably, somewhere in Java, the visitor will come across a *wayang* performance of some kind. *Wayang* literally means "shadow," but since all theatrical forms are, in a sense, abstractions, *wayang* has become a handy expression embracing most types of theatre in Java.

Wayang kulit is the theatre of the flat leather shadow puppets; *wayang golek* is the theatre of three-dimensional wooden puppets; *wayang wong* (Javanese) or *wayang orang* (Indonesian) is the human theatre; and *wayang topeng* is human theatre in which the actors wear masks. Separate again is classical dance, once the exclusive prerogative of the Javanese courts, but now an important element in *wayang wong* performances. In all forms of *wayang* the dialogue (whether spoken by the *dalang* or the actors) is in Javanese or Sundanese, and the chants are often in *kawi*, the Old Javanese language. Bahasa Indonesia is sometimes used in humorous exchanges between the clowns, or in direct repartee with the audience, but except in the modern *ludruk* plays it is never used as

from where he manipulates the puppets, directs the *gamelan*, intones or sings special songs, narrates story outlines, and provides the voices for every character. The puppets are arrayed to the left and right of the centre of the screen, stuck into the soft pulp of the banana trunk: the "goodies" are on the *dalang*'s right hand, the "baddies" on his left. The audience, as it chooses, can sit on the *dalang*'s side of the screen (the best place to appreciate the colours of the puppets and their master's extraordinary skills) or on the

the main language.

A *wayang kulit* performance requires a white cloth screen, a puppeteer or *dalang*, a *gamelan* ensemble (the size varies), the trunk of a banana tree, a light source to cast the shadows (once an oil lantern in the shape of a garuda or sun-bird, now generally an incandescent bulb), and of course the puppets. All are assembled on one side of the screen, the *dalang* sitting cross-legged on the floor

Preceding pages, a *wayang orang* performance at the Mangkunegaran Court in Solo. **Above, left and right**: *wayang kulit* can be viewed from both sides of the screen.

"shadow" side of the screen, a marvellously exciting world of hard-edged blacks and subtle, wavering, ghostly greys.

In addition to his other skills the *dalang* is also a master of improvisation. He works from a basic story outline or *lakon*, but there is no formal "script" in any *wayang* performance. The outline naturally dictates much of the content of the dialogue, but it is the *dalang* who injects originality, humour, satire and even social commentary into the presentation.

A performance begins at 8.30 or 9 p.m. at night (though daytime shows are not uncommon). The first 3 hours up to midnight introduce characters, establish the story line and provide occasional skirmishes and conflicts. At midnight the second part begins, invariably introduced by the *panakawans* (clowns), and this is always the most vigorous and enthralling segment of the play. Some 3 hours later, after a multitude of battles and sundry adventures, the resolution of the action and plot takes place, and the performance ends just as the sun is about to rise.

Wayang golek performances follow a similar pattern, though naturally without the need for a screen, and the audience normally sits facing the *dalang*. Daylight performances of *wayang golek* are quite common.

a *dalang* who chants songs and conducts the *gamelan* orchestra, but his role is less important than it is in the puppet plays. The human players move with rigid adherence to stylised steps and actions, many of which are astonishingly similar to those of the puppet characters.

Dance has a very important role in *wayang wong*, and although some of the verbal encounters which help set the scene are boring to look at (but full of philosophical subtleties to anyone who understands Javanese) the dancing more than compensates for the dull patches. Every town of any size has a resident *wayang wong* troupe. Sriwidari performs each night in Solo, and is the oldest and most

Shadow puppets are most popular in Central Java, where they enact episodes from the *Ramayana* and *Mahabharata* cycles; wooden-puppet plays are much less common, and normally tell stories from the Amir Hamzah tales. In West Java, *wayang golek* is far more popular than *wayang kulit*, and follows the *Ramayana* and *Mahabharata* repertoire.

Wayang wong (or *wayang orang*), with live actors, is extremely popular throughout Java. As in the puppet theatre, the plays are mostly based on the Hindu epics, though there is a considerable store of tales from East Javanese history and legend. *Wayang wong* also uses

famous troupe in Java, acknowledged throughout the island as the best.

Good presentations of *wayang wong* are brilliantly colourful spectacles, with sumptuous costumes and a golden glitter of bracelets, armbands and head-dresses. For the visitor the *Sendartari* (an Indonesian acronym for art-drama-dance) performances on the open-air stages at Prambanan, 16 km east of Yogya and at Pandaan's Candra Wilwatikta 45 km from Surabaya are exciting introductions to a complex but superbly alive world of theatre. In both instances the dialogue has been dropped, so that the dancing and the music become all-absorbing.

Wayang topeng is now seldom seen as a full length performance, though a revival is taking place in Cirebon in West Java, and *wayang topeng* Cirebon can sometimes be seen in Jakarta.

A variation of *wayang topeng* is *tari topeng* (literally "mask dance"), in which two or three masked dancers perform short excerpts from the *Panji* stories (see page 92). These are invariably danced with great skill, and the beautiful, stylised masks seem to acquire a living, mobile quality. The *Panji* cycle is also of probable historical interest, representing a unique Javanese synthesis of indigenous with Hindu elements.

Until the early years of this century Java-taught outside of the old palaces…though dancing masters at Yogyakarta's *kraton* can be seen instructing their pupils as they must have done for centuries.

Pure dance, as opposed to the dance dramas, still exists in two famous forms, the *serimpi* and the *bedoyo*. Both are danced solely by girls, and both are exquisitely subtle in their grace and elegance. The *serimpi* is a stylised combat between two pairs of girls, and is apparently based on the old Amir Hamzah stories. The *bedoyo* is a beautiful series of undulating and gently flowing movements performed by nine girls. The *serimpi* and the *bedoyo* are still danced within the Solo court, and can also be seen in Yogyakarta

nese classical dance was not seen outside of the courts, where it had developed over the centuries into a serenely stylised and immaculately precise form. Originally of ritual and religious significance (Siva was more easily propitiated by dance than by any other form of worship) it became one of the most highly regarded and polished of all Java's arts. Happily for today's visitor many of the movements of court dancing can now be seen in the *wayang wong* dance dramas, and the formal art of classical dance is now

Left, *wayang golek* puppets, in the style of Yogyakarta. **Above**, *tari topeng*.

at special functions held by relatives of the sultan or by members of the old aristocracy, though dance performances are no longer staged within the *kraton*. Any opportunity to see either of these beautiful dances should not be missed.

Ketoprak and *ludruk* are two other theatrical forms that might be encountered. The *ketoprak* repertoire is based largely on indigenous East Javanese tales (part myth, part history), and the acting style is essentially realistic; dance and singing may be used at the opening of performance, but not within the fabric of the play. *Ludruk* was created this century, and is the closest thing in Java to modern Western theatre, with plots generally based on conflicts arising out of the generation gap or thwarted love trysts. Female roles in *ludruk* are played by men.

The most famous folk-dances in Java are the *reog Ponorogo* (in which the lead dancer wears a horrendously heavy tiger mask) and the *kuda kepang* "horse trance dance" which is sometimes seen in conjunction with the *reog Ponorogo* but more often seen alone. It is known by several different names, but the action is essentially the same: dancers, astride "hobby horses" of plaited bamboo, whirl themselves into a state of complete trance, during which they dismount from their steeds

must always lose) than a recognition of the perpetual ebb and flow of the spirits of darkness and light. They are far older, and far more popular, than Chaucer's *Canterbury Tales*, but like the Tales they are filled with action, wit and imagination. Their partly religious, partly philosophic content has remained absorbing and relevant because it has been presented in such a consummately entertaining manner.

In the *Ramayana* the chief characters are Rama, his wife Sita, his brother Laksmana, the monkey general Hanuman, the demon king Rawana, and Rawana's brother Wibisana. In the *Mahabharata* the "good guys" are the five Pandawa brothers, of whom

and proceed to eat unhulled rice, glass or anything else that is offered to them.

The two main stories informing Javanese theatre and dance are the *Ramayana* and the *Mahabharata*. Both are moral tales, full of instructions and examples on how to lead the good life; both praise the rectitude, wisdom and perseverance of the noble *satriya* or warrior class; both stress faithfulness, integrity and filial and fraternal devotion; and both acknowledge that the trek along the path of virtue demands humility, self sacrifice, deprivation and compassion. They are cautionary tales, like *Everyman*, but are less a battle between good and evil (in which evil

Arjuna and Bima are the best loved, and the semi-divine Krisna; the "bad guys" are the hundred Korawas (99 brothers and a sister).

Arjuna and Rama have certain characteristics in common: both are semi-divine (Arjuna is descended from the god Indra, Rama is an incarnation of Visnu), and both are consummate archers; Rama, however, does not have Arjuna's awesome predilection for the fairer sex, but devotes himself to his only wife, Sita.

The most popular figures of all are the four *panakawans*, the clownish servants of the Pandawas: Semar the father, "short-legged, fat, hermaphroditic…flat-nosed, with a hypertrophic jaw, a wise, tired eye, an enormous rear part, a bulging paunch, and heavy, almost feminine breasts" (Claire Holt), and his three sons Gareng, Petruk and Bagong. They are much more than clowns. Whilst they are often up-roariously funny (even to those who can't understand a word of Javanese), their role is akin to that of the medieval courtjester: a source of wit and humour, and also of valued counsel. Semar, especially, appears to carry the accumulated wisdom of the ages. Although Arjuna is semi-divine, he is not impervious to the displeasure of the gods. Yet gross, grotesque Semar, with his rheumy eyes, not only confronts the gods but often bests them: he alone could have the

Although many participants in the larger "crowd scenes" will be nameless monkeys warriors or crude, destructive giants and demons, there are still dozens of leading characters whose identity is established visually according to age-old precepts. The clue may be the way in which a dancer moves, the shape of his head-dress, the colour of his face or his mask (*wayang topeng*). Wooden and leather puppets can be unmistakably identified in the same way. These visual characteristics, however, tell much more than "who", for they also illuminate the personality of the character.

Rama and Arjuna are obviously of noble birth for they move in a refined (*halus*) man-

effrontery to throw the great god Brahma into a well.

In a complete set of *wayang kulit* figures there may be as many as 400 individual puppets. In the course of a village performance of *wayang golek* upwards of a hundred characters might be seen. Even *wayang wong* calls for a large number of human actors, and the Prambanan *Ramayana* troupe puts a hundred people on stage.

Left, sounding the gongs at a *wayang kulit* performance. **Above left**, *kuda kepang*, the "horse trance dance" and **right**, *wayang golek* puppeteer prepares his charges.

ner. Even in battle they are graceful and delicate, using their minds as much as their muscles, whilst their demon foes rant and rage with the fury of a wounded bull elephant. As dancers, they are always slimly built. As puppets, they have long, straight downward-pointing noses and narrow downcast eyes, both symbols of nobility, and their faces are generally gold in colour.

Arjuna and the twin brothers Nakula and Sadewa always wear their hair in an upward-curling roll like a scorpion's tail: their elder brother, Yudistira, wears a flatter, more compact style, denoting his more gentle, introspective nature.

Bima is stupendously strong. He is also impetuous, generous, loyal, and a ferocious warrior. In *wayang kulit* he towers above his four brothers, and has wide-awake eyes and an upturned nose similar to his Korawa opponents, though his "scorpion-tail" hair style automatically marks him as royal. In *wayang wong* he moves with abrupt, angular steps resembling vigorous isometrics. His most singular feature is a pair of huge, thumbnails, fearsome weapons in time of war.

Krisna, a god incarnate, is an ally of the Pandawas. As a shadow puppet he has a black face, is small, and has the long straight nose and narrow eyes of the gentleman warrior. His brother Baladewa, who sides with

The *raksasas* and *butas* (giants, ogres, demons) who inhabit both the epics normally have red faces, huge round eyes and bulbous noses.

Voices, too, are helpful in identifying a type, if not a specific character. The *halus* characters speak in a soft, often inaudible monotone (delivered by the actors in *wayang wong*, or by the *dalang* in puppet plays). The *kasar* characters variously shout, rage, scream and bellow. Wheedling ministers (*patih*) and ill-meaning teachers (*guru*) often whine and sniffle.

In their homeland, the vast subcontinent of India, the *Ramayana* and the *Mahabharata* have been known for 3,000 years. With the

the Korawas has a rose or red face, is much taller than his brother, but nonetheless has a refined nose and almond-shaped eyes: he is not a complete ogre.

Rawana, Rama's implacable foe, thrusts and struts upon the stage, every step filled with menace. His head turns sharply with each movement, his legs move like pistons in the *gagah* or *kasar* style which is an attribute of all demon nobles. His eyes are fixed rigidly ahead of him symptomatic of intractability; his face (whether a grease-painted human one, a mask, or a puppet head) is an impassioned, furious red in keeping with his aggressive, hostile nature.

spread of Indian religions and culture through Southeast Asia, the two epics became part of the mythology of Burma, Thailand, Laos, Cambodia, the Malay Peninsula, and especially of Java and Bali. Both epics are long and complex, even in the barest outline. Thus, the following synopses offer a thread, but not the rich texture.

The *Ramayana*: Rama, Laksmana and their half-brother Barata are the sons of the king of Ayodya. An accomplished bowman, Rama wins the hand of beautiful Sita in an archery contest, but through the interven-

Rama and Sita in a Yogya style performance.

tion of Barata's mother, Rama is prevented from succeeding his father as king. Rama, Sita and Laksmana go into exile, refusing Barata's entreaties to return. In the forest they meet a sister of Rawana, king of the demons (*raksasas*); she falls in love with Rama, is spurned, and then turns to Laksmana who promptly cuts off her nose and ears.

Rawana, determined to avenge this indignity, sends off a servant in the form of a golden deer. Rama stalks the animal and kills it. Its dying cries sound like Rama calling for help, and Laksmana, taunted by Sita, goes in search of his brother though he has been forbidden to leave his sister-in-law. In his absence Rawana appears as a holy beggar and confronts Sita, who refuses his appeals to desert Rama. Rawana assumes his natural terrifying form, abducts Sita, and flies off with her. The gallant bird Jatayu attempts to rescue her but is mortally wounded. Before dying he tells Rama and Laksmana what has happened.

Searching for Sita, the brothers meet Hanuman, a general in the kingdom of the apes, who takes them to meet Sugriwa, his king. Sugriwa who has been usurped by his brother, seeks Rama's aid in regaining his throne. Rama kills the errant brother, and the grateful monkey king places his army at Rama's disposal. Rama and Laksmana set off with Hanuman and the white ape army, and learn that Rawana has carried Sita across the sea to the island of Langka, Rawana's homeland. Hanuman undertakes a daring reconnaissance of Langka and finds Sita in a garden of Rawana's palace. He gives her a token from Rama, and Sita in turn gives Hanuman one of her rings, but Hanuman is discovered by Rawana's guards, is captured after a desperate fight, and is sentenced to be burnt at the stake. With the pyre blazing, he wrenches free, his tail a mass of flames, and sets fire to the palace before fleeing from Langka.

Hanuman carries Sita's ring to Rama, and the ape armies gather on the shore opposite Langka and build a giant causeway across the sea. On the island a tumultuous battle ensues. One of Rama's magic arrows eventually fells Rawana, and the victors return home with Sita to a boisterous welcome. In the kingdom of Ayodya, Rama receives the throne from his half-brother Barata.

The *Mahabharata*: The 99 Korawas, led by the ambitious Suyudana, believe that the kingdom of Ngastina should belong to them and not to their cousins, the Pandawas. Egged on by the evil chancellor Sakuni they resolve to destroy the Pandawas: Yudistira, Bima, Arjuna and the twins Nakula and Sadewa. Although brought up together under the regent of Ngastina, and instructed by the same teacher Durna, the cousins have never been close, and the superiority of the Pandawas in any kind of contest has only heightened the resentment and jealousy of the Korawas.

Plot follows plot. Arjuna is poisoned, but revived by the gods, Yudistira is imprisoned, but released by Bima, the greatest warrior amongst the famous five; and finally a drastic attempt is made to burn the Pandawas alive. Tiring of torments, the Pandawas and their wives take to the forest for some years and form an alliance with Krisna. Yudistira has married the beautiful Drupadi, oft-wed Arjuna marries Sumbadra (Krisna's sister) by whom he has a son Abimanyu, and Bima has married the giantess Arimbi and produced a son Gatotkaca, who, like his father, is a fearsome warrior but who has also inherited from his mother the ability to fly.

A truce is reached with the Korawas, but the peace is short-lived. Yudistira, an inveterate gambler, is inveigled into a rigged dice game and loses everything (palace, wife, himself and his brothers) to Suyudana. The Pandawas are forced into a 13-year exile. On returning they find that Suyudana will not return them their little kingdom as promised. They hold a council of war with Krisna. The Bharatayuddha, "The War of the Bhatatas," begins.

In 18 gory days the cream of the Bharata nobility is destroyed. The Pandawas' losses are heavy, and of the Korawas there is only one survivor.

In microcosm, the Bharatayuddha is the arche-type of the fratricidal conflict: the House of Lancaster against the House of York, Union against Confederacy. Yet the whole cycle is filled with soft interludes, with humorous tales of mistaken identity, with reflections on the court life of the Pandawas.

Arjuna Wiwaha, "The Wedding of Arjuna", is one of the most popular stories in the cycle, relating the temptations imposed on Arjuna during his ascetic devotionals on Mount Indrakila, where he has gone to seek strength and guidance for the forthcoming battle against a demon king who threatens the abodes of the gods (the gods, in many of these tales, are far from infallible, and frequently seek human aid in thwarting the demons and netherworld creatures who assail them). In ordinary life a redoubtable warrior with a fatal charm with women, Arjuna is tempted by seven divine nymphs, whom he resists; the god lndra tests him further by promising *nirvana*, but Arjuna persists in his ascesis; he is attacked by one of the demon's giants, defeats it, and then joins forces with the gods in a series of escapades which bring

victory…and as a reward spends a month with each of the nymphs.

Three other legends (part myth, part history) are popular to varying degrees in different parts of Java.

Panji is a royal prince who loses his beautiful bride Candra Kirono (Kirana), a princess of Kediri, on the eve of their wedding. Panji's subsequent adventures in searching for his true love have been embroidered and embellished in scores of variations on the simple theme. There are disguises, the inevitable lusting demon kings, innumerable cases of mistaken identity, wild battles, false leads…in fact, everything that "True Love Stories" could ever hope for. Candra Kirono, though deeply in love with Panji often manages to complicate matters by assuming the role of a warrior, but love always wins out.

The *Panji* cycle probably developed in East Java about 500 years ago. Today it is most often seen as a mask play (*wayang topeng*) or in shorter mask dance versions (*tari topeng*), and is a popular and apposite entertainment at wedding parties: guests may be treated to a half-hour episode featuring Candra Kirono in a white mask, Klono (an ardent but ill-fated kingly suitor) in a red mask, *Panji* in a beautiful golden mask…and a clown who will have the guests in tears of laughter as he mimics the delicate movements of Candra Kirono and the bold severity of Klono (waving a feather duster instead of a *kris*) until the *gamelan* refuses to play for him and he feigns sleep in the middle of the floor.

Damar Wulan, another semi-historical tale from East Java, is a favourite in the *ketoprak* repertoire. Nephew of the prime minister of the Majapahit queen, Ratu Kencana, Damar Wulan is employed at the court as a lowly grasscutter, but he falls in love with and secretly marries his beautiful cousin Dewi Anjasmara. The handsome couple are discovered and imprisoned, but Damar Wulan wins his freedom and honour when he succeeds, after many adventures, in vanquishing Menak Jingga, the "Red Knight", who is advancing with an army on the palace of Ratu Kencana. (Menak Jingga, though classically cast in the bad-guy mould, is interesting and colourful enough to warrant stories of his own.)

Amir Hamzah is a fanciful interpretation of Persian history and the rise of Islam in the 7th century. It was probably composed about 800 AD. during the reign of Haroun al Raschid, and reached Java (along with Islam) in the 15th century. Amir Hamzah, also known as Menak, relates the trials and tribulations of the Prince and mainly consists of battle after battle after battle, interrupted by frequent love affairs. The noble prince is credited with laying the groundwork for Mohammed's warrior missionaries, and his boisterous adventures are by far the most popular stories in the *wayang golek* theatre of Central Java.

Left and right, scenes from the *Ramayana*.

Java packs an incredible amount of diversity into a small area, with geography, cultures and even the climate changing every few kilometres. Visitors parachuted separately into individual areas – the sodden rain forests of the west, the cold, misty Dieng Plateau, maritime North Coastal ports, Metropolitan Jakarta and the African veldt of the eastern salient – and asked to record their impressions would seemingly describe wholly distinct environments, like a group of blind men describing an elephant. This book divides Java into five regions, roughly following geo- and ethnographic boundaries. The sequence – west to east along the southern roads with an optional sojourn along the north coast – corresponds to the most common routes travellers take through Java. Most visitors arrive in **Jakarta**, Indonesia's capital, a city so large, economically important and culturally distinct and that it is treated in a separate section. Casual visitors may be put off by Jakarta, and dismiss it out of hand. But anyone who looks beyond the noise and traffic chaos will find a fascinating Asian city. **West Java**, the western third of the island, is also somewhat neglected. But the region contains some of the most spectacular scenery and vibrant traditional culture on Java. West Java includes the historic pepper port of Banten, the world-famous Krakatau volcano and the pristine, barely-accessible nature reserve of Ujung Kulon as well as some fine beaches and cool highlands. **Central Java** is the tourist heartland of Java. It is here that the great ancient and modern empires left their mark

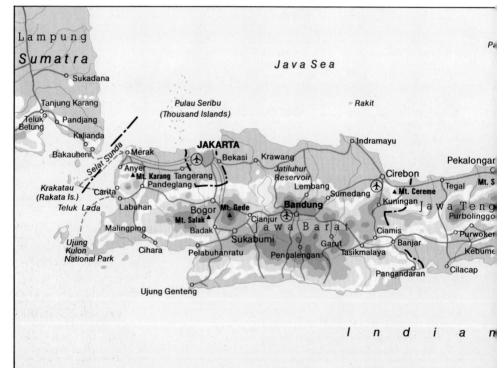

on the land and people. Most people appropriately devote the major portion of their stay to Central Java, the most heavily-populated and culturally-sophisticated region of the island. Yogyakarta – a part of Central Java although administratively a separate province – also has the most highly-developed tourist infrastructure of anywhere on the island except Jakarta. **East Java** requires a bit of effort and expense to experience properly. Predominantly rural and isolated, East Java is the little-visited backwater of the island. Almost every tourist makes an obligatory stop at Mount Bromo for the sunrise before continuing to Bali , but few stay to discover the antiquities, remote nature reserves and colonial charm of the province. **The North Coast** is treated separately, as an optional extra. As the most convenient and rewarding route across Java lies predominantly in the south, most visitors bypass the north entirely. In fact, they miss little, as the area offers scant reward for a casual tourist. But those who wish a complete their picture of Java can return to their starting point along the north coast highway, stopping at areas of interest to let their imagination recreate Java's glorious mercantile past.

Preceding pages: an awe-inspiring cluster of volcanoes, including Bromo (left foreground), Batok (centre) and Mahameru in the distance; at work in the *padi*-fields; downpour on the Dieng Plateau; a riot of colour in Cirebon Harbour.

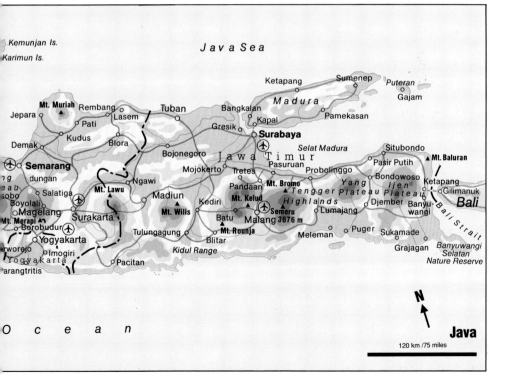

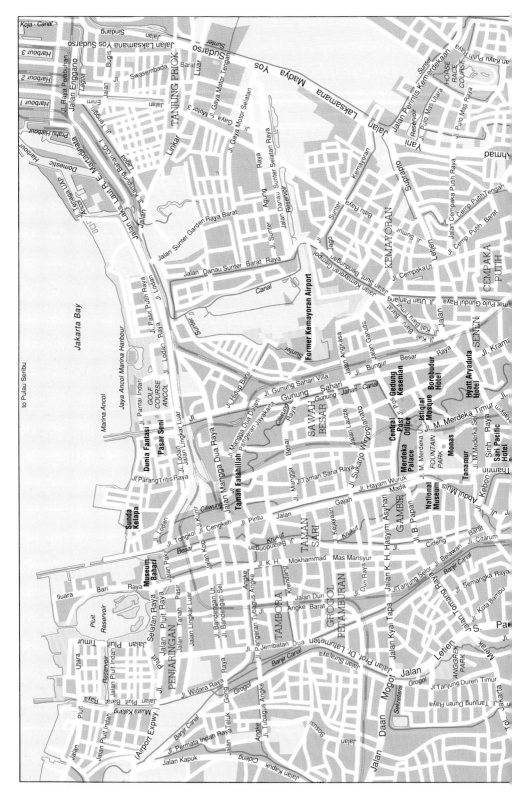

Jakarta

1600 m / 1.0 miles

At first sight, Jakarta does not seem an attractive place to visit. The dirty-brown pall of smog you see blanketing the city from the airplane window, the blast of humid heat as you leave the arrival hall and the snail's-pace traffic on the road to the hotel put off even the most hardened and adaptable travellers. Most upmarket tourists regard Jakarta as an expensive, boring stopover. Backpackers add the city to their repertoire of road-war stories, along with 96-hour bus rides through monsoon-flooded roads and unpleasant encounters with officialdom.

But Jakarta, Java's major gateway and the hub of air, land and sea transport, is largely unavoidable. So a visitor should use the opportunity to explore this fascinating, if frustrating, city.

Situated on a broad alluvial plain, which every year thrusts farther northwards into the sea (part nature, part reclamation), it has no attractions in geographic terms. Not until the foothills of the Parahyangan (Preanger) District, 50 km to the south, does the landscape begin to offer any natural beauty.

It has also grown too fast. Its population has multiplied several fold since the 1960s and there are now thought to be more than 9 million people living in Jakarta. To accommodate this growth the city has sprawled outwards rather than upwards (most high-rise buildings are hotels or offices, not apartment blocks). Jakarta streets during business hours are one long parking lot, and the telephones bring whole new meaning to the term "communication breakdown."

For all its geographic and infrastructural shortcomings, Jakarta remains the heart and soul of modern Java and Indonesia. As Indonesia prepares for its immanent jump into full industrialisation, Jakarta, the economic and political headquarters of the archipelago, represents the present and the future of this great island. To experience Jakarta, whether pleasant or unpleasant, is to round out your perspective of Java.

Aerial view of Jakarta, with Fatahillah Square in the foreground, the Station and the Domed Mosque prominent on the Horizon.

It is likely that the mouth of the Ciliwung River (modern Kali Besar) has been settled for thousands of years. By 1500 it was Pajajaran's port town, known as Sunda Kelapa, and it was herein 1522 that the first Europeans made contact with a Javanese kingdom. The Portuguese, aware of the turmoil in Central Java, thought (erroneously) that the struggles were religious rather than political, and sought a trading alliance with the Hindu kingdom of Pajajaran. This was granted. Returning 5 years later the Portuguese found that Pajajaran's control of Sunda Kelapa had been destroyed by Islamic troops led by Falatehan (Fatahillah) on 22 June 1527. The name of Sunda Kelapa was changed to Jayakarta, or "Great Victory," and the date is still celebrated annually as the birthday of Jakarta.

As a vassal town of the powerful Banten sultanate, Jayakarta survived virtually unmolested for almost a hundred years.

In the first decade of the 17th century, Dutch and English traders established posts in the town. The presence of the interlopers was initially peaceful. Then, in 1618, Sultan Agung of Mataram destroyed the Dutch post at Jepara. The Dutch fortified their trading centre in Jayakarta. In a rapid series of events the Sundanese posted a gun battery against the Dutch, who in turn destroyed the battery and the English trading post; Banten captured the town but not the Dutch fortification, which the beleaguered garrison named Batavia; on 28 May 1619 the Dutch governor-general, Jan Pieterszoon Coen, arrived from the Moluccas with a fleet and soldiers which, 2 days later, sailed forth to capture and destroy the old town.

Jayakarta remained in Dutch hands for the next 330 years.

A massive shoreline fortress was built on the northeast bank of the Ciliwung River. The fortress survived a critical attack by Sultan Agung in 1629, and a new walled town slowly developed within the protective range of its guns. The rigorously geometric layout of that town, laced with canals, is still preserved in the streets of "Old Batavia."

About 1730 "the pestilence" arrived in the form of decimating malarial plagues. The appalling death toll over the next century, encouraged by the lack of proper sanitation, greatly hastened Batavia's spread to the south. Many citizens moved into more salubrious dwellings along the southern reaches of the Ciliwung and in the new suburb of Weltevreden or "well contented," and in 1741 the governor-general moved out of the old castle to a healthier clime.

The old town nevertheless maintained some of its former grandeur. Captain James Cook, who landed there in October 1770 and stayed almost 3 months, left a detailed and generally favourable account of the town, its suburbs, the countryside and the people. At one place in his journal he wrote:

"The environs of Batavia have a very pleasing appearance and would in almost any other country, be an enviable situation. Gardens and houses occupy the country for several miles, but the former are so covered with trees, that the advantage of the land having been cleared of the wood that originally covered it, is almost wholly lost while these gardens and the fields adjacent to them are surrounded by ditches which yield a disagreeable smell; and the bogs and morasses in the adjacent fields are still more offensive. For the space of more that thirty miles beyond the town, the land is totally flat, except in two places, on one of which the governor's country-seat is built, and on the other they hold a large market; but neither of these places is higher than ten yards from the level of the plain. About forty miles from the town the land rises into hills, and the air is purified in a great degree: to this distance the invalids are sent by their physicians when every other prospect of their recovery has failed, and the experiment succeeds in almost every instance, for the sick are restored to health; but they no sooner return to the town, than their former disorders revisit

Early (1787) map of Batavia Harbour.

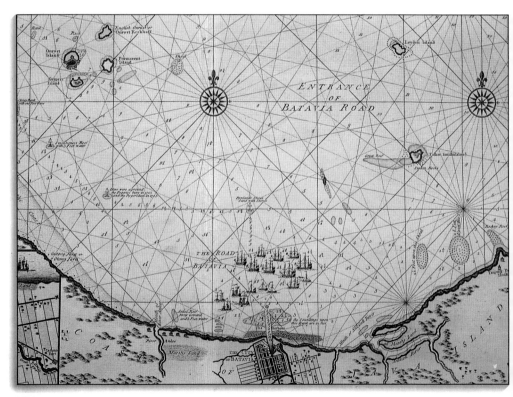

them. On these hills the most opulent of the inhabitants have country seats, to which they pay an annual visit. Those who reside constantly on the hills, enjoy an almost perpetual flow of health; and most of the vegetables of Europe grow as freely there as in their native ground."

During the 19th and early 20th centuries Batavia's life was centred around Weltevreden and Kiningsplein – "King's Square" – the area which is now Medan Merdeka, dominated by the 137-metre National Monument capped with a flame of pure gold – 37 kg of it. In the 1920s and '30s new residential streets were laid out in the Menteng area to the east of present-day Jalan Thamrin. Later during the Japanese occupation, the name "Batavia" was changed to "Jakarta" an abbreviated form of the older name for the city "Jayakarta." After Indonesia's independence was secured the Republican Government moved back to Jakarta from Yogyakarta and in 1966 the city was proclaimed as the *Daerah Khusus Ibukota*, literally the "Special Region of the Mother City." In spite of grumbles about the heat, the telephones and the traffic (from everyone foreigners or Indonesians) and the occasional regret that the Dutch never decided to shift the capital permanently to Bandung, Jakarta is here to stay as Indonesia's capital and primary city.

Many visitors experience Jakarta without seeing **Taman Fatahillah**, the heart of "Old Batavia." It is reached by heading straight north from Jalan Thamrin to Jalan Gajah Mada and Jalan Pintu Besar Utara. On the southern side of this square, newly renovated and now a popular venue for theme parties and receptions, is the old **Stadhuis**, the town hall built in 1710. The building now houses the city's Historical Museum and it contains a rich collection of antique furniture, European porcelain and stoneware, portraits, maps, old tombstones, weapons, coins and other paraphernalia dating right back to periods of prehistory. Special sections of the museum are also devoted to the successive kingdoms that once controlled the Jakarta area. Admission to the museum,

Rooftops in Jakarta's Chinatown.

as is the case with every government-subsidised museum in Jakarta, is still amazingly cheap.

On the east side of the cobbled square is the **Balai Seni Rupa Jakarta**, which serves as the city's art gallery, as a repository of a fine ceramic collection and as a storehouse of information about the arts. The Balai's gallery is perhaps the best example of contemporary Indonesian painting. This museum is housed in a restored neo-classical building dating from the Dutch period.

Directly across from the Balai and northwest from the old Town Hall is one of Indonesia's most fascinating special purpose museums, the **Wayang Museum**. Here's where the great complexity of the *wayang* tradition in Indonesia is captivatingly displayed. Short *wayang* performances are held on Sunday mornings.

On the north side of the Square, the the colonial-style Restaurant Fatahillah is a suitable place to battle museum fatigue with a cool drink or a tasty Indonesian rice or noodle dish.

A short taxi ride from Taman Fatah-illah is **Pasar Ikan** and the adjoining area known as **Sunda Kelapa**. This is a fascinating area: fish from each day's catch is sold beginning at the first light of dawn (a good and cool time to visit) and vessels from the world's last great commercial sailing fleet can be visited and explored.

The Pasar Ikan area is full of myriad lanes, bursting with stalls selling all manner of nautical gear: ropes, chains, pulleyblocks, winches, sail-cloth, hooks, lanterns, and tackle of all descriptions.

The ongoing restoration of historic parts of Jakarta includes refurbishing a line of splendid old Dutch warehouses, one of which now houses the city's maritime museum (called the "Museum Bahari"). The oldest warehouse at the back of the Bahari complex holds a laboratory for archeological studies, and another wing contained a permanent exhibit of naval models and maps.

The most enthralling part of the Sunda Kelapa area is undoubtedly the sailing ships. The area abounds with photo op-

Bugis schooners dockside at Pasar Ikan.

portunities of splendid full-rigged sailing ships and coolies hauling cumbersome bags of fish or grain along narrow gangplanks. Some of the bigger *pinisi* are over 200 tonnes dead-weight, built entirely of teak by craftsmen who use no nails and work to no plan except what they carry in their heads. If you're game, persuade the crews to let you scramble up the monkey ladders affixed to the mainmasts of these vessels. The view is sensational but hold on tight!

Many travellers moved by an adventurous spirit try to arrange passage on the schooners to other destinations in Indonesia. Although most captains consider starry-eyed Joe Conrads more trouble than they are worth, one of these proud, independent sailors might not mind a foreign passenger for a few days.

Jakarta's sea-faring past is also kept alive in **Kali Batu**, about 10 km east along the coast road. This port area has none of the restored and rather orderly atmosphere of Sunda Kelapa; on the contrary it is raw harbour life. A rigid distinction is traditionally preserved between the mooring places for Buginese sailing ships and those for the Madurese *lete-lete*: at Kali Batu Madura sailors tie up singlemasted, wide-beamed ships that bring in salt from Gresik, near Surabaya. For the nautically-inclined these intricately carved and painted ships are something not to be missed.

Also to the east of Sunda Kelapa but much closer is an interesting reminder of past European influence in Java: the old **Portuguese Church**. The church, located on Jalan Pangeran Jayakarta No. 1, was completed in 1696 and was once used by the many Portuguese descendents who then lived in Batavia. The pulpit is elaborately ornamented, and the inside of this plain-looking edifice is an unexpectedly beautiful example of baroque art, a testament to the variety of peoples attracted to the Indies.

Museum Nasional (formerly Museum Pusat) is found to the south of the old Kota area on the west side of the huge **Medan Merdeka**. Housed in an old Dutch neoclassical building, once

Scenes from Kali Batu.

known as "Gedung Gajah," the Museum is the nation's repository of historical and cultural artifacts. The central courtyard is filled to overflowing with stone friezes, reliefs and free-standing statues from the Hindu and Buddhist periods. Examples of traditional architecture, musical instruments and household items from each of Indonesia's 27 provinces are presented in the right ground floor gallery. A fine library completes the ground floor attractions while upstairs is a treasure chest of bronze dieties and Hindu artifacts.

There is also an outstanding collection of Chinese porcelain in the Museum. The expert in Tang horses and Sung platters will be disappointed but the devotee of Chinese porcelain made for export will find himself confronted with one of the finest collections in Asia. Every piece has been located somewhere in the archipelago, and anyone thinking of buying Chinese porcelain in Jakarta or elsewhere in Java will be doing himself a good turn if the examples in the Museum are studied closely.

The best part of the National Museum undoubtedly is its treasure room, which is opened on Sundays, revealing gold ornaments from various Javanese kingdoms and other precious artifacts. The Museum deserves a full day. The Ganesha Society sponsors guided tours in several languages. Hours are: 8.30 a.m. to 2 p.m. on Tuesdays, Wednesdays and Thursdays; 8.30 to 11 a.m. on Sundays; and 8.30 a.m. to 1 p.m. on Fridays. On the second and fourth Saturdays of the month all night *wayang kulit* performances are staged at the museum.

On the north side of the Square is the brilliant white **Presidential Palace**, formerly a merchant's mansion. It is only the official residence of the current Indonesian President however; President Suharto actually resides in a relatively modest home on a small back street in Menteng.

Other Medan Merdeka attractions include the **Istiqlal Mosque** which is known to be the largest in Southeast Asia, with its celestial but massive white

Hindu sculpture at the National Museum.

dome and rather rakish minaret.

The vast headquarters of the Pertamina Oil Company is on the northeast side and from every angle **Monas**, the National Monument, towers above the Square: it can be visited each day from 9 a.m. to 5 p.m. The Monas has a lift up to the top of its tower and a series of relief murals depicting the struggles of the independence war may be viewed in the ground area.

The other structure of interest on Medan Merdeka is the **Immanuel Church**, a building evoking Jefferson's Montecello in Virginia with its circular expanse and strict neoclassical porch. It is on the eastern side of this vast square. Both it and Istiqlal can be visited, but with the latter it is best not to go during Friday's prayers and to ask directions at the gate. (Remember to always remove your shoes when entering any mosque.)

An entertainment area, in the broadest sense of the word, is at **Ancol** (pronounced "Anchol"), in northeast Jakarta by the coast. A fabulous complex of drive-in-cinemas, golf courses, bowl-ing halls, marineland, type aquarium called the Gelanggang Samudra, a Disneyland theme park and an eight-storey hotel, the Horison, which offers a fine seaside buffet breakfast. Art and handicrafts, mainly souvenir quality but with some worthwhile articles, are for sale at the open-air art market.

Although a detailed shopping guide to Jakarta would need dozens of pages, there are some areas which you cannot afford to miss. Although all the international class hotels (and there are many now in Jakarta) have curio shops, some of them quite good, a better bet for the cost-conscious and/or adventurous is an excursion to places like **Jalan Kebon Sirih Timur Dalam** (running perpendicular to Kebon Sirih and Wahid Hasyim) and **Jalan Ciputat Raya** in South Jakarta.

A staggering array of some really first-class antiques, ranging from colourful Madurese guardian ducks carved from teak to elaborate Chinese influenced canopied beds, is found on Jalan Majapahit, especially in "N.V. Garuda."

Prayer time in magnificent Istiqlal Mosque.

Jalan Surabaya is probably the largest special purpose market for antiques and bric-a-brac in Jakarta: it's located off Jalan Diponegoro in Menteng. Although it has been flashed up with permanent aluminium roofing and is somewhat rather overrated now, it's still possible to find a bewildering assortment of domestic vanities: heaps of old Delftware porcelain from Holland, great collections of "Chinese porcelain" (most of which are copies from a Bandung factory), old coins, hot-out-of-the-mold bronzeware, eastern Indonesian textile and other goodies. Try to come early to Jalan Surabaya, well before the tourist buses that now make regularly scheduled stops at this once-chaotic, now-tame market.

Fabrics are found in many shops, a good start can still be made in the **Pasar Baru** area (within sight of Istiqlal on the west side of Jalan Dr Sutomo) and *batik* stores are scattered around town. Batik Keris, the country's largest *batik* producer, has a flashy multi-storey shop on Jalan Cokroaminoto in Menteng.

There is also Batik Danar Hadi, an excellent shop on Jalan Raden Saleh Raya, just east of the Menteng area. There is also a variety of *batik* boutiques in the smarter suburbs such as Kebayoran Baru, Kemang and Menteng, and it is easy to find out where they are, find them in the yellow pages of the telephone book.

There are not many single stop shops in Jakarta but an exception is the government-run Sarinah department store on Jalan Thamrin, close to the Hotel Sari Pacific, and the private Sarinah Pasaraya in Blok M. For the traveller with only a little time in Jakarta, both Sarinah stores offer the totality of Indonesian handicrafts at set-out reasonable prices.

Any traveller to Asia worth his salt is attracted to the life and pace of open air markets, whatever their wares. The Jakarta city administration has zealously tried to impose some order on the more choatic markets, mainly by building some rather dreary multi-storied concrete leviathans to house the small traders. Fortunately the bustle of Jakarta's main markets has survived these transplant operations, and the large general markets (such as **Pasar Cikini** and **Pasar Minggu**) are as alive as ever.

One special purpose market is **Pasar Burung**, one of the real attractions of Jakarta. Located just off Jalan Pramuka in an area called Kayu Manis, ornithologists will experience heaven or (if they happen to be conservationists too) suffer agonies. Here are captive birds from all over Indonesia: macaws, parrots, the Javanese *perkutut* and other tropical curiosities, almost all captured illegally. At the junction of **Jalan Mahakam** and **Jalan Melawai** in Kebayoran Baru is a flower market that is cheap and refreshing, set among the trees of a small park.

On the cultural side Jakarta has really come of age in the last few years. One of the many pleasurable things about Jakarta is that a night's hunt often yields unexpectedly rewarding insights into "cultural life," in its broadest sense: interesting things are going on in the most unlikely of places.

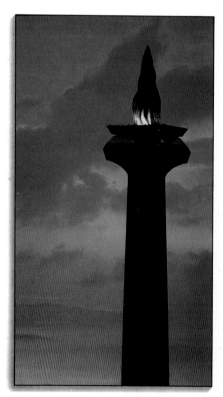

Monas, the national monument, towers above Medan Merdeka.

Pride of place for strict *haute couture* goes to the **Taman Ismael Marzuki** on Jalan Cikini in Menteng. Nearly every night T.I.M. offers a solid programme: exhibitions of Indonesian painting, overseas jazz groups, Surabaya ludruk comedy troupes or the latest piece of Indonesia's vibrant and emerging theatre. Monthly programmes for T.I.M. are distributed in hotels and travel agencies, or a copy can be obtained directly from the T.I.M. office. Don't miss it.

The *Gedung Kesenian* near the main post office is a renovated colonial-era theater now offering a mixed bag of local and imported cultural events. The revived glory of the building itself is worth the trip. *Wayang* and other cultural performances are held most weekends in the open-air amphitheatre at the *Pasar Seni* in Ancol. The *Jakarta Post* daily English language newpaper contains a listing of events around town.

Wayang wong is the Javanese word for live theatre using actors. Although developed long after the puppet *wayang* form, *wayang wong* has adapted the legends of the *Ramayana* and *Mahabhrata*, and mixed them up with a lot of indigenous Javanese lore. The result, even for the non-Javanese speaking, is enthralling, particularly the scenes of combat and courtly dance. The best place to see *wayang wong* in Jakarta is still at the **Bharata**, a cinema-style building on Jalan Kalilio No 15, near Pasar Senen, that has a huge *kali* head over its front entrance. Performances begin at 8 p.m. every night except Mondays and Thursdays. The Java Pavillion at the Taman Mini Indonesia has *wayang kulit* demonstrations every other Sunday, beginning at 10 a.m. and lasting about 5 hours. Finally, the National Museum organises *wayang kulit* performances every other Saturday which last the whole evening. Literally.

The best foreign cultural centres are the German and Dutch institutes, located on Jalan Matraman Raya 23 and Jalan Menteng Raya 25, respectively. Printed monthly programmes are available on request, or from the respective embassies. To their credit these institutes help

Jakarta's skyline at dusk.

foster indigenous artistic expression by giving exhibition and stage space to local artists and performers.

To round off the cultural side of Jakarta are two Indonesian organisations. The first is Lingkar Mitra Budaya Jakarta, a group of well-heeled persons, mostly Indonesian, who are interested in the arts. A programme of the Lingkar's monthly activities can be obtained from its pleasant office and exhibition centre at Jalan Tanjung 34, in Menteng. The second group is the Balai Budaya, a group with an exhibition hall on Jalan Gereja Theresia 47 in Menteng, used almost exclusively for exhibitions of painting. Drop in and discover the arts scene in Indonesia.

If you find yourself attracted by some of the work of Indonesia's carvers and contemporary painters you may even consider purchasing a representative sample of their work. There are many studios of varying description and quality, many of which as you might expect, sell little more than fast buck "Bali" paintings or forest-nymph type wood carvings. For peerless quality in contemporary Indonesian painting visit the **Duta Fine Arts Gallery** at Jalan Kemang Utara 55.

Jakarta, like any other city, is really more a matter of mood than a recitation of whistle stops. Many visitors do not sample the atmosphere of even one urban *kampung*, an oversight that robs them of a feel of the city as it is known by the great majority of its population. The Jakarta Municipality in recent years has worked hard to upgrade basic services and the result in many areas are closely settled but often very charming *kampung* which are pleasurable to visit. One of the best examples of these Kampung Improvement Projects is in the Menteng Sukabumi Kampung on the southeast side of Menteng bordering a railway shuttle line. Any cabdriver knows the area, and a wander through will add an extra dimension to your memories of the city. Have no fear: the natives are especially friendly and it is easy to find your way in and out.

Jakarta's mood is also captured in the

Jaya Ancol theme park.

following places: nighttime food stalls along the entire length of Jalan Peconongan in the fascinating Kebon Kelapa area of town, just across a drainage canal from Bina Graha, the President's working office; the Glodok Chinese quarter sandwiched in between Jalan Gajah Mada and Jalan Mansyur just south of the old Kota area; the open book-stalls which spring up each night at about 5.30 p.m. in Pasar Senen; and not least the Tanjung Priok port area where first class sea food places, modest in appearance, rub shoulders with shadey night spots and ubiquitous billiard halls.

Jakarta is also filling in time a glass of plain tea at any one of the seemingly thousands of *warung*, canvas-topped street stalls that can (and often must) pick up and move at a moment's notice, just out of reach of a police sweep of "illegal" traders. Alternately, a two-dollar cup of Nescafé in a hotel coffee shop will bring you into contact with the rapidly-expanding, westernised middle class of Jakarta. As Indonesia continues its non-stop economic boom, most deals go down in the Hilton, Mandarin or new Grand Hyatt hotels. Many hotels, notably the Sari Pan Pacific, also offer early evening cultural performances in the lobby bars.

Trendy Jakartans spend much of their leisure time at discos. Though many clubs tend to open and close regularly, perennial favourites are the Hilton Hotel's Oriental and the Sari Pacific's Pitstop. The Jaya Pub on Jalan Thamrin and Pete's Tavern on Jalan Gatot Subroto, offering good pub food and live music, are popular with both foriegners and locals.

No night on the town is complete without stop at the Tanamur, Southeast Asia's longest-running disco. Recently expanded and redecorated, if that is the word, as a sort of post-modern air-raid shelter after a near miss, the Tanamur is the only club attracting clientele from all levels of Indonesian and expatriate society.

One very underrated (and occasionally overrated) attraction is Jakarta's

Traditional Sumatran house at Taman Mini.

Taman Mini Indonesia Indah ("Beautiful Indonesia in Miniature"), which is located on the southeast side of the city and is reached by taking the first turn-off from the Jagorawi toll expressway. For all its obvious play for tourist dollars it does provide a good introduction to the country's variety and is well worth a visit.

Taman Mini is consciously designed to capture all of Indonesia's local culture in one single complex. Stretching over nearly 100 hectares the park provides the visitor without too much time in Indonesia with exciting insights into the complexity of this vast country. The 27 provinces of Indonesia (the most recent inclusion being East Timor) are each represented by a pavilion. Each of these buildings, constructed in the distinctive style of the various regions, presents inside the decorative skills and local art forms of each province, including textiles, carvings, metalwork, traditional dress and panoramas depicting scenes of everyday life. Each pavilion has its own programme of cultural performances, ceremonies and dances, all of which is noted in the monthly Taman Mini programme, available free from most hotels.

Equally impressive are the various special purpose buildings at Taman Mini such as the new museum (opened in 1980) and the superb performance centre facing the entranceway which is styled after the aristocratic Javanese *pendopo* form. There are also buildings following the distinctive architecture of each of Indonesia's five accepted religions: Islam, Protestant Christianity Hinduism, Buddhism and Catholic Christianty. There is even a wonderfully austere building with an exquisitely carved interior for the adherents of the various forms of Kebatinan, a form of mystically-inclined religious practice found chiefly in Java.

To cover the distances inside Taman Mini one can choose for transport horse-drawn carts, a mini-train, buses or a cable-car that crosses the park and the artificial lake that is carved in the shape of a gigantic map of the archipelago. **Happy faces at the zoo.**

114

There are restaurants and several shopping areas, and even a miniature Borobudur Temple. Next to the park stands the **Keong Mas Imax Theater**, which presents wrap-around-sound film tour of the archipelago several times a day on the largest movie screen in the world.

All in all, even though Taman Mini is undoubtedly "touristy" it is also a superior attraction and well worth the visit.

The **Ragunan Zoo**, also at the extreme southern end of Jakarta, offers a good introduction to Indonesia's astonishingly diverse and threatened wildlife. This delightfully-chaotic garden zoo has an interesting population of exotic and mundane for Indonesia residents including Sumatran tigers and a Komodo dragon. Young orangutans are seen in the trees near the zoo's small orangutan rehabilitation and research project. This visit is particularly pleasant as most animals are not kept in cages but in landscaped enclosures, not very different from their natural habitat.

If you look out the window when flying to Jakarta you will most often see a large number of coral islands lying off Java's north coast. These islands, known as **Pulau Seribu** are Jakarta's marine attraction. Pulau Seribu (the "thousand islands") actually consist of slightly over 300 islets, some privately-owned and most uninhabited. Close to the Jakarta port, the islands of Pulau Onrust and Pulau Ayer are popular for day outing, as both have coral shores that abound with shells.

Pulau Onrust was the staging point for Jan Peiterzoon Coen's final assault on Jakarta in 1619. During the 18th century Onrust was an important shipyard, and James Cook had the "Endeavour" careened there in 1770: the bottom of the ship was thoroughly repaired, and much to Captain Cook's satisfaction, who bestowed great encomiums on the officers and workmen at the Marineyard; in his opinion there is not one in the world, where a ship can be laid down with more convenient speed and safety, nor repaired with more diligence and skill. The island was later a fort, and a

Muscling in for a mooring at one of the "thousand islands".

quarantine for *hajis* (pilgrims) returning from Mecca. Part of the island is now under cassava cultivation, but its woods, shoreline, old ruins and foundations, and a cluster of vine-covered 18th and 19th-century tombstones, make it a relaxing spot.

The nearby islands of Kelor, Kahyangan and Damar also feature in Jakarta's history. Pulau Bidadari's name, which means "Heavenly Nymph Island" was cruelly ironic considering it was the site of Jakarta's leper colony. This island, like many others, is now a resort.

Further out, away from the industrial and human pollution of Jakarta Bay, most of the islands larger than a sandbar have been developed. The majority are in private hands as weekend getaways for the Jakarta elite. The Jakarta Municipal government recently clamped down on private ownership, and has forbid purchases or resales. Anyone already owning an island is now permanently struck with a palm-fringed island in a turquoise sea.

For the rest of us, several larger islands have developed as up-market tourist resorts. Pantara Timur and Pantara Barat, developed in cooperation with Japan Air Lines, are Asian yuppie paradises with marble bathrooms and beaches swept clean every morning. Pulau Putri and Pulau Pelangi are the most popular islands, with simple cottages and live entertainment on weekends. Even these islands are expensive for what you get, but all offer reduced weekday rates. Pulau Sepa has simple cottage with shared Indonesian-style bathrooms. In all cases, shopping facilities are limited to basic necessities, so you should bring along your own supplies including food if you balk at the high restaurant prices.

A better deal are the islands popular with the snorkeling and diving set. Despite the tourism development, the islands's coral reef remain suitable for diving and snorkeling, though they cannot compare to other areas in the archipelago. Snorkeling gear is widely available, and several companies offer diving packages for qualified divers.

Marine life includes turtles, moray and garden eels, rays, pelagic and reef fish, nudibranches, anemones, giant clams, sea fans, soft and hard corals. Reef sharks are more curious than aggressive. Dolphins and flying fish can often be seen during the boat trip from Jakarta.

Papa Theo, set up as a dive camp, offers very basic facilities and excellent fresh fish in the restaurant. Though scuba divers and snorkelers predominate, Papa Theo is also popular with Jakarta expatriates on a weekend and foreign families. The generator shuts down soon after dark, creating an excellent ambience for stargazing and other nocturnal activities.

Scheduled ferries leave from the Ancol marine daily at 7 a.m., taking 2½ hours. The ferry leaves the islands at 2.30 p.m. More expensive alternatives are speedboats, a hydrofoil and charter flights to the strip at Pulau Panjang. Any travel agent in Jakarta will be able to give you details on accomodations and transportation. For Pulau Putri and Pulau Pelangi, deal directly with the Pulau Putri Company on Jalan Thamrin 9 (in the Jakarta Theatre Building).

Left and right, Islands in the sun: a great getaway from city life.

In their haste to leave Jakarta many travellers make a bee-line for Yogyakarta, Bali and other points east. Apart from, perhaps, a cursory glance at Bogor or Bandung, they totally ignore Sunda, the western part of the island.

That is a shame, because West Java is different and offers a variety of landscapes and vistas seldom found in the East: from the majestic volcanoes around Bandung and Tasikmalaya, to the rugged west coast, to the wilderness of Ujung Kulon and Pangandaran, to the gardens and plantations of Bogor and Puncak, there is enormous potential for lovers of the great outdoors. Yet it is understandable that most travellers find West Java extremely time consuming: the beauty of the landscape can be savoured only once in a blue moon, perhaps at the end of the dry season, roads are frequently bad and often require a four-wheel-drive vehicle. Standards of accomodation jump from very few expensive hotels to mosquito-infested *losmen* where you are advised to bring your own bedding and in some cases food.

The culture of the Sundanese has remained alive despite continual depredations and sporadic warfare. Unlike the refined Javanese, the Sundanese value earthy excess and power, and they possess a strong sense of humour that is easy to enjoy. Cultural performances, however, are often confined to remote villages, not nearly as accessible as the organised performances of Central Java.

Casually dismissed as the "Mountain Javanese" by the people of the heartland, the Sundanese have developed a strong culture of their own that actually predates the great empires to the East.

West Java's recorded history begins with what is perhaps the earliest known written record found in the island: an inscribed stone, dating from around 415 AD, which records the royal presence of Purnavarman, king of Taruma.

The Sanskrit inscription suggests an Indianised ruler, one of the first in Indonesia, but there is a yawning gap in West Java's recorded history for the next thousand years.

As the Islamic city ports gained control of the northern coast, from Pasuruan in the east to Banten in the west, Pajajaran emerged for a brief moment in history's spotlight. The kingdom of Pajajaran was located in the hills around Bogor, with a secondary town and port at Sunda Kelapa. It is believed that the rulers of Pajajaran were Sivaistic, and were forced inland by the growth of the Muslim coastal states during the 15th century. Within a hundred years the kingdom was destroyed, overrun by the forces of the Banten sultanate. The history of West Java, however, has left few tracks on the rugged landscape, adding very little to the list of tourist attractions. Sunda remains a place for nature lovers and backpackers.

Preceding pages, Banten was the first Dutch settlement on Java. **Left**, an extremely rare Javan rhino.

BANTEN AND
THE WEST COAST

Four hundred years ago **Banten** was a princely state of great wealth and splendour. Banten town was an energetic maritime city; and the countryside it controlled (also known as Banten) embraced a huge slice of Sundanese territory, from the Java Sea to the Indian Ocean, and eastwards from the Sunda Strait to the borders of Sunda Kelapa in the north and the bay of Pelabuhan Ratu in the south.

The name still covers that great area, but the glory has long faded. The present day town of Banten, far from being a splendid city, is now little more than a few picturesque ruins, masses of coconut palms and strings of shabby, tiny villages lining tidal creeks and canals.

The Portuguese were the first Europeans to visit Banten, arriving early in the 16th century when the great Javanese commander Falatehan at the behest of the Sultan of Demak, was completing his conquest of the area. Banten rapidly grew in importance, defeating and finally dispersing the Hindu forces of Pajajaran who sought refuge from Islam in the rugged hills and mountains to the southwest of Bogor, and around the port of Sunda Kelapa.

Banten's grip on the entrepot pepper trade was the source of its wealth. Some of the pepper grew within Banten, but most came from Sumatra, and by the middle of the 16th century, when the Portuguese were granted limited trading rights, more than 1,500 tonnes of the precious spice were leaving Banten every year in ships bound for India and China.

This was Banten's hour of glory, its brief century-long strut upon the boards of history.

At the time Banten was almost synonimous with the archipelago, and in many maps and European travel accounts of the period Banten is the only name to be recorded. The year 1596 proved to be fateful for Banten, and ultimately for the entire archipelago.

Banten, Dutch architecture in tropics.

On 22 June four Dutch ships, commanded by Cornelis de Houtman, dropped anchor in Banten's road-steads after a voyage which had lasted 14 months and cost the lives of almost half the fleet's complement of 250 men. The survivors were the first "Hollanders" to set foot on Indonesian soil.

The Dutch were soon followed by the English, and by Danish and French traders. The tiny English community, about 14 men at any one time, fought and brawled in the streets with the "Flemings," but loved them nonetheless for they were all brothers in an alien environment.

The fortunes of the invaders, and of Banten itself, waxed and waned. Plot followed plot, blockade followed blockade, and one sea skirmish led to another as men fought and died in a constant struggle for economic hegemony. But by 1684 the Dutch had, more by accident than design, assumed control of Banten from their base In Batavia and had embarked on the construction of a massive fortress, Fort Speelwijk, to protect their interests. Banten's role as an independent sultanate thus was finally eclipsed.

For the tourist coming from afar, Banten should be treated as a one day excursion from Jakarta. The road is good, but uninteresting, and the traffic is very heavy on weekends.

At **Serang**, 90 km west of Jakarta, a surfaced road leads 10 km north to Banten. About 2 km short of your destination, on the right-hand side of the road, is the tomb of Maulana Yusup, the third ruler, who died in 1580. Nearer the present village, on the left-hand side, are the remains of Istana Kaibon, a palace built for one of Banten's princes, lived in by the mother (and guardian) of another prince, and destroyed in 1832. Nothing more than a pile of bricks remain, but the inevitable watchman will spring out of nowhere with his ubiquitous "visitors book" and a polite request for a contribution.

Across a narrow river, and a little to the northwest, is the sprawling one-hectare site of the Surosawan, the high-walled and heavily-fortified palace compound which was built, wrecked in a bloody civil war and rebuilt, all during the reign of Sultan Abulfatah Agung (1651–83). Its final destruction, ordered by the Dutch about 1810, was carried out reluctantly over a period of 30 years, but grass-covered mounds and hillocks mark the sites of storerooms, dwellings and casements, and shrub-crowded holes lead down into intriguing passageways now blocked by debris. The great walls, still 3 to 4 metres high, look good for another thousand years.

On the northern side of Surosawan lie the brassy plain of the *medan* and the imposing white *menara* (reputedly designed by a Chinese Muslim) built by Maulana Mohammed in the closing decades of the 16th century. A narrow, simply-ornamented doorway leads to a spiral staircase, the steps of which, worn and rutted by tens of thousands of feet, follow a tight, shoulder-wide circuit up through the walls of the tower to two high balconies offering superb views of the *medan*, the mosque (with its pool and adjacent cemeteries), Surosawan

and the flat coastline to the north.

If you wish to climb the minaret, make sure nobody is coming down or wants to follow you up, otherwise you might find youself in a dangerously claustrophobic situation. The mosque is on Java's pilgrimage circuit, and a large number of warungs, souvenir stalls, and a resident colony of beggars are ready to receive the busloads of pilgrims that descend on the site each dawn.

A kilometre away to the northwest are the ruins of **Fort Speelwijk**. The fortress, built in 1682, was extended in 1685 and in 1731, and finally abandoned by Governor-General Herman Willem Daendels at the beginning of the 19th century. It originally stood on the sea's edge, but is today separated from the sea by more than 200 metres of sand-silt marsh and coconut palms. A single watchtower stands high on the perimeter wall its triangular loopholes offering a dispiriting vista of littoral marsh and, perhaps, in the distance the buff-coloured sails of solitary *prahu*. Fifty metres through the eastern gateway of the

Sunrise and tranquility at the Banten mosque.

fort, in a bleak tangle of brambles, are the ravaged tombs of another era.

More recent is a red and yellow Chinese temple opposite the entrance to Fort Speelwijk. It is probably 200 years old, but has been recently renovated and is totally uninteresting. There is no casual accommodation in the tiny villages of "Banten Town"; overnighters should head for nearby Serang, Cilegon or Merak.

Banten will be of interest only to the historian or the Jakarta resident that has already exhausted all the possiblities for a weekend out of town. The area, however, still has much to offer for along the shores of the Sunda Strait there are attractive resorts and beaches where the waters are generally calm, though during the monsoon season metre-high waves are not unusual. For ornithologists and nature lovers there's a worthwhile half-hour boat-ride from Banten to the island of **Pulau Dua** where between March and July an amazing variety of migratory birds arrive for a season of squabbling, mating and nesting.

About 20 km northwest of Serang, at **Cilegon**, you can branch north to the hilly coastline around Merak and Pulau Rida (also known as Florida Beach) or south towards Anyer. Cilegon itself is dominated by the vast Krakatau Steel plant. This corner of Java, close to the coalfields of Sumatra, has become a heavy industry area, with Cilegon yet another expatriate enclave.

Because of this economic development, the coast is a difficult area for budget travellers, so if you are travelling penny-wise pack a picnic lunch and treat the western beaches as a day trip. If you're looking for a *losmen* or similar inexpensive accommodation, you'll invariably be told to try the Hotel Cilegon, a somewhat seedy and mosquito-ridden hotel in the center of town. Down the coast, the Carita Krakatau Beach Hotel has a few budget rooms at the back.

At Serang, there are some modest accommodation, but apart from its proximity to Banten town it is in the middle of nowhere.

Today's Banten harbour is a far cry from the busy port of the 17th century.

South of Cilegon, running down the coast, there is a spate of activity in and around **Anyer**. There are pretty bays and long stretches of beach, but development plans suggest that this might become the Miami of West Java, including a newly-opened marina and plenty of industry thrown in for good measure. The most comfortable place to stay is the new luxurious Anyer Beach Motel, formerly owned by Pertamina. Seven kilometres short of the Motel a red hill was bulldozed into the sea to make a breakwater and a barge wharf for a new off-shore rig-platform assembly plant. Other industry, including a ship-building yard, is also slated for the area.

If you're in the mood for a minor voyage of discovery the Motel can arrange the rental of a boat with an outboard which can get you across to **Sang Hyang**, a seldom-visited 700-hectare island an hour to the northwest of Anyer. It is almost deserted, and there is no accommodation available, but it's an exciting and rewarding experience.

The southeast coast offers a few small sandy beaches, with calm shallow water inside a reelline only 50 metres from the shore, but mostly the coast consists of strands and banks of shells and coral thrown up by the tides. Not all is white. Much of the dead coral retains its brilliant hues of vermilion, crimson and carmine, or pale blue darkening to indigo, its delicate honeycomb cells a masterpiece of organic engineering. There are shells by the hundreds of thousands, and even amongst the tide-wrack you can find excellent specimens which have not lost their porcelain sheen. However, all that is on the rough, crumpled shore. Beneath the island's clear leeward waters are reefs of layer upon layer of fan coral, brain coral, coral trees and a treasure trove of cowries, volutes, turbans, cones, clams, spindles, murexes, conches...the world!

When you've had your fill of diving and snorkeling and exploration, you can satisfy the inner self with the superb mangoes, papayas and bananas which

Pulling the nets at Sang Hyang.

are part of Sang Hyang's abundance. mosquitoes are also abundant, so be prepared.

Back on the mainland it's about a 6-km run south from the Anyer motel to **Karang Bolong**, a huge stand of rock which forms a natural archway from the land through to the sea. Some of the natural beauty around Karang Bolong has been lost with the erection of a chain-wire fence and a cluster of unattractive warungs, but it is nonetheless an imposing sight.

Besides the coastal road link between Anyer and **Labuhan** (41 km long), the latter can also be reached by the inland route through Serang and Pandeglang, a 63-km drive. The attractive Labuhan coast offers launches for trips to Krakatau and Ujung Kulon. Be careful, though, many smaller boats are badly-maintained. The Carita Krakatau Beach Hotel will recommend seaworthy boats for trips to Krakatau and the game reserve at Ujung Kulon.

For several centuries **Krakatau**, an unimportant and uninhabited volcanic island 40 km off the Sunda coast, had lain dormant. Then, in 1883, it achieved instant and lasting infamy. A series of cataclysmic explosions ripped the island and blew out so much ash (almost 16 cu km) that the earth's crust collapsed forming a monstrous 41-sq-km submarine caldera. The sea rushed in, boiled on contact with the molten rock, and then tidal waves up to 30 metres high swept the coasts on a voyage of destruction that claimed more than 35,000 lives. The explosion was heard more than 3,000 km away in Australia, and stygian blackness covered the land for 160 km around. Ash is believed to have drifted around the earth three times, producing spectacular sunsets as far away as England.

In the decades following the catastrophe, undersea volcanic activity continued, and a new cone with a gaping half-crater emerged from the drowned bed of the caldera: Anak Krakatau, "Child of Krakatau," smouldering and steaming, a son following his father's habits.

Fishing near the smoking Krakatau.

Of the islands visible from the Anyer-Labuhan coast, Krakatau is the gently sloping cone lying farthest to the south, with **Krakatau Kecil** ("Little Krakatau") smoking away to the north and Anak lying between and a little behind these two. The main island, on which meagre vegetation is once more gaining a foothold, can be visited in a long one-day launch trip from Labuhan. Good travel agents in Jakarta can arrange the details for you, though it is possible to do it yourself in Labuhan. There are no regular launch services to Krakatau during the monsoon season, from the end of November through to the end of March.

Labuhan is also the take-off point for the long launch ride (more than 12 hours) to **Ujung Kulon**, an outstanding wildlife and nature reserve on the far southwest corner of Java.

Prior to 1883 Ujung Kulon was lushly enveloped in a thick mantle of jungle, impenetrable and economically unexploitable. What was left of the peninsula's growth after Krakatau's explosions and tidal waves was smothered under a blanket of volcanic ash and dust, and in the years that followed all that grew there was rough pampas grass and low, hardy scrub. The area became a paradise for the *banteng*, the fast and dangerous wild ox which still roams there. Now, almost a century later, the jungle is creeping back and the future of the banteng concerns naturalists and preservationists. Even greater concern is lavished on the one-horned rhinoceros, an increasingly rare beast found in few other countries, and in Indonesia limited to the 510 sq km of Ujung Kulon where it enjoys the protection and encouragement of the World Wildlife Fund.

Most of the reserve's other animals and birds can be seen in the other game parks in Java, but nowhere else is there such a concentrated array of different species: monkeys, crocodiles, pythons, peacocks, panthers, mouse deer, boars, bats and countless other denizens who crash, thump, whoop or glide through this untouched wilderness of swamp, grassland, forest and jungle, of plains, hills, valleys and estuarine shallows.

Volcanic rock – evidence of violent past.

Ujung Kulon is accessible only by boat from Anyer or Labuhan, or by helicopter from Jakarta, for the narrow isthmus separating the peninsula from the mainland is a trackless marsh. A brief there-and-back visit will probably whet your appetite, and you should try to allow at least 5 days to make the most of your adventure.

There is very limited accommodation in Peucang, where there is also a watch-tower, nevertheless if you plan to move around take camping gear: light-weight tropical tent, insect-netting and repellants, groundsheet, jungle boots, machete or *parang*, a change of clothes, and enough food and drinking water. The sea bordering the peninsula is a delight for conchologists and coral-watchers: take snorkel or scuba gear if you can, or at the very least borrow a facemask.

Permission to enter the reserve must be obtained beforehand from the Forestry Department (Bagian Perhutanan), Jalan Juanda 9, Bogor. If you're arranging your trip through a good travel agent he should be able to look after these details.

An alternative route from Labuhan to Jakarta, or a straight-on route if you're planning to head east by road, is through Pandeglang, Rangkasbitung and Jasinga to Bogor. Another option, if time is no object and you enjoy rough but beautiful back-country journeying, is the route from Labuhan east to Ciandur, south to the coast at Cilangkahan, east again past the Cikotok goldmines to Pelabuhan Ratu (Samudra Beach), then north to Bogor or farther east to Bandung.

Half of the 100-km journey from Rangkasbitung takes you through a magnificent landscape or rubber trees, rolling hills and high ridges. Beyond Jasinga the country changes again as you plunge down onto rich river flats green with *padi*, dominated in the distance by the rugged peak of Gunung Salak.

Of special interest for the anthropologically-minded is the "Badui territory" to the south of **Rangkasbitung**.

Approximately 3,000 of these reclusive people live in 39 villages within the

The pristine wilderness of Ujung Kulan National Park.

51 sq km embraced by the boundaries of Desa Kanekes. This territory lies a little more than 35 km south of Rangkasbitung in hilly country ranging from 300 or 400 metres in height to mountain passes, near Gunung Kendeng, which are crossed at 1,200 metres.

In one sense a "lost tribe" also exists, for within the larger Badui community, near the southern-most boundary, are three villages inhabited by 400 Badui Dalam ("Inner" Badui people); they are completely surrounded by a protective buffer zone of Badui Luar ("Outer" Badui people), and deliberately shun all contact with the world beyond their group. Each of the three Badui Dalam villages is headed by a *puun*, a hereditary spiritual and temporal leader whose person is sacred (the notion of inherited leadership is unknown in most Javanese villages); the land within Badui Dalam territory is also regarded as sacred, and outsiders, including the Badui Luar, are forbidden to till its soil or settle there.

The Badui Dalam are not permitted to wear any cloth but the rough white homespun they weave themselves. They may not cultivate cash crops, use fertilisers, eat any four-legged animals, domesticate any livestock apart from chickens, or use any medicines except their own herbal preparations. Their agriculture is limited to *ladang*, "shifting cultivation," which relies on the natural fertility of newly-cleared ground and which is seldom productive for more than two seasons.

Similar taboos and restrictions apply to the larger group of Badui Luar, but are less rigidly observed. Although obliged to wear only their homespun blue-back cloth, and forbidden to wear trousers, some of the Luar people now proudly sport the colourful sarongs and shirts favoured by their Sundanese neighbours. Other elements of "civilisation" (toys, money, batteries) are rapidly infiltrating, especially in the villages to the north, and it is no longer unusual for an outer Badui. to make the journey to Jakarta, or even to work outside as a hired hand during the rice-planting and reaping seasons; some even

A Badui mother nurses her baby.

work in big towns and cities like Jakarta, Bogor and Bandung. Animal meat is eaten in some of the outer villages where dogs are trained for hunting, though animal husbandry is still forbidden.

The origins of the Badui are obscure, though ethnically they appear to come from the same ancient stock as the Sundanese and Javanese. It has been suggested that they are remnants of the last Hindu kingdom in West Java, Pajajaran, but this fails to account for the unique nature of their religion, which shows no Hindu influence. Rather the religion is a strange blend of animism and certain Islamic elements, with some original ideas thrown in for good measure. The ultimate authority is vested in Gusti Nu Maha Suci, who originally sent *Nabi* (prophet) Adam into the world to lead the life of a Badui, and *Nabi* Mohammed to organise the world's religious affairs. The Badui's most hallowed ground lies on Gunung Kendeng in a place called Arca Domas, which is visited annually (and only) by the *puun* of the inner communities.

The Badui wear homespun indigo clothes.

The lives of the Badui are hardly idyllic, though the beauty of the country in which they live suggests another Shangri-la. Many hardship, abound. Nevertheless, there is great vitality in their *angklung* music (the sound of rattled bamboo tubes is often accompanied by the deeper tones of goatskin drums) and in sonorous rhythms beaten out on hollow rice-pounding logs.

The Badui also have a formidable reputation as medicine men, and their herbal preparations are eagerly snapped up by country and city dwellers alike, and many itinerant *tukang*, with the streets of Jakarta as their beat, claim to be genuine Badui.

If you are genuinely interested it is possible to visit some of the villages on the northern rim of the Badui area. The most easily accessible is **Desa Kaduketug**, which is a good 4-hour hike from Leuwidar (24 km south of Rangkasbitung). Do note that permission must be obtained beforehand from the *Kantor Kabupaten* ("District Office") in Rangkasbitung.

BOGOR, PUNCAK AND THE SOUTH

South of Jakarta, the coastal plain rises into the Parahyangan Highlands, a popular weekend escape for Jakarta's oppressive heat and humidity. **Bogor**, at the end of a 60 km tollroad, is either an easy day trip from the capital or the first stop of a journey into the highlands. Because of its proximity to Jakarta, Bogor's hotels and *losmen* are invariably overpriced, undermaintained and crowded, so few choose to stay the night. But Bogor is worth an hour or two on the way to the Puncak and beyond or could be destination of a day excursion from Jakarta.

The Jagorawi Toll will get you to Bogor in 40 minutes, as thousands of commuters do every day, but an alternate route will send you head first into the chaotic, congested secondary roads of Java. After fighting your way through 50 km of gradually thinning traffic, the road to Bogor leads slowly uphill through a tunnel of huge trees. At the top, an 18th-century landscape painting springs to life: beyond a pair of handsome wrought-iron gates can be seen an imposing, porticoed residence surrounded by sweeping lawns where herds of white-spotted deer graze. A sentry-box houses a smartly turned out 20th-century soldier, comfortably attached to an automatic rifle. This is the summer palace of the President of Indonesia. Suharto, however, is seldom here, as he prefers to spend his time on his own experimental farm located in the nearby hills.

Although only 290 metres above sea level, Bogor is appreciably cooler than Jakarta (54 km to the north), and it is easy to imagine the pleasure of Governor-General Baron Gustaaf van Imhoff when in 1744 he left Batavia's malarial plain and reached this spot. Nothing now remains of Buitenzorg ("Free of Care"), the country house he built, though the present palace was built on the same site in 1856, and from 1870 to 1942 was the official permanent residence of the Governors-General of the

Dutch East Indies.

In the years following independence the palace and in particular a small pavilion within the palace grounds became a favourite haunt of the late President Sukarno. The palace still contains a large part of the huge art collection which he amassed, and is close to the public; can be visited if you make arrangements through a good travel agent. Nearly all the pieces in his collection feature scantily dressed ladies or explicit erotic scenes. The kind of "art" you expect to find in the house of a provincial meat monger who suddenly acquired wealth.

Raffles lived there well before the arrival of those art pieces, and fell in love with the place. He wrote in 1811 that "I have now from my window a prospect of the most delightfully picturesque scenery – a valley filled with rice, with a romantic little village at the beginnings of a stream which rushes down by twenty torrents and roars booming over rocks innumerable; in the background a magnificent range of mountains, wooded to the top and capped in clouds."

Pangrango and Gede, two 3,000-metre peak in that "magnificent range," still dominate town. The stream, too, still runs clean and clear through the grounds of Bogor's world famous Botanical Gardens before coming to a sad end in the viscous black waters of a canal at Pasar Ikan.

Bogor's real glory is the Botanical Gardens, **Kebun Raya**, which originally surrounded the palace but are now separated by a fence. They are open every day, and on Sundays and public holidays become Jakarta's playground, when brightly coloured clothing vies with flaming borders of canna lilies as hundreds of families picnic on the grass under the shade of trees up to 30 metres in height. Hordes of brown-and-white-uniformed schoolchildren on a class outing strip down to their knickers, or less, and gambol among the rocks and eddies of a swift-flowing stream; giant "Victoria Amazonica" sit on tranquil ponds waiting for the Frog Prince; and

Preceding pages, Bogor's Botanical Gardens. Below, the stately palace of Bogor.

"Rafflesia," the world's largest flower, hailing from Sumatra, opens its metre-wide bloom in Bogor each October. Bogor was once the most important botanical gardens of the East, but decades of mismanagement and lack of funds here reduced it to little more than a public park. Remnants of the colonial past, however, are evident everywhere.

A cobbled pathway leads to a tiny cemetery locked in a thicket of wrist-thick bamboo. The names on the tombstones are mostly Dutch, though an English sea captain made his last landfall here in 1835 and was buried, "much regretted by his relations & friends," only a few hundred metres from the back of the palace. On the placid surface of an ornamental pond are the shimmering reflections of elegant white columns, the facade of the palace rising above an expanse of immaculate lawn.

Close by is a small Grecian-style cenotaph in memory of Olivia Mariamne Raffles (who was in fact buried in Batavia). Her arrival in Java was marked by a conflict with the wives of many of the Dutch officials: she objected to their habit of wearing the kebaya, "adorning themselves with vulgar jewellery and chewing sirih." Happily, an amicable settlement was reached and the good ladies duly bowed to "proper" English taste.

Raffles has often been credited with laying out the Kebun Raya, but the honour belongs to Prof. C.G.L. Reinwardt and his assistants from Kew Gardens, James Hoper and W. Kent. The gardens were officially opened as "Land Plantentuin" in 1817, and gained international repute during the 19th century for their range of botanical specimens and for research into such cash crops as tea, cassava, tobacco and cinchona; although oil palm was not developed commercially in Southeast Asia until this century, a small plaque identifies the oldest and probably the tallest oil palm in the region, brought from the west coast of Africa in 1848.

Although the research station and once-great orchid gardens are shuttered

Ferns and tree ferns thrive in the cool climate of Cibodas.

and forgotten, the thousands of tree species from thoughout the world planted in these gardens during the last 175 years have grown to stately splendour under the tropical sun. The gardens, though now a botanical backwater, still possesses the finest avenues of trees in the world. Sadly, the legions of fruit bats that used to nest in the high branches during the hot afternoons have dwindled to a few scraggly specimens.

While parts of Bogor display a stately elegance, the atmosphere of the hills around **Puncak** ("Summit") can be bucolic. Eco-tourism is becoming a popular activity, as the tea plantations and rainforest beyond are easily accessible.

The road to Puncak climbs steadily from Bogor, winding its way through a manicured landscape of tea plantations, punctuated by the vivid colors of flower gardens glimpsed through the open gates of weekend homes. Beyond the top of the high pass the descent opens up a vista of pines and conifers on steep hillsides. Nestling amongst the trees on the more gentle slopes are dozens of hotels, guesthouses and "weekenders," and the roadside is crowded with restaurants which cater for cool-climate appetites with (amongst other things) tasty ikan mas or golden freshwater carp.

At the very summit, before the road tips downward like the awful first plunge on a roller-coaster, most travellers stop to catch their collective breath at the Rindu Alam, a roadside restaurant with a commanding view of the entire pass and on a rare, clear day, to the sea at Jakarta.

The view is even better from the massive shattered rim of **Gunung Gede**, which juts almost 3,000 metres into the sky. Raffles climbed Gede in 1815, and carried a thermometer so as to judge the height of the volcano on the basis of the drop in temperature. His estimate of 2,000 metres was well short of the mark, but his description still holds: "We had a most extensive prospect from the summit – Batavia roads (i.e. harbour), with the shipping so distinct that we could distinguish a ship from a brig on one side, and Wine Coops Bay (Pelabuhan

The Victorian folly of Cipanas, once a favourite retreat of Sukarno.

Ratu) still more distinct on the other; the islands all around were quite distinct and we traced the sea beyond the southernmost point of Sumatra; the surf on the south coast was visible to the naked eye. To the eastward we included Indra Mayu point in the prospect, and Cheribon Hill rose high above the rest."

The starting point for the day-long climb to Gunung Gede and back is 5 km south of Cibodas at the **Cibodas Botanical Gardens**. This extention of Bogor's Kebun Raya has taken over the latter's research functions, and provides a good introduction to the type of rainforests that once covered most of Java. The temperature is sensibly cooler than in Bogor, and the Dutch planted many trees suitable to the temperate climate, that now grow side by side with great tree ferns and tropical epiphites. To climb Gunung Gede, it is advisable to take a guide, as a cold night lost in the mountains is not the object of eco-tourism. Enquire in Bogor at the *Lembaga Biologi Nasional* (LBN, the National Biological Institute).

The road to Cibodas is lived with the summer homes of wealthy Jakartans, and the nurseries that cater to their gardening needs. Both are a delight to the plant lover and add interest to the excursion to Cibodas.

Cipanas (literally "Hot Water"), a little before Cibodas, is famous for its hot springs. Governor-General van Imhoff, that indefatigable traveller of the 1740s, commended the healing properties of its waters and established a health resort there that was heavily patronised despite the 4 days' bone-shaking ride from Batavia. On the outskirts of the town stands a quaint little "palace" with elegant wrought-iron columns and deep, low-spreading eaves which marry the styles of a classical Javanese *pendopo* and a Victorian "folly." Once part of the health resort, it is now a seldom-used country house for the President.

The southern coast of West Java, beautiful but dangerous, is also within easy reach of Bogor. The most accessible spot is **Pelabuhan Ratu**, where the

Exotica from various parts of the world are grown at Cibodas.

ragged, wind-lashed Indian Ocean foams and crashes onto black-sand beaches, grey-gold beaches, and onto rocks sculpted and hollowed by salt spray, rain and sun.

Pelabuhan Ratu is just 90 km from Bogor, 160 km from Jakarta (through Bogor), 155 km from Bogor through Puncak and Sukabumi, or 160 km from Bandung.

The road south from Bogor follows a winding route over the pass between **Gunung Salak** (2,211 metres) and **Pangrango** (3,022 metres), where the valleys and hillsides are a lush garden of rubber trees, tea plantations and terraced *padi*-fields. If you were to go no farther, you could say that you had seen Java in the proverbial nutshell, for this wonderfully varied landscape embraces most of what the island offers in scenic attractions and spectacular views. Even the minor distractions are a delight: yet another breed of *dokar* or horsecart, quite unique and resembling the back half of pre-war automobiles which have been neatly guillotined.

Perhaps the most appealing of all are the unspoiled fishing villages along the coast. "Unspoiled" is often a cliche designed to hide a multitude of unattractive sins, however at Pelabuhan Ratu, there is real freshness and vitality in the village life. The fish market does a roaring trade in the mornings, with freshly caught fish of every imaginable shape and size with some easily exceeding a metre in length. The coastline itself, backed by steep hills, is raw and varied in its beauty.

From the village of Pelabuhan Ratu, past a series of small, pleasant weekend "bungalow" hotels, the road follows the seashore through handsome natural forest to the site of the Samudra Beach Hotel, an island of tacky modernity in otherwise unchanged surroundings. The hotel has long been popular with Jakarta's outdoor set (who like their comforts as well), and is generally heavily booked at weekends, but on weekdays it is quiet and restful.

The beach is pretty. The surf is treacherous and unpredictable. Many

Tea plantations and vegetable gardens around an artificial lake.

people, ignoring the admonitory legend of Nyai Loro Kidul (Queen of the Southern Ocean), have discovered to their cost that swimming in the ocean is dangerous, so it's better to enjoy the hotel pool.

If the sea is best left to Loro Kidul, the rivers near Pelabuhan Ratu offer a thrilling alternative. Regular rafting expeditions are operated on the Cimandiri and Citarik rivers, the first is suitable for novices and families, the other, a turbulent Class-4 in many sections, is for experienced paddlers only.

About 5 km west of the hotel, at Karang Hawu, a towering cliff looks out over a tangled mass of rocky reefs. Farther west is the tiny fishing village of Cisolok where a hot spring gushes forth from a small riverbed.

For a breath of adventure, you can head on towards **Cikotok** where Java's most important gold and silver mine is operating. Cages plummet down into two 50-metre shafts, and you should be able to arrange with the management for an exciting descent into the netherworld.

The coast road beyond Cikotok is outstandingly beautiful and seldom used. It does not always stick to the coastline, but plunges inland at various points, scaling saddles and ridges through heavy forest before nosing back to the ocean front. With four-wheel drive, good weather and accurate information about road conditions it is possible and rewarding to make this gruelling trip, which will eventually land you back in "civilisation" at Labuhan on the west coast of Sunda above the Ujung Kulon peninsula.

A less demanding four-wheel safari can take you south of Pelabuhan Ratu to **Ujung Genteng**, one of Java's less-well-known game reserves. It's advisable to check with the police or the hotel in Pelabuhan Ratu before setting out because the road is rough, and could be impassable.

Heading east from Pelabuhan Ratu in the direction of Bandung and Central Java the best route goes through Sukabumi. The attractive drive winds through hilly country before linking up with the main highway at Cianjur.

Fishing village at Pelabuhan Ratu.

BANDUNG

From Puncak to **Bandung** it is only 120 km. Beyond Cipanas the country changes abruptly. The vistas of terraced hillsides, plains of *padi* and forests of pine give way to massive limestone outcrops. The population has expanded tremendously in recent years, and the road is lined with houses and shops all the way through, seemingly an extension of Bandung itself. The monotony is interrupted by the occasional pottery stall and smoke-belching kilns producing bricks from limestone mined in nearby quarries.

If you are heading straight to Bandung from Jakarta there is an alternative route which avoids the hills around Puncak and is much faster. By road or rail the route is almost the same. The K.A. Parahyangan express, with comfortable allocated seats and a restaurant service, does the 3-hour trip five times a day (try to book a day ahead, and be at the station half an hour before departure time: Gambir Station, on the east side of Jakarta's Medan Merdeka, is the most convenient station). Views from the train are at times spectacular, especially when crossing slender steel bridges that span yawning ravines; below, stepped *padi*-terraces as little as a metre wide climb up and down almost vertical slopes and nestle alongside huge boulders strewing the riverbeds.

By car, the road east is fast and furious along the expressway cutting through the endless ricefields. At the eastern terminus, an older arterial road takes traffic south into the highlands. At Jatiluhur is a huge hydro-electric and irrigation dam, completed in 1965, where calm waters are ideal for boating, water-skiing and fishing. Beyond Jathiluhur the foothills of Java's central mountain range are covered with teak forests which disperse the sunlight through gold-green leaves. The temperature grows cooler when the road cuts through a forest or rubber plantation. In Purwakarta, you can buy excellent local pottery (including big water jars with shiny black glazes

and buff-coloured decoration). A little farther south, and slightly higher, carefully tended rubber plantations make leafy tunnels across the winding road. After about 2 hours of winding mountain roads you are on the outskirts of Bandung.

As Java's cities and towns go, Bandung is comparatively new. It was established by the Dutch in the early years of this century in the northern foothills of the enormous Bandung plateau, enclosed by high ridges and peaks with magnificent views of pretty countryside. The city rapidly acquired importance as a commercial and educational centre (Sukarno received his engineering diploma from the famous **Bandung Institute of Technology** in 1926). Its attractive tree-lined streets on the hills north of the railroad cutting through its centre are the epitome of suburban respectability, and the pleasure of living there, in a mild upland climate, can be easily imagined. It is still a pilgrimage point for nostalgic Dutch visitors, and seems to hold a spot far closer to Dutch

Preceding pages, a children's angklung orchestra shows its stuff in Bandung. Left, stopping with style at the Savoy. Right, Gedung Sate.

hearts than most other towns in Java. It does have a certain polish and veneer of old-fashioned colonial civilisation which somehow refuses to die; it is ironic that Bandung was the site of the Afro-Asian Conference in 1955, a time when many of the participants were shrugging off the yoke of colonial masters.

Parts of the city today exude a somewhat jaded air, but the abiding impression is one of bustle and vitality, appropriate to Indonesia's third largest city. The population is now about 2 million, as many as 4 million if the immediate Bandung environs are included. The industrial expansion of the '80s made Bandung one of the world's fastest growing cities in Asia and today it is decidedly an industrial town, with textile factories, electronic assembly plants and even an airplane factory. Bandung is also an artistic and intellectual center, but these merits are hardly appreciated by the casual traveller who only notices the heat, noise, pollution and traffic. For most, Bandung is an overnight stop enroute to Yogyakarta,

or a base for exploration into the spectacular Parahyangan highlands.

There is little in the way of architecture that predates 1900 in Bandung, and in fact little of substance was built before a great residential expansion of Dutch people between 1920–40. Some splendid examples of Art Deco survive: the **Savoy Hotel** replete with furniture and fittings from the era has been recently refurbished, and now offers modern conveniences to complement the Jazz Age elegance. The Grand Hotel Preanger, has also managed to upgrade itself without losing its charming character.

Novel designs with stained glass and tile in the art nouveau style can also be found in some of the older Dutch housing. The landmark of Bandung, Gedung Sate, was built in 1920 to house government offices. The atmosphere of the period lives on in Jalan Asia Africa and Jalan Braga, the main shopping district.

The Bandung Institute of Technology is Indonesia's equivalent to M.I.T and its students have a reputation for outspokenness and activism. The Institute

Tangkuban Parahu dominates the valley of Bandung.

("ITB" is the Indonesian abbreviation) also boasts one of the country's best fine arts schools; many of Indonesia's prominent artists received their initial training here. The principal campus complex of ITB is architecturally the most interesting of all Indonesia's centres of higher education, comprising a number of buildings designed by MacLaine Pont that attempt to blend local architectural forms with western techniques. The result is often stunning. One of the favourite local pastime is to ride past ITB to the **Dago Tea House**. Here you can enjoy the cool late afternoon breezes from the highlands north of the city, and appreciate the beauty of both the city and inhabitants (Bandung women are reputed to be the most beautiful in Java). There are several other pleasant spots in the upper reaches of the city, including the Babakan Siliwangi, the first and probably best "kurung" style restaurant in Bandung. In this updated version of traditional Sundanese cuisine, you choose a live fish from the pond at the entrance, then retire to a table set up in an open pavilion while your meal is cleaned and grilled over open coals.

There are several **museums** in Bandung, including a military one reserved for the history and exploits of the Siliwangi Division of the Indonesian Army (which is based in Bandung) but they are of scarce interest to the foreign visitor. A museum unique to Indonesia however is found in the massive old headquarters of the office of the Geological Survey of Indonesia. The Geological Museum is open from 8 a.m. until 1 p.m. every day except Sunday, and it displays an extraordinary array of fossils, rocks, maps and some first-class models of volcanoes.

The real attractions of Bandung lie not in the city, but in the highlands to the North, where you will find hot springs and a volcano with an asphalt access road right to the crater.

From Lembang, once a mountain escape, now a busy suburban area, to **Tangkuban Parahu**, the famous "Upturned Boat" mountain and its three

Downtown Bandung, with Jalan Asia Africa lined with colonial buildings.

craters, is a steep, winding 16 km on a good but narrow road. Hardy Sundanese farmers traverse this road, and others, at a steady jog-trot, delicately balancing shoulder poles slung at each end with a 50-kg basket of cabbages. Higher up the road, where vegetable plots vanish and tall pines reach for the sky, the baskets give way to rough-hewn wooden slings filled with lengths of sweet-smelling white pine and toted at the same heart-pounding pace.

Early morning is the best time to see the main and most accessible crater on Tangkuban Parahu, when the mist swirls around nearby peaks and ridges and a glancing ray of sun turns it to quicksilver. The vegetation is harsh and scrubby, complementing the dormant threat of the far-from-dead volcano.

The floor of the volcano's main crater, looking like a giant grey pancake, still squeaks and steams and bubbles, sending sulphurous odours up to the 1,830-metre rim. Souvenir sellers, occasionally engulfed in these noxious vapours, pluckily combat the fumes and the morning cold on the lip of the crater; they sell brilliant yellow lumps of crystalline sulphur, and strange monkey-like objects which have been fashioned from tree-fern fibre. Depending on the crater's mood, guides may be able to take you down into the depths for some moonscape sightseeing; on the other side of the crater ridge they can also guide you to hot springs and sulphur holes. The inevitable fauna of parasites living off tourists can be at times as annoying as their balinese counterpart, but a price has to be paid for a chance to see a volcano without the sweat of the climb.

Stomping around a cold mountain top can sharpen the desire for food and for a hot bath. The latter is well catered for at **Ciater**, where there's a choice of public or private hot pools, warm enough (though not scalding) to relax the most travel-weary limbs. Head back down the road from Tangkuban Parahu, turn left at the tollgate and you'll find Ciater about 7 km farther on.

Closer to Lembang are the **Maribaya**

The crater of Tangkuban Parahu.

Hot Springs (4 km east), tucked snugly into a high-walled, sun-trap valley. Trimly landscaped, its small park is a glory of hillocks, dells, cascades, swings and slides, pools, streams and bridges …the perfect spot for family outings and family snapshots. If you happen to be at Sukarandeg, on a Sunday, you might care to take time out to watch a ram fight:

"A big black and white ram strains at his leash. Magnificent horns curl back from the crown of his skull and encircle his ears. His proud, heavy head looks out of place above his long, spindly shanks. His opponent, white and lighter horned, stands with his handlers on the far side of the 10-metre sq. The leashes are dropped. For almost a second the two warriors glare at each other across the hard-packed earth. Then there's a mad blur of speed and a heart-rending crack as two lumps of flesh and bone meet head-on."

They back off with a slow, deliberate step, their gaze never faltering. They stop momentarily, and charge again.

Crack! The white ram staggers, then drops to his knees. A tinge of pink stains his snowy crown. The handlers separate them and they return to their corners. The white ram, his Irish up, comes out like a berserk locomotive. Crack! They back off, pause, and strike again. This time it's black and white who falls. He half rises, and falls again.

The spectacle takes place every Sunday morning, starting around 10 a.m., in a small glade set among towering bamboo on the road between Lembang and Maribaya about 1 km short of the springs. There are usually 20 matches, but only rarely is an encounter fatal. Two southern trips may be of interest before you take the road to the east. At Ciwedey, 30 km to the southwest on the way to Gunung Patuha, you'll find cottage industry craftsmen working with iron and turning out a fascinating range of hand-forged knives and daggers with carved wooden hilts.

Depending or road conditions you may be able to cut across country from Ciwedey to **Pengalengan** (also reached

Ram fights keep Sunday mornings busy.

by taking the road due south from Bandung through Banjaran). The attractive hilly country leading up to Pengalengan provides the usual picture of mixed crops, with bananas, rice and cassava fighting for space in a verdant jumble. This, however, hardly prepares you for the formal iron gateway and neatly clipped hedges like the entrance to a seigneurial estate, or the seemingly endless vista of rolling hills smothered under a mantle of tea bushes, or the ordered rows of spick and span houses clustering amongst the greenery, that greets you at Pengalengan.

A number of government controlled tea estates are located in this area, generally better known, broadly, as the Malabar Estate after the nearby 2,300-metre peak of Gunung Malabar. Farther to the southeast you can drive to within striking distance of Gunung Papandayan, which offers magnificent views if you are prepared for the long but not too arduous walk to the peak. **Papandayan** is an active three-sided crater, still boiling but safe, which blew out its fourth side in a catastrophic explosion in 1772 that killed more than 3,000 people.

Sundanese culture is less refined than the high court culture of Central Java, and it is characterised by an earthiness which is often lacking further east. Although the best place to experience Sunda dance and music is the hundreds of highland villages, Bandung also presents many of these varied offerings.

Jaipongan, is a popular dance form that started life in the early 1970's in seedy nightclubs and hostess bars. Based on a mixture of traditional dances, this diversion for middle-aged businessmen and teenage taxi dancers caught the eye of professional choreographers who wanted to inject some vitality into the tradition-bound court dances. Today, *Jaipongan* troupes perform "traditional Indonesian dance" world-wide, while the original "*Jaipongan* Palaces" are still going strong.

In West Java *wayang golek* is preferred to the *wayang kulit* or shadow plays, although both forms feature well-known stories from the *Ramayana* and *Mahabharata* tales. Unlike the flat leather figures of Central Java, the *wayang golek* puppets are three-dimensional wooden figures, brightly-painted and clothed in rich fabric. Under the influence of kung fu and western action films, many leading *wayang golek* spice up their performances with special effects. A decapitated warrior will spurt crimson blood, a poisoned minister will vomit green bile before collapsing out of sight.

Angklung, a popular Sundanese musical form, may be heard at almost all the hotels and in many other venues around town. The sound of the word "*angklung*" suggests something about the nature of this form of indigenous music: delicate hollow notes reverberating in bamboo tubes. Originally tuned to a five-note scale and played on ceremonial occasions only, the *angklung* is now more often heard in western octaves, but the effect in either scale especially when the *angklung* is accompanied by the Sunda flute (the *suling*) is hauntingly beautiful.

Left, Sundanese *topeng* **dancer. Right,** *wayang golek.*

FROM BANDUNG TO YOGYA

Outstanding *batik*, wild windswept beaches, superbly-situated mountain temples, wildlife reserves, steaming craters, triple-canopy jungle and exquisite picture-postcard landscapes are among the reasons for giving time to the countryside between Bandung and the cities of Central Java.

For the devotee of scenic beauty, the lover of folk arts, the explorer, the beachcomber, the historical romantic...for all of these, the border country between west and east Java can be an absorbing interlude.

The administrative line separating West Java from Central Java is, a fuzzy one. Although there are notable cultural and linguistic differences between the two provinces (Sundanese is spoken in the west, Javanese in the centre) there are no distinct geographical features or major towns demarcating the border, and one province blends imperceptibly into the other.

Bandung, in round figures, is 150 km by road to the west of the border; east of the border, Semarang is 200 km away, and Yogyakarta 280 km. In describing routes between these cities it would be arbitrary to fix a cut-off point at the official provincial boundary just because it happens to be there. The following pages, cover a little of West Java and a little of Central Java in setting out a logical link in your travels from west to east, and offer three basic routes.

The "north coast route" is the fastest and, in most respects, the least interesting: it runs through Bandung or Jatibarang to Cirebon, then on to Tegal, Semarang and down to Yogya. (See page 225: the North Coast)

The "south coast route" is the slowest, but it offers many scenic compensations en route through Bandung, Tasikmalaya and Kebumen.

The "middle route" is quite fast and is the most attractive. It begins with either the south coast or north coast route, and then blazes a new trail a little east of the

border: you head south from Tegal or north from Buntu, and then in both cases swing east from Banyumas along the mountainous road through Wonosobo.

It is possible to drive straight through from Jakarta to Yogyakarta in as little as 14 hours; but it's tiring whether you're driving or being driven, and a more leisurely pace is recommended. There are numerous variations on the three basic routes, though if you're planning to take any back roads be sure to check first on road conditions with the local police or military.

The journey through south **Parahyangan** is the "slow boat" route to Yogyakarta. Eight peaks over 2,000 metres high make the area south of Bandung a demi-paradise for nature-lovers, bushwalkers and amateur volcanologists, and there's some wonderful exploring to be done. Nature's charms were less obvious to the Dutch and their Ambonese mercenaries when they first fought their way through this natural guerrilla terrain in the early l680s and reached the shores of the Indian Ocean: their steel

Left, a duck herder in Central Java. **Right**, pretty *padi*-field patterns.

breastplates, sweltering buckskin jerkins, and moisture-prone black-powder flintlock muskets didn't make good jungle companions. Even today it is utterly believable that Parahyangan (Priangan or Preanger) was a no-man's land between Mataram and Banten. Between Bandung and Garut almost every sideroad leads to a mountain or crater or hot spring.

One of the more spectacular mountains is **Gunung Guntur**: leave the main road at Cicalengka and go south through Majalaya and Paseh. Walking up to the mountain's steaming array of holes and gaping craters will take you through beautiful, sun-dappled forest. "A deep silence reigns in this fairy wood where the huge old trees are clad with soft velvet-like mosses," observed a travel writer some 50 years ago.

To nominate the "picturesque" heart of Java is to play with fire, but if there had to be such a nomination, the long, winding stretch of country through Garut and on to Tasikmalaya could stake a claim. Although lacking the rugged majesty of Bromo or Dieng, it encompasses all of the gentle cliches of landscape, embroidered with deftly worked threads of green and gold, set up for viewing in a jolting, breathtaking package. There are naked children lolling on the greasy wet backs of mud-bathed *kerbau*, a hot sun burning down on a sea of ripening rice, and plumes of feathery bamboo dipping and nodding in an afternoon breeze like long-necked waterbirds. There's a powder-pale sky, hinting at pink, reflected on the surface of a flooded, unplanted *padi*-field. A flash of sunlight transforms a column of water into a band of silver, dropping from one rice-terrace to another. There are little towns, more spacious than those in the north. White dolls' houses, trimmed with curlicues of equally white icing, cool within deep, colonnaded verandahs. The *becak* are cleaner and brighter and (if it's possible) more colourfully and lovingly decorated than anywhere else on the island. The ponies, bedecked in a jangle of polished silver "horse brasses" and scarlet pompoms of Napoleonic

Terraced rice fields of Garut.

regimental style, strut with a higher step. Their carriages (to call them carts is unkind) shine like cherished old walnut desks. Even the presence of people, people and more people at every twist and turn of the road, is here less a reminder of precarious overcrowding than a symbol of warmth and bucolic vitality.

Garut is the starting point for this idyll. Appropriately, the cone of nearby Gunung Cikura, a little off the main road to the southwest, is as perfect as a volcanic cone can be. Off to the east, Gunung Telaga Bodas, also worth a visit, has a crater lake alive with sulphur which is 50 percent pure and easily extracted; the lake has become one of Indonesia's principal sources of this valuable element.

Beyond Garut, man-made volcanoes in the form of sky-spearing chimney-stacks mark the site of kilns where earthenware pipes and roofing tiles are churned out in hundreds of thousands. Tiles are another of Java's minor surprises. The tropics, and especially the idealised tranquil village, suggest a world of thatched roofs. But Java's houses (with the singular exception of some in the Banten area), from the mansions of Menteng to the tiniest plaited-bamboo dwelling, are carefully topped with tiles, a 19th-century innovation designed to eliminate plague-carrying rats that liked to bed and breed in the nooks and crannies of a sun-warmed palm-thatch roof.

Tasikmalaya, 7 km east of Garut, is the centre of a prolific weaving trade in rotan, pandan leaf and bamboo, and its finest wares adorn the shelves and windows of souvenir shops throughout Java. Less well known is its smaller but exciting *batik* industry, where the local predilection for detail produces some of the most colourful and attractive floral motifs in the *batik* catalogue. An engaging memento of Tasik, combining the workmanship of both crafts, is a finely woven solar topee, Raj-style, covered with *batik* (wear it, if you dare!). For woven-on-the-premises purchases it is worth diverting about 12 km north

Early morning mist at Tasikmalaya.

to the village of Rajapolah where many of the weavers live and work. At Banjar, 42 km east, is the turn-off to Pangandaran.

Back on the main road and heading east from Banjar there is little more of interest. Minor notes: huge panniers, filled with snow-white cassava chips, and spread out over dozens of sunny slopes; **Majelang**, where the pasai bulges with attractive pottery and basketware; **Wangon**, acclaimed as the cleanest and prettiest town in Central Java, and looking just that with its neat houses set well back from the road behind whitewashed fences of split bamboo; **Buntu**, where a road junction can take you 9 km north to Banyumas and the start of the "middle route" through Wonosobo; and looking south, on your way to Gombong, the knobbly hills of **Karangbolong**, bump after bump like a giant set of filed-down shark's teeth washed up on the coast, where limestone caves yield a valuable crop of edible swallows' nests for the famous soup.

Local transport, as ever, bespeaks regional differences. Here the *oplets* are battered Chevy ranchwagons; the woven-roofed bullock carts have a carved and fretted back panel not seen anywhere else; and in the pony-cart "*caravanserai*" at Kutowingangun the harnesses are topped not with pompoms (as in Garut and Banjar) but with feathered plumes like those worn by a grenadier. One labour-intensive result of all these carts, gigs, wagons and carriages is a multitude of *tukang* who earn their livings as wheelwrights, wainwrights and blacksmiths. Shoeing a horse is a skill still much in demand though the humped oxen wear tie-on sandals made from old tyres.

At Purworejo, on the last leg of the journey, you have a choice of driving northeast to Magelang and then south again to Yogya; or you can head southeast through Wates which saves 40 km.

One of Java's more easily accessible game reserves, **Pangandaran**, is almost 60 km south of Banjar, through Banjarsari and Kalipucang.

A stream falls in the sea from the Knobby Hills of Karangbolong.

Monkeys, banteng, tapir, small deer and powerful, bright-beaked hornbills abound in the heavy forest which clings to the slopes and hills of the Pangandaran peninsula and envelops three grassy upland clearings where the wild ox roam. The strangest sights along the narrow bush trails are the small bands of sweepers and hackers who keep the pathways free of leaves and trim at the edges. The narrow neck of land linking the reserve to the mainland is only a kilometre across, but seawards the peninsula breaks out and then closes back again like a flat onion.

East along the coast, the water is calm within the shelter of Pangandaran Bay, where the nets of fishing traps hang lazily from their bamboo platforms, and where a few fishermen patiently work their seine-nets along the shore. The sheltered waters make this a good swimming beach. To the west is the flat sweep of surf-pounded grey sand which stretches 15 km to **Batu Hiu** and beyond. This is fast gaining popularity as a surfing beach, but without reliable transportation there, is destined to remain largely undiscovered.

There are two tollgates at Pangandaran. The first, at the village, allows you the privilege of enjoying the east and west coastlines. The second, at the barrier fence on the neck leading to the reserve, lets you into the game park. At weekends, and during holiday periods, a few portable warungs do brisk business near the entrance, but in-between times the peninsula is blessedly quiet and relaxing.

Accommodation is simple, spartan, and inexpensive on the east side of the peninsula, more expensive on the west. There are several good Chinese seafood restaurants, and most places serve standard backpacker fare to the steady stream of young travellers who stop over. A few enterprising souls are also running a lucrative souvenir trade which includes handsome shell necklaces and an amazing range of stuffed and mounted animals: the pairing of taxidermy and a wildlife reserve apparently holds no contradictions.

The narrow isthmus of Pangandaran is graced by sand beaches on both sides.

When somebody says he is in love with Indonesia, he probably means two things: either he is in love with Bali or Yogyakarta (or both). No other place in the archipelago holds the same fascination for westerners as these two small places that have so much in common: a manicured man-made landscape dominated by volcanos, distinctive art and culture, and a holiday atmosphere that seems to be created just for the tourists but is in fact the result of indigenous traditions.

The culture of Bali was the result of the immigration of the Javanese elite, following the conquest of the island by new Islamic rulers, and the fertile plains of Yogyakarta have been the cradle of that Javanese culture.

In the radius of a few kilometres around Yogyakarta are found some of the most spectacular sights in all Asia, both natural and man-made, including Borobudur, Prambanam and countless other masterpieces of Asian architecture.

Despite their conversion to Islam, the people of Yogya, a term many consider to be the Javanese for "excellence," have managed to maintain a strong link with their Hindu past. This is evident not only in their theatrical tradition – one of the main attractions for the visitor – but, more importantly, in their character and manners.

The role played by Yogyakarta during the struggle for independence, and the firm stand taken by Sultan Hamengkubwono IX against the colonial oppressors, both Dutch and English, have reinforced the status of the town amongst their fellow countrymen and many regard Yogyakarta as the cradle of the new independent republic. Thanks to the far-sighted and heroic ruler, the Republic has allowed the Sultanate to survive as an autonomous enclave, and the survival of the court has contributed substantially to the preservation of ancient traditions that date back to the time when Borobudur and Prambanam were built.

The traveller who does not have months to spend on the island should get a connecting flight to Yogya as soon as he lands in Jakarta. Yogya encapsulates the best of Javanese culture and is the most convenient base for excursions to the temples nearby as well as more adventurous treks to the volcanos of Central Java.

The twin antagonist of Yogya, Surakarta (both were born of the split of the Mataram Kingdom) has a similar history and culture but a far less enjoyable atmosphere and should be regarded as an excursion from Yogya rather than a destination of its own.

Preceding pages, typical village near Yogyakarta. **Left**, the face of nobility.

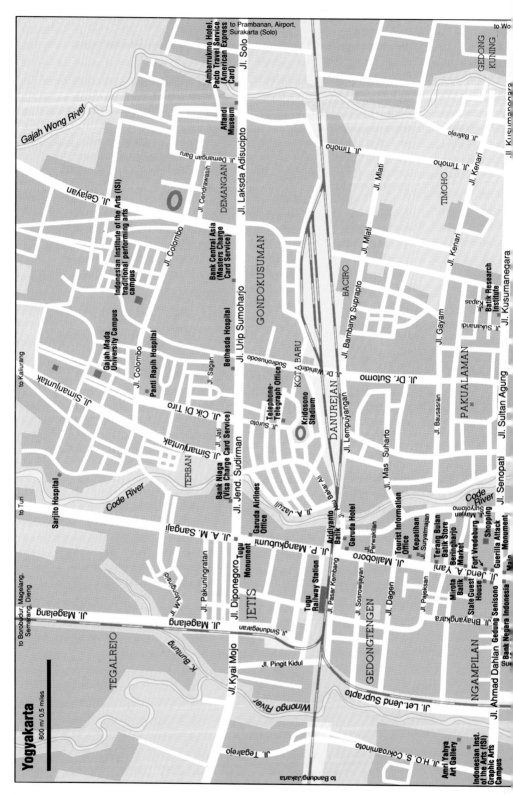

Yogyakarta

800 m / 0.5 miles

to Prambanan, Airport, Surakarta (Solo)

to Wo

Jl. Solo

GEDONG KUNING

Amberrukmo Hotel, Pacto Travel Service (American Express Card)

Affandi Museum

Gajah Wong River

Jl. Demangan Baru

Jl. Laksda Adisucipto

Jl. Cendrawasih

DEMANGAN

Jl. Kusumanegara

Jl. Balirejo

Jl. Timoho

Jl. Timoho

Jl. Kenari

Jl. Gelayan

Jl. Colombo

Jl. Miati

Jl. Miati

TIMOHO

Jl. Kenari

Indonesian Institute of the Arts (ISI) traditional performing arts campus

Bank Central Asia (Masters Charge Card Service)

GONDOKUSUMAN

BACIRO

Jl. Bambang Suprapto

Batik Research Institute

Jl. Kusumanegara

Jl. Sukanandi

Jl. Kapas

to Kaliurang

Jl. Simanjuntak

Gajah Mada University Campus

Jl. Colombo

Panti Rapih Hospital

Jl. Colombo

Bethesda Hospital

Jl. Sagan

Jl. Urip Sumoharjo

Sudirohusodo

Jl. Dr. Wahidin

KOTA BARU

Jl. Dr. Sutomo

Jl. Gayam

PAKUALAMAN

Jl. Sultan Agung

Sarjito Hospital

Jl. Cik Di Tiro

Jl. Jati

Jl. Simanjuntak

TERBAN

Bank Niaga (Visa Charge Card Service)

Telephone-Telegraph Office

Jl. Surjo

Sudirohusodo

Kridosono Stadium

DANUREJAN

Jl. Lempuyangan

Jl. Senopati

Code River

Jl. Jend. Sudirman

Jl. A. Jazuli

Jl. Mas Suharto

Jl. Bausasran

to Turi

Garuda Airlines Office

Jl. A. M. Sangaji

Jl. P. Mangkubumi

Ahidiyanto Batik

Garuda Hotel

Tourist Information Office

Jl. Perwakilan

Kepatihan

Jl. Suryatmajan

Terang Bulan Batik Store

Code River

Mayen Suryotomo

Jl. Senopati

Jl. Sultan Agung

Guerilla Attack

Shopping

Tugu Monument

Jl. Pakuningratan

Jl. Diponegoro

Jl. Pasar Kembang

Jl. Malioboro

Jl. Beringharjo

Fort Vredeburg

Main Monument

JETIS

Jl. M. Moh

Jl. Morojaid

Jl. Magelang

Jl. Sindunegaran

Tugu Railway Station

Jl. Sosrowijayan

Jl. Dagen

Jl. Pajeksan

Mirota Batik

State Guest House

Jl. Jend. A. Yani

Gedung Senisono

Bank Negara Indonesia

Su

to Borobudur, Magelang, Semarang, Dieng

Jl. Magelang

TEGALREJO

K. Bunung

GEDONGTENGENG

Jl. Bhayangkara

NGAMPILAN

Jl. Ahmad Dahlan

Jl. Kyai Mojo

Jl. Pingit Kidul

Winongo River

Jl. Let. Jend Suprapto

Jl. Tegalrejo

Jl. H.O.S. Cokroaminoto

Amri Yahya Art Gallery

Indonesian Inst. of the Arts (ISI) Graphic Arts Campus

to Bandung/Jakarta

to Wonosari, Baron

I. Gembira Loka

Gajah Wong River

Jl. Veteran

Jl. Veteran

Jl. Jantruan

Jl. Glagahsari

Jl. Babaran

Jl. Pandean

Jl. Veteran

UMBULHARJO

Jl. Celeban

Jl. Batikan

Jl. Menteri Supeno

Jl. Taman Siswa

MERGANGSAN

Jl. Ngeksiganda

Jl. Kemasan

Tom's Silver

Silver Craft Stores

KOTA GEDHE

Jl. Watugilang

Jl. Perintis Kemerdekaan

Jl. Gambiran

Jl. Modorakan

Jl. Tepal Gendu

Jl. Imogiri

Jl. Imogiri

to Imogiri

Bus Terminal

Jl. Pramuka

Jl. Nitikan

Jl. Tegalturi

Jl. Sorogenen

Jl. Sorosutan

Code River

Jl. Sisingamangaraja

Jl. Sisingamangaraja

to Imogiri

Tjokrosuharto Craft Store

Jl. Ireda 66

Puro Wisata, Sasono Suko

Jl. Ireda 66

Dalem Pujokusuman

Jl. Kol. Sugiyono

Galar. Museum

Gallery

Hanoman's Forest Garden Restaurant

Jl. Prawirotaman

Palm House

Jl. Parangtritis

Jl. Menukan

Jl. Siwojajar

Jl. P. Mangkurat

Pagelaran

Godod Sutejo Gallery

Ngasem

Rotowijayan

KRATON

Jl. Gamelan

Sasono Hinggil

South Square

Jl. Mayjen Sutoyo

Jl. Gading

GADHING

Panjaitan

Tulus Warsito Studio

Slamet Riyanto Studio

Batik Home Industries, Antique Stores

Jl. Tirtodipuran

Jl. Mantrijeron

Jl. Mangkuyudan

Jl. Jogokaryan

KRAPYAK

Jl. Parangtritis

to Parangtritis

Kraton Museum

Jl. Rotowijayan

Jl. Ngasem

Bird Market

Jl. Nyasem

Taman Sari (Water Castle)

Batik Artists' Colony

Jl. Polowijan

Jl. Taman

Jl. Ngadisuryan

Jl. Nogosari

Jl. Let. Jend. Haryono

Indonesian Institue of the Arts (ISI) Music Campus

Jl. Suryodiningratan

Jl. Wakhid Hasyim

Jl. Bantul

Letjen S. Parman (Taman Sari)

Sugeng Jeroni

GEDONG KIWO

Agastya Art Foundation

Winongo River

Jl. Bantul

to Samas, Glagah, Bantul, Kasongan

to Samas, Glagah, Bantul, Kasongan

THE GENTLE PULSE
OF YOGYAKARTA

In **Yogyakarta**, more than in any other of Java's towns, the presence of an old and highly-developed culture can be felt and heard. It is easy (and commonplace) to describe that culture as a hothouse flower, or a bloodless survivor from an aristrocratic past with as much relevance to the present as a fly preserved in amber. Such judgements are trite and unfair.

These two elements, patrician and peasant, meet and blend in Yogya: in its arts, life-style, and being. And this, perhaps, is why most visitors fall in love with Yogya.

One of the delights of this city is that things are always happening in a quiet and subtle way, and this can be most rewarding. You can spend hours relaxing around the markets. You can go to any dancing school, from the *kraton* to the smaller schools around town, and watch the kids practising traditional dances. You can even wander past a house and see young children learning to play the *gamelan* orchestra in the garage. You can watch *batik* artists at work, go to the *dalang* school and see *wayang golek* or *wayang kulit*. All this is happening so much of the time in Yogya – the continual practising and perfecting of fine arts and other aspects of Javanese culture.

However, Yogya is not just Java. The lively artistic and intellectual life of Yogya attracts Indonesians from all regions of archipelago. A sizeable percentage of Yogya's population is non-Javanese, giving a cosmopolitan air to this small town. These days, the most important segment of Yogya's inhabitants is the floating population of tourists and resident foreigners. Slowly, the world is discovering that Indonesia is not just Bali, and the rich, sophisticated culture of the Javanese is drawing increasing numbers of visitors.

Like the Balinese, the Yogyanese have applied great ingenuity to the task of building a tourist center without de-

stroying the elegant charm of this venerable court city. Far from being isolated in concrete, highrise tourist ghettos, foreigners are absorbed into Yogyakarta like water into a sponge, staying in residential neighbourhoods converted into simple boarding houses or small hotels. University students become instant tour guides, and even a few of the ubiquitous pedicab drivers have learned simple English. Artists have thrived, as even the marginally talented can churn out enough moon-rising-over-the-ricefields schlock to feed their families.

Every night, hawkers, street entertainers and harmless hustlers of every description rub shoulders with students, middle class families and tourists on Jalan Malioboro, turning this one-time royal processionway into noisy, bustling street fair. This art-colony-cum-university-town had a carnival atmosphere long before the first tourists arrived, and the sometimes outlandish foreigners are just one more ingredient to the bubbling Yogya stew.

Since the town itself is the main attraction, the best way to experience Yogya is to walk aimlessly, *jalan-jalan* as the locals say. Even in the most remote neighbourhoods, you are welcome to stroll about as long as you dress modestly and greet everyone pleasantly. However, there are a few "must-sees" for the first-time visitor, so you should apply a little direction to your wanderings.

"When a man is tired of London," said the inimitable Dr. Johnson, "he is tired of life." The same can be said of Yogyakarta, for there is enough within the city and in the surrounding countryside to satisfy most tastes.

The **palace**, the hub of old and new Yogyakarta, is a good starting point for your peregrinations. From the bottom end of Jalan Malioboro take a straight line to the south. You'll reach a large grassy square, the *alun-alun lor*, dominated on the west by the Masjid Besar (Great Mosque). In the centre of the square are two *waringin* trees, between which white-robed plaintiffs once sat

164

when they wished to make representations to the sultan.

At the southern end of the *alun-alun lor* lies the **Kraton**, the palace compound of the sultans of Yogyakarta.

Kraton Ngayogyakarta-Hadiningrat, like most things Yogyanese, is a gentle experience, for behind its massive walls there is a single-storeyed world of grace and delicacy where elegant *pendopo* reign supreme.

Construction of the palace began in 1755, following the division of Mataram, and continued for almost 40 years during the long reign of Hamengkubuwono I. The innermost group of buildings, Proboyekso, was completed in 1756, and is still the private domain of the sultan and his immediate family; it also houses the revered *pusaka* or sacred heirlooms. Sitihinggil and Pagelaran, the pavilions and buildings facing the *alun-alun lor* (and now used by several faculties of Gajah Mada University) were finished the following year. Dono Pertopo and Kemagangan, the two great gateways to the central courtyard, were completed in 1761–62; the Masjid Besar in 1773; and the Beteng or great wall in 1777. The glory of the *kraton*, the splendid reception hall known as the Golden Pavilion or Bangsal Kencana, was finished in 1792.

Structurally, very little has been altered in the intervening years. The closing decades of the reign of Hamengkubuwono VII and the accession of Hamengkubuwono VIII in 1921 saw a flurry of decorative activity. Half a century ago the gilt-framed mirrors, crystal chandeliers, cast-iron columns, stained glass, Italianate bronzes and marble floors were the last word in palatial decor. Resolutely European in taste, these items today strike a charming, anachronistic note, recalling the spirit of a gracious if somewhat artificial life.

It is not a feast of splendid oriental gaudiness. Somehow, these rococo fantasies sit well amongst the severe, classical proportions of the *pendopo*, the white-washed walls and the massive gateways; even a strange little band-

Yogya offers enough variety to suit most tastes.

stand rotunda, decorated with stained-glass images of musical instruments, has a patrician air about it.

Even the young guides who now help the courtly retainers handle visitors do not dispel the illusion that time has stood still within the palace walls. There is an unhurried grace and deference that evokes a feeling of calmness, reflecting the mood of the sunwashed well-swept courtyards.

In the **Sri Manganti** courtyard two *pendopo* hold a collection of carved and gilded palanquins and sedan chairs, and four sets of *gamelan* instruments: Kyahi Gunturlaut and Kyahi Keboganggang, both dating from the Majapahit period; Kyahi Gunturmadu, which once belonged to the 16th-century Demak sultanate; and Kyahi Nagawilaga, an 18th-century copy of a second Demak set (the original is owned by the court of Solo). Beyond a gateway flanked by two silver-painted guardians is the **Pelataran Kraton** courtyard, the site of the magnificent Golden Pavilion. On the other side of the courtyard a passageway leads

through to the museum, filled with fascinating paraphernalia: gilt-metal copies of the sacred *pusakas*, royal portraits by Raden Saleh, a superb saddle richly ornamented in velvet and gold and silver thread, gifts given by European monarchs and the titled elite. In a nearby *pendopo* is a bed decorated with pink and blue Murano glasswork and mirrors.

Kraton festivals highlight the Yogya year, the largest being the three Garebeg ceremonies, Maulud, Sawal and Besar (check with a tourist office for exact dates). Royal guards in traditional uniforms escort the gunungans, mounds of rice, from the *kraton* to the mosque.

The streets and lanes outside the *kraton* walls should be explored slowly, in a *becak* or on foot. To the west especially they hide unexpected pleasures, for this in days gone by was the equivalent of an address in Mayfair or the East Sixties, and there are still many beautiful old buildings and *pendopo* where court-sponsored *wayang* performances are sometimes held.

The Golden Pavilion in the *kraton* of Yogyakarta.

Staying with things royal, the restored *pendopo* in the grounds of the **Ambarrukmo Palace Hotel** is another entrancing link with the past. The palace was built in the 1890s by Hamengkubuwono VII as a country retreat, and the hotel stands on what was once the palace orchard.

The evocative ruins of **Taman Sari**, the "Water Castle," lying a little to the west of the *kraton*, would have gladdened the hearts of those romantically inclined 18th-century gentry who erected crumbling "Gothick" towers wrapped about with moss and creeping tendrils. This huge and once magnificent pleasure park was begun in 1758. One popular story says it was built by Spanish slaves, though research suggests that the faintly Iberian flavour was injected by an architect of Portuguese descent who lived in Batavia.

The vicissitudes of time, climate and temporal powers, helped along by an earthquake in 1865, have reduced much of Taman Sari to an intriguing collection of roofless halls, eerie underground passageways and shattered arches. A small part of the huge palace has been partially restored, and is now a museum. The rest are ruins scattered though the town. Birds-and-flowers stucco ornamentation, weathered kala gargoyles, and a gilded stone screen can be found amongst the lush growth. Bananas, bamboo and papayas surround the dozens of kampung houses that have sprung up along once-royal pathways and against equally regal walls. Small *batik* workshops flourish in this labyrinth of tropical foliage and ancient glory, a wonderful place to browse and buy.

Close to the *kraton*, in the northwest corner of the *alun-alun lor*, is the **Sono Budoyo Museum**. This should be compulsory viewing for anyone interested in Central Java's rich artistic heritage. Built by a Dutch architect, T. Karsten in Javanese style, it contains such varied masterpieces as an 18-carat gold Buddha unearthed in a rice-field in 1956; another Buddha, slightly larger, with gold-inlaid lips; a superb array of household goods fashioned from bronze

Left, mythical figure at Taman Sari. **Right**, an old palace guard.

and brass; an exuberantly worked *gamelan* set from Cirebon; and some excellent *wayang kulit* figures. Try to spare at least an hour.

The city fathers of Yogya have given a modest boost to man's age-old quest to beat the world's swords into plowshares. After forming an Arts Council, they proceeded to Commandeer Vredegurg, an old Dutch garrison on Jalan Malioboro near the Post Office. The fort is now a museum, devoted to the struggle for independence.

Cultural performances: From the very first moment you set foot in Yogya, you will not escape the sound of the **Gamelan**. You'll hear its insinuating, liquid melodies floating over a white-washed wall in a quiet, sunlit street, or bursting forth from a transistor radio at a *warung*; you may hear it as you stroll through the yards and forecourts of a palace, or in the lobby of a hotel; and *gamelan* is an integral part of Javanese dance dramas and the ever-popular puppet shows.

The number of instruments in a *gamelan* orchestra may vary from as few as 13 to as many as 75. They are almost all percussion instruments, ranging from the large gongs, "kettles" and resonating slabs of bronze to smaller pieces like the *gender* and the *gambang* or xylophone. A *rebab* (two-stringed viol), a *celempung* (a kind of zither) and occasionally a *suling* (flute) are the only string or wind instruments. The larger and more sonorous pieces carry melodies with long notes, whilst the smaller and lighter instruments carry melodies with shorter notes and (generally) a faster tempo. To foreign ears the most curious aspect of *gamelan* is the tuning, which normally combines a five-tone system (*slendro*) and a seven-tone system (*pelog*).

An appreciation of *gamelan* music is of course a very personal experience: people attuned to the vigorous Balinese form often find the Central Javanese version soporific; lovers of Central Java's style often decry West Java's as monotonous and unimaginative. Although describing music with words is a dangerous occupation, the following much-quoted quotation, cited by Jaap Kunst in his Music of Java, seems to sound the right chord: "(*Gamelan*) is comparable to only two things: moonlight and flowing water. It is pure and mysterious like moonlight and always changing like flowing water...it is a state of being, such as moonlight itself which lies poured out over the land."

Visitors to the *kraton* are welcome to attend the *gamelan* rehearsals on Monday and Wednesday mornings and for just a small fee you may tape the music. The smaller Pakualaman palace has adopted the soft, lilting style of Yogya's rival, Surakarta. Concerts are staged there every fifth Sunday on the date *Minggu Pahing* (ask, or check a Javanese calendar). Music begins at 10 a.m. Ambarrukmo Palace and Garuda hotel play *gamelan* concerts in the lobby everyday.

Of all Yogya's arts, **Wayang Kulit** is probably closest to the hearts of its people. The bemused Westerner, lost in a welter of seemingly unidentifiable characters and a rapid flow of incom-

This mask, at the *kraton* entrance, helps to ward off evil.

prehensible Javanese, may view *wayang kulit* as an ancient picture show, and leave it at that. In fact, the visual aspect, enchanting though it may be, is only a part of the *wayang kulit* performance, for the interplay of music and the amazingly varied character voices of the *dalang* are even more important to a Javanese audience.

Wayang shows are still used today to disseminate information about government programmes and play a role in the moral instruction of the younger generation. While a particular theme may be deemed suitable to keep off evil spirits and played as an exocistic ceremony for a child struck by bad luck or illness, another may be staged for a selected audience of juvenile criminals to improve their moral standards.

Night long performances are regularly staged in conjunction with major religious occasions and palace festivals. As pure entertainment, *wayang kulit* still enjoys great popularity, but is also being adapted to the changing times. As modern urban audiences do not have the time to watch an entire all-night show, many *dalang*s are experimenting with compressed versions, 2 to 3 hours long. Many audiences insist on back-to-back action scenes instead of drawn-out dialogues on philosophical issues.

The traditional *blencong*, the oil lamp, has been replaced almost everywhere with a strong electric bulb. The brighter light enable larger audiences to enjoy each performance, but has changed the atmosphere as the flickering light made the shadows come alive.

Some *dalang* in the meantime are experimenting with modern techniques, receiving mixed reviews and reactions from the public. Gasman, a Yogyanese artist and *Wayang* carver, has staged experimental performances in which two *dalang*s, sitting on opposite sides of the screen, train colored spotlights to add tone to the shadows. Most of the puppets he employs deviate substantially from the rigid tradition as does the dance paraphernalia that Gasman creates for equally innovative dance shows.

Ancient *gamelan* set in the Pakualaman Palace.

Even visitors with a limited time in Yogya will have a change to watch a performance, as occasions abound; the best shows are held in a special pavilion at the *kraton*'s South Kemangan courtyard on the nights after a Garebeg festival. Every second Saturday of the month, night-long shows are staged at Sasomo Hinggie Dwi Abad, in the South Square.

Tourist shows are presented in several hotels and restaurants; the Agastya Art Foundation (Gedong Kiwo M J 3/327) has shows every afternoon, and Ambar Budaya (opposite Ambarrukmo Palace) on Monday, Wednesday and Saturday mornings. **Wayang Golek**, in which life-like wooden puppets generally act out tales from the Arabic Menak stories, has never held the same appeal for the mystically inclined Javanese as the flickering, highly symbolic *wayang kulit*. Performances are less common than those of *wayang kulit*, but can be seen at the NITOUR office (Jalan K.H.A Dahlan 71, every day except Sunday, from 11 a.m. to 1 p.m.), at the Agastya Art Founation (Saturday, 3 to 5 p.m.) and several hotels and restaurants, including Ambarrukmo Palace and Hanuman's Forest Garden.

Yogyakarta's style of *golek* is quite distinctive, with thick velvet jackets and less elaborate headgears. Most of the puppets sold in the curio shops, however, are the production of Bandung craftmen, or at least imitate their style.

Yogya's indigenous form of dance theater, called **Wayang Wong**, is infrequently performed, restricted nowadays to the anniversaries of the leading dance schools. Designed to be staged under the roof of an aristocratic *pendopo* by a vast corps of dancers drilled to recite set lined in archaic Javanese and to execute complicated mass maneuvers and battles amidst the teak pillars, it could never become a medium of nightly entertainment. In Solo, however, a different dramatic format set on a proscenium stage and consisting mostly of improvised, colloquial dialogue became a model for *wayang* troupes throughout Java. The dancing is only rudimentary, a pale shadow of the elaborate Yog-

Dance lessons under the master's watchful eye.

yanese choreographies, but the level of stagecraft achieved is remarkable.

Wayang wong Solo-style and *ketoprak* (similar, but based on events and legends of Javanese history) draw regular crowds at THR, Yogya's engagingly seedy amusement park (Jalan Briglen Katamso). The performances are woefully inferior, yet still colourful and amusing. The action starts around 9 o'clock.

Dance is one of the highlights of Yogya's culture. Some dances are performed on special occasions, others are performed regularly; some are resolutely classical, some again are ancient in inspiration but modern in choreography and style. All of them enjoy a devoted following, and should you stumble on a rehearsal, a visit to one of the city's dancing schools might suggest that everyone between the ages of 5 and 15 is a dance student.

Classical court dancing, fluid yet superbly controlled, originated in the *kraton* and is still taught there. A practice session (Sunday mornings at 10 a.m.) is fascinating not just for the insights it gives on the subtleties of Javanese dance, but also for the delightful atmosphere of the *kraton* and the painstaking care with which the old dancing masters coax along their young charges. Classical dance is also taught at Krido Bekso Wiromo (the first school to teach court dancing outside the *kraton*) and at Siswo Among Bekso. The most active schools of strict Yogyanese classical technique are Mardawa Budaya and Pamulangan Beksa Ngayugyakarta; classes are in the late afternoons and evenings.

The state dance academy (ASTI) combines all of Indonesia's traditional dance forms into its curriculum. Modern and modernised classical dances can be seen at Bagong Kussudiarjo's studio. (Singosareu, Jalan Martaolimete 9, tel 2982)

The full beauty of Javanese dance is best appreciated in an actual performance. Special make-up, glittering jewels and elaborate costumes transform young girls into ethereal nymphs from the Southern Ocean; young men don a

A scene from the *Ramayana* at Dalem Pujokusuman.

topeng (mask) in the role of a lovesick prince preparing to meet his beloved; clowns tumble with athletic agility; and forbidding giants strut ominously.

Several of the hotels in Yogya provide evenings of Javanese dance for their guests' enjoyment: The Ambarrukmo Palace hotel, the Arjuna French Grill Restaurant, Hanuman's Forest Garden Restaurant and other tourist oriented establishment in Jalan Prawirotaman. The best shows, however, are staged thrice a week (Monday, Wednesday, Friday at 8 p.m.) at Dalem Pujokusuman, the art school of a respected member of the royal family, Sasminta Mardawa.

For most visitors, however, the **Ramayana Ballet** is the perfect introduction to classical dance in all its mythical wonder and drama. Held at an outdoor theatre in Prambanan, 16 km east of Yogya on the road to Solo, with the magnificent Loro Jonggrang temple as a backdrop, the Ramayana Ballet presents a memorable enactment of one of mankind's greatest epics.

Unlike many dances in other countries which have lost much of their vitality and flavour in being commercially packaged and sold like soap powder, the Ramayana Ballet has stayed remarkably true to its origins in *wayang wong*. The static verbal encounters have been snipped out (even the Javanese often find these boring) and greater emphasis has been given to the dancing. The result is spectacular "theatre": Rawana, high-stepping, angular, always menacing; Rama, smooth, couth, cool; and Sita, liquid grace, delicately tossing the trailing ends of her selendang. The engaging but slightly haphazard corps de ballet (variously demons, monkeys and fish), and the use of dramatic stage lighting are of course recent innovations, but they are effective.

It is said that the inspiration for the Ramayana Ballet came from a gentleman in the employ of Cook's Tours. He took his idea to the late President Sukarno, who said "yes." From this unabashedly commercial inception the venture grows in reputation and appeal with every performance. The reasons are obvious: four clear nights on and around the full moon, each month from May through October; a large outdoor amphitheatre and more than 100 assorted dancers and *gamelan* musicians; a shirt-sleeve tropical night, a thousand-year-old temple of inspiring beauty as part of the scenery; and a story of gods, giants, mortals, monkeys and beautiful women. For 2 hours, from the moment the spotlights turn the temple to antique silver to the last deep-throated note of the gongs, you'll be enthralled by a succession of visual and aural delights. Brilliant costumes, dramatic confrontations, tumultuous battles, hypnotically sinuous music, extraordinary displays of acrobatic skill and dancing.

This version of the *Ramayana* epic, unfolding over four successive nights, leaves out many of the complex stories-within-stories found in the original tale. If you've only time for one performance, try for the second night when all the leading characters have a chance to show off their dancing skills before being killed off.

Left, Rama and Sita. Right, Serimpi dancers at Dalem Pujokusuman.

Koperasi Angkutan TAXI Pariwisata Yogyakarta

"PATAGA"

TAXI CHARGE

N⁰ 007843

Jl. Malioboro 89 (72) Yogyakarta Phone : 66353 (5 Lines)
TELEX : 26174 NAHOGA 1A PO. BOX 42 INDONESIA

ROOM NO. :

NAME :

DESTINATION : Kaliran Bron

DRIVER : Pop Insan

CAR / POLICE NO. :

TIME ARR. :

TIME DEP. : 9.45

AMOUNT Rp. 7.000.-

TOTAL HOUR :

TOTAL : Rp.

GUEST :

DATE : 8 - 5 - 94

SIGNATURE :

CLERN :

DO NO WRITE IN BELOW SPACE

SHOPPING IN YOGYA

Yogya is a treasure-house of attractions for the curious, probing shopper, and its fascinations are almost endless. Silver, *batik*, antiques, curios and *wayang kulit* will be at the top of most shopping lists, though once you hit the browsing and buying trail you'll find plenty more, from the sublime to the vulgar, to excite your fancy.

Kota Gede is the centre of the **Silver** industry. There are two major workshops and a handful of ones where (buying or not) you can pass an intriguing half hour watching the hammering, beating, cleaning and polishing of the metal. Deft fingers create spider-web filigree; anvils clang till your head rings; gentle hammer-blows tap out elegant repousse work. The temptations are enormous, and even if a superb miniature of Yogya's royal coach is beyond your means, there's a wide range of rings, bracelets and pendants, coffee sets, ash-trays, flatware and occasional pieces of modern jewellery to choose from, at more moderate prices. At the new, expanded Tom's Silver (Jalan Ngeksiganda, Kota Gede) visitors are welcome to watch one of Yogya's premier workshops process and design high-quality silver.

Back in town, at Jalan Mas Sangaji 2 (just north of the Tugu monument), there's a house and workshop of Tan Yam An where good copies of modern silver designs are made. Prices for silverwork and for combinations of stones set in silver are reasonable; they will even retrieve your stone and melt down the silver and start again if you're not happy with the design. An unusual sideline is the sale of old *kebaya*, once worn by Java's older generation of Chinese women but now seldom seen. Made of fine lawn or muslin, with handworked lace and embroidery, the *kebaya* are showpieces of Javanese traditional handicraft.

Batik is one of Yogya's great drawcards. Unless you class yourself with the connoisseurs, it's a good idea to begin at *Balai Penelitian Batik dan Kerajinan* (Batik and Handicraft Research Centre) in Jalan Kusumanegara, east of the main post office, for a comprehensive and well-displayed introduction to the staggering variety of patterns and colours to be found throughout Java. An individual guided tour costs nothing, and in the course of it you'll see every step of the *batik*-making process: designing, *canting*- and *cap*-waxing, dyeing, cleaning. It is essentially a research centre though part of what is made there is for sale, including sample cloths showing the different designs.

Batik cloth is sold all over Yogya. There are several shops on Jalan Malioboro (besides the market) that offer the usual range of ready-made *batik* clothes and traditional *batik* lengths. Terang Bulan, with fixed prices (*harga pas*), will give you a good idea of what is available. The several large and well-appointed shops along Jalan Tirtodipuran offer every possible item that can be "batiked," plus clothing and *batik* lengths, both modern and traditional that come in various sizes (remember this when buying). Good modern *batik* and such popular style clothing as T-shirts and singlets can be found at Batik Ardiyanto and

Tobal Batik. Dressier (and pricier) clothes are designed and displayed at several famous art galleries.

Many of the city's better-known artists, and a number of aspiring ones, also produce *lukisan batik*, paintings made in the usual wax-and-dye manner but specifically designed for framing and hanging. You'll quickly notice a preference for the rather repetitive Hanuman-visiting-Sita-in-the-garden themes (though some classically inspired work is fresh and exciting) or the more vital and certainly more varied essays in abstract impressionism and pure abstraction. Try Gallery Amri, Bambang Oetoro, and Sapto Hudoyo and the smaller galleries in Taman Sari.

The art of **Painting** is fairly active in Yogya, though standards, themes and techniques vary considerably. During the revolutionary and immediate post-revolutionary years Indonesian painting was strong and vigorous; sometimes crudely executed, these works nevertheless projected an almost explosive vitality. Today, much of that groping, grass-roots urgency has disappeared. Many painters seem more interested in technique, and in the interplay of form, colour and texture. The result is attractive, if somewhat derivative, work which owes much to Western norms. However, some recent work is exploring the surrealistic fantasies which seem to find fertile ground in the Javanese psyche. The Cementi Gallery on Jalan Ngadisuryan has a good selection of contemporary painting, as does Nyoman Gunarsa's gallery on Jalan Wulung 63.

The works of Affandi, Indonesia's "grand old man" of contemporary painting until his death in 1990, is now sold exclusively through the Direx Gallery, across Jalan Solo from the late artist's large studio-cum-gallery overlooking the river.

To see where the up-and-coming generation is moving in painting, sculpture and handicrafts, you'll be very welcome at ASRI (Academy of Fine Arts) in Gampinean. opposite Gallery Amri.

For **Antiques** and **Curious** the hunting grounds include the many shops that line Jalan Malioboro and one more

Pasar Beringharjo.

across the tracks on Jalan Mangkubumi, the streets to the south and west of the *kraton*, a handful of small shops near the Ambarrukmo Palace Hotel, and Pasar Beringharjo for cheap handicrafts.

Among the things that may catch your eye are carved and gilded chests for herbal medicines, or a pair of polychrome Loro Blunyo wedding figures; a handful of copper coins with the Dutch East India Company's cipher, VOC, or thin silver pieces from Zeeland, Friesland and other provinces; an ornately carved, roofed and "walled" bed, or the gilded panels of birds and flowers that once adorned these huge pieces of furniture. There are naga-wreathed stands for *gamelan* gongs; bronze statuettes of Durga, Nandi, Siva, Ganesa and Agastya, of Buddha and innumerable bodhisattvas; crude *wayang klitik* figures, delicately lacquered boxes; and porcelain from Annam and China.

Highly-concentrated perfume and fruit essences may take your fancy. Beknamol is flowery; santol oli has a sandalwood fragrance. Make your choice

at Pantja Karya, Jalan Jen. Achmed Yani 72; or at Apotik Sanitas, Jalan Jen Achmed Yani 64 (both located at the "bottom" of Jalan Malioboro).

The southern end of Jalan Malioboro also introduces **Pasar Beringharjo**. One of Java's biggest markets, it will assail you with sensual pleasures: golden arrays of brass pots, pans and pestles; narrow passageways filled with stalls of *batik* and antiquated sewing-machines (have a *sarung* run up in half a minute); hanks of rope and strands of string ideal for macrame work: herbs and spices and odiferous roots destined for a *jamu* concoction; earthenware pots and sets of miniature terracotta cooking ware (children's toys); and always the busy and often raucous clamour of Yogya's women doing their shopping.

Farther west, in the quieter streets of Pasar Ngasem, are dozens of small shops selling biscuit-coloured charcoal braziers, water-jars, pottery moneyboxes (often brightly painted), and handsome leather moneybelts and pouches. Nearby is the fascinating **bird market**, the cages

The bird market.

swinging on high poles.

Yogya's **Leather Goods** are attractive and figure prominently in Malioboro's night market. Buff-coloured hand-tooled leather, decorated with floral motifs and sometimes with *wayang* figures, is available in a wide range of suitcases, overnight bags, briefcases, pocketbooks, sandals, belts and money pouches. Leather ages to light mahogany color. Check stitching and hardware closely; weak fastenings fail long before leather does. BS and Kusuma in the Ngasem area stock the best quality, strongest constructed goods in this style.

For the best in *Yogya Gucci* quality leather goods, visit the shop of Yamin Makawaru in the Hotel Ambarrukmo. Yamin pioneered the technique of binding Kalimantan rattan with quality leather, producing durable fashion and business accessories.

Leather is also the starting point for ***Wayang Kulit*** figures (though the thin, semi-translucent buffalo hide or *kulit* should properly be called "parchment"). The finest pieces, as delicately worked as guipure lace and as finely coloured as a butterfly's wing, are indisputably examples of craftsmanship becoming art. Prices vary, depending on the quality of the parchment, the standard of the gold paint (there are three grades used), and the complexity of the figure. An outstanding *gunungan* (mountain) incorporating the tree of life will take at least a month to make.

The *wayang kulit* puppeteers, the *dalang*, are still the main buyers of the best figures. Nevertheless, superb pieces are occasionally made for display rather than for use. There are quite a few *wayang kulit* workshops in and around Yogya, though some are hard to find. Two of the best places to watch puppets being made and to see a good range of high quality work are Ledjar's (near Malioboro street) and Moeljosoehardjo's (Jalan Taman Sari 37 B).

Masks and **Wooden Puppets** for use in topeng dances and in *wayang golek* performances are also good buys. Many pieces are hastily put together for the tourist trade, and their quality is dubious.

Left, a wayang kulit figure. Right, a mask maker tries on his creation.

For the finest work, made by one of the few remaining craftsmen who still carves for the actors and *dalangs*, rather than for casual visitors, visit Pak Warno Waskito.

Pak Warno is a shy, gentle old man who's been plying his craft for more than 50 years. He never went to school, and taught himself to use the keenly-honed knives and chisels that litter his workbench. Around him, unpainted heads sit in rows above a shoulder-high wall like headhunters' trophies; a sharp-nosed Panji mask regards the world with a permanent half smile, wooden lips parted over wooden teeth; and in dim corners you may find ancient puppets of unknown vintage, perhaps a little battered and scarred by time and use, but Pak can perform miracles of rejuvenation if you ask him to restore a piece. He accepts special orders, but doesn't speak English.

To reach Pak Warno's secluded hideaway, take the Bantul road south from Yogya, turn right at the 7.6 km marker, walk about 300 metres, turn left, and stop at the first house on your right. Signposts will guide you.

You can combine a visit to Pak Warno with a call at Desa Kasongan for cottage industry **Pottery**. On your way back to Yogya, turn left at the 6.5 km post (a sugar-cane trolley track crosses the road at this point) and follow the side-road for about a kilometre. If you've admired the jauntily coloured moneyboxes in the form of elephants, roosters, mythical beasts and mounted cavalry which can be found in Yogya, especially around Pasar Ngasem, Kasongan is where you can see them being modelled by hand, fired in an open blaze of roots and palm leaves, and then painted with a verve and panache that's almost Mexican in feeling. Kasongan sprawls, and there is no real centre to the village, but almost every household you come to will have a potter. It is possible to have items made to order; allow up to a week or 10 days for a "special." If you prefer unpainted pieces, remember that the love ochre ware has been fired only once, and is fragile; double-firing gives a more durable result, but the colour will be grey-black.

Pottery makers at Kasongan.

TO THE GREATER GLORY OF THE GODS

Borobudur, one of the world's greatest Buddhist monuments, was built some time between 778 and 842 AD during the Sailendra dynasty. Ironically (though in perfect accord with the Buddhist doctrine of ephemerality) the centre of power had, by 1100 AD, shifted to the eastern end of Java and Borobudur was being engulfed by vegetation.

Raffles visited Borobudur in 1815, and ordered that the site be cleared of undergrowth and then thoroughly surveyed. The work was carried out, but it was not until 1907, when Dr. Th. van Erp began a massive 5-year restoration project, that real progress was made. It was then found that the structure of Borobudur was not in fact solid, but merely a casing of unmortared stone enclosing a natural hillock. Although the original builders had incorporated many spouts to carry off rainwater, and despite van Erp's great care, seepage within the newly exposed monument became a serious problem. Soil and rubble from the inner hillock were gradually washed down against the retaining walls of each terrace, building up enormous pressure which threatened to burst the whole structure like a fermented orange. Chemical salts, too, were slowly eroding the reliefs and carvings.

With UNESCO helping to raise money, almost US$23 million, the gigantic task of rescuing Borobudur was launched in August 1973. Work was completed in 10 years and President Suharto officially reopened Borobudur on 23 February 1983.

Borobudur is only 41 km northwest of Yogya: 31 km will take you a little north of Muntilan, where a sign-posted side road leads to the site; if you're coming from the north, there is another turn-off 7 km south of Magelang.

Borobudur, as a classical *stupa*, is both a *meru* (mountain) inhabited by the gods, and a replica of the three divisons of the Mahayana Buddhist universe: *khamadhatu*, the lower sphere of the everyday world; *rupadhatu*, the middle sphere of form, spiritually superior to the world of the flesh; and *arupadhatu*, the higher sphere of total abstraction and detachment from the world.

There were originally 10 levels at Borobudur, each falling within one or other of the three spheres. At the bottom, now only partly visible, was a level with bas-reliefs depicting the delights and damnations of *khamadhatu*, the physical world; this level was probably covered even before the completion of the temple, possibly to buttress the monument, possibly because the unholy realities of earthly lusts had no relevance to a pilgrim.

The next five levels (the outer processional path and the four square terraces) show, in their reliefs, the life of Prince Siddharta on his way to becoming the Gautama Buddha, his previous incarnations, and episodes from the life of the *bodhisattva* Sudhana. These are within the sphere of *rupadhatu*, and are the most absorbing and delightful of the Borobudur sculptures: ships, family life,

musicians, dancing girls, saints and heavenly throngs.

The square terraces end. Above, three circular terraces support 72 latticed *dagobs* (miniature stupas), most of which are still whole. Most contain a statue of a *dhyani* Buddha, but one *dhyani* stands alone, bereft of his shell, gazing out towards the strange mountain range of Menoreh which seems to echo the silhouette of Borobudur and where one series of lumps and knobs is said to be the profile of Gunadharma, traditionally the temple's architect.

These three terraces are a transitional step between *rupadhatu* and the tenth and highest level, the topmost *dagob*: the sphere of *arupadhatu*, of formlessness and total abstraction. This crowning *dagob* contains two pyramidal chambers. The movement upwards from the material world to the realm of Sublime Reality would suggest that the two chambers were originally empty, the ultimate symbol of absorption into the supreme spirit, yet a *kris* and an uncompleted Buddha statue were found in the lower and large chamber during the 19th century when there was a gaping hole (since sealed) in the side of the *dagob*. Had the statue been there for a thousand years? The *kris* could not have been, but who had placed it there, and why? There are not yet answers.

Borobudur was probably erected for the glorification of the Ultimate Reality, the Lord Buddha, and as a tangible, tactile lesson for priests and pilgrims, a textbook on the path to enlightenment.

Once a year, on Waicak Day (the celebration of the Lord Buddha's birth and death), the temple relives some of its past splendour as thousands of saffron-robed Buddhist priests perform a grand processional by the light of the full moon, offering flowers, incense and prayers. Even non-Buddhists revere the statues of the *dhyani* Buddhas, silently shrouded within their latticed *dagob*, and good fortune is assured if you can touch a figure through one of the square or diamond shaped holes.

Experiences of Borobudur can vary. Most visitors are impressed by its size,

Borobudur's various terraces are plainly evident.

184

and delighted by the reliefs. Others find the immense scale a little too much to cope with. Everybody remember the crowd, the heat and the steps, unless they have been among the first visitors to cross the gate at 6 a.m.

Candi Mendut was built about the same time as Borobudur, but it is not a *stupa*. It resembles most Central Javanese temples with its broad base, a high central body and a steep pyramidal roof once crowned by a large *dagob* and a series of smaller ones. The superbly carved panels on the outer walls depict various *bodhisattvas* and Buddhist goddesses, and are the largest in Indonesia. On the outside of the staircase balustrade small panels relate charming folktales, many of which, in the manner of Aesop's fables, are about animals. The walls of the passageway to the antechamber and the interior of the temple are also decorated with fine reliefs of the tree of heaven surrounded by pots of money and *kinnaras* (half bird, half man), and with two beautiful panels of a man and a woman amidst swarms of playful children. It is thought that these represent a *yaksa* and a *yaksini*, child-eating ogres who converted to Buddhism and became protectors instead of devourers.

The Mendut panels are delightful in their artistry and detail, but they hardly prepare you for the stunning impact of the temple interior and three of the finest statues to be found in the Buddhist world: a magnificent 3-metre high figure of Buddha as Sakyamuni flanked on the left and right (of the viewer) by the *bodhisattvas* Lokesvara and Vajrapani. This is, as Bernet Kempers says, "one of the greatest manifestations of Buddhist spiritual thought and art.... For many visitors to Mendut a silent sojourn in the interior must be one of their most impressive contacts with a higher world."

Many people respond with an equal or greater joy to **Prambanan**, a temple complex (16 km east of Yogya) named after the village which thrusts up to the southern boundary of the temple group. Prambanan is best seen shortly after dawn or in the late afternoon when slant-

The interior of Candi Mendut.

ing sunlight picks out details with a rounding, golden touch. But it is still beautiful at any time.

Prambanan was completed about 900 AD. It was deserted within a hundred years, and collapsed about 1600. Preparations for the restoration of the central Siva temple began in 1911; work started 19 years later, and was completed in 1953. The Brahma temple was completed in 1987, and the Visnu temple in 1990. Reconstruction is still carried out on minor buildings.

The highest courtyard contains the principal edifices. Entering from the south you pass a small "court temple." On your left (west) are three larger temples: the first was dedicated to Brahma, the second and largest to Siva, and the third to Visnu. Opposite these are three smaller temples which contained the "vehicles" of the gods: the gander (*hamsa*) of Brahma; Siva's bull (*nandi*), a monolithic, amazingly relaxed beast carved with consummate skill, and unfortunately the only "vehicle" remaining; and the sun-bird (*garuda*) of Visnu.

At the far north is a second "court temple." Beyond the central courtyard, at a lower level, there were once 224 minor shrines or temples, almost all of which are still in ruins.

The largest temple, the masterpiece dedicated to Siva, is also known as Loro Jonggrang ("Slender virgin"), a name sometimes given to the whole Prambanan temple complex. As legend tells it, Loro Jonggrang was the daughter of Ratu Boko (Eternal Lord). Wooed by an unwanted suitor, she demanded that the man build a temple in one night, and then frustrated his almost successful effort by pounding the rice-logs in a premature announcement of dawn. Enraged, he turned the maiden to stone. She remains at Prambanan as Siva's consort, Durga, a statue in the northern chamber of the main temple. Other major statues include Agastya, the "Divine Teacher," in the main temple's southern chamber; Ganesa, Siva's elephant-headed son, in the western chamber; and an outstanding 3-metre figure of Siva in the central chamber. There is

Celestial beings adorn the walls of Loro Jonggrang.

also a multi-faced Brahma in the Brahma temple.

One aspect of Loro Jonggrang's appeal is its glorious symmetry and grace. Another is its wealth of sculptural detail: on the base of the main terrace, the so-called "Prambanan motif" in which little lions in niches are flanked by trees of life and a lively menagerie of *kinnaras*, hares, geese, birds, deer and a host of other endearing creatures; on the outer balustrade of the terrace, animated groups of singers and dancers, and panels of relaxed, beautiful celestial beings; on the main wall of the temple, the regents of the heavenly quarters; and finally, on the inner wall of the balustrade, the wonderfully vital and utterly engrossing Ramayana episodes which end (on the Siva temple) with the arrival at Langka of Hanuman and his ape army.

The positioning of the reliefs is formal. The movement within each panel is free-flowing, filled with fascinating detail. Even the most tumultous scenes include lovingly rendered touches: monkeys in a fruit tree, birds robbing a grain bin, kitchen scenes. Prambanan's beauty and variety demand more than one visit.

Candi Sewu, also undergoing reconstruction, is at the far end of the fenced Prambanan complex about 1 km from the main group. Sewu, the "Thousand Temples," was built about 850 AD, with a central temple surrounded by 240 minor shrines. The central temple is now being reconstructed, and the walls of the smaller temples reveal a tantalising array of Buddhist deities. The large monolithic temple guardians have been a constant source of inspiration for Javanese artists. Replicas also adorn the courtyard of the *kraton* in Yogya.

Candi Plaosan is another buddhist temple, probably built between 835 and 860 AD. Plaosan originally consisted of two large, rectangular temples. Both were two-storeyed, three-roomed buildings, bounded by a multitude of little shrines and solid stupas. One major temple has been restored, and contains a number of beautiful *bodhisattvas*, very fine *kala* heads above the windows (an unusual feature), and reliefs which per-

Left, loose stonework peppers the ground around the main Prambanan complex. **Right**, deity on an exterior wall at Candi Sewu.

haps depict donors who helped finance the building.

Candi Sari, prettily set amongst banana and coconut groves in a small hamlet (200 metres north of the 14.4 km post from Yogya), is similar to the Plaosan temples, with two storeys, windows, internal cuttings for wooden joists supporting the floors, and superb external reliefs of heavenly beings. Temples like Sari and Plaosan were probably also monasteries where priests, votaries and pilgrims lived above the sanctuaries. Some of Candi Sari's relief statues show traces of "diamond plaster," hard and stone-like, which helped preserve the carvings, enabled sculptors to add fine detail, and provided a base for the bright paintwork that once lit up these temples like immense, multi-faceted gems.

Remnants of fine, yellowed plasterwork can also be seen at **Candi Kalasan**, 50 metres off the main road at the 14 km post. An ancient inscription dates Kalasan at 778 AD, but the existing structure is probably a century younger. The outstanding feature is a huge, ornate *kala*-head above the southern doorway. If you can stand the sweet-ammonia stench of bat droppings, the inner chamber of Kalasan reveals the overlapping blocks of an extraordinarily high and steep pyramidal structure it once housed a huge bronze statue of Buddha.

The area around Prambanan is the most prolific site of temples in Central Java: more than 30 lie within half an hour's walk: some is little more than a small shrine, some are just foundations, others have just been reconstructed, like Candi Banyunibo; more are being discovered.

Candi Sambisari was unearthed only in 1966, and is now completely reconstructed – like the houses of Pompei, it was covered by volcanic ashes which preserved it for 11 centuries, and now lies in a 4-metre deep pit. Built in the first half of the 9th century, Sambisari was a Sivaitic sanctuary: the central temple still contains a Lingga. The external walls are decorated with images of Durga, Ganesha and Agastya. To reach Sambisari turn left (from Yogya)

beyond the 10.2 km post and continue north for about 2 km – the diversion offers also a chance to see bucholic rural villages and lush farmland.

For those who love, within the mind's eye, to reconstruct history, **Ratu Boko** is a dream. Ratu Boko although seldom visited, deserves attention, both because of its location and its historical significance. This was a Royal Palace, probably occupied by members of the Sailendra dynasty and incorporating pre-existent religious structures. Ratu Boko was built on a 200-metre plateau overlooking the Prambanam plains. From its northern edge, on a clear morning, one can enjoy a spectacular view over the temple-studded plain, with the volcanoes at the back, and understand the symbolic significance of the palace as well. As the King considered himself a link between the Gods and the earth, it was befitting to live in a recreated model of the abode of the Gods – the Mount Meru – well above his subjects. The ruins can be reached on foot by a steps path starting opposite the 18 km post, or by car though a long winding road that only locals can find.

The first group of ruins encountered is the monumental gateway to the palace, and to the left of it, a strange square platform that was possibly a cremation site. The second group is 15 minutes away; continue along the path beyond the gate and then turn right, passing through a village built with ancient stones from the palace. Just outside the kampong, there is a recently reconstructed stone platform enclosed by a wall. Just behind it the ruins of the palace, that the villagers describe as "the harem" including a number of pools carved out of the live rock. These pools are still filled with fresh water, and used by the locals for bathing. They offer evidence that pleasure gardens were part of the palace complex, a concept not very different from that of Taman Sari, built 10 centuries later. It is difficult to escape the vision of the ancient king gazing at his girls swimming naked in the pools, and once again one regrets to have arrived in Java a thousand years late.

There is much to be admired at Candi Sari.

SIDE-TRIPS FROM YOGYA

Six kilometres away to the southeast is the town of **Kota Gede**, famous for its silver workshops. It is a compact little town, its main street lined by an honour guard of shop-houses which give way, near the river, to a shambly array of once-stately architectural fantasies: columns where columns don't make sense, strange lead-glass windows, outbursts of coloured tiles, and gateways that seem to lead nowhere.

Kota Gede was founded in 1579 by Senopati, also the illustrious founder of the second Mataram dynasty, who now lies buried in a small moss-covered graveyard only half a kilometre from the town's central market. A broad pathway and two enormous *waringin* trees herald a secluded courtyard through which a narrow pathway leads on to an ancient mosque and a maze of lesser courtyards and decorated doorways. In the midst of this serene labyrinth lies the tiny, high-walled cemetery. Offerings of flowers, petals, incense and cigars strew the worn stone steps in front of the large, weather-grained wooden door leading to Senopati's tomb.

Senopati's original *kraton* is believed to have stood a kilometre farther on. The site is now occupied by a beautiful garden cemetery established by Hamengkubuwono VIII. The main gateway, small and unobtrusive, is inscribed Hasta Renggo (Eight Founded). Beyond a second and more ornate gate is a lovely walled garden, filled with roses, jerberas and small frangipani trees, and the well-kept graves of many members of Yogya's royal house.

In the square outside the cemetery is housed a lump of polished black rock, the size of a double bed. It is variously described as an executioner's block, or as Senopati's throne. Next to it are three large balls of yellow stone, ranging in size from a shot-putt to a volley ball, and reputedly used for juggling.

Another and more splendid link with Yogya's past is at **Imogiri**, 20 km to the

south along a narrow road linked with others (to Parangtritis, 26 km, and Bantul, 12 km) by even narrower lanes that crackle across the landscape like the fine fractured-wax lines on a piece of *batik*. Occasionally you may have to stop as a stumpy yellow diesel engine, or a little black coal-burner with a Casey Jones smoke-stack, rattles and sways across the roadway on its narrow-gauge track, dragging behind it an unsteady train of cane-trucks.

Imogiri has an ancient, sturdy air about it. Close-packed houses made of fired brick are roofed with S-profile terracotta tiles; tall wooden shutters covering the shopfronts are unpainted or faded, adding to a pervading feeling of sun-drenched cleanliness. A little beyond the village the road ends in a tiny square containing a single *warung* and an old *pendopo*. Ahead, a broad pathway leads off through an avenue of trees, the starting point for the climb to the royal tombs.

The famous Sultan Agung was the first of his line to be buried there, interred

Left, rice farming in the shadow of Gunung Merapi. *Right*, silversmith in Kota Gede.

in 1645 on the top of a small rocky outcrop that springs from the plain roughly halfway between Yogya and the sea. Since then almost every prince of the house of Mataram, and of the succeeding royal families of Yogyakarta and Surakarta, has been laid to rest at Imogiri.

A visit to this venerated site takes on the air of a pilgrimage (which indeed it is for many Javanese), for the 345 shallow-tread steps of the wide, formal stairway will exact considerable penance. Happily, even at midday the steps are shaded for most of the way, and there's a touch of magic as shafts of sunlight drop through the overhanging trees and catch eddies of smoke from burning leaves, or the bright colours of a *kebaya*.

The tombs lie within three major courtyards at the top of the stairway: in front are those of Mataram; to the left, those of the Susuhunans of Solo; to the right, those of the Sultans of Yogya. Each great courtyard encloses smaller courts containing the memorials and tombs of the princes: Entry into the smaller courts, and viewing of the tombs, is permitted briefly only on Mondays and Fridays after noontime prayers, and you must wear formal Javanese court costume to visit them. This is less demanding than it may sound, and the necessary garments can be hired on the spot for a low fee.

Although the forecourts and inner courts are closed at other times, the long, high-walled walks along the front of each complex are always open, and their tranquil and relaxing atmosphere, like that of a medieval cloister (with tropical sunshine and shade), makes the climb worthwhile. At each end of the front gallery an archway leads through the walls to a pathway which reaches the real summit of the hill. It's an uneven but easy 10-minute walk to circle the complex, and the views are magnificent: Yogya and Gunung Merapi to the north, an agricultural kaleidoscope to the west, and to the southeast a low rim of ragged, treeless hills which suddenly plunge seawards to Parangtritis.

The royal tombs of Imogiri.

The shore at **Parangtritis** is linked with an ancient tradition which may have flourished in pre-Hindu times as a fertility cult, and which was later observed symbolically by Sultan Agung and his successors. Legends claim that Senopati was married in fact (not fantasy) to Raden Loro Kidul, the "Queen of the Southern Ocean" whose domain, also known as the region of death, is beneath the waters of the Indian Ocean. Ritual observances of the marriage are still performed in the Central Javanese courts: a special dance, the Bedoyo Ketawang, takes place in Solo on the anniversary of the *susuhunan's* accession, and until recently could be witnessed only by the *susuhunan* and the closest of his nobles, for the dance symbolises his marriage to Raden Loro Kidul. In Yogya, on the occasion of the sultan's birthday, a special Labuhan ceremony involves the distribution of sacred nail- and hair-clippings, together with *melati* flowers which have been offered during the year to the royal *pusaka*, at rituals held on the slopes of

Gunung Merapi and Gunung Lawu, and on the shore at Parangtritis.

Raden Loro Kidul, "Queen of the Southern Ocean," may be the consort of kings, but she has a malevolent disposition. Swimming on her rough southern coast is tantamount to entering her territory without a permit, and offenders frequently drown. She has a special predilection for young men dressed in green (her colour).

Legend or no, the rips and violent currents, and a heavy surf, make swimming dangerous on most of Java's southern coast. At Parangtritis this seascape is backed by a forbidding shoreline of jagged clIffs and great dunes of shifting, iron-grey sand. Desolate, angry, weirdly beautiful.

The spell closes in. Extraordinary twists and curls and subtleties of masses of dunes; clearly defined yet melting divisions between black and grey on huge sand-slopes. The dunes won't be the same tomorrow; they'll even change today, sand moving and shifting. Black, grey, another grey, black. An intricate

harmony of patterns like taffeta or watered steel.

Its expressions change. Black sand, a heavy sky waiting to fall, a pewter sea. On the ridges a sudden eye-opener as late light catches a solitary figure on the way from nowhere to nowhere. Even in the brightest sunlight, when the heat is scorching underfoot and the sky is cool blue above, the sand retains its stunning black menace.

Farther afield are the twin beaches of **Baron** and **Kukup**. Baron is a narrow, long bay hemmed in by modest cliffs and small coves which can be reached from the main beach along pathways traversing the intervening ridges. Kukup, a kilometre to the east, is more open, with an exciting mixture of rocky islets, a couple of caves and stretches of weed-slicked limestone shallows jutting out into the surf. Both are a little safer for swimming than Parangtritis, though caution is still essential.

The route to Baron will take you 55 km south-east of Yogya on a good though narrow road. Turn south off Jalan Solo at the "Solo 60 km" post, and turn south again at Wonosari for the last 22 km through country which is both pretty and ragged: rock-fringed hillocks of the "Thousand Mountains," Gunung Seribu, jut up from the limestone landscape, with black cave- mouths grinning from scrub-strewn slopes.

Less attractive than Baron, Kukup or Parangtritis is **Samas** (variously Somas or Somos), but it has the advantage of being closer to Yogya. The road is good, small chalets and eating places are shooting up, but there's little more to he said. The surf, spectacular to look at, is dangerous because the beach shelves abruptly; the treeless dunes and reed-fringed inland lagoons are bleakly attractive, but the black sand underfoot can get very, very hot. It's no tropic isle, though for landscape watchers it is magnificent on a stormy day.

The beauty of most of the coastline south of Yogya is well matched, and more, by the mountains crowding In from the north, where you can choose between the cool and peaceful relaxa-

Cliff fishing at Baron and Kukup.

tion of a hill station like Kaliurang, or lace on your stoutest shoes or climbing boots for a tough volcano trek.

Kaliurang, 23 km due north of Yogya, offers plenty of guesthouses, two swimming pools, a tiny herd of deer from Bogor and a beautiful 2.5-km lung-exercising walk to "Overseer Point." The weather can be unpredictable: even if Merapi is crystal clear from the lowlands it may be shrouded in cloud by the time you reach the lookout at Plawangan (1,275 metres).

Near the summit of Plawangan the path traverses a narrow ridge where tree-clad slopes fall away steeply on both sides, splashed with fiery red and yellow lantana blossom. Normally there is nothing to be heard but the sound of birds, though if the mist comes down you'd swear the spirits of the volcano were abroad: softly swirling vapours creep through the trees, and through the silvery grey light floats the eerie sound of *gamelan*, the disembodied wailing chorus sounding like the denizens of the crater itself.

On a clear day **Gunung Merapi** can be seen in all its glory. Watching it is a full-time job at the Plawangan seismological station where the volcanologists, armed with binoculars and seismographs, work in month-long shifts before moving on to Gunung Kelud or Ijen or wherever else Java's crust is growing restless. Merapi is the most volatile of the island's volcanic tribe, and tops the dangerous list: the closing months of 1973 were marked by a series of minor lava flows and the ensuing (and more damaging) lahar streams of water, mud and ash; the last serious eruption occurred in 1954. To keep the volcano quiet, the Javanese regularly bring him offerings, on the anniversary of the sultan's coronation.

Another good observation point is to the west of the mountain. A small sideroad, well sign-posted in English, branches off the main route to Muntilan at 23 km from Yogya and creeps slowly through tunnels of bamboo and tall stands of pine before revealing the ravaged western slope of the volcano,

Different transportation modes on a country road.

scarred and twisted by a continuing series of lava flows. At night, dull red globs of molten rock can be seen through the darkness, oozing slowly over the rim like monstrous science-fiction slugs, sometimes accompanied by bursts of sparks and flaming cinders. By day, when clouds and mist swirl around the crater's pinnacled rim, huge boulders flung from the core bounce and bound down a steep, grey gulch, raising plumes of ash and smoke as they strafe the slope.

That is one view of Merapi. There is another, from the rim itself.

To stand on the rim of Merapi, gazing down on the world from a height of 2,900 metres, and down into the Dantean crater as well, is probably the most exciting mountain experience in all of Java. Bromo, in East Java, is usually given more attention for it is easier to get to. At Bromo, you walk. At Merapi, you climb.

The climb should be made with the assistence of guides and experienced people. Treks are organised by the Kar-

tika Trekking Service (Jalan Sosrowijayan 10), by the Agung Guesthouse in Yogya, or by Fle Vogel Homestay in Kaliurang.

Although the climb is heart-pounding, the starting point is easily reached. Head east from Yogya to Kartasura just 8 km short of Solo), take the northwest junction to Boyolali and turn off there at Jalan Merbabu (not at Jalan Merapi). The road leads to the great saddle which links Merbabu and Merapi, and on to the little village of Solo where another volcanology post is located. The men on duty will let you rest there, and if you are not on an organised trek, can arrange for your guides. Spare mattresses are generally available. A reasonable payment must be made to the guides, and a donation to the professional volcano-watchers will be greatly appreciated. Solo is the easiest approach. The direct route from Kaliurang is much more difficult.

Merapi can be a daylight trip, but it is best to start the adventure at 2 a.m. in the morning to have a chance to catch the only moment of clear visibility at sun-

Below and right, Merapi remains the most volatile volcano on Java.

rise. As soon as the sun is up, the haze will cover much of the hills. Snug-fitting boots or shoes are essential, and you should take warm clothing, a good torch and a supply of water and energy foods in case you get hungry. You may feel hot to start with, but up near the rim it's tooth-clacking cold.

The trek from the volcanology post to the crater rim and back will take roughly 7 hours. With one exception the climb is steep all the way. It starts through pretty, grassy country dotted with cassias; snakes upwards through a realm of flowers, wild raspberries and stunted bushes; and finally inches onto slopes which are bare of vegetation. Here, on a small plateau, you can make your peace with the world.

In the clear, clean dawn light this is paradise indeed. To the west, the peaks of Sumbing and Sundoro, Dieng's guardians, and beyond them the crown of Slamet, 140 km from where you stand; eastwards, Lawu and farther again to Wilis; the Java Sea to the north, the Indian Ocean to the south; and below you,

a million black and silver mirrors, the glass of *padi*-fields trapped in the sky's first light, as cold and shining as teardrops scattered upon the pristine Earth. For the sure-footed there is one more goal: the crater rim. The guides mutter "*berani*," and follow you as far as they dare (*berani* usually means "brave," but in the context of where you're going it translates more aptly as "crazy"). Don't try to fight the mist if it comes down: less than a metre's visibility, with instant cremation lurking somewhere in the gloom, is not to be toyed with.

The slow climb takes you over razor-sharp rocks, warm rocks, hot rocks. Sulphurous vapours swirl around your ankles. And there, a death's fall below you, under treacherous ledges and jutting rocks, is the devil's well where all the trouble starts: plunging cliffs, a terrifying roar of steam, and a stomach-churning sense of ferocity and power which (you might feel) must be an answer to the world's energy problems. It's time to scuttle back to the safe white walls of Yogya's *kraton*.

DIENG PLATEAU AND GEDUNG SONGO

From your comfortable base in Yogya, you can make an excursion into the heart of Java. Temples are again the official label but the real rewards are stunning landscapes and a good insight into the life of rural Java.

The **Dieng Plateau**, its temples and lakes, and the surrounding mountains, are among Central Java's great scenic rewards: a landscape of constantly changing moods, swathed in mist at one moment, alive with sunshine the next.

From Yogyakarta, to Dieng and back is a long day trip. Better to spend a (freezing!) night in Dieng as the plateau is often clear of mist only in the early morning. Or better still, stay overnight in Wonosobo, where accommodation and food are much better, and leave the little town early in the morning. Dieng is half an hour away.

The road from Yoyga passes Borobudur and Magelang, an unkempt little place like so many Javanese towns, before climbing into mountains covered in tea and tobacco. Gunung Sumbing (3,371 metres) on your right and Gunung Sundoro (3,135 metres) on your left, a handsome pair of sleeping volcanoes who haven't bothered anyone for years. Kledung, the pass between them, is crossed at almost 2,300 metres, and the views are beautiful. The last major town before Dieng is Wonosobo, a pleasant, busy town and a popular base for tourists visting Dieng.

The scenery is magnificent. The country becomes more steep and rugged, and the people change with it. They're a hill breed, tough and stocky.

In Kejajar, 16 km from Wonosobo, the morning market is a festival of colour and (to the outsider) confusion: pale green cabbages the size of beach- balls, coconuts from the lowlands, cakes of boiled rice, saucer-sized pats of *gula jawa* (brown sugar).

In the next 9 km the road climbs more than 700 metres. The terraces become ragged, groping for a foothold here, a

toehold there, as they straggle up the precipitous slopes. The road noses upwards into what must be a dead-end gorge. Suddenly there's a narrow downhill defile, and there in an other worldly light, lies the plateau. Straight ahead, the cluster of ancient, weathered temples.

The existence of demons, spirits and wrathful giants seems not only plausible but probable as grey skeins of mist envelop the surrounding ridges of the Dieng Plateau. The noonday sun, so clean and bright only half an hour before, shrinks from sight behind black fingers of cloud. The cold rain falls, sarong-shrouded figures hurry through the gloom, and darkness covers the face of the earth.

The eerie strangeness of Dieng Plateau, its proximity to the heavens, may have been among the reasons that men laboured there to erect the series of temples that still dominate the plateau. Built to honour Siva, and probably constructed in the early decades of the 8th century, the Dieng temples are remarkable for their simplicity and their spare sculptural ornament.

The main group of temples is named after heroes and heroines of the *Mahabharata* though the names may have been given only a little more than a hundred years ago. **Arjuna**, **Puntadewa**, **Srikandi and Sumbadra** stand in the centre of a flat field, accompanied by the squat, ungainly servant, Semar. The ground about them looks firm enough, but it's mostly deceptive marsh, and any attempt to reach the temples except by the raised causeway is a guarantee of black mud to the ankles or knees (lines of small raised dikes appear to intersect, but there's invariably a more-than-jump-sized gap between them). A millenium ago the marsh was drained by a complex series of tunnels; the remains can still be seen on the northwest corner of the field, but they no longer work.

Candi Gatokaca stands alone at the southern end of the plain, and farther south on a hill embraced by slender acacias is **Candi Bima** with its unique sculpted heads in horseshoe-shaped roof

Preceding pages, the scenic road to Dieng Plateau. **Below**, the main group of temples at Dieng.

niches. Near the main group are the foundations and outlines of what may have been dwelling places for priests and pilgrims.

In the early morning, when the air is still cold, a walk along the wooded pathways encircling **Telaga Warna** ("Coloured Lake") and **Telaga Pengilon** ("Mirror Lake") is enchantingly peaceful and beautiful, and colours sing: orange lichens on tree trunks, translucent blood-red leaves, brilliant apple-green fern fronds, milky green water where drowned hot springs bubble to the surface. Knolls and dells, straight from a Chinese brush painting, hide small caves and grottos still popular as retreats for meditation. Goa Semar is reputed to be the very center of Java, and the dwelling place of the ancient god Semar – charged with power, the place is said to here been chosen by President Suharto to meditate and get inspiration in difficult moments. Beyond the lakes to the south, 2 km along a bumpy but passable track, a never-ending billow of steam marks a fissure where boiling mud plops and splutters in a scalding dance.

There are two other temple sites high on mountain slopes of Central Java: Sukuh and Ceta on Gunung Lawu and the **Gedung Songo** or "Nine Buildings" group on the southern slopes of Gunung Ungaran above Bandungan.

The latter deserves a place as the most beautifully-sited group. You can have Gedung Songo three ways. With sunshine, with mist, or with a combination of both.

The latter is a dream, for in the strange half-light the landscape takes on the sculptural quality of a naked body: smooth hills, shadowy valleys, dark clefts and long upland plains. The first to met is a small, simple structure, flat surfaces lightly ornamented with squares and triangles of ancient memory, roof corners picked out with little dagobs, exterior wall niches long since robbed of their statues. You nose forward through the light mist, following a path above a steep winding gorge, with patches of greyish rubble in the bracken swathing the hillside.

The lakes of Dieng encircle the very centre of Java.

The ground underfoot, if you take to the ridges, is soft and spongy with peat moss. The pungent smell of sulphur, carried by mists from heights you know are there but cannot see, assails your nostrils. The light plays strange tricks, and you might feel you're suspended in a world of ethereal magic: a sudden updraft thins the mist, a flash of sunlight outlines moving figures on a ridge and reveals another shape softly etched against the skyline, another temple visible for seconds and then wrapped again in a shroud of shifting grey silk.

And so it goes. Mist, silver sunlight, temples, more silver, the shrill cries of mountain birds in gullies below you. A temple complex. Three reasonably intact buildings in a sea of rubble. In three niches, battered but appealing statues of an eight-armed childlike statue of the elephant god secreted away, below eye-level, in a base niche. Scattered around are finials and *linggas* and *yoni* pedestals. A roaring ravine, high-walled and narrow with treacherous soft patches of grey-blue, grey-mauve mud, filled with little springs of water far too hot to touch. A hole, reaching back into the bowels of the earth, whistling and shrieking. Green moss, framing a tiny fissure which steams and hisses like an angry cat.

The mist may have cleared by the time you reach the final temple on the final ridge, a great breast of land thrusting into and above the broad plain where shallow lake Rawapening lies under the shoulder of Merbabu and the hills and peaks to the south, the valley a patchwork quilt of intricate *padi*-terracing and fallow land.

To the west, under a cloud cap, the pillars of Sumbing and Sundoro, the gateway to Dieng. Behind you, to the north, trees and shrubs cling to a vertical rock that backs the gorge you've climbed and skirted. Around you, visible from the spur on which you stand, are the other temples on their small spurs, a ring of perfection, serene and enchanting.

The Siva temples of Gedung Songo were built about the same time as those on the Dieng Plateau (some 60 km west-

Temples of Gedung Songo, with view of volcanoes in the distance.

wards as the *garuda* flies) in the early years of the 8th century. Five of them are easily reached and explored in a 2-hour hike, and even if you don't care for temples, the walk and the views are magnificent.

Gedung Songo is accessible from Ambarawa, on the northeastern route from Magelang to Semarang (from Dieng is half a day drive). In Ambarawa, take the clearly sign-posted 7-km road to Bandungan and turn left at the T-junction at the top of Bandungan's main street (marked by a mass of hoardings advertising local hotels and guest-houses). Turn right (north) up the new 5-km road from Bandungan to the temples. **Bandungan** is a pleasant hill-station, very popular with the Semarang crowd who comes here to enjoy the fresh air. A number of decent guest houses and small hotels offer adequate accommodation. If there are room available, try to stay at the Rawa Pening, an old mansion with a spectacular view on the volcanos, and visit the temples early in the morning.

Not so long ago the temples could only be reached after a solid half-hour climb; now they are very easily accessible, as the road ends just below the first temple. Following the gully trails beyond this point the best route is left (south) up a narrow ridge to the main temple, where you carry on with a circular route on clear but slippery paths past the sulphur gorge and back to where you started.

Lovers of ancient locomotives (as opposed to ancient temples) will find a windfall in **Ambarawa**. After the Indonesian State Railways completed their changeover to diesel power, 21 of the best examples of railway "big iron" were preserved in the Ambarawa Railway Museum. The highlight is a 1905 vintage cog-railway taking steam buffs to Bedono, 7 km distant. It is possible to arrange for a special outing through the State Railways (PJKA) office on Jalan Thamrin (behind the Pertamina office) in Semarang, or see the station-master at Ambarawa. A good tour operator should be able to look after details.

Terraced orchards at Gedung Songo.

Surakarta, or **Solo** as it is better known, is an easy 1-hour drive from Yogya. The countryside between the two cities is a glorious patchwork of agricultural endeavour and small towns. Prambanan, with a view of Loro Jonggrang rising above river-side trees; at Klaten, a fast by-pass through rich tobacco fields and counter-balanced well buckets standing like storks in a field; at Gondang, a huge factory dated 1860, a remnant of Java's early industrial revolution; before and beyond, 100-metre thatched "longhouses" for drying tobacco; Delanggu (or Jalanggu), famous for its woodcarvers, but more immediately notable for the masses of *tukang gigi* signs (a *tukang gigi* is less a dentist than a maker of false teeth: the signs are a dream for the collector of pop art); Kartasura, once known as Wanakarta, and for six decades the capital of Mataram, where only a crumbling brick wall recalls former glories; then a final 8-km to Solo's main street.

Solo is a city loved by students and scholars of Central Javanese culture, for it was here that royal patronage brought that culture to its greatest flowering. Although at first glance the flat, sprawling city seems even less a royal capital than Yogya, Solo rewards patience.

The early years of the 1740s were tumultuous ones for the island of Java. A massacre of Chinese merchants and traders in Batavia sparked off a frightening chain of events, bewildering in their complexity and repercussions. Chinese and Javanese combined forces, seized some of the port cities in the east, laid siege to others, and annihilated the Dutch garrison in Kartasura, the seat of the Mataram dynasty. The Madurese prince Cakraningrat, nominally a vassal of Mataram, sided with the Dutch in putting down the revolts. The *kraton* at Kartasura was reduced to ruins, Pakubuwono II was deposed, and a pretender was placed on the throne as Hamangkurat V. In an ironic twist of fate, the pretender's reign lasted a mere 6 months and Pakubuwono was returned to his throne in 1743 under the aegis of the Dutch. Cakraningrat received nothing for his loyalty.

Kartasura had been the capital of Mataram for only 63 years before the destruction of the *kraton*. The *susuhunan*, Pakubuwono II, nevertheless decided to move his capital. A new site, hopefully more auspicious, was selected 8 km farther east on marshy ground along the banks of the Bengawan Solo, the Solo River. Two years of preparation followed, and on 17 February 1745 a wondrous day-long procession followed a flower-and banner-bedecked route from Kartasura to the new capital of Surakarta.

Leading the procession were the royal *waringin* trees, wrapped in silk and destined for the northern square (*alun-alun lor*) in front of the new palace. There followed the Bangsal Pangrawit, a special audience chamber which would be ready to receive the "emperor" (as the *susuhunan* was called by the Dutch) on his arrival. Next came the emperor's elephants and horses, the first group of

officials, the court artisans (goldsmiths, tailors, armourers, coppersmiths), the keeper of the royal seal, a group of ministers, five troops of soldiers, the crown prince and his retinue (including Major van Hogendorp, representing the Governor-General), regalia bearers, religious officials, mounted relatives of the emperor, the royal guard, more bearers of regalia, and then the *susuhunan* himself.

"Just then came the king, dressed as a bridegroom in the royal wagon Kyahi Grudo accompanied by high-ranking officials and other regalia carriers. The soldiers of the Tamtama (royal bodyguard) were on the left and righthand side of the king, 200 men on each side. In the rear were the officials Martalulut and Singanagoro carrying the wadungs (knives) of the king, called Kyahi Pangarab-arab and Kyahi Buta Mancak wrapped in silk."

There was more. The royal ladies, wives and relatives; the emperor's *pusakas* and his library, carried on palanquins; the cooks and utensils for

Preceding pages, busy Solo street. *Below*, Pakubuwono X reigned for 46 years.

206

creating the royal meals; the two *waringin* trees for the southern square (*alun-alun kidul*); the *gamelan* sets; and finally the wealthy traders and merchants, the animals belonging to the royal family, the official hunters and fisherman, and a huge crowd of people from the northern coastal districts who helped carry the emperor's cannons.

The emperor arrived at his new palace. The portable audience chamber had been set up, the queen and the court ladies were despatched to their quarters, and Kandjeng *Susuhunan* Pakubuwono addressed his people:

"Adipati Pringgoloyo, Sindurejo and all my subjects. Hear and obey that this day I have the wish to change the name and status of the village of Sala and make it into the capital city of my kingdom with the name.... Surakarta Hadiningrat. May it be spread to all the people of the whole country of Java."

Court dancers perform at Mangkunega-ran Palace.

The promise of that magical journey was short-lived. Within 12 years the Empire of Mataram was in a terminal death throe. Pakubuwono II was dead.

In 1755 his son and successor, Pakubuwono III, could only watch helplessly as his domains were fragmented: his uncle, Mangkubumi, became the first Sultan Hamengkubuwono of Yogyakarta; his cousin became Mangkunegoro I, controlling a small domain within Solo's remaining territory; and politically, the Dutch held the reins.

The famous "Division of Mataram" was also a blessing in disguise, at least for posterity and today's traveller. The *susuhunan*, although politically emasculated, was still permitted to receive revenues from his lands. Art flourished in the court of Surakarta as it had not done for a hundred years in Mataram. With incoming revenues no longer destined for their war coffers, the *susuhunan* gave their gold to the development of dance, *wayang kulit*, *gamelan* music, *kris*-making and *batik*. It was perhaps an aristocratic hot-house culture, but the culture (if not the power and the glory) survives even now.

The **Kraton** of Solo, Keraton Sura-

karta Hadiningrat, lies just to the south of the eastern end of the city's main street, Jalan Slamet Ryadi. The road south runs a short distance to the *alun-alun lor*, down between the two royal *waringin* trees, and stops in front of the pale blue Pagelaran pavilion with its shining expanse of cool marble tiles and the glassed-in audience chamber, Bangsal Pangrawit, from which Pakubuwono II addressed his subjects in 1745.

At the back of the Pagelaran a broad flight of steps, guarded on each side by iron railings and old cannons, leads up to the Sitinggil pavilion originally faced onto the *alun-alun lor*. The great *pendopo* now contains a sacred cannon, Nyai Setomi, once part of the Portuguese defences in 16th-century Malacca and later captured by the Dutch.

Since 1976, the Pagelaraii has been converted to offices for a major Surakarta university.

The main body of the *kraton* is enclosed in a series of courtyards behind the immense gate-house of Kori Kamandungan Lor. Here, shaded by groves of leafy trees, between which flit the bare-shouldered *abdidalem*, the female attendants, is the large audience hall of the *susuhunan*. The columns supporting the roof are richly carved and gilded, but are hung with protective drapes which are removed only on special occasions. Crystal chandeliers hang from the rafters, marble statues line the walkways, wrought-iron columns and ornately glazed Chinese flowerpots vie for one's attention. A superb stained-glass screen bears the arms of Pakubuwono X who, during a 46-year reign (1893–1939) was responsible for the main decorative elements that now delight the eye in every corner of the *kraton* complex. Most of what you see today, however, is a replica. The palace, in fact, was destroyed by fire in 1985 and has been faithfully reconstructed.

The museum associated with the *kraton* was established in 1963 and contains many interesting artifacts but is in deplorable state of maintenance. The museum also displays some re-

The reconstructed throne hall of the Susuhunan Palace.

markable figure-heads from the royal barges, including the huge-nosed visage of Kyahi Rojomolo, a giant of surpassing ugliness who decorated the prow of the *Susuhunans'* pirvate barge.

The Solo River is the longest in Java. From an unpromising beginning in the harsh limestone hills near Donorojo it traces a torturous course north and northeast for more than 350 km, before breaking into a number of estuaries on the Surabaya Strait. As a navigable link between the rich, rice-growing heart of Central Java and the coastal trading ports (Gresik, Sedayu, Surabaya) it played a vital role in Java's recorded history.

Of all the vessels that made the long voyage from Solo to the north coast, Kyahi Rojomolo was the most splendid. Over 35 metres long, with a 7-metre beam, it contained four rooms and a dining hall that could seat 30 people. It began its service during the reign of Pakubuwono IV (1788–1820), made the return voyage to Gresik three times, collected the Madurese bride of Pakubuwono VII (1830–58) from Bojonegoro, and was finally retired from service towards the end of the 19th century.

The *kraton* and museum are open daily 9 a.m. to 12.30 p.m. (Fridays, 9 a.m. to 11.30 p.m.).

There is a different but equally absorbing museum in the **Mangkunegaran Palace**, north of Jalan Slamet Riyadi at the top end of Jalan Diponegoro.

At the palace only the museum and the huge front *pendopo*, built for Mangkunegoro IV early in the 19th century, are open to visitors. The *pendopo*, is reputed to be the largest in Java. The ceiling, from which are hung huge chandeliers, is elaborately decorated with color patches designed to keep off specific evils, and associated with the Javanese Zodiac. The *pendopo* houses four grand *gamelan* sets; one of them is regularly used for concerts and dance performances, the others are reputed to possess magic properties and are played only on special occasions. Dance rehearsals and *gamelan* concerts are held

Left, palace attendants play a traditional game while watching the museum at Mangkunegaran Palace. **Right**, dance paraphernalia from the palace collection.

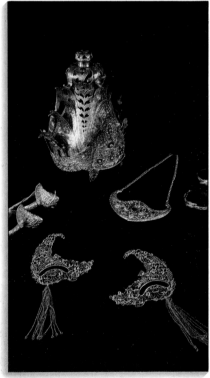

every Wednesday at 10 a.m. and are open to the public.

The museum is in the main hall of the palace building, immediately behind the *pendopo*. A regal flight of steps leads past an array of gilded statues into the hall (open from 9 a.m. to noon daily, except Sundays; entry Rp.300, or Rp.150 for nationals).

The collection recalls that of an 18th-century gentleman, the sort of inspired amateur who filled his cabinets with a pot-pourri of fancies. There are gold-plated dance ornaments, pieces of miniature furniture in filigree gold and coloured enamels, a *sirih*-set in silver-mounted agate; there are dozens of Hindu-Javanese bronzes (mirrors, bracelets, bangles), cases of gold jewellery and superb rings. The palace also has a fine collection of *wayang topeng* masks, and one of the oldest sets of *wayang kulit* surviving.

At Sriwedari Park, on Jalan Slamet Riyadi, is the **Radyapustaka Museum**, the only museum not established by the Dutch. It has a good though not out-standing collection, and the food stalls outside are a pleasant place for lunch. It is open from 8 a.m. to 12.30 p.m.

The Sriwedari Park boasts the most accomplished *wayang wong* group in Java. There is a performance every night from 8 p.m. to midnight. Dance rehearsals and occasional performances may be seen at the Akademi Seni Karawitan Indonesia (ASKI) and the Pusat Kebudayaan Jawa Tengah, both near the main *kraton*.

The two *kraton* hold important yearly festivals whose exact dates must be checked with a travel agent or hotel, because the Javanese year follows a lunar calendar. Most important are the Sunaii ceremony, Sekaten (with its month-long night market) and the Garebeg Maulud festival.

Halfway between Jalan Slamet Riyadi and the Mangkunegaran Palace, on the righthand side of Jalan Diponegoro, is **Pasar Triwindu** (Pasar Windu Jenar), Solo's "flea market."

For the devotee of bric-a-brac, curiosities and honest junk, this is paradise

Solo's busy shopping area.

indeed. Five minutes' browsing will whet your appetite. Fifteen minutes of plunging from one stall to the next will have you in rhapsodies over stoneware bottles, Japanese teacups, glit-brass uniform buttons with the ciphers of Solo's royal houses, *naga*-buckles inlaid with brass, garnets and brilliants (or at least passable pastes), lovely old bell-jars with cut-glass finials and etched "MN" initials, brass *sirih* sets, charcoal-heated irons, and a wonderful selection of refurbished hanging oil lamps.

Pasar Triwindu's supply of lamps, of varied ornateness and size, seems to be the best in Java, and apparently limitless mainly because most now on sale are reproductions faithfully modelled after the originals. "Flowers and baskets" are at the lower end of the price scale, but "lions and palm trees" and similarly extravagant motifs are more expensive; larger lamps, some with as many as six branches, are of course more highly priced. If you're considering buying a lamp in Java (most visitors are entranced by them) don't forget that the metal

counterweight will add a good 5 to 10 kg to your baggage.

Lamps aside, there are possibilities for decorating a dozen houses in fond remembrance of the 1920s, another dozen in nostalgic 1930s style, and a handful with a regretful salute to the last days of Europe's gilt-and-candelabra era circa 1910: there are plates, cups, incomplete dinner services, tiles, glasses, goblets, statuettes, *baig-noires*, chafing dishes, silver-plated cruet sets, vases, lamp-bases, inkwells, ash-trays, teapots, salvers and rolling-pins.

There's also plenty of out-and-out junk (empty plasma bottles, chipped enamel bedpans), but even amongst the debris you might find quaintly labelled tins that once contained dubious nostrums, old medicine bottles in startling green glass, or an ornate temperature-gauge which in 1913 decorated the bonnet of a long forgotten automobile. Prices at Pasar Trewindu depend a lot on one's bargaining expertise, though it is the kind of place where you may feel that whatever you buy is a bargain.

Pasar Triwindu.

On the trail of exotica you can indulge yourself in **Dancers' Requisites** at Toko Bedoyo Serimpi on the corner of Jalan Hayam Wuruk and Jalan Ronggo Warsito. These are theatrical suppliers' retail outlets, not souvenir shops, but of course you are welcome to inspect and buy a glorious range of anything and everything connected with the dressing of *wayang wong* and classical dance.

There are costumes, monkey masks with moveable lower jaws for Hanuman and the ape army, spangled golden headdresses, the checked cloths worn by the clownish *panakawan*, gilded bracelets and armbands, painted or unpainted *topeng* masks, coloured gloves and matching tights worn by the various monkey regiments, and stage *kris* of menacing realism. There are even a few old-fashioned buckles, though most items are new.

Solo has long enjoyed a reputation as one of Java's most important *batik* centres, and calls itself the City of *Batik*. To discover why, pay a visit to the huge **Pasar Klewer** at the eastern end of Jalan Secoyudan, under the shadow of the west gate to the *alun-alun lor*. The entire market is devoted to fabrics, with hundreds of neat stalls jammed together along narrow passageways on two floors. *Batik* is overwhelmingly predominant, though some stalls specialise in *lurik* of various grades and a few offer *kain ikat* and other materials.

Although the company now concentrates on commercial textiles, a *batik* pioneer, **Batik Keris**, maintains a sort of "living museum" at its factory in Solo. Two dozen women sit around a common heated wax pot tracing intricate designs while next door, men use heavy copper stamps to imprint repeating designs on lengths of fabric. In an adjacent building, men stir huge vats of boiling water to extract the wax from finished cloth. The Victorian sweatshop ambience is a far cry from the showplace exhibits of Yogyakarta's *batik* shops.

Across town, one small *batik* factory continues the aristocratic traditions of fine, painstaking craftsmenship. At Hardjonagoro's workshop on Jalan Kratonan 101, exquisite *batik tulis* is produced in a setting more elegant than the now-touristed *kraton*. Hardjonagoro's talented blacksmith forges *kris* using traditional methods. Viewing is by appointment only.

A two-stringed *rebab*, with a beautifully turned neck and delicate tuning-screws, can be bought or made to order at the **Balai Agung** on the *alun-alun lor*. There is also a big selection of the various kinds of percussion instruments that make up the rest of the *gamelan* orchestra.

Many kinds of Javanese music, *gamelan* music with or without vocal accompaniment, and the music which accompanies the many forms of *wayang* (from puppets to people), are now available on pre-recorded cassette tapes. If you like browsing and strolling, a walk down Jalan Secoyudan, the goldsmiths' street, can be entertaining: not just for the dozens of *toko mas* with their golden baubles, but also for some of the names ("King Kong" sits uneasily as the name of a jeweller's shop).

Left, a shop sign. **Right**, a blacksmith at Hardjonagoro workshop blesses his newly completed *kris* with holy water.

SIDE-TRIPS FROM SOLO

Directly to the east of Solo lies the 3,265-metre bulk of Gunung Lawu, its gently rolling foothills smothered with *padi* and peanuts, its higher slopes clad with pine forests, virgin hushland and, frequently, swathes of dense white mist. The main road eastwards to Madiun and Surabaya skirts the northern edge of the mountain, but there are two reasons for travelling up or even over Lawu: the first is for a glimpse of one of Java's most mysterious temples; the second is for some inspiring scenery.

Candi Sukuh, 910 metres up on Lawu's western Rank, is sometimes billed as "Java's only example of erotic temple carving." If erotic means the explicit presentation of a stone penis or two, then the description fits, though don't expect the convoluted couplings found in some Nepalese and Indian art. Sukuh's appeal lies in its blend of mystery, of dark disarray, of almost satanic majesty, presented in a superb setting. It is utterly different in mood and in structure from temples elsewhere in Java, and this alone makes it worth seeing.

Five kilometres east of Solo take a right fork off the main road towards Karangpandan and Tawangmangu. Just through Karangpandan, a few metres beyond the "TAW-12" km post there is a side-road to the village of Kemuning. Follow this road for 5 km and turn off at the Candi Sukuh signpost for the steep climb up to the temple. The road is surfaced all the way. If you do not have your own transport, you must charter a bemo from Karangpandan, as there is no guarantee you will find transport back from the site.

Built in the middle of the 15th century during the twilight years of glorious Majapahit, on a site which may once have been occupied by a temple dedicated to ancestor worship, Sukuh strikes a disquieting, alien chord with its flat-topped "Egyptian" step-pyramid and its

Candi Sukuh on the slopes of Mount Lawu.

"Mayan calendar" carvings. Only after a while do the familiar *panakawan* clowns, carved in the distorted *wayang kulit* style found in East Java, emerge intelligibly from the crude reliefs, weird and shocking after the sculptural finesse of Loro Jonggrang.

At the top of the first stairway leading through a split gateway you'll tread on (or over) a large phallus aimed at a plump *yoni* and surrounded by browning rose petals left by previous supplicants. Farther up the grassy terraces, at the edge of the main temple complex, a well-endowed boar (once part of a splendid high-relief frieze) gazes stonily down his snout at an even grander elephant. Under the shadow of the central temple and its guardian trees a headless gentleman clutches a club in one hand and his own bell-bedecked penis in the other.

In its setting of steep, pine-clad hills, Sukuh possesses an impressive grandeur. In the main courtyard are interesting sculptures, enhanced by the eclectic styles.

Three enormous flat-backed tortoises stand like sacrificial altars on a stone-flagged courtyard. A roughly hewn demon glares balefully at the world, a sharp-beaked *garuda* is a hovering angel of death one one side of an obelisk, an anthropomorphic elephant is the proud proprietor of a blacksmith's shop hung with krises and swords. Figures crowd one another within the stylised outline of a womb. The unadorned pyramid squats heavily, four-square on the ground.

Sukuh poses many questions that remain unanswered. Were its builders religious refugees from East Java? Were they the locally-born, mountain-dwelling inheritors of an ancient faith? Were they, perhaps, the survivors of the great Central Javanese kingdoms of the 9th and 10th centuries? What were the origins of their diverse and seemingly unrelated sculptural styles?

We don't know, though that hardly matters, for not knowing enhances Sukuh's spell.

The surrounding landscape, steep and pine-clad, is the perfect complement to

A relief from Candi Sukuh.

Sukuh's allure. There are a number of trails which begin close to the temple and lead high up the forested slopes of Lawu. Just to the right of the temple grounds there is a small, clean *pondok* which will sleep four people, and which makes an ideal "base camp for exploratory walks. There is no fixed price for accommodation; a nominal fee is asked.

Candi **Ceta,** with its Bima figures and numerous terraces, was built about the same time as Sukuh, but is less interesting. It lies beyond Kemuning, some 600 metres higher up the mountain than Sukuh, reached by a bad track.

Back at Karangpandan the road climbs up towards Tawangmangu, a pretty hill town which seems to be filled with white-painted guesthouses. To go farther you'll need a car with plenty of heart: the grades are alarmingly steep, and some of the bends are real hairpins. Neat terraces give way to counterpane plots of cabbages and corn that dip and roll with the hillsides, tended by farmers in black jackets and half-trews, or in sarongs of deepest indigo.

Cultivation disappears. The road gropes ever upward through groves of wild acacias and banks of wildflowers into a sea of mist and dense forest where strands of pale green lichen drip from the trees. In places the road's paving stones are covered with layers of moss, or grown through with stubbly grass.

It's wild, primeval and magnificent. The road eventually crawls over a ridge and winds through the grey light. Woodcutters, ghost-like in the mist as they trim freshly cut logs and pare sticks for their charcoal kilns, may perhaps encroach on the solitude. Soon market gardens appear. The road drops sharply, twisting around sharp bends, and finally reaches **Sarangan**, a popular cool-climate weekend resort for people from Madiun and the surrounding area. A couple of dozen *losmen*, hotels and guesthouses cluster at the northern edge of Telaga Sarangan, many of them offering superb views across the small lake with its background of soaring wooded peaks. Boating, riding, bushwalking and working up an appetite in

Stone guardians at Candi Sukuh.

the crisp mountain air are the main diversions in Sarangan, which is easily approached from Madiun if you prefer to avoid the low-gear route over Lawu from Solo.

Only 5 km below Sarangan the little village of **Ngerong** nestles at the head of a pretty valley. There are a few *losmen*, though you may like to stay at the small, modern guesthouse run by Ibu E.M. Anugrah Damajhanty behind the *rumah makan* Anyar. Ibu's back garden is a masterpiece of terracing, and is filled with roses, pumpkins, jerberas, orchids, bonfire salvia, fresh young lettuces and a natural stream that tumbles through a steep gully almost straight beneath your breakfast patio.

Before or after breakfast, take one of the tough local ponies ("tough" sometimes means "stubborn") and explore the local trails through forests and vegetable gardens, meandering from one cobble-stoned village to the next. The experience is one facet of heaven on earth, and the hire of a pony is quite cheap.

With 2 or preferably 3 days to spare, your jaunt to Candi Sukuh, Tawangmangu and Sarangan or Ngerong can be extended to include a surfing beach, harshly beautiful landscapes, a *gamelan* "orchestra" with lime-stone stalactites for instruments, and a hundred hills looking like giant cupcakes.

The destination is **Pacitan**, across the border in East Java on an estuarine plain where the Kali Grindulu runs into the sea and meets long lines of rollers sweeping into the broad bay.

With Solo as your point of departure and return there are several possible routes. You can go east around Gunung Lawu to Madiun, or across Lawu to Sarangan; in both cases you then head south to Ponorogo and on to Pacitan, and complete the circuit by coming back through Wonogiri for a total of roughly 300 km. An alternative is the southern route direct from Solo through Wonogiri to Pacitan, and back the same way.

The road from Ponorogo follows a torturous, tough course along the corkscrew turns of the Grindulu valley, rid-

Phallic sculpture at Ceta.

ing high along cliff-tops and sheer hill-sides, crawling under rocky over-hangs, plunging into tight gullies crowded with teak or plots of corn. Ragged terraces of cassava scramble to the tops of blunted hills; a landslide has exposed a great red scar of earth and rock; seams of blue-grey clay are scoured for lodes of abrasive pumice; and immense boulders cling precariously to weathered hill-sides, others lie like devil's marbles where they have come to rest on the valley floor. This is a spare, dry, hand-some beauty.

A rapid series of bridges, a widening valley, then the plain, then Pacitan. Check with the *bupati* (the *kantor kabupaten* is one of a group of buildings backing the grassy square at the southern end of town), and you may be able to stay the night at the *pasanggrahan*, a kind of lodge, 7 km beyond Pacitan on the southwestern side of the bay. The cost is quite reasonable and the two-bedroomed cottage can sleep four comfortably and six at a pinch; take your own food. Fifty metres away is a large,

clean public swimming pool which is usually deserted on weekdays. If the *pasanggrahan* is unavailable, there are clean *losmen*-style rooms in Pacitan.

The cottage, though a mite jaded, can be enjoyable, with a constant roar of crashing surf and a tree-framed view of a long crescent of grey-gold sand, white foam and dull green waves. The beach is accessible down a side-road about 2 km back towards Pacitan, or can be walked and waded to from the cottage. The surf, which breaks heavily some distance from the shore, is quite safe closer to the beach. On the sand above the high-tide mark salt-bleached outriggers, looking utterly unseaworthy, huddle in a sem-blance of shipwreck.

On the way from Pacitan to the cot-tage, in a wilderness of windswept grass and odd sticks of cactus, is a Greek temple. Severe, classical, unbelievable. At the south end the pediment is in-scribed "R.I.P."; at the north end, *Gegaan maar niet vergeten*, "Gone but not forgotten." A coffin-shaped sar-cophagus lies amid the fluted columns,

Left and right, just another day in Java.

218

its long, well-chiselled inscription still unscarred, still legible, and utterly incomprehensible: it is in code from start to finish.

The most imposing view of the coastline is from a rubble-strewn ridge about 15 km out of Pacitan on the 105-km route to Wonogiri. The road soon loses itself in a crazy jumble of low, rounded hills, terraced with rock walls right to their summits, sometimes blistered with exposed faces of limestone, sometimes blackened by the jagged mouths of caves which have, over a thousand years of history, sheltered kings, guerrillas, rebels and revolutionaries.

Gua Tabuhan, one of the finest caves, is said to have provided refuge for Prince Diponegoro during his 5-year war against the Dutch. Purely as a cavern, hung with grey-white columns of quilted, rippled limestone (some of them still dripping, still growing) it is impressive. The vast antechamber, spattered with brilliant moss, seems to end abruptly in a dark dank corner until the flickering yellow light of bamboo torches reveals a small opening leading to another 50 metres of eerie, shiny-wet tunnel where hordes of little boys, acting as guides and guardians, will make you feel like Snow White making a royal progress through the Seven Dwarfs' mine. The tunnel floor is uneven and slippery, and the ceiling is skull-cracking low in some places.

The big event at Gua Tabuhan is the "orchestral" performance in the main chamber. There is one small double-ended drum, with drummer. He sets the beat. There is one old man and six young boys, all clutching hard lumps of rock, and almost hidden behind an organ-pipe cluster of hefty stalactites; three of the smaller boys are wedged into crevices two or three metres above the floor, and only their feet can be seen. Then the music starts. Pure *gamelan* melodies clinking and resonating in perfect pitch as rock strikes rock, each stalactite vibrating and booming and singing like a monstrous tuning fork. The old man has the pick of the instruments: two blows, struck a handspan

An explosion of limestone at Gua Tabuhan.

apart on the same column, produce two notes in perfect harmony. Ten minutes, three melodies. This is no free concert so do a little friendly bargaining.

Other boys, perhaps less accomplished as musicians, sell souvenirs: fist-sized lumps of hard, brilliant white quartz. Broken down into wearable chunks, the quartz is attractive set in silver as a ring or pendant, or some other item of jewellery.

The road leading to Gua Tabuhan is a *desa* track in much better condition than the main road. The turn-off is well signposted: approaching from Pacitan it is 3 km beyond Punung; from Wonogiri, it is 2.7 km beyond Donorojo. The track runs one km in from the main road, and another signpost guides you left for the last 1.5 km to the cave entrance.

Donorojo is famous for two things: agate and *wayang beber*. Agates are found in the gullies and river-beds of the surrounding area, and a thriving cottage industry cuts and polishes the stones. They are for sale.

Wayang beber is an ancient and almost extinct form of storytelling in which the tale literally unwinds on a series of painted scrolls. The last remaining practitioner of this art, the *dalang* Pak Samen, lives in a village near Donorojo and performs about seven times a year. His scrolls carry episodes from the Panji tales, and the responsibility for their care is shared by families in the area. Experts agree that the scrolls are extremely old. Although it is impossible to date them conclusively, there may be some truth in the local belief that the scrolls once belonged to the royal dynasty of Majapahit, and were given for safekeeping to Pak Samen's ancestors when Muslim Demak was rising to power in the north.

The co-operative care of the scrolls means they are not always in the same place, and they may take some tracking down. If you speak to the *camat* (head of the sub-district or *kecamatan*) at his office on the main road in Donorojo, you may be able to see the scrolls; finding them will probably take a couple of hours. You might even be lucky enough to see a performance.

A little beyond Donorojo, still within the hills and heading towards Wonogiri, the road crosses the border between East and Central Java. In case you miss the boundary maker, a large painted emblem of the Diponegoro Division – "Central Java's Own" – will tell you where you are. This is the northern edge of the coastal range. Below you, the road winds down onto the plains and into a familiar landscape of *padi* and palms.

Shortly before Wonogiri there's a seemingly precarious ride across a long railway bridge: the "roadway" timbers on either side of the railway lines are splintered, cracked and even missing, however, the prospect becomes less nerve-racking when you realise that fully-laden freight trains make the crossing.

If you're still in the mood for scenic vistas and an energy-consuming climb, a high pinnacle of rock, at the back of Wonogiri, offers superb views across the plains to Merapi, Merbabu, Lawu and the hills to the south.

Illustrative style of a *wayang beber* scroll (<u>right</u>) takes its inspiration from the *wayang kulit* puppet (<u>below</u>).

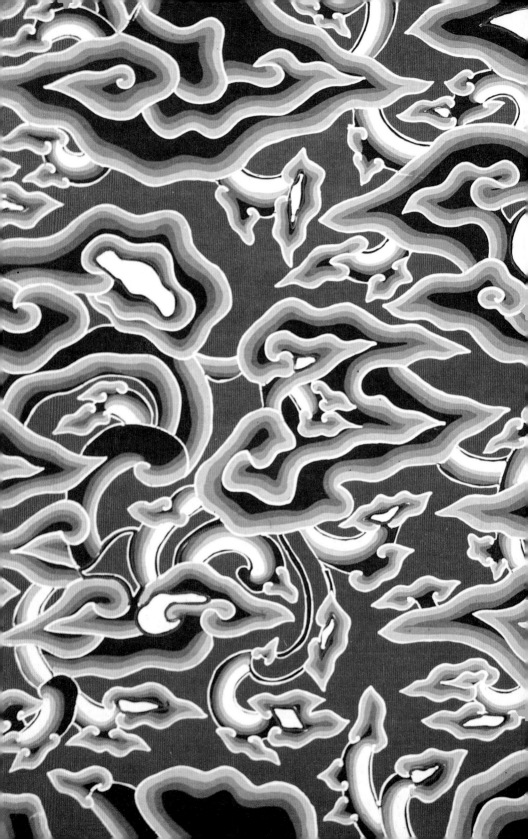

THE NORTH COAST

The journey through the North Coast region is likely to be more satisfying as a voyage of the spirit than as a physical encounter. Two *kraton* and a few mosques and temples are scant return for hours of playing cat-and-mouse with hurtling buses and plodding tanker trucks on the hot, congested North Coast highway. But armed with a little knowledge and an active imagination, a short jaunt along the coast will give you a more complete view of Java.

Indonesians refer to the north coast of Java as the *pasisir*, meaning fringe. The ethnocentric Javanese, comfortable in their fertile heartland, preferred to deal with the outside world through these coastal vassal states. Because of the *pasisir*'s favourable location and the enormous food surpluses generated in the heartland, the coastal settlements became a popular stopover for trading ships plying the route between China and India. As *pasisir* residents developed trading contacts with most of Asia, a cosmopolitan culture developed in marked contrast to the introspective heartland Javanese.

But the Javanese aristocracy could not keep outside influence bottled up in the *pasisir*. In the vibrant coast regions, foreign values and culture would be adapted to Javanese tradition, and would then spread into the heartland. The most powerful of this new influenced was Islam, brought by Indian traders in the 15th century, which was adopted by the *pasisir* populations and propagated southward.

During the 16th century, the fortunes of the *pasisir* settlements skyrocketed with the first Europeans. As the focal point for the spice trade, where clove, cinnamon and nutmeg from the Outer Islands would be exchanged for Chinese silk, Indian textiles and European gold, Demak, Kudus, Cirebon and Jepara grew into powerful city states, eventually dominating the decadent inland empires.

By the mid 17th century, the resurgent Mataram Empire under Sultan Agung had conquered the *pasisir* cities, and a century later the Dutch gained control over the entire North Coast as the price of assisting Surakarta's *susuhanan* to control his fragmenting empire. The *pasisir*'s importance faded as cash crops from the heartland replaced the spice trade. The *pasisir* cities became merely transshipment points for coffee and sugar, and then backwaters as the shallow harbours silted up and trade shifted to Batavia and Surabaya.

But the *pasisir* has left its mark on modern-day Java. That *batik* still exists is largely due to the commerical acumen of *pasisir* enterpreneurs who developed mass production and marketing techniques for this traditional textile. The ubiquitous clove-flavoured *kretek* was developed in Kudus, a modern-day adaptation of the city's former role as spice port.

Now, the *pasisir* is booming again as modern industry spreads outward from Jakarta and Surabaya. As in the past, the new values, attitudes and culture of the outside world are being nurtured and adapted in the *pasisir*, soon to spread to the heart of Java.

Preceding pages, the cloud and rock motif-Chinese inspired – is common along the North Coast. **Left**, sprucing up a fishing boat at the *pasisir*.

TRAVELLING ALONG THE PASISIR

At the far western end of the pasisir the ancient sultanate of **Cirebon** is best approached from Bandung via a slower and more attractive route than the flat and boring coastal plain. The road meanders down through tree-clad slopes to Sumedang (depending on the time of day, stop for a snack or meal at Restaurant Tampomas Baru) and disgorges onto the plain at Kadipaten, a jumping-off point for wild boar hunting in the Ljungjaya area. Keep an eye open for crowds around an improvised stage in the villages, for you might catch a *wayang topeng* (masked dance) with Panji confronting his red-visaged adversary Klono. *Wayang topeng*, once famous around Cirebon, came close to extinction, but a grass-roots revival is gaining momentum. As a stranger you may become an impromptu player or a source of comic relief.

Rugged limestone hills, gouged and quarried, announce Jatiwangi. Huge lime kilns look like medieval battlements during a siege. Dusty figures carry rock-laden baskets up treacherously crumbling stairways to the lip of the furnace mouth. In the smoke-filled air they look like harried but loyal defenders shoring up a breach. Farther on, lovers of colonial architecture will find a cluster of tiny gems in the neat, compact town of **Jambelang**, all wide eaves and columns and big shutters. Near Weru there are *warung* selling simple rattan furniture.

Cirebon, with Javanese, Sundanese and some Chinese elements in its culture, is an interesting potpourri. Crawfurd, in his famous *Descriptive Dictionary* of 1856 noted that "perhaps its name (is) correctly Charuban, which in Javanese means mixture," and many people still speak a local dialect which blends Sundanese and Javanese. Its popular name, *Kota Udang* or "Shrimp City," is a tribute to the local fishing, but does scant justice to Cirebon's turbulent past.

Warred over by Hindu Pajajaran and Muslim Demak in the 15th century, sandwiched between the kingdoms of Banten and Mataram in the 17th century, and conquered and re-conquered, Cirebon finally became a restless fief of Batavia in 1705, jointly administered by three sultans whose courts rivalled those of Central Java in opulence and splendour. The present sultan, deprived of his royal revenues in these democratic days, is appropriately a banker.

Two of the ancient *kraton*, Kesepuhan and Kanoman, are open to visitors. In the southeast corner of the city, adjoining a striking tiered-roof mosque, **Kesepuhan**, with its low-walled grassy forecourts, exudes the bewildered air of an Edwardian dowager deserted by her maids and butlers. Blue and white Delft tiles dot vertical white-washed surfaces like stamps in an old album with foliated borders.

The small dusty museum (opened on request) has some marvellous but ill-kept treasures and curiosities, including wicked spiked bludgeons used in dis-

Left, stucco work on the walls of Kesepuhan Kraton draws inspiration from *batik* motifs. Right, Dutch tiles adorn both the inside and the outer walls.

plays of magic invulnerablity. Across the courtyard, a gilded coach carries such a mixture of mythic symbols that a griffin seems human. The dragon's head, elephant's trunk, eagle's wings and bull's forelegs illustrate the syncretism of Chinese, Hindu, Islamic and Buddhist influences that distinguish Javanese court iconography.

The Chinese-influenced "rocks and clouds" decoration on the chariot is a recurring motif in Cirebon's arts. The motif occurs in woodcarving, plasterwork and *batik*, but for exuberant embellishment nothing matches the ruins of **Candi Sunya Ragi** (about 4 km out of town on the southeastern bypass). First built by a Cirebon prince early in the 18th century, its present weird form was put together by a Chinese architect in 1852. It is a grotesque amalgam of plaster, red brick and concrete put together like a child's sand-drip castle and honeycombed with tunnels, grottos, secret chambers, doors for dwarfs and staircases leading nowhere. The now-dry watercourses and empty planters

indicate that the site was once a natural pleasure garden or mediation retreat. A small amphitheatre beside the parking lot is used for Prambanan-style *sendratari* performances every September.

Five kilometres north along the main Jakarta road, is the sacred tomb of Sunan Gunung Jati, one of the nine great *wali* who helped establish Islam in Java. Pilgrims burn incense and perform their worship at the doorway leading to the inner sanctum, closed to everyone save the tomb's caretakers. A maze of courtyards filled with gravestones surround the holy tomb and cover the slopes of the small hill across the road.

Artistically, Cirebon may seem to be in a decline. This is more apparent than factual, as a glance at the activities board in the cultural centre, *Kantor Pembinaan Kebudayaan*, will quickly show. The office of the cultural centre is housed in a pillared, low-eaved building on one side of the city's *medan*, and here you can find an impressive list of regional acts and dances which take place in the surrounding area. There is no perma-

The cloud motif so typical of Cirebon appears again on the roof of the *kraton*.

nent performing arts venue in Cirebon itself. *Wayang topeng Cirebon* and a local version of the horse trance dance are both popular in the district, and so too is *angklung*. The latter is hardly a new fad, for the Java Gazette described way back in 1813 "a native band which after playing some minutes on their different instruments eritirely composed of bamboo tubes, and accompanying them with their voices, commenced a Malay dance."

The local **batik** industry is flourishing, notwithstanding claims by some *batik* merchants in Central Java that Cirebon *batik*-making is in decline. It is true that the cream of the Cirebon crop ends up in cities like Jakarta, its price magnified as much as 400 percent by enterprising entrepreneurs, but in the numerous cooperatives around Cirebon, mostly within 5 km to the west near the village of Trusmi (Weru), you can find outstanding examples of the *batik*-maker's art. For a view of the finest *batik*, pay a visit to Ibu Masina's studio. Almost opposite the office of the *keca-*

matan in Weru is a signpost pointing south to "Sumber 6 km"; take the opposite road north for one km, and you'll find Ibu Masina's place along the edge of a narrow lane, housed in a long, low white building directly across from a grassy clearing.

The shop, now run by her daughter, sends most of its output to Jakarta and Denpasar. Nevertheless, you should have the chance to see some extraordinarily fine hand-drawn *batik*s, including superb blue and red bird designs and the handsome classical Cirebon motif of "rocks and clouds" in magnificent tones of blue.

Farther east along the coast the prospect is generally dull. Occasionally there are small estuarine towns where colourful boats ride easily on the tide. High-peaked prows adorn the boats like painted dorsal fins; tall three-pronged rowlocks wait to receive the long rudder oars; and hulls are ablaze from stem to stern in a riot of colour. Rolled nets, stacked between the thwarts, shimmer in the bright sunlight like giant cocoons

The Sultan's coach in the Kesepuhan Kraton.

of silk. Downriver, homing craft with great sheets of squarish sail rigged to port and starboard look like butterflies gliding on their tails.

Farther along the coast the market of Brebes, devoted to small red onions, is doing a roaring trade. At the next whistlestop you might chance upon an afternoon performance of *wayang golek* celebrating a circumcision ritual: the puppets are magnificent, and the price of admission is cigarettes for the *dalang* and his musicians.

Across the fields of sugar-cane and *padi* to the south of Tanjung, shimmering in the heat, is the blurred outline of a range of hills. At the eastern end of the range the second highest mountain in Java, Gunung Slamet, thrusts its 3,428 metres in the sky.

Except as a road junction, and as a centre of fishing and mechanised weaving, **Tegal** has little to recommend it, though pottery and handicrafts enthusiasts may be tempted by the excellent ochre-ware which includes teapots decorated with brass strap-work and paired with pierced-brass trays; roadside stalls about l0 km on the southern road out of Tegal are the best hunting ground.

What the north coast lacks in scenic beauty it makes up for in *batik*. **Pekalongan**, like Cirebon, is another famous *batik* centre. Quite apart from the retail stores along Jalan Hayam Wuruk, Pekalongan justifies its sobriquet as *Kota Batik* ("*Batik* City") with the presence of dozens of independent hawkers who will descend upon you the moment you set foot in town or enter a restaurant. Competition is fierce but good-natured, and you should be able to have the initial asking-prices (or do even better) with a little care and some judicious bargaining. There is *batik* in Pekalongan, hand-waxed, stamp-waxed and even machine printed, which you won't easily find in other parts of Java.

The pilgrimage point for the true connoisseur is the small workshop of Oey Soe Tjoen, the source of the most exquisitely wrought *batik* in the whole of Indonesia. Take the road south from Pekalongan to the village of Kedung-

A Pekalongan *batik* drawn during the Japanese Occupation.

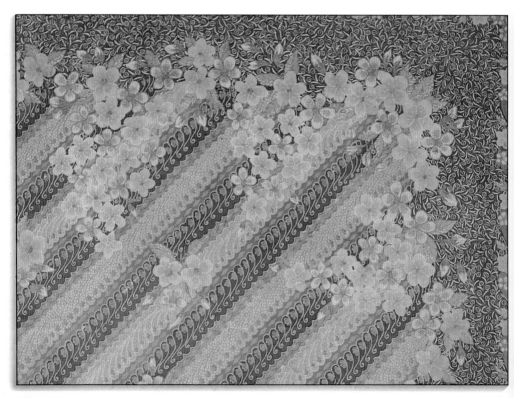

wuni, 9 km away. About 200 metres before the village police station (a reminder in case you miss the unpretentious house) is No. 104 Jalan Raya. This is where the cream of Jakarta's society comes for its *batik*. If the wives of ministers, generals and diplomats don't actually make the journey themselves, they make sure they see the wares somehow. They invariably buy the expensive pieces.

Each length (*sarong* or *kain*) takes around 9 months to complete. Ibu Oey does the designing and *tulisan* waxing, with detail so intricate that it's hard to believe this is handworked (until you see a sheet of cloth in progress and can examine every dot and line of wax). The dyeing, in gentle tones of mustard-ochre, olive and corn-flower blue, pale rose pink, dull orange and mauve, is done by her son. It's a family business that still continues to produce bird, flower and butterfly designs of such finesse, and colours of such delicacy. In response to requests (especially by foreigners), Ibu also makes smaller pieces of *batik* which are ideally suited as wall hangings. Even if you're not buying, visit the workshop just to see what really fine *batik* is all about. It is customary in the Pekalongan area for *batik* workers to take their holiday on Fridays.

For half the distance between Pekalongan and Semarang the road runs fast and smooth through teak plantations, gently rolling hills, and villages of neat houses with wooden facades and shallow verandahs. Then there's rice and sugar-cane, and finally **Semarang**.

The decline of the great north coast ports, which reached its nadir during the turbulent course of the 17th century, was hastened by the growth of the inland state of Mataram, the Dutch control of coastal waters, and the slow flow of silt from land to sea which filled in harbours and made rivers unnavigable. Demak was once a port. So too was Pati, its vassal and salt centre. And less then 500 years ago a navigable channel separated Gunung Muria, northeast of Jepara, from the mainland. Today the channel is filled with *padi* and salt pans. Deprived

Residential area of Semarang, spread over the hills.

of their trade, the entrepot ports had no money for men or for dredging. The mud thickened, and overcame. So the fortunes of Semarang rose, in a sense, from the mud. Eclipsed as a port by its stronger and wealthier neighbours during the 16th and 17th centuries, it nevertheless offered a small, calm rivermouth; and, its roadsteads were sheltered enough to provide safe refuge for trading vessels which swung at anchor whilst bum-boats and barges ferried cargoes to and from the shore.

In the course of the 18th century it rapidly gained ascendancy over the older, mud-choked ports. Today Semarang still flourishes as the capital city of the province of Central Java. Modern Semarang has few relics of an illustrious past. Those remaining bear witness to the presence, in bygone days, of a large population of Dutch traders and officials, and a fair sprinkling of Chinese merchants: old buildings with exterior wrought-iron staircases, great warehouses, colourful temples and solid churches.

On Jalan Let. Jen. Suprapto, a little south of Stasiun Tawang (the main railway station) is **Gereja Blenduk**, a fine example of 18th-century church architecture: a shallow Greek-cross floor plan, a high drum and a huge copper-clad dome, now a dingy ocher above the white-washed walls and the heavy columns of the porch. The church was consecrated in 1753, and is probably the oldest remaining Christian church in Java after the "Portuguese Church" built in Jakarta around 1696 (the Gereja Tugu near Jakarta's Tanjung Priok was probably built in the 1760s). Semarang's church is still in use, and visitors are welcome inside, the baroque organ is a mad swirl of cream and gold angels, though its pipes no longer sing: a modern organ was installed behind the facade some 70 years ago. The streets in the area are dotted with old balconied buildings of shabby charm.

There are also a number of old and not-so-old Chinese shop-houses, though unhappily, in many parts of the city, their sugar-icing frontages are being

Left, Gereja Blenduk. Right, a guardian at Sam Po Kong Temple.

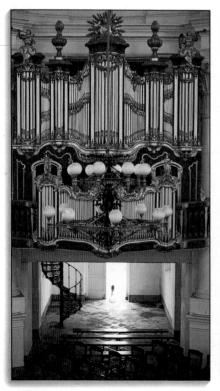

given a ravaging face-lift which destroys their character. In many cases this is unavoidable as the the shopfronts are lopped off entirely in order to widen narrow streets that have become major thoroughfares.

Heading farther north up the river towards the coast, through the old section of town and along Jalan Pekojan, you'll find Gang Lombok, a tiny canalside lane full of excellent Chinese eating-houses, the shops of scrap-iron merchants and a small square enclosed on two sides by the buildings and halls of the **Tay Kak Sie**, the city's largest Chinese *klenteng*, or temple. The main temple, built in 1772, has beautifully carved beams on its high ceilings, and the interior is full of carved and painted gods, ritual objects, oil lamps, brassware and the pervasive aroma of incense. Unlike many more recently built Chinese temples, this one is mercifully free from the garish gold paint usually applied with more vigour than artistry.

Although Semarang is not a *batik*-making centre, an excellent range of Pekalongan *batik*s and a smaller selection from Cirebon and Solo can be bought there. Two good shops are GKBI on Jalan Pemuda, and PPIP at B. I2 Jurnatan shopping centre on Jalan Haji Agus Salim.

Farther west, on the main road to Kendal, is the large red and yellow **Sam Po Kong** temple, also known as **Gedung Batu**. It traces its history back to the middle of the 15th century when a small cave (the central and most holy shrine in the present complex) was dedicated to the memory of Chinese Muslim Admiral Zhenghe, a high-ranking envoy from the imperial court of the Ming dynasty, who visited Java in 1406 and again in 1416. According to tradition, he landed at the site of the temple, which was in fact on the shore of a small cove 500 years ago.

The presence of this shrine confirms recent studies about the role of Chinese Muslims in the spreading of Islam through the North Coast. Its eclectic decoration, on the other hand, is proof of Javanese syncretism: at Sam Po Kong

Tay Kak Sie Temple.

chinese figures stand side by side with ancient Hindu temple guardians. To reach the temple, turn left (south) at Jalan Salaman immediately after crossing the new bridge on the main west road, and follow the tar-sealed side-road for almost 2 km.

A few kilometres farther along the west road is the well-kept cemetery honouring the many Dutch civilians who died in Japanese internment camps during the occupation.

On the lighter side, Semarang caters adequately for nightlife. There are a number of nightclubs and massage parlours. For Javanese theatre the best place is Ngesti Pandowo at Jalan Pemuda 116. *Wayang wong* is the main attraction, though *ketoprak* is performed once a week. At Sri Wanito, as the name *wanito (wanita)* suggests, all the roles are played by women. Leaving Semarang, and taking the road south towards Yogya, you'll pass through Candi Baru, the "new town" built on rising hills at the back of the old city. Many of the houses and gardens are beautiful, a pleas-

ant change from the shabbiness of much of the city's central area. The views, as the road climbs higher, include superb panoramas of the harbour and the coast. Near Gombel, the Nyonya Meneer *jamu* company has established a museum illustrating the history of the herbal concoctions available on every street corner in Java, and now in attractively-packaged single-dose foil packets in overseas supermarkets.

With Semarang as your base, 1-day return trips to Demak, Kudus and Jepara can be done comfortably. These towns can also be visited if you're travelling straight through to Surabaya, a route which runs through Demak, Rembang, Tuban, Babat and Gresik on a road that is generally wide, tar-sealed and often appallingly congested. The optional route from Rembang through Blora and Bojonegoro to Babat is shattering in more ways than one, and is not recommended; the stretch from Blora to Cepu on the border of East Java has some attractive, heavily timbered teak forests, but at both ends of both routes (and at the Gresik end in particular) the vistas are relentlessly boring: flat and mostly treeless rice plains, desolate salt pans, and scarred and quarried limestone ridges.

For more than 50 years **Demak** was the undisputed *nonpareil* amongst the coastal states, conquering Cirebon in 1475, and Palembang and Jambi shortly afterwards; it became a Muslim sultanate under Raden Patah in 1511, its forces had destroyed the feeble and shadowy successors of Majapahit by 1520, and in 1526 Falatehan (also known as Sunan Gunung Jati, and perhaps Demak's most illustrious son) established the sultanate of Banten before capturing Sunda Kelapa, the site of modern Jakarta, in 1527.

The end came in 1546 when Demak succumbed to its once quiescent vassal and rice port, Jepara. Its vast *alun-alun* is today dominated by the three-tiered Grand Mosque, reputedly founded jointly by the Wali Songo and now the holiest mosque in Java. Legend and history aside, the interior is cool, lofty and disappointingly bland.

The mosque of Demak.

In **Kudus**, 24 km to the east, the past is more tangible. The oldest part of the town, Kauman, lies a little west of the river on the road to Jepara and is the site of a mosque founded by Ja'far Shadiq (**Sunan Kudus**). The tall red-brick minaret, its third level marked by a horizontal line of Chinese export porcelain dishes and its roof capped by a more recent pillared pavilion and an anachronistic clock from Arabia, dates from the early 16th century and may once have been part of a Hindu-Javanese temple structure. The mosque is strange mixture of Mojopahit architecture and persian shapes. A very unpredictable combination which is neither beautiful nor captivating, but somehow sums up the history of the northern coast.

Behind the *menara* (minaret), through a maze of walls, tiny doorways and secluded corners, is the tomb of the *sunan*, surrounded by the many graves of his descendants. Even today there are townsfolk of humble means who proudly carry the title of *raden*, denoting their blood ties with the great *wali*. His mausoleum is hung with a fine curtain of lace which all but obscures the delicate lattice-work carving on honey-coloured stone walls; a small doorway, skilfully carved and chiselled, and hung about with gold embroidered cloth, leads through one wall to an inner chamber and the grave.

The name Kudus comes from the Arabic *al kuds* (holy), and the town is the only one in Indonesia with an Arabic name. This is the holiest mosque on Java, and seven pilgrimages to this mosque are equal to a trip to Mecca. A tradition decreeing that cows should never be slaughtered in the town may be legacy of a Hindu past.

The character of the narrow streets around the old mosque is unabashedly Muslim and even Middle Eastern in feeling. Certainly it is not the Java of bamboo-walled *desa* dwellings. Here the houses stand tight and tall, always hidden behind high stone walls. A prosperous town, many of these family compounds display and engaging mix of architectural styles, with ornate carved

teak traditional houses standing proudly beside art-deco main houses that could be a set for an RKO musical. Kudus is not the place to spend a long holiday, but a 2-hour strolls around the labyrithine lanes behind the mosque will provide a good insight into the history of the north coast, and reveal a Java completely different from the one we have come to understand in Yogya and Solo. The old houses of Kudus, now treasured by collectors for their precious carvings, are secluded from the world like those of an Arab town and although decidedly Javanese in style, they are monuments to the spirit of Islam.

Most of town's prosperity derives from the aromatic clove cigarette known as *kretek*, More than one hundred businesses, large and small, help account for roughly a quarter of Indonesia's annual production of *kretek* cigarettes. A small museum jointly established by the leading companies (the turn-off sign is on the road to Demak) illustrates the history of this typically Indonesian smoke.

The *kretek* industry explains two unusual things that you may notice in Kudus. Carts, wallowing like galleons in a gale, and laden fearsomely high with straw-coloured bundles, are carrying maize-sheaths. And buxom young women, streaming through a gateway as though hell-bent on a feminist demonstration, are nothing more alarming than *kretek*-wrapping factory girls making the most of a work break.

From Kudus, a reasonable side-road can take you 33 km to **Jepara**, long famous for the skill of its woodcarvers. Although many of Jepara's artisans have been drawn to the bigger cities, and bigger money, this small town is still an active carving centre. Faithful copies of antique chairs and tables are still dowelled, slotted, tongued and joined without a nail to be seen, and there is apparently a heavy demand for extremely detailed and finely worked decorative panels depicting scenes from Javanese mythology and legend.

Most of Jepara's portable products, especially boxes of various sizes, are available in curio-cum-souvenir stores

Left, a traditional house in Kudus. Right, itinerant *batik* seller.

in the larger towns and cities. Less well known are the handsome teak and ebony chess sets: the inlaid board doubles as a carrying case; and every pawn, every piece, is carved by hand and has a unique and delightful character. Prices keep rising, but even so the value of Jepara's carved wood is outstanding.

Two of the town's daughters have achieved enduring fame. The queen of Jepara, Ratu Kali Nyamat, widowed about the time Jepara overthrew the Demak sultanate, laid siege to Portugal's Malacca stronghold in 1551 and again in 1574 with doubtful support first from Johore and then from Aceh. Although unsuccessful in both campaigns, she succeeded in scaring the Portuguese witless.

Raden Ajeng Kartini belongs to modern Indonesia's pantheon of heroes, a place earned through her spirited espousal of emancipation and freedom. Her writings, published as *Letters of a Javanese Princess*, are famous throughout the country: "Conditions both in my own surroundings and in those of others around me broke my heart, and made me long with a nameless sorrow for the awakening of my country." Born in 1879 in Mayong, a small *desa* outside of Jepara, Kartini was the daughter of the regent of Jepara. She married the progressive regent of Rembang, and died at the age of 25 shortly after bearing a son.

Both Kartini and Ratu Kali Nyamat are buried in the grounds of the old mosque at Mantingan, about 19 km south of Rembang on the road to Blora. The original mosque was built at the instigation of Ratu Kali Nyamat, and some of its finely carved reliefs were preserved during reconstruction in 1927.

Around Jepara, and farther east towards **Rembang**, the roof-ridges of many houses are stunningly ornamented with black glazed finials, inlaid with what looks like mother-of-pearl, and sometimes shaped like a *fleur-de-lys*. The same delight in glitter and mirrorwork can be seen in the rigging of fishing boats drawn up on the beach at Rembang, where coloured fringes and tassels, and strangely curved rigging poles, evoke ancient sailing glory.

Distinctive fishing boats of the North Coast.

EAST JAVA

It is true that East Java suffers in some respects from comparisons with other parts of the island. Its many temples do not quite match the majesty and grandeur of Borobudur or Loro Jonggrang. Its kingdoms (Kediri, Singosari, Majapahit) are preserved in a few pieces of ancient bronze and terracotta but not as extensive living palaces like the 18th-century *kraton* of Mataram's descendants. The vestiges of East Java's great cultural wealth are also less well preserved than those of West and Central Java, and the mighty coastal cities, once amongst the finest ports of Asia, have little to show of their former glory.

But what East Java does have is raw, natural beauty of peerless variety. Exciting, bewildering, surprising. It is a mass of contrasts and extremes, with desolate salt marshes and perfect southern seacoasts; it is the grand gesture, given without compromise, with sweeps of thorn-tree veld plucked from Africa, steep jungle trails brilliant with butterflies, and sulky smouldering volcanoes. It is a place for the walker, the explorer – though it does have its quieter and more restful moments. It is more demanding, physically, than the other provinces, and that too is part of the appeal of East Java.

A frequent corollary to outstanding scenery is a lack of accessibility and creature comforts. Though the Regional Tourist Development Board, an active and energetic body, has done and is doing much to improve accommodation facilities, access roads and the like, what is worth seeing in East Java is often hard to get to. By building a bull-racing stadium at Bangkalan on the west coast of Madura and by encouraging *reog* and *kuda kepang* dance groups in Surabaya, the Tourist Development Board has brought these three attractions closer to the tourist. But even Mohammed had to go to the mountain, and if you want East Java to reveal its charms you'll have to do a lot of the footwork yourself.

East Java is not all high adventure and trail blazing exploration. Several of the sprawling plantations cater to visitors, offering a taste of life in the heyday of colonial splendour, and the hill towns, hot springs and resorts cater to the bone-weary traveller.

There are so many possible routes, day-trips, circuits and voyages of exploration through the hinterland of East Java that a categorical statement on where to go and what to see would be presumptuous. With that qualification in mind, and with up to 4 or 5 days to spare, you'll find an interesting choice of tour bases between 55 and 90 km south of Surabaya. Beyond this point, heading east or west, "mod cons" virtually disappear and road conditions vary from reasonable to appalling: 40 km on your map, anticipated as an hour's journey at most, may well turn into a 2-hour spine jolter.

Of all Java, this is the one place where if you don't already have your own car or jeep you should hang the expense and hire one.

Preceding pages, mist-covered mountains of East Java. **Left**, country stroll.

SURABAYA

Surabaya is one of the few places in Java which, as a mere name to the outsider, is likely to evoke Conradian visions: square-riggers in full sail and lusty, brawling seamen drawing knives over a bag of gold or a handful of black pearls; the smells of spices and sandalwood, the reek of caulking pitch and sea-drenched hemp hawsers and copra drying in the sun; dusky maidens and peg-legged, eye-patched skippers; and legendary Surabaya Sue (who really existed).

Today's reality is mundane: Java's and Indonesia's number two city with a port second only to Jakarta's Tanjung Priok in size and importance; capital of East Java, and a vital, progressive centre for trade and manufacturing. Almost nothing remains of the colourful past, though an early-morning stroll along the wharves at Kali Mas (Golden River) at the far north of the city, the world of black-sail Macassar schooners, will whisk you back to the closing decades of the 16th century when Surabaya (once known as Ampel or Ngampel) was master of Sedayu, Gresik, Jaratan, Pasuruan, Panarukan and Blambangan before bowing to the onslaught of Mataram.

It was impossible to forestall the inevitable, and in 1625 Surabaya fell to Mataram's superior numbers after a prolonged and gallant defence, echoed 320 years later in some of the most savage fighting ever seen on Java's soil.

The "Battle of Surabaya" began on 10 November 1945, less than 3 months after the Proclamation of Independence had been read in Jakarta:

We the people of Indonesia hereby declare Indonesia's independence. Matters concerning the transfer of power, and other matters will be executed in an orderly manner and in the shortest possible time. In the name of the Indonesian people: Sukarno/Hatta.

The transfer of power meant one thing to the Indonesian leaders and quite an-

Jalan Tunjungan, Surabaya's main street.

other thing to the British troops who landed in Surabaya in September with the ostensible purpose of disarming the Japanese occupation forces (which the Indonesians had already achieved) and repatriating them, releasing Allied prisoners-of-war, and assuming a caretaker role until the Dutch could reclaim their estate. The result was a confusing and frightening tragedy of errors which led to the murder of the British commander, Brigadier-General Mallaby, in October and to reprisal bombing raids and finally a full-scale British invasion.

The Indonesian forces, hastily assembled, hastily armed, hardly trained (if at all) rallied to the cry *merdeka atau mati*, freedom or death! The British police action became a war of attrition, punctuated by atrocities on both sides, until the invaders" tanks overwhelmed the defenders' rifles and the Surabaya "rebels" were driven from the city into the hills. The British phlegmatically acknowledged the tenacity of resistance; the outside world, hauling itself out of the wreckage of a disastrous war, was also impressed; and the Indonesians themselves were a little surprised and more than little proud: *merdeka* could be, and would be, fought for.

The Tenth of November is now celebrated nationally as Heroes' Day, and Surabaya is honoured as "The City of Heroes," with a tall commemorative monument standing aloof and proud in the centre of the main city square.

The city's ancient reputation as a major trading port is still upheld. It enjoyed preeminence during the Dutch regime, and only since independence has Tanjung Priok in Jakarta taken the lead. It is unfair to say that Surabaya is bereft of cultural compensations, but no doubt the last few hundred years of merchant mentality have given the arts little encouragement.

Surabaya's cultural diversions are mainly related to dance, and mostly to forms of dance which are deeply rooted in traditional folklore. The oldest of these is probably *reog Ponorogo*, named after the town lying to the south of Madiun where the dance was once most often performed, though its origins are obscure. There may be a grain of truth in the *reog* adherents' claim that the venerable Balinese *barong* dance was derived from *reog* following the dispersal of Java's Hindu powers in the 16th century (a suggestion hotly disputed by the Balinese), but this of course begs the question of its real origins. Both *reog* and *barong* perhaps owe something to the celebrated Chinese lion dance, but even this is conjecture.

The most striking aspect of *reog Ponorogo* is the huge and ponderously heavy head-dress worn by the main dancer: a tiger mask of ferocious mien surmounted by a magnificent fan of peacock tail-feathers. The mask weighs between 40 and 50 kg and is mainly supported by a mouth-strap clenched in the dancer's teeth (it is said that a *reog* dancer can be identified by an outstanding muscular neck). Other participants include a small group of *kuda kepang* (bamboo horse) dancers and sometimes a trance dancer who does the usual grass-and-glass eating act. *Kuda kepang* can also be seen as a separate dance.

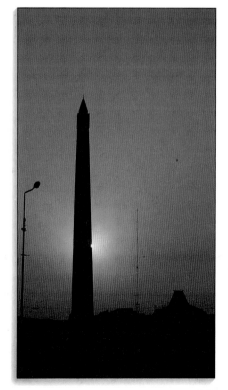

The Heroes' Monument dominates the main square.

Both dances were and still are traditional town and *desa* activities of considerable ritual significance, but waiting in a remote village for a performance *au naturel* is generally only a little less frustrating than waiting for Godot. However, a number of *reog* and *kuda kepang* dance groups are on permanent call in Surabaya, and special performances can be organised, but try to give a few days notice if possible. The East Javanese Regional Tourist Development Board (BAPPARDA Jawa Timur) at Jalan Yos Sudarso 3 (near the City Hall) will be happy to help you with the details, or ask a travel agent or hotel. One *reog* group, that of Pak Amari Hamzah, is at Jalan Pucang Anom 53.

Although the *Ramayana* and *Mahabharata* have become the common cultural property of the whole of Java, the eastern province may properly claim two of the most popular *Mahabharata* episodes as its own: Arjuna Wiwaha, in which Arjuna is tempted by seven delectable nymphs, was composed in the Old Javanese language during the reign of King Airlangga in the 11th century; and the tumultuous Bharatayuddha (when the Pandawa brothers and the Korawa family finally stop talking and start fighting) was the work of another Kediri poet some hundred years later.

Both of the great classics are regular fare at the *wayang wong* theatre in THR (People's Park), leavened with offerings of stories based on East Java's own historical and legendary sagas: Damar Wulan (a hero of Majapahit days), Menak Jinggo (the sworn adversary of Damar Wulan, villainous enough to warrant stories in his own right), Sawunggaling (a 19th-century freedom fighter). *Ketoprak* and *ludruk* are also performed.

Classical dance versions of these tales are on the programme of the season of East Javanese "ballet" staged at the open-air **Candra Wilwatikta** amphitheatre at Pandaan, 45 km south of Surabaya on the road to Malang.

Candra Wilwatikta, with the almost-perfect cone of Gunung Penanggungan in the background, was opened in Sep-

The ferry to Madura is heavily utilised.

244

tember 1971 as the venue for the First International Ramayana Festival in which a number of dance groups from Asian countries performed national versions of the ancient epic. The theatre has since then been the site of a regular ballet festival held on the full moon nights of the months June through November.

Comparisons between the Pandaan and Prambanan (Yogyakarta) ballet festivals are largely irrelevant. The latter is exclusively devoted to one version of the *Ramayana* story as it unfolds on the panels of the Prambanan temples, and is performed serially over four consecutive nights. The Pandaan season includes performances of a shorter, one-night version of the *Ramayana* based on a series of reliefs found on the main temple at Penataran (in East Java), but more than half of the annual programme consists of dances based on East Java's indigenous tales.

Theatre apart, Surabaya has little to hold the visitor. The chinese quarter is worth exploring: The **Hok An Kiong** temple, built in the 18th century, is on Jalan Slompretan. At **Klenteng Dukuh** Temple Fukien hand puppets perform everyday. Jalan Panggung presents a curious mixture of arab and chinese shops, and further north the arab quarter clusters around the **Mesjid Sunan Ampel**, the city's oldest Mosque. The zoo (Kebun Binatang) in the southeast corner of the city is well stocked and offers the famous "Komodo Dragon," the world's largest lizard which grows to more than 3 metres in length.

The shopping along Tunjungan is good (some electrical goods are cheaper here than in Singapore). There's water-skiing and boating at PORAS (Surabaya Watersport Club) near the harbour, or you can rent a prahu at Kenjeran. You might even make a call on Joko Dolog, the statue sculpted at the close of the 13th century to commemorate Prabu Kertonegoro, king of Singosari, and which now stands in front of Government House (Joko Dolog translates regally enough as "guardian of young teak," though many Surabayans irreverently but affectionately refer to the statue as "fat boy").

Scenic Surabaya Harbour.

SIDE-TRIPS FROM SURABAYA

There are also some interesting **Side-Trips** to be made: Gresik and Giri, a short distance to the north-west; the museums at Mojokerto and Trowulan on a good road to the west the island of Madura and its famous bull-races, and Tretes in the hills to the south.

Only 55 km south of Surabaya, **Tretes** is one of the prettiest and most pleasing of Java's mountain resorts. The air is fresh, the nights are cool, and the views of mountains and walks through the hillside tracks are incredibly beautiful. There's a range of *losmen*, guesthouses and hotels to suit every pocket, from the cheap to the expensive – which offer all meals, modern private bathrooms with hot water. It is the sort of place for horse-riding in the morning (perhaps to visit one of the three lovely waterfalls, all within easy riding distance), a nap after lunch, a huge pot of tea or coffee enveloped in a well-padded tea-cosy at four in the afternoon, and a general feeling of well-being after the heat of the plains.

If you enjoy the motley and the bizarre, drop in at **Iboe Djaja** about half-way between Tretes and Pandaan, a rather extraordinary house-and-garden crammed with treasures and kitsch: classical stone carvings, bottled snakes, embroidered Chinese wedding robes, fossils, grotesque statuary and precious Ming platters. Room after room of aesthetic disasters and collector's delights. The latter include some beautiful goose-and-gander couples in carved, poly-chromed wood, once common in the homes of wealthy East Javanese but now seldom seen outside of antique shops.

The geese of the carvings, the legend goes, were once human, once man and wife. The husband unbeknown to his spouse, was *au fait* with the language of animals. Somehow (this is not explained) she caught on to his mysterious power and demanded to know what two *cicak* (house lizards) were saying as they chattered in the rafters. The reluctant husband ignored her pleas, but when his good wife threatened to kill herself the husband capitulated. The *cicak*, he said, were exchanging words of love. At which point husband and wife became gander and goose. End of story.

Candi Jawi, 7 km downhill from Tretes on the Pandaan road, is worth a quick visit. It was built about 1300, after the death of Prabu Kertonegoro, and sometime later (possibly after the earthquake of 1331) a Buddhist *stupa* was added to the top level of what was basically a Sivaistic structure. The story behind the attractive reliefs on the temple base is still a riddle.

There are also a number of terraced temple sites to be found on the slopes of **Gunung Penanggungan** (in fact, something like 81 sanctuaries at heights of 750 to 1,500 metres dating variously from 977 to 1511). They are difficult to track down, though the hunt is an excellent excuse for horse-riding and hiking, and some of the horse guides know a few of the sites.

Left, gaily decorated Madurese bull before a race. **Right**, 14th-century Candi Jawi.

The most striking are the remains of **"Airlangga's Bathing Place"** at **Belahan**, approached from about 5 km north of Pandaan on the road to Surabaya. It was from here that the superb and controversial "portrait" statue of Airlangga as Visnu-on-Garuda (now a brilliant gem in the collection of the Mojokerto Museum) was taken in the early 19th century, but there are still two interesting "spout" figures identified as Sri and Laksmi, Visnu's wives. Another ancient pool is found at **Jalalatunda**, near the village of Trawas. This romantic site is the starting point to follow the ancient pilgrimage trail up to the summit: to visit the temples (the majority of which are located around the 1,000-metre line) you need a guide and camping gear, as the expedition will take a couple of days.

It is safe to assume that within East Java the decline of Hinduism and the rise of Islam were not marked by bloodshed. Certainly, there were wars, but these were political rather than religious, and no *jihad* (holy war) seems to have been waged in the early days of Islam's establishment in the northern coastal ports.

Tome Pires, a peripatetic Portugese who lived in Malacca between 1513 and 1517, described **Gresik** as "the jewel of Java in trading ports where the ships at anchor are safe from the winds, with their bowsprits touching the houses…it is called the rich people's port (where) many foreign merchants have settled." The great trading vessels have long since gone, but in the narrow streets of the old town, where houses with iron-barred windows stand tightly packed and women in white head shawls flit silently by on their way to the masjid, it is not difficult to recall Gresik's ancient role as a frontier post of Islam. Maulana Malik Ibrahim (or Magribi), one of the great Islamic *wali*, lies buried in Gresik, alongside his wife and children. His tomb, dated 1419, is generally regarded as the oldest Muslim gravestone in Java (a claim is made for one of the modest stones in the ancient cemetery at Troloyo which reputedly dates from 1376).

Jalalatunda Bathing Place.

At **Giri**, 2 km to the south of Gresik, is the tomb of *wali* Sunan Giri who, like most of his brethren, combined spiritual and temporal powers. He was the founder of a long-lived dynasty (referred to by visiting Europeans as "the Popes of Grise") which survived as a *desa perdikan* or holy tax-exempt village until overwhelmed by Mataram in 1680, long after the other coastal states had fallen.

The 18 km route to Gresik and Giri is bleak and desolate, a seemingly endless sweep of ugly but economically important grey-and-white salt pans. Their harvesting has a long history, and more than 300 years ago foreign traders noted that "on these sea roads come also the junks which come from the Molucca Islands and take in some salt until they have a full cargo…for there are many salts pans everywhere."

There is salt, too, on the neighbouring island of **Madura**.

A regular car and passenger ferry service operates from the L.C.M. dock (Jalan Kalimas Baru) at Tanjung Perak, Surabaya's harbour: 25 minutes will get you across the narrow strait to Kamal on Madura and this is still the only way to get to the island, as there are no airports on Madura.

The Madurese have long enjoyed a reputation for toughness, and the mere sight of black-moustachioed Madurese sailors was once enough to strike terror into the hearts of the mainlanders.

The independent spirit of its people (whose language is quite distinct from Javanese and Sundanese) meant that Madura never took kindly to invaders and overlords. It was a fractious ally and (later) a vassal of Majapahit. It was conquered by Sultan Agung's forces in 1624, when the puppet Raja of Sumpang was put on his throne, but under Prince Trunajaya during the 1670s it was a thorn in the side of both Mataram and the VOC (Dutch East India Company). A divided state after 1705 when the Dutch controlled the eastern half of the island, Madura became an ally and later a sworn enemy of Batavia under Cakraningrat in the 1740s, and was a supporter of Prince Diponegoro in his

Old Dutch houses of Madura.

heroic but futile "rebellion" of 1825. Together with Surabaya and Pasuruan it harboured an enduring hatred for Sultan Agung and all his successors, and was partly responsible for the eventual division of Mataram in 1755.

The harshness of Madura's rubbly, limestone terrain may account for the resilience of the Madurese.

Inland, ragged cores of rock thrust up between spindly clusters of trees in an inhospitable landscape. Crops struggle for a foothold on the poor, stony soil; straw and pandan leaf stacked in tree boles are like huge nests. Many houses, often little bigger than a double-bed, are still being built "colonial style" with high tipped roofs and thick white columns that should survive Armageddon. Women carry everything on their heads (mostly in green and white enamel washbasins or, in the north, on white enamel trays) unlike their sisters in Central Java who tote their baskets in a back-slung shawl or *selendang*; Madurese women walk with a comely grace, and many are extraordinarily beautiful.

Along the southern coast the fishing villages exude a solid but slightly jaded Mediterranean air. Fishing boats lie gunwale to gunwale in narrow estuaries, logs in a seemingly irreparable logjam. Salt-water marshes are reaped of their only possible harvest: money-earning salt, dried on vast pans of blinding whiteness, then packed into bright blue sacks. At Tanjung the *prahu* carry huge triangular sails, wide-striped in orange and dusty brown, brick red and yellow ochre. White outrigger dugout canoes sit on trestles above the sandflats like ready squadrons of giant seagulls.

At Camplong there's a swimming beach at the end of a long avenue of graceful casuarinas. Far across the smooth water cottonwool clouds surround the invisible mainland peaks of Arjuna, the Tengger group and the mass of Ijen.

While Pamekasen is the administrative center, the historical centre of Madura is Sumenep, where there are several interesting remains from the golden

Madurese sailing boats anchored in a creek.

age of coastal trade: the *kraton* of Panembahan Sumolo, the Jamik Mosque, and the Royal graveyard at Aste Timmggi.

Madurese architecture, and its highly prized furniture, shows a characteristic blend of Chinese and baroque elements, combined with a strong use of color that is decidedly local.

Madura is also the home of *kerapan sapi*.... Ten-thirty in the morning. A pair of big tan bulls, coats sleek and smooth, eye-whites flashing in spasms of fear and excitement. Nostrils snort and tug at nose-ropes and the dry ground soaks up a stream of creamy saliva. A shoulder heaves and a cloven hoof paws the white line. Ten strong men, sinews popping, thrust back against 600 kg of taut, anxious flesh. A burning sun glints on a sequined head-dress, lights up the pale green shafts of the trailing sled and the crimson satin of the rider's hunched, half-crucified figure, spreadeagled between the rippling tonne of stud stock. The red flag falls. Whips crack.

In roughly 10 seconds two pairs of bulls, their sleds and riders bucketing and swaying, cover 130 metres and drive a foaming wedge of muscled fury into the crowd bunched behind the finishing line. Somehow nobody is killed. Miraculously nobody is injured. This time.

It's a strange sport, this *kerapan sapi*. As the Madurese tell it, it began long ago when plough-team was pitted against plough-team over the length of a rice-field. Part work, part play. Today, stud-bull breeding is big business on an island where the land is too wretched and poor for any more than the scantiest agriculture, and the races, with progressively bigger and better prizes offered by local govemment, have become a real incentive for stock improvement. Only bulls of a certain standard (condition, weight, colour) can be entered: from August onwards heats are held at district and regency level until the cream of the crop fight it out for the crown, the cups and the money at the grand final in Pamekasan, the island's capital.

Nine in the morning. The bulls parade before the throng as courtiers before Louis XIV, a-jangle with colours and

Easy rider at the bull races.

finery, accompanied by fife and gong; hawkers set up their stands; the crowd surges in a mass of purple and yellow, pink and green, ochre and orange; sellers of *pandan* hats slice their wares into shapes-to-order (take a conical hat like an ancient Portuguese helmet and apply a razor-sharp knife: the tightly bound pandanus fronds spring into new, bizarre shapes).

Ten in the morning. The bulls, stripped of their parade regalia, wait calmly behind the scenes with their handlers and supporters. When their moment comes they'll tense like steel springs. Now, they placidly blink their big, bovine eyes and look pretty in their sparkling headbands. Soon, the tornado.

Bull-racing is very partisan. Though it lacks the rattle-and-scarf crew of English soccer and the baton-twirling beauties of college football, it's district against district, regency against regency (even *desa* against *desa*) as far as the adoring crowd is concerned. This home grown enthusiasm can obscure the fact that one race is pretty much like any other, a flat-out straight-down-the-track contest. But it's superbly colourful.

The final bull-race meeting held at Pamekasan is the biggest and most colourful event, but races can also be seen during August and September in Pamekasan and at nearby Sampang. An impressive new bull-racing stadium has recently been completed on the outskirts of Bangkalan, at the far western end of the island only 16 km from the ferry terminal at Kamal, and races will be held there on the first Sunday of every month.

The northern corner of the island is pretty with coconut groves, sandhills and real golden beaches. Pasongsongan and Pasean are photogenic fishing villages: colourful *prahu* (but plain sails); dried fish, husked corn, cucumbers and mauve and purple *kue* in the market. From Sotaba to Ketapang the desolate hinterland encroaches. Beyond Ketapang you can continue round the coast via Arosbaya on a dirt road, or cut through the centre to Sampang.

Impressions: goats, cactus (the ruin-

Vintage horse carts are still plying the routes of East Java.

ous "prickly pear"), Muslim graveyards perched on rocky outcrops, green plaited-bamboo *tempat kue* for carrying selamatan offerings, horsecarts with immense 2-metre wheels, a few thatched-roof houses, white face-powder turning women's faces mortuary grey, white cranes standing in rare fields of green *padi*.

At Arosbaya, 11 km short of Bangkalan on the northwest coast, ask the *bupati* for permission to visit the tombs at Air Mata (4 km inland). The main attraction is the large, ornately carved *gunungan* headstone on the grave of Kanjeng Ratu Ibu, consort of Cakraningrat I (1546–69), though the whole setting on a terraced hilltop, with beautiful views across tiny valleys and a feeling of cloistered peace, is worthwhile in itself.

One hour's drive to the west of Surabaya, **Trowulan**, the capital of Majapahit, ancient Java's greatest empire, is little more than the main road, a handful of houses, and the museum. Unless you're careful you can be through

it in a minute and not even know it.

Justly famous for its Majapahit terracotta statuary, the museum sits splendidly in a large garden crowded with frangipani trees and brick-bordered garden beds filled not with flowers but with thousands of archaeological rejects: lumps of ornamented terracotta, weather-ravaged stone carvings and countless shards of celadon-glaze and blue-and-white pottery.

Inside the museum, the collection consists mainly of articles made from fired clay. There are dozens of small portrait heads, many unmistakably Chinese in mien; a figure wears what looks like a European frockcoat; and one delightful fragment shows a dog biting the heel of a fleeing person. There is a big, roughly modelled, but expressive, headless torso of a heavily pregnant woman; there are dozens of miniature step-roofed *candi*s with intricate incised designs, which may have been builders' or architects' models; and there are water vessels in the form of cockerels, or shaped like a mythical half-fish, half-frog. There

Candi Bajang Ratu, once a bathing place, is one of the few remains of the Majapahit capital.

is also some good stone sculpture, a collection of bronze statuettes and domestic artifacts (a marvellous beaker with *wayang kulit* ornament), a mixed bag of silver coins and Chinese porcelain, and a few fascinating pieces of woodcarving.

Everything in the Trowulan museum has reputedly been found within a 10-km radius, an area which was probably the seat of Majapahit power. A detailed table-top map on the porch of the museum is a useful guide to nearby sites and remains, including Wringin Lawang, a gateway which may have led to the residence of Gajah Mada, the kingdom's famous prime minister.

Two of the more interesting remains are **Candi Tikus** and **Candi Bajang Ratu**. The pretty country lane that leads to them is lined with trees and white brick fences with temple-roof gateposts; behind the fences are small, neat, whitewashed and mostly windowless plaited-bamboo houses, their verandahs stone-paved, their verandah posts of unhewn wood, their doors often providing a colourful splash of yellow and green.

Neither Candi Tikus nor Candi Bajang Ratu is in fact a *candi* in the sense of being a temple. Tikus is an ancient bathing place, once resplendent with three water-filled pools which were fed through a series of stone *kala*-head spouts. Bajang Ratu, about 500 metres from Tikus, is a fine, tall red-brick gateway with striking terracotta *kala* heads.

Another cemetery of far greater historical importance is located at Troloyo, roughly 2 km south of Trowulan. Here, in a summery setting of coconut palms and banana trees where pigeons coo and grasshoppers clack in the dry grass, are the gravestones of some of the later members of the Majapahit dynasty. Recent research shows that the oldest headstone dates from 1376 (1298 according to the ancient Javanese saka calendar); it is thought to be Muslim and, if so, would deprive the tomb of Maulana Malik Ibrahim (1419 AD) in Gresik of its claim to be the oldest Muslim grave in Java.

Back on the main road, and heading east out of Trowulan, a further 10 km will bring you to **Mojokerto**. The town straddles yet another arm of the mighty Brantas River, and offers a number of pleasures: in the old quarter, west of the main street, are charming traffic-free alleys (or *gang*) lined with miniature canals; there are many imposing columned houses from "the Dutch time"; and on Jalan Jen. Achmed Yani there is an excellent museum of Majapahit stone carving and sculpture. The finest work, however, is probably a thousand years old: a magnificient "portrait statue" of King Airlangga as Visnu mounted on a huge and formidable *garuda*, once the centre-piece of a sculptural group which decorated the Belahan bathing place in the foothills above Pandaan.

There are other pleasures and treasures in the Mojokerto museum: a "figure-head" water-spout of a slender, nubile young lady of astonishing sexiness; a pair of princes casually holding hands; and a series of stylised landscape panels, from Trowulan, filled with rivers, fields, forests, rice-terraces and animals.

Left, a Majapahit miniature in Mojokerto museum. **Right**, modern-day "candi," features a universal symbol.

TEMPLES & THINGS

A quest for temples can be one of the great joys of East Java. Ranging south from Surabaya it is possible to see the best of them in one day by tracing a long and tiring circuit through Malang, Blitar, Kediri, Mojokerto and back to base, but a more leisurely journey is recommended.

Even if old stones leave you cold you'll be well on the trail to some of the most beautiful country in East Java as you follow remote *desa* tracks, tiny back lanes overhung with forests of bamboo, roads where there's never a bus to be seen.

Malang, 90 km south of Surabaya, is a perfect base for "temple tripping": a charming, clean, attractive town with a mild climate. You may however be tempted by the surprisingly named Hotel Niagara in **Lawang**, 18 km north of Malang on the main road.

In the years just before the Great War of 1914–18 a wealthy Chinese exporter of *kayu jati* (teak), Lim Siang Yew hired a Brazilian architect by the name of Senhor Pinitu. Together they conceived and built a stately five-storey house on the outskirts of Lawang, nestling in the gentle foothills at a cool 491 metres under the eastern shoulder of Gunung Arjuna. Into this mansion with its five-metre ceilings went a sizeable fortune in teak, red brick, brass handrails, wrought-iron balustrades and a cage-like electric elevator. Wall tiles, terrazzo floors and stained glass transom lights display the sinuous *art nouveau*.

In 1963 the Lim family sold their inheritance. It became the Hotel Niagara, furnished throughout with *meubel antik Jepara*; the elevator, grudgingly, still works but pauses between floors; there is a swimming pool; fresh white and yellow arum lilies, perfect partners to the stained glass, sit on the tables in the bar ("sorry mister, no whiskey, only Black & White"); incense is still burned before Buddha and his attendants who huddle inside glassed-in niches on the flat rooftop with its magnificent views

of Gunung Arjuna; and there is a story of three female ghosts who haunt one of the rooms.

It's not a Hilton. It's not a *losmen*. But it's the kind of place you could fall in love with. The only blemish is a new but mercifully small addition on the road frontage: modern, no doubt necessary, but fortunately begun well after Senhor Pinitu paid a brief return visit in 1971 at the age of 97.

Malang has often been described as the most attractive town in Java (a missionary, on learning recently that a confrere had been posted to Malang, was heard to remark with a touch of most unmissionary-like jealousy, "Ah, he is indeed one of God's chosen"). The town's fortunes date from the closing years of the 18th century when coffee was successfully established as a cash crop; today, tobacco and an important cigarette industry also add to its prosperity.

Its attractions are obvious. Unlike many Javanese towns which lie dead straight along a dreary, shuttered, down-

at-heel main street, Malang sweeps and winds over gentle ridges and gullies along the banks of the Brantas River, offering unexpected views and quiete backwaters that demand to be explored. It is kempt and clean, with a strong feeling of civic pride: neat houses and an attractive town centre, and even the canary-yellow *becak*, all have a fresh-scrubbed look about them. There is also one of the most modern and well-cared-for museums in Java, the **Musium Brawijaya** at the southern end of Jalan Besar Ijen. Named after the kings of the Majapahit dynasty, it houses momen-toes, weapons, colours, documents, pho-tographs, battle plans and other memo-rabilia associated with the VIII Brawijaya Division, the third of Java's KODAM or Military Area Commands.

A couple of blocks to the south of the main square is **Pasar Besar**, the huge new central market. It is full of exciting corners (including a clothing section where light filtering down through glass skylights evokes the feeling of a Middle Eastern bazaar). At the southern end,

amongst an enthralling jumble of sec-ond-hand goods (*barang bekas*) you can unearth old Dutch china, brass cur-tain rails, Chinese incense burners, finely etched *sirih* sets, *wayang klitik* puppets and dozens of other minor treasures. The fruit section (depending on the sea-son) is full of locally-grown apples and grapes, and masses of cheap avocados.

Still shopping, you might be tempted by the varied delights of a small *toko tembakau* or shop for smokers' requi-sites across the road and about 200 metres down from the YMCA Hotel in Jalan J.A. Suprapto (the main road north to Surabaya). Apart from an astonishing range of *kretek*, virginia cigarettes and vast bundles of tobacco for every con-ceivable purpose (shag, black, navy-cut, twist, wad, curly), there are the Pop Art phantasies of the *jamu* packets. *Jamu* is an all-purpose herbal preparation which apparently cures most ailments known to man. The individual ingredi-ents are available throughout Java, haggled over by housewives in every *pasar*, but it also comes as a powder in

Market day in Malang.

a flat little sachet somewhat smaller than a packet of instant chicken-noodle soup, and revels in brand names. The selection at Malang's little tobacco shop is breathtaking, every one of its different packs, perhaps a range of 50 in all, featuring a unique, multi-coloured 1950s comic label.

Malang's YMCA is anything but the hostel one might imagine. It is one of the most modern hotels in town, others being the Splendid Inn and Hotel Pelangi. An important side-note; YMCA is pronounced "Imka." A recent addition is the stylish Tugu Park Hotel, which in a short period of time has come to be regarded as one of the nicest hotels in Indonesia. For food, European style, the best spot is Toko Oen in Jalan Jen. Basuki Rachmat (opposite the big new Sarinah shopping complex). It's a charming anachronistic survivor from colonial times, and amongst other delicacies it serves good *wienerschnitzel*, *broodjes* and *uitsmijter* (Dutch variations on a sandwich), and home-made ice-creams.

Lawang is a cosy hill town.

Another good base for temple-tripping is **Selecta**, a popular town-sized hill resort set high on the southern side of Gunung Arjuna (5 km north of Batu, 20 km west of Malang). The climate is pleasantly cool, the apples excellent, and there are good swimming facilities. Above Selecta, through a world of wild orchids, huge trees and damp clouds, the tiny mountain village of Sumber Brantas sits astride the source of the huge Brantas River.

The course of the Brantas, as it flows southeast, south, west, north, northeast and finally east into the Madura Strait, is also the course to follow in pursuit of East Java's ancient kingdoms, for its fertile valleys and its great delta were well able to support the sizeable populations that must have built the many temples in the area, many of which are extant and worthwhile visiting.

To reach **Candi Singosari**, look for the Garuda Bioskop on the northern outskirts of the town of Singosari between Malang and Lawang; turn left (west) at the cinema and another 600

metres will bring you to the temple.

Candi Singosari was one of the last religious-cum-commemorative monuments erected by the blood-spattered Singosari dynasty, and was built about 1300 shortly after the violent death of its last king, Kertonegoro. The main structure of the temple was completed, but the sculptors and masons responsible for the decoration (working downwards from the roof, as was the custom) never finished their task, due perhaps to civil strife and the dissension over royal succession. The stark, bald strength of the undecorated bulging-eyed kala heads above the doorways of the gods' chambers is more powerful and threatening than the finely carved *kala* on many other temples. Of the statues which once inhabited the temple's chambers only one remains: Agastya, the "Divine Teacher" and mentor of Siva.

About 200 metres beyond the temple is a pretty sweep of close-cropped grass and huge shade trees, a rural village green, unremarkable were it not for two monstrous carved figures of *raksasa* or *dwarapala*, the club-clutching guardians stationed at the entrance to a town or temple. One seems to be resting languidly under a giant *waringin* tree, his hand raised in a half-threatening *noli-me-tangere* attitude. The other, a short distance away, lies buried to the navel in hard-packed soil, leaning slightly askew as though struggling to hoist himself from his ancient grave. Although only 3 metres high, the terrible twins with their fangs and clusters of skulls seem twice as large, especially when smothered under an ant-like swarm of village children. It has been suggested that they once guarded the main gateway of the Singosari kingdom, but there is a lack of decisive archaeological evidence.

Candi Jago (or Jajagu) offers a fair share of conundrums. It also has some marvellous reliefs in the two-dimensional *wayang kulit* style which is characteristic of much East Javanese temple carving, and includes some of the earliest known representations of the *panakawan* or servants (variously grotesque, obese, deformed, dwarflike)

Candi Singosari's celebrated guardian.

260

who, as Semar, Petruk, Gareng and Bagong, are still amongst the most popular of all Java's *wayang* characters.

From the village of Blimbing, now virtually a northern suburb of Malang, take the sign-posted road east to Tumpang. Just 100 metres short of the Tumpang market (dominated by huge trees and dozens of horse traps) a small road to the left leads straight to the temple. There, for a small tip, the caretaker will be happy to escort you on an anti-clockwise tour through the five fascinating levels of reliefs which decorate the retaining walls of the three terraces and the temple itself: these depict the immortal sagas of the Pandawas and Korawas, of Arjuna's meditation and temptations, of Krisna.

It's easy to spend hours there, unravelling the complexities of who is doing what to whom (and why), or delighting in the homely delineations of everyday life which crowd the panels. Between episodes the guide will regale you with the terrible tale (true enough) of an archaelogical official who stole

into the temple grounds in the dead of night and disappeared with seven of the finest free-standing statues of various Buddhist and Sivaistic deities. The culprit was apprehended but the statues have not yet been replaced.

Candi Jago was started in 1268 as a memorial to another Singosari king, Vishnuvardhana (the only one who died of natural causes). Changes and additions may have been made until as late as 1343, and further confusion is encountered in the form of Indian influences: Pala sculptural styles and the Nagari script.

A little over 5 km to the southeast of Tumpang is **Candi Kidal**, honouring yet another of Singosari's bloodily deposed monarchs, Anushapati, and completed around 1260. The route to Kidal is picture-postcard pretty, and the temple, in contrast to the history of the king it honours, sits like a gem amid banana trees and coconut palms: utterly serene, utterly perfect. It is not large, but for many people it summarises in miniature all that is best in Singosari temple art:

Left, Candi Jago's gate. **Right**, Candi Kidal, a jewel of East Javanese architecture.

the tall, slender profile and stepped roof with its ornate carving, the bold, outstanding kala heads above the niches; the bas-relief medallions and especially the portraits of Garuda on three sides of the base.

The 80 km south and then west from Malang to Blitar and **Candi Penataran** (11 km north of Blitar) will take a good 2 hours by car. Between Kepanjen and Wlingi the road twists and turns through teak plantations, passes the massive vertical slab of the Karangkates dam, and zooms through small towns and villages where the gateway of every house is identically moulded and painted in the form of a large "1945" and where the women's woven hats have a flattened top to make basket-carrying easier (the carry-all *selandang* of Central Java loses out in the east to the more stately, straight-backed goods-on-the-head technique). The turn-off to Penataran is clearly sign-posted at the eastern entrance to Blitar.

The Candi Penataran complex is, in Broadway's *patois*, a sleeper. It gathers momentum slowly, gradually dissolving the feeling of anticlimax which is a typical first reaction: it has no soaring Loro Jonggrang pinnacle, no stupendous mass like Borobudur, and its steel fence and iron-roofed entrance pavilion elicit about as much fervour as an amusement park on a wet day.

The gradually rising terraces cover long distances, flattening one's sense of perspective. Draw closer, and the individual delights and distractions begin to take shape. A broad, seemingly bare platform suddenly reveals its sculptured comic-strip saga, filled with wit and vitality as it unfolds the story of the fat and thin ascetics, Bubukshah and Gagang Aking. Farther on, the finely detailed carving on the roof of the perfect little Dated Temple reveals itself. On the next level the heavy, sinuous snakes of the Naga Temple envelop the squat, square structure with the palpability of living pythons. Another level, and the magnificent boldness and bravura of the main temple commands the vision. And then there are the enthral-

Candi Penataran, with the decorated platform in the foreground.

ling *Ramayana* reliefs.

Suddenly it all fits. The flat vista of the beginning becomes a wonderland of new details, new discoveries.

Penataran's stones were cut and carved and assembled over a period of some 250 years (between 1200 and 1450) though most of the important surviving buildings date from the great years of Majapahit during the 1300s: the Dated Temple of 1369 (now the emblem of the VIII Brawijaya Division), the main sanctuary with its guardians dated 1347, and the decorated platform of 1375. The somewhat random arrangement of the whole complex is similar to many Balinese temple sites today, and it is assumed that most of the structures were roofed with wood and thatch (perishable materials which have not of course survived) which would have made a great difference to the existing skyline; the actual body of the main temple, which originally topped the three terraces, has been reconstructed at ground level and now sits alongside its three-tiered base.

The superb reliefs on the base of the sanctuary tell only part of the *Ramayana* story, but happily a part which is filled with action and excitement: followed anticlockwise the panels (interspersed with medallions of birds and animals) unfold the drama of Hanuman's secret mission to Rawana's palace on the island of Langka (yesterday's Ceylon, today's Sri Lanka), his capture, his escape, and finally the ferocious battle in which the death of the giant Kumbhakama anticipates the eventual demise of Rawana on the sharp end of one of Rama's magic arrows. (This is the excerpt from the *Ramayana* danced with all its fury and derring-do at Pandaan's Candra Wilwatikta).

The bold, formalised *wayang* style of the *Ramayana* panels is quite .different from the more naturalistic style of the Krisna stories on the second terrace, where more realistic people topple headlong from war chariots and soldiers do battle with dagger-like weapons which are the first known visualisations of the famous *kris*.

A hundred metres or so to the rear of the temple there's a small bathing place which ought to be filled with naked nymphs. Steps lead down to cool, inviting water, and the walls of the pool are lushly carved with birds, beasts and flowers. It bears the date 1415, which probably makes it the oldest still-used bathtub in Java.

A short way outside of Blitar, on the right-hand side of the road leading to Penataran, is a small, well-tended cemetery for heroes and patriots (Taman Makam Pahlawan), one of many such cemeteries in Java. The small white headstones briefly record name, rank, number and unit, and only the dates link these quiet tombs with celebrated military actions writ large on Indonesia's battle colours.

But dominating these quietly-dignified final resting places is an enormous mausoleum of glass and marble. Although he specifically requested in his will to be buried in a simple grave with the inscription "Here lies the voice of the Indonesian people," Ir. Sukarno, the graduate in civil engineering who, as

One of the *Ramayana* reliefs at Penataran.

President of Indonesia, led his people from colonial oppression to proud nationhood lies for eternity in a monument as grandiose and tasteless as the "social realism" monstrosities he erected in Jakarta. A subject of almost religious adulation during his lifetime, Sukarno's grave is a major attraction for local tourists.

Musings on these and other ironies of life could well lead you to Tulungagung and the cave hermitage of **Selamangleng**. Hacked and hewn almost a thousand years ago out of solid rock, the square-cut cave looks over a small, lush valley dominated on the far side by an immense slab of eye-tooth rock (a landmark visible for miles, and the best guide to the cave site). If you turn your back on the view, you'll find the walls of the retreat decorated with a charming selection of episodes from the Arjuna Wiwaha: celestial nymphs, enticing and delectable creatures, are sent at Indra's behest to tempt the untemptable Arjuna who is wrapt in penance and ascetic devotionals on Mount Indrakila (a suitable subject for a hermit's home, though the unknown sculptor was lighthearted and human enough to depict one of the nymphs relieving herself in a handy stream).

Tulungagung is 33 km west of Blitar through a land of cane-fields and coconut plantations. From here you can dash north to Kediri, or continue westward towards Ponorogo on a bumpy, meandering route where back-lane exploring has some minor rewards: small, cool waterfalls in narrow, tight-ended valleys; a bamboo ferry being hauled across a river by rope and muscle-power, the shallow deck awash with muddy water which wets the feet but not the spirits of its passengers; and everywhere the local hat shaped like a lampshade or inverted flowerpot, and invariably painted dull green with odd traces of blue and yellow decoration.

In Ponorogo, if you check first with the *bupati* at the *kantor kabupaten* on the west side of town, you may be lucky enough to catch a performance of *reog Ponorogo* in its original environment.

Although Kediri has figured largely in Java's history and legend (in particular as the inevitable, implacable foe of nascent dynasties) the present town has nothing to offer and need only serve as a whistle-stop en route to **Pare** and the nearby temples of Tegowangi and Surowono (Pare's immortality has been assured by its pseudonymous role as "Mojokuto," the town so thoroughly analysed by Clifford Geertz in his classic study *The Religion of Java*).

The temples of **Candi Tegowangi** and **Candi Surowono** were both founded in the late 14th century by relatives of Hayam Wuruk, the last king of Majapahit before the beginning of its rapid decline and dissolution. Only their square base-platforms remain, but in both cases these are divertingly decorated with animated and amusing reliefs. Tegowangi is unfinished on one side, and on another a broad flat pilaster carries the beginnings of two sculpted heads (one male, one female) which seem totally unrelated to the rest of the structure; on some of the panels there are superb landscape views of temples in a heavy tropical setting.

Surowono has some appealing vignettes: a boar hunt, an assortment of gross *panakawan*, a lady by the name of Sri Tanjung astride a huge fish, and a motley assembly of fornicating animals.

If you've not already seen the Majapahit museums and remains at Trowulan and Mojokerto, a reasonably fast road will get you from Pare to Jombang and the main route to Surabaya. If you're heading back to Malang, there is a beautiful but at times very rough road running east from Pare. The 75-km route encompasses most of Java's landscapes: a varied kaleidoscope of ricefields, dense forest, mountain peaks, waterfalls, high passes, rocky riverbeds, uncertain bridges, even worse roads, and a selection of visual delights that will mean at least a couple of rolls of film. Monkeys, pine forest, apple orchards, huge watermelons, orchid farms, more of those "1945" gateways, a swimming pool and *losmen* tucked into an idyllic corner. If beautiful landscapes are your idea of an ideal journey, you will be well rewarded on this trip.

Fish from an ancient tale decorates Candi Surowono.

264

BYROADS TO BALI

Below Surabaya, along the southern shores of the Madura Strait, the wrist and bunched fist of East Java thrust out towards Bali. Of all the province's territory this is in turn the most desolate and forbidding, the most ravishingly beautiful, the most haunting, the most rewarding.

Here, in the 200 crow-flown kilometres between Malang and the warm waters of the Bali Strait, are more than a dozen of Java's mightiest peaks (six of them over 3,000 metres high) capped by the splendour of Gunung Semeru, the "cosmic mountain."

You can fly over them on the 30-minute flight from Surabaya's Juanda Airport to Bali. You can skirt them by train; the Mutiara Express makes two journeys daily from Surabaya to Banyuwangi and the Bali ferry. You can even avoid them by taking the northern road through Pasuruan and Pasir Putih, a rather bleak and dispiriting route which should only be taken if you're really in a hurry.

But this exciting hinterland should be explored (by car, on horseback, by foot, or by a combination of all three). The rewards are those of free, untrammelled natural beauty, not those of tangible human history: there are no visible remains of the many incursions and invasions that wracked ancient Blambangan, the old name that once embraced the land from Malang to the east coast, but which now defines only the remote peninsula probing thumb-like into the sea in the far southeast corner.

It was amongst the peaks and high valleys of Blambangan that Hindu Java fought a stubborn rearguard action against Muslim Mataram, and it must have seemed that all was lost in 1639 when Sultan Agung's troops swept through to the coast and even subjugated part of Bali which bounced back as though nothing had happened, pushed the invaders into the sea, and regained much of Blambangan as well. For the next hundred years the area was a fa-vourite haunt of rebellious vassals who constantly harassed and harried a waning Mataram: Prince Trunajaya of Madura in 1674 (who sacked the *kraton* and drove Hamangkurat I into exile), the Balinese ex-slave Surapati in 1705 (curiously allied with Hamangkurat III against the VOC), and a mass of predatory Balinese who once again overran Blambangan during the shaky reign of Pakubuwono I in the early years of the 18th century. As late as 1715 Surapati's sons were busy building themselves a little kingdom where Malang now stands, and it was not until well past 1750 that the Dutch finally cleared the area and enforced the peace in a drastically depopulated land.

Outside of the rich river valleys and large towns like Bondowoso, Jember, Probolinggo and Pasuruan, the population is still sparse (at least by Javanese standards), and even along the busy north coast road there's one long stretch with not a single building to be seen. Seeing the country, it's not difficult to understand why.

The North Coast is very sparing in its favours, and about as visually charming as an empty parking lot. Pasuruan offers a few gems of colonial architecture; a monstrous, turreted, gabled edifice (a perfect setting for an operetta *circa* 1910) now used by Palang Merah, the Red Cross; and an interesting *pasar* where you might find Madurese silver anklets. Probolinggo's contribution is the turn-off to Bromo. There are patches of mangroves and occasional outrigger *prahu*. Then suddenly, with a sigh of relief, you're in **Pasir Putih**.

The sand is more grey than white, but the string of clean, comfortable hotels squeezed along the beach-front between the five fingers of Gunung Ringgit and the sea are a mecca for Surabaya's weekend sun 'n' sand worshippers (the big city is only 175 km away). If you stay overnight, the following day should start with breakfast on your balcony. It will be the first, positive step to a memorable day.

Fish from the first-light haul, charcoal grilled; hot sweet tea with a hint of cardamom; the sun catching the loose sails of outriggers swinging gently on top of the tide, ornately carved and coloured helmsmen's backrests mounted slightly to port of the stern (the boats are for hire); farther out to sea large fishing *prahu*, five pairs of long oars driving them easily over the smooth water as the net drops away behind (images of an armed galley, bristling with hostile pirates bent on booty – you're glad of your swivel-mounted brass eight-pounder, packed with grapeshot and good dry powder); a swim, time out to float over the top of the luminous coral gardens, and a doze in the sun. Why move?

Then on through a flat parched land and vistas of sugar-cane. **Situbondo** with its neat little stone-fronted houses, four sturdy stone columns and a deep verandah black with shade, dolls' houses built to last forever. **Asembagus**, wooden-panelled porch balustrades neatly carved and fretted. A brief stretch of green, green *padi*, a last gasp of emerald before you're engulfed in a wilderness of stunted scrub and a colour spectrum that shifts from dun to drab olive to dun and back again. It's time to pull out your Stewart Granger safari hat with the zebra-hide band in readiness for the **Baluran National Park**.

Feet swish and crackle through the dry, flattened tussocks. A brace of quail, startled, sweep into the air from a grassy hollow almost under your step. A small herd of deer, barely visible through the shimmering heat haze, moves across a rise, the antlers of the big buck still visible after the fine heads and ear tips of his does have disappeared. Under a thorn tree, far out on the plain, a mob of wild water buffalo jostle sluggishly in the shade. Two hawks circle lazily, one beat of their wings catching an updraft as they call to each other in shrill two-note cries. Close to the shoreline, where mangroves embrace small yellow beaches, and hermit crabs and mudskippers go about their business in the sun-bleached tide-wrack, monkeys shift uneasily then settle back to their eating and chattering and nit-picking.

The dried-out water courses would not be out of place in Africa or the Australian bush; the gnarled savannah growth and sweeping stretches of straw-coloured grassland are a far cry from the *padi* of Central Java and the humid jungles of Papandayan; the mists of Tangkuban Prahu and Dieng Plateau belong to a different world.

The entrance to the game reserve is at Wonorejo village, 55 km east of Situbondo, and 37 km north of Banyuwangi. At Wonorejo, 2.2 km from the main road, contact the Game Reserve officials (*Pengawas Pelindungan Alam*) for permission to enter. They can provide transport in the park. About 12 km within the reserve, on Bekol Hill, there is a small guest house, a lookout tower, and a number of well-plied tracks that will enable you to see the wildlife but keep you clear of the fast, dangerous banteng or wild ox. August to November are best, for in these dry months, the animals must stay near the permanent water holes.

Baluran's physical aspect is exciting in itself: hot, thorny, and dry. Deer, buffalo and banteng are easily seen, especially at first light as they amble slowly from the wells near the watchtower and drift across the pampas seeking solitude and shade.

For birdwatchers it's another paradise: peacocks, tiny finches, golden-breasted honey-eaters, masses of wood pigeons, black and white fantails, parrots the colour of young rice shoots. It's the sort of place where binoculars and long lenses are essential, though it's possible (through stealth and a kind wind) to get within 100 metres of a herd of deer.

It's an absorbing diversion by day, but as the animals are best seen (or at least more easily seen) at dusk or at dawn it's a good idea to spend the night there if you don't mind roughing it.

Banyuwangi is less than an hour away to the south on a road dominated by coconut groves, coarse rocky outcrops and the looming 2,800 metres of Gunung Merapi, the extreme eastern shoulder of the Ijen plateau. The Bali ferry actually departs from Sukawidi, 7 km north of Banyuwangi. It leaves hourly (arrive an hour early if you're travelling by car).

In the hills above Banyuwangi, at Kaliklatak, a coffee plantation has been opened to visitors. The plantation has 14 spotless bungalow style rooms, each named after a different fruit. The plantation tour takes 4 hours.

The **Southern Route** from Surabaya to Banyuwangi, 375 km, is longer and slower than the northern option. Yet the beautiful country makes this an excellent route for those going on to Bali.

Below Malang the road traces a long arc southeast then east through Turen and Dampit, gathering up small ridges and then hills and then mini-mountains as it goes. The vegetation is as lushly tropical and varied as you could wish for. In between wondering whether or not the road will really succeed in tieing itself into a modern Gordian knot you can take in Kodachrome views at every bend and corner: coffee trees, dark ripple-edged leaves with a rich sheen; coconut palms against a vertical hillside splashed with impossible terraces of *padi*, magic staircases tumbling to the

Skittish deer freeze at the approach of visitors.

bottom of the valley; a sudden blaze of canna lilies, hibiscus with the spread of a dinner plate, and giant yellow daisies.

The ingredients of this landscape are familiar, but here, somehow, it's almost as though every corner, every gully, every hint of a hillock, has given of its best for the world's most spectacular Barnum and Bailey horticultural display. Or it may all be a tribute to **Gunung Semeru**, the abode of the gods, the source of life-giving streams, the magic mountain.

For a while it's a game of hide-and-seek. Around one bend, and there's the enormous slope of the western shoulder, striped with grey-black, purple-black seams like a half-opened umbrella. The next corner, a brief glimpse of the peak. Another bend, and where the peak should be there's a mass of cloud. Then suddenly (about 65 km from Malang), you're running along the top of a crescent-shaped ridge, the rim of a broken rice bowl, and there to the north, clear, cloudless, unobstructed and less than 15 km away, is the whole majestic heap.

Gunung Semeru is, at 3,676 metres, the highest mountain in Java. Although it tops its nearest rival, Gunung Slamet in Central Java, by a mere 250 metres it was obviously considerably higher in its more youthful days.

As the ancient legends spin the story, it appears that the gods were in need of a suitable abode in Java, and arrangements were made to transfer Mahameru from the Himalayas and deposit it in West Java. Unfortunately, the gods, with their usual touch of almost human fallibility, had underestimated the enormous weight of the mountain. Java was thrown off balance, and a hasty decision was made to shift the new arrival farther towards the east. Speed overrode caution, and on the way Mahameru was the victim of "damage in transit": large chunks broke off from the base, and when finally put down on its unsteady footing Mahameru teetered and slipped to one side and lost its top as well. The top is Penanggunan (the beautiful small cone near Tretes); the base fragments, running east to west, became Welirang,

Basic accommodation at Baluran.

272

Kawi, Kelud, Wilis and Lawu.

Despite these tribulations the old peak has aged well, and there's a certain jaunty air to the plumes of white smoke that spasmodically billow forth from the crater. On a calm day these puffs have all the awesome perfection of an atomic mushroom: dense white clouds rising with extraordinary languor then hanging suspended in space, seemingly motionless but imperceptibly spreading and softening and finally disappearing like a wraith.

Towards dusk the runnels and fissures and deep seams fill with blackness, hard and sharp against the pale eggshell blue sky. The immense sweep of the western slope moves from grey to mauve to purple, a line of gold shimmers briefly on a ridge cap, the black furrows blend with the coming night.

Out of the darkness come crimson fireflies dancing an Irish jig on a trampoline. You think about getting your eyes checked. Darkness again. A glob of red light appears in the distance and expands like a balloon of fiery bubble-gum. It pops. The mountainside, black against a black sky, explodes in a cascade of scarlet stars as the lava oozes over the crater rim and plunges down.

The less exciting remainder of the trip passes tobacco plantations near Jember, crops of cassava and coffee, teak forests, a lovely road to Kalibaru and rubber plantations.

The **Middle Way** is more a bundle of suggestions than a fixed itinerary. You can leave the soulless north road at Probolinggo and head south through teak forest to Klakah, a green-belt of corn and tobacco, and a flat but pleasant run along the dike-top of a huge irrigation canal to Jember. Staying on the Klakah road as far south as Lumajang you'll enjoy some superb views of Semeru (though not as exciting as the backdoor sunrises from Malang). Just beyond Besuki, on the way to Pasir Putih, there's a good road south which wriggles upwards through ragged, handsome country to the agriculturally rich Bondowoso plateau and then through to Jember.

Mahameru is the highest mountain in Java.

ON THE TRAIL

There are two side-trips off the Surabaya-Banyuwangi-Malang circuit which demand jolt-proof bones, a taste for the wilds and a modestly adventurous spirit. The first, **Ijen Plateau**, is highly recommended to mountain buffs and hikers; the second, Sukamade, is grist for coast-watchers. Both are spectacular, and about the only thing they have in common is coffee.

The Ijen Plateau can be reached through Bondowoso from either the northern or southern coast: the former is faster, the latter more attractive, and in both cases it's wise to make an overnight stop nearby in readiness for an early start and a full day (try Pasir Putih or Jember for reasonable accommodation; Bondowoso has clean *losmen*).

Sukamade is possible but gruelling as a 1-day venture, and really needs at least 2 days. Your arrival time is not important, so you could spend the previous night in Banyuwangi to the northeast, or in Lumajang (after Semeru) or Jember to the west.

Not so long ago (geologically speaking) Ijen Plateau was an active crater complex of gigantic proportions: 134 sq km of fire and fury, the easternmost chimney in Java's long chain of volcanoes. Today the bowl is home to 7,400 people who earn a living on the coffee estates that cover most of the valley floor. The ubiquitous acacia or cassia, coffee's parasol, is almost outnumbered by huge trees of Falstaffian girth which climb up and over the plateau's steep lip and drop away as deep, silent forests on the outer slopes of the ancient volcano: wild, rugged and utterly magnificent country which doesn't quite fit the usual image of Java. It's the Black Forest; it's where the spirit of Paul Bunyan walks abroad.

Ijen is dormant, not dead. In the far southwest corner of the plateau, Gunung Raung (3,332 metres) rumbles and frets; on the northeastern edge, 20 km away and less than 500 metres below the 2,800 metre peak of Gunung Merapi,

the **Kawah Ijen** crater lake broods with menace and malice afore-thought: to boil or not to boil?

From Sempol (a coffee estate village in the heart of Ijen) to Kawah Ijen and back is a solid walk of 4½ to 5 hours, plus another 20 minutes or so at each end for road transport from the village to the start of the trekking point. A guide is essential, and the estate *kepala* (headman) can arrange this for you.

With luck (which means an absence of fallen trees blocking the track) you'll be able to drive as far as a small bridge. Then it's feet, feet, feet. The trail twists and winds and climbs through groves of casuarinas, across rocky streams, through thigh-high sword-grass and masses of purple morning-glories. From a small grassy clearing you'll catch sight of a white building high on a hill, half an hour away up V-shaped pathways filled with slippery grit. The "house" an old *pondok*, is a 2,200-metre home for 30 or 40 men and boys who carry shoulder baskets of pure sulphur from a "quarry" on the lake's edge under the shadow of the sheer walls of the crater. The labour, and the living conditions, are pure Dickens.

Beyond the *pondok* the track forks: to the right the trail is well defined, stamped hard by the hundreds of bare feet padding up and down its twisting length from dawn till dark; to the left it becomes a seldom-used pathway of rough grass strewn with fallen pine branches.

The right-hand trail is the easier of the two, despite a few wooden ladders that have to be ascended with caution. The left route is better suited to a mountain goat, for after lurching around bluff after bluff of pines and bracken it suddenly reveals not just a shattered, jagged, hell-fire landscape but also the semblance of a pathway: the trail inches its way across gaping crevices and frightening glissades, traversing almost vertical sheets of loose rubble, bouncing over one-plank "bridges" no more than 20 centimetres wide. Underfoot, the ground has turned to ball-bearings.

Ten minutes. A lifetime. It all feels the same.

Then, at 2,400 metres, the south-

The inaccessible but attractive Sukamade coastline.

western rim of the crater. And the crater itself. A sheer-walled chasm of grey and mauve and red, scarred and harrowed, plunging into a lake of pale green milk; a line of yellowish sulphur scum above the waterline like the high-tide mark on a dirty bathtub; in a remote corner an evil mingling of smoke and steam, scalding out from beneath a precipitous overhang; and in the air the pungent stench of sulphur.

It is appalling, terrifying, stupendous. Weirdly beautiful.

If your nerves hold out you can totter 75 metres down the crumbling remains of a concrete-and-steel stairway to the lake's edge where a safety-valve dam has been built. Despite the hot fumes and smoke wafting across from the other side of the lake, the water is cool, and along the foreshore on the inner side of the dam's wall there are strange slabs of compressed sulphur mud and pockets of crystals embedded in rust-coloured rock.

Below the dam the land drops away in a tumultuous cascade of rock and rubble into the tops of a pine forest, the start of a yellow-coloured but otherwise clear stream which is crossed a couple of times, in its lower reaches, by the trail back to Sempol.

The right-hand route is less alarming, but presents its own set of difficulties at the far end in the form of noxious white fogs of sulphur dioxide which billow forth from gaping slits and holes. A deep breath, taken at the wrong time. will have you wishing for a gas mask.

Vapours or not, the trek is rewarding. for this is where the sulphur comes from, oozing out of the cracks and fissures at the lake's edge in turgid red streams which soon harden into solid yellow shapes of exquisite sunny brightness.

The heavier lumps, broken with a hammer are the daily bread of the *pondok* people. Although sulphur is extracted from the crater lake at Telaga Bodas near Garut (West Java) in far greater quantities, the mineral at Kawah Ijen is purer and is worth commercial exploitation despite the horrendous labour

Gunung Raung as seen from the nearby hamlet of Jampit.

involved: Java's "home-grown" sulphur is a natural source of sulphuric acid, in great demand in the oil-refining business and in the production of fertilisers.

The lighter pieces of sulphur sometimes come in the shape of beautiful drops, stalactites and other curious formations. If you have a shapely stick handy you can make "instant" coral branches in vivid yellow: dip your stick in a pool of molten sulphur (try not to asphyxiate yourself in the process), bring it out, let it cool, and there you have it. Don't wrap your treasure in any good sweater or natural-fibre material for protection on the long journey back, or a day or so later your equally precious clothing will look as though it's been invaded by an army of hungry moths.

The road to Sempol, and on to Kawah Ijen, leads off the main Bondowoso-Situbondo route, 2 km north of the little market town of Wonosari. The 48 km will take close to 2 hours over a surface which is, in parts, unbelievably punishing and strewn with great lumps of axle-cracking volcanic rock; it's almost as though some netherworld demon, with a grim sense of humour, had sprinkled the route with handfuls of granite tetrapods. Excluding bumps, the high forest country is quite beautiful.

Depending on what time you reach Sempol, the jaunt up to the crater and its lake can be done easily in a day's outing, though if you like early-morning starts limited accommodation is available in the village. The *pasanggrahan* or guesthouse can be used if prior arrangements have been made with the *Direksi Perkebunan* (Estate Management) in Jember, 41 km south of Wonosari. This is the only official accommodation, but for around Rp.500 per person it's possible to stay in the village at the *Asrama Polisi*, the police hostel a few hundred metres beyond the estate checkpoint. Very basic accommodation can also be found, within an hour's walk of the crater rim, on a small plateau which is the first staging post for the loads of sulphur on their way down from the *pondok*; the "sulphur road," plied by pack horses and really little better than a footpath heads down to the southeast over the outer rim of the Ijen caldera. If you enjoy toting a back-pack this is a tough but interesting exit route which takes around 6 hours before reaching the nearest roadhead near Licin, roughly 10 km to the west of Banyuwangi.

Bondowoso and Situbondo are both well known for bull-fighting (bull against bull, not bull against man), and it's worthwhile checking in either town in case your trip coincides with a fight. More peaceable, and fun, is an exploration of the colourful animal market in Wonosari, jam-packed with bulls, goats, sheep and every villager from miles around. The covered section of the pasar has an astonishing array of goods (it is, after all, the village "supermarket" and general store combined). If you enjoy squatting in the dust and haggling for a quarter of an hour or so you could wind up with a couple of colourful plaited rope *sapi* whips for a very reasonable price. If you still feel rugged enough, you might like to change from craters to crashing surf.

Coffee is big business at Sukamade.

The **Sukamade Baru** estate was founded in 1927. Today it covers (in round figures) 1,100 hectares of which 310 hectares are planted with coffee, 350 with rubber and 100 with coconut palms for copra; what remains is river beds, the estate compound, a village, a bunch of almost inaccessible jungle-clad hills, and a stretch of some of the most attractive coastline in Java.

To get there you turn south at Genteng on the main road between Jember and Banyuwangi, but you'll need some preparation for the next 67 km, for on most maps Sukamade doesn't exist.

Borrow, hire or otherwise commandeer transport with a high clearance and preferably four-wheel drive; pack a couple of changes of clothing, swimming gear, a "cold bag" and plenty of colour film; then head due south.

For the first 32 km to Pesanggaran you spin happily along a pretty canal-side road lined with banana trees, coconut palms, contented villagers bathing *au naturel* and other picture-postcard scenes. Pesanggaran itself boasts several of the finest old Fords in captivity: they started running in 1929 and still carry goods and people; the fact that they still work is not so remarkable: that they should stay alive on the roads they ply is astounding.

The next 35 km west to Sukamade takes a good 2 hours over potholes, narrow bridges, river fords, a minor hill through a rubber plantation, a major hill through towering natural jungle (broken occasionally by views of the jagged coastline) and finally a 50-metre ford across the Sukamade River just 5 km short of the estate compound. (About 24 km out of Pesanggaran the road nudges the back edge of a long, sweeping beach of fine grey lava sand; the surf runs heavy and uneven, but it's safe for swimming if you don't venture out too far, and deliciously refreshing. On a busy day you might see one or two fishermen, but most of the time it's deserted.)

At the estate you will be made welcome by members of the managerial staff of the company, who know at least a little English. Then at the estate's *pasanggrahan* (no official prices yet, though there will be a charge), the surprises start. You'll be shown to a clean, spacious room (albeit spartan) with sheets top and bottom. The bathrooms are big and hygienic, and when you have cleaned up you will be offered a *bir yang dingin sekali* (ice-cold beer). There are many things to do and see on the estate, which bustles with activity: 1,600 people live in the estate village, 750 of them active workers earning low wages plus rice and helping produce 235 tons of rubber and 325 tons of coffee beans annually.

The estate is in the heart of **Meru Belizi National Park**, officially declared in 1982 to protect the east remaining tigers in Jore. These are now extinct, but small jungle cots still abound. The *macan tutul*, or spotted panther, and a number of sleek, long-bodied wild cats which take scant notice of headlights as they saunter saucily across the rough tracks.

And there are turtles. Big, heavy ladies, tipping the scales at around 200 kg,

The inlet to Sukamade's "Blue Lagoon".

who emerge wet and glistening from the pounding surf and chug laboriously up the beach-head as they seek a "nesting" place beyond the high water mark. On the beach there is a conservation station, that make sure that the eggs are protected and properly hatched. This is one of the few remaining turtles beaches in Indonesia.

At night, after a gargantuan meal in the finest Javanese "home cooking" tradition it's a jeep-trip to turtle territory, patrolling the beach in search of the telltale "tank tracks" while you side-step skirmishing attacks from armies of crabs who roam the sand.

The next morning you can have your cold storage bag filled with beer or soft drinks from the refrigerator before heading off with one of the estate's jeeps, a driver and a "porter" or two for Green Bay to – a tiny landlocked cove backed by jungle where 200 metres of pale yellow sand sweep down into a surf which is an impossible, unbelievable green. En route over the mountain road you'll see families of the Black Monkey

The coast features a rich array of tropical vegetation.

with their strange "granny bonnet" fringes of grey hair, or groups of kingfishers in startling combinations of green turquoise and yellow, or grey and white lace-wing butterflies by the hundreds.

The 20-minute walk from the jeep track to the beach is a jungle jaunt through an array of vines, lianas, and the whole spectrum of tropical growth (Rafflesia, giant among flowers, grows in the area). The trail is narrow, steep and slippery, but your goal is breathtakingly beautiful, and the swimming superb though do be careful of the undertow at high tide.

Back at the ford you can explore the sandbanks for the pugmarks of panthers and the footprints of monkeys. The estate has on record a 20-centimetre tiger pad, which is big for a mere cat. Keep your eyes open too for giant hornbills which flap slowly past like incoming B-52s. One last point. The estate can accommodate 30 people, and its policy is to care for visitors as though they were personal friends.

BROMO: BETWEEN HEAVEN & HELL

The ride is slow and black through air heavy with the fragrance of pine and acacia blossom, accompanied by the soft clop of unshod hooves on unseen earth, the creak of saddle leather, and a feeling of riding into eternity. You pause, shivering, on the precipitous heights of the Munggal Pass as the landscape comes to life for another day: the bare sweep of the Sand Sea, a misty olive and grey surf of tussock, a ribbon of silver first-light catching the shifting sand of a dried-out watercourse; a sudden daub of luminous yellow ochre splashing the face of Batok, the black walls of the Tengger basin against a cold salmon sky, the ominous mass of **Gunung Bromo**.

Or you might be huddled in your blanket on Bromo's rim. On one side the hiss and rumble from the volcano's core. Later, when light spills into the crater and catches the smoke and steam with the brilliance of a magnesium flare, a shift of wind exposes a monstrous circular shaft, plummeting downwards, a gaping elevator-well, express to the netherworld…where, as the Tenggerese know, departed souls take the swift underground route to Mahameru, "the highest temple." On the other side, a faint jangle of harness as horses move restlessly down where the mud of ancient lava-flows has been racked by wind and rain into a labyrinth of Wild West gulches and cliffs.

It's a place where colours take on a new bloom, a new depth which suggests that three dimensions just aren't enough. If you time your trek to coincide with the last days of the full moon you'll even find the old goddess, in all her luminous glory, sliding down the flank of Batok: a moonscape within a moonscape.

The sunrise can be seen from two vantage points, both spectacular, both quite different: the first is the crater rim of Bromo itself (approached from

Like a scene from a science fiction film, Bromo is eerily beautiful.

Ngadisari to the northeast), the second is the 2,340-metre Munggal Pass (approached from **Tosari** to the west).

Both mean getting up in the very early hours of the morning. From Ngadisari to Bromo across the Sand Sea and back again takes roughly 4 hours by horse or on foot. It's possible to take a jeep as far as the edge of the Sand Sea, though the grades on both sides of the pass from Ngadisari are very steep.

There are now a couple of good modern hotels in the Ngadisari area, including the upmarket Grand Bromo, as well as a cheaper one at Sukapura, the village before Ngadisari. In Ngadisari itself there are a few *losmen*, and above the village near the edge of the Sand Sea, the Hotel Bromo Permai.

The trek from Tosari is more strenuous, taking about 8 hours for the round-trip. Even with a horse (and you will surely need a guide) you'll have to walk down the steep slope of the Munggal Pass on your way to the Sand Sea (and stagger up on your way back). There are

a couple of modest *losmen* in Tosari where you'll feel like a member of the family, drinking coffee and hearing tales of the strange man who reputedly runs around the mountains in little more than a loincloth, living on bread and finding ancient Hindu bronzes (everyone knows where he lives, but he's never at home when anyone calls).

The circular trip, which involves a lot more walking, is thoroughly worthwhile. You can start from Ngadisari, sit on Bromo's rim and watch the sun come up, then take the horses as far as the foot of the Munggal Pass and hike back through the hills and forest to Tosari. There, a cabbage truck can carry you back to "civilisation" (with a car and driver you can naturally forget about the cabbage truck). Of course, the circular trip in reverse can also be done, but this is less exciting.

There is another outstanding view of the crater complex, with Semeru glowering in the background, from Gunung Penanjaan (2,770 metres) on the north side of the Sand Sea. The best approach

Catching some rays at the crater complex.

is from Ngadisari.

The Tosari turn-off is just south of Pasuruan on the road to Malang. The Ngadisari turn-off is 1.5 km short of Probolinggo (34 km east of Pasuruan) on the main north coast road. Both are well sign-posted.

Gunung Bromo, relative to its surroundings, is not high. It looks, in naked daylight, like a wrinkled, crabby, preposterous toad, reluctantly squatting on the edge of its pond, reaching out for the lotus-bud of Batok. Veined and tired, it has often been the victim of mistaken identity, and it is not unusual for visitors to greet their first view of Batok with the cry "There's Bromo, folks!"

Statistically, too, it is unimpressive. A crater within a crater, standing a fraction more than 2,300 metres above sea-level at the highest point of its narrow rim. Next to it is Gunung Batok, an almost perfect cone with a cut-off top and neatly seamed slopes. Both lie on the southern shore of the Sand Sea, a flat expanse of iron-grey sand and patches of scrubby grass, almost 2,200 metres

high and enclosed by high-walled ridges which were once the rim of an ancient and enormous volcano (now dead) on the northern slope of the Tengger massif. To the south, hills stretch away to become the slopes of Gunung Mahameru, also part of the Tengger range (virtually another country, the highland home of 300,000 Tenggerese).

And yet, in that long hour before the sun comes up, when the chill morning light has killed the stars and your fingers are blue with cold, Bromo's naked, haunted, tortured landscape is enchanting; later, in full sunlight, it glowers with a forbidding power in which beauty and ugliness become inseparable.

The story of the creation of Bromo, Batok and the Sand Sea is similar to other mountain-origin tales in Java: a smitten lover, an unwilling princess, a task to be performed between sunset and sunrise, the crowing of rudely-awakened roosters signalling a false dawn, and the frustrated suitor slinking off into the darkness. The princess in Bromo's case decreed that a great in-

land sea should be dug around the volcano's mouth. The tool used was the hard half-shell of a coconut which, flung away at the dawning hour, became Gunung Batok. The broad trench became the Sand Sea.

There is also the legend of the onions. Kyai Dadaputih, ancestor of all the Tengger people, lived with his wife in abject poverty, barely eking a livelihood from the soil. The gods, from their seat on Gunung Mahameru, promised him an everlasting abundance of food, in the form of red and white onions, if he sacrificed his youngest child in the crater of Bromo. The new vegetables flourished, but Dadaputih and his spouse (sometimes identified as the princess of the Batok tale) were naturally reluctant to meet their side of the pledge; then the gods threatened total catastrophe, and their twenty-fifth child was duly flung into the chasm (one version of the story says that this son was plucked from the cauldron and taken to live with the gods).

This also explains, in non-agricultural terms, why there is no *padi* in Tengger, and why the hills around and above every Tenggerese village are a huge market garden: onions, cabbages, maize, carrots, leeks, potatoes, cauliflowers.

Terrace upon terrace, plot after plot, creep up steep slopes, encircling compact villages of brown-black tin roofs where permanently burning brick hearths warm the kitchens and dry the vegetables hanging from the rafters. Clumps of liquorice-smelling fennel spring up along the mountain pathways, wild edible berries hang in luscious clumps, racks of corn-cobs (bleached by the sun) hold their seed for the next planting.

There's a strong element of Shangri-la in Tengger, a tangible sense of bucolic bliss. It would be naive to suggest that everything is perfect, though many people, anthropologists amongst them, have commented on the apparent contentment of the Tenggerese. Their life is hard and frugal. Religion, a curious blend of animism and Hindu beliefs, is simple. A flat smooth rock and two large overhanging trees are a shrine, and ritual gifts of vegetables and chickens are offered annually to the gods of the crater at the midnight ceremony held on Bromo's rim on the 14th day of *kesada*, the last month of the Tenggerese year. A primitive gesture of appeasement, perhaps, but hillside cuttings reveal layer after layer of ancient volcanic ash sandwiched between even shallower layers of soil. Bromo is not always quiescent.

The trek to Bromo is an intensely personal experience. Sunrise over its savagely beautiful landscape is part of it. So too is the same blistered wilderness in the full light of day. It is the releasing, joyous solitude of the Sand Sea, the sunlight discovery of gardens and enchanting pathways you passed in darkness. It is saddling-up before dawn and wondering, on windswept ridges, if you'll ever feel warm again (gloves and a genuinely windproof jacket are recommended). It is an unheralded white plume from Semeru's distant crater, turning pink in the dawn light. Strange, enduring, exhilarating. Another aspect of what Java is all about.

Left, "moonscape within a moonscape". **Right**, high in the saddle on the Sand Sea.

TRAVEL TIPS

GETTING THERE

Despite small recent improvements, Indonesia is still a land of red tape and bureaucracy, and this inevitably affects travel arrangements as well: all traffic to and from Indonesia must come through a few selected ports of entry, disregarding their distance from your place of origin.

Air travel to Java must pass through the Sukarno Hatta airport of Jakarta (Cikareng, 20 km from the city) or through the Ngurah Rai airport in Bali. From there you must get a Garuda connecting flight to your destination. There are no direct flights from overseas to major business or tourist destinations such as Surabaya or Yogyakarta.

The Sukarno Hatta airport is modern and spacious, and relatively efficient. Custom and immigration formalities were speeded up in the "Visit Indonesia Year" (1991) and the horror stories of old travellers are now a thing of the past. Still, business-lounge services are minimal, exchange counters, information desks and other basic facilities have erratic business hours and phone calls are a major undertaking.

Transportation to downtown Jakarta is usually by taxi: the fare is about US$10, including the highway toll (US$3), and if traffic is normal it takes about 40 minutes to get to your hotel. Air-conditioned buses are available at cheaper rates but their service is erratic and a long wait may be involved.

Departure tax from Sukarno Hatta for international flights is 11,000 rupiah, 4,000 for domestic flights. All baggage is screened at the entrance, and further screening is done at the gate for hand luggage. It is safer not too carry film in the luggage; ask the officer on duty to inspect your film personally. They are usually friendly and cooperative.

BY SEA

Nowadays few travellers arrive, like Conrad, by ship, although PELNI, the state-owned shipping company, has now a modern fleet going to every corner of the archipelago and to Singapore.

From Singapore, there are frequent motor launches to Tanjung Pinang. They usually leave in the morning, and the trip takes about 6 hours. From there you can transfer to the KM TAMPOMAS

(Pelni line) and in two days you will be smelling, like Conrad, the odours of the Java sea. The unforgettable experience is completed with custom formalties at Tanjung Priok harbour and possibly a bus ride through Gadjah Mada Road to get into town.

Luxury cruises are another story, and they still exist; the *Pearl of Scandinavia*, run by Mansfield Travel in Singapore; (Tel: 7379688), offers a 14-day Indonesian cruise which begins and ends in Singapore; however, on this you get to see little of Java and a lot of the Java sea.

Real adventurers may like to join one of the 3,000 Bugis ships that sail across the archipelago. Trips can be arranged by direct negotiation with the shipmasters at Pasar Ikan.

PELNI Lines Head Office, Jl. Gadjah Mada N 14 Jakarta, Tel: 343307, 361635 or 344342, Fax: 3810341 or 345605.
Jakarta Sales Office, Jl. Pintu Air N. 1, Tel: 358398.
Singapore Sales Office, 50 Telok Blangah Road, 02-02, Citiport Centre, Singapore 0409, Tel: 2726811, 2715159 or 2718685.
Surabaya Sales Office, Jl. Pahlawan 20, Tel: 21041.

TRAVEL ESSENTIALS

All travellers to Indonesia must be in possession of a passport valid for at least 6 months after arrival and with proof (tickets) of onward passage.

Visas have been waived for nationals of 30 countries for a visit not exceeding two months. Those countries are: Australia, Austria, Belgium, Brunei, Canada, Denmark, Finland, France, Greece, Iceland, Ireland, Italy, Japan, Liechtenstein, Luxembourg, Malaysia, Malta, The Netherlands, New Zealand, Norway, Philippines, Singapore, South Korea, Spain, Sweden, Switzerland, Thailand, United Kingdom, United States of America and Germany.

Entry and exit must be through the airports or seaports of Jakarta, Bali, Medan, Manado, Biak, Pontianak Ambon, Batam, Surabaya; the Pekanbaru and Balikpapan airports; and the seaports at Semarang and Riau. For other ports of arrival and departure, visas are required.

Visas are free also for registered delegates attending a conference which has received official approval.

Taiwan passport holders are also given visa free entry but only at the airports in Jakarta, Medan and Bali.

For citizens of countries other than the 30 listed above, tourist visas can be obtained from any Indonesian Embassy or consulate. Two photographs are required and a small fee is charged.

Visa-free entry is not extendable; if you plan to stay in Indonesia for more than two months you must obtain a visa: "Visitors visa" are normally given for a 4-5 weeks initial stay, but they can be extended up to 5 times for one or more month's duration each time, for a total of 6 months.

"Business visa" allows a stay up to 30 days, and can be extended to three months. It is then more convenient to enter with a regular visa. Writers, journalists and photographers require a special permission; it is a long procedure and the visa may be refused. Unless you need to be accredited officially, it is advisable to enter as tourists, and do not state your profession.

"Surat Jalan": A *surat jalan* is a letter from the police permitting the bearer to go to certain places. It is advisable to carry one when travelling in some of the outer islands, but in Java only in such out-of-the-way places as the Ijen plateau. If in doubt check with a good travel agent. In Jakarta a *surat jalan* may be obtained in an hour or two at Police Headquarters (Markas Besar Kepolisian Republik Indonesia) in Jalan Trunojoyo (Kebayoran Baru).

MONEY MATTERS

Changing Money: Foreign currency, in banknotes and traveller's checks, is best exchanged at major banks or leading hotels (though hotel rates are slightly less favourable than bank rates). There are also limited numbers of registered money changers, but avoid unauthorised changers who operate illegally. Banks in many smaller towns are not necessarily conversant with all foreign banknotes, so it is advisable to change most currencies in the cities. Your *rupiah* may be freely converted to foreign currencies when you are leaving the country.

Traveller's cheques: Traveller's cheques are a mixed blessing. Major hotels, banks and some shops will accept them, but even in the cities it can take a long time to collect your money (in small towns, it is impossible). The US dollar is recommended for traveller's cheques. Credit cards are gaining increasing acceptance. All hotels except the cheapest *losmen*, most tourist shops and many restaurants accept VISA and MasterCard, though a few will tack on a three percent surcharge. Most smaller shops balk at American Express because of that company's high discount rate.

Foreign Banks in Jakarta

Algemene Bank Netherland NV, 23-24, Jl. Ir. H. Juanda, Jakarta, Tel: 362309.

American Express Bank Ltd., Arthaloka Building 2, Jl. Jend. Sudirman, Jakarta, Tel: 5702389.

Bank of America/NT & SA, 17, Jl. Merdeka Selatan, Jakarta, Tel: 348031, 347031.

Bank of Tokyo Ltd., Jl. Jend Sudirman Kav-10-11, Jakarta, Tel: 5780709.

Bangkok Bank Ltd., 3, Jl. M.H. Thamrin, Jakarta, Tel: 366008.

City Bank NA, Gedung Landmark, Jl. Jend. Sudirman, Jakarta, Tel: 5782007.

Deutsche Bank (ASIA), Gedung Eurasbank, 80, Jl. Imam Bonjol, Jakarta, Tel: 331092.

Standard Chartered Bank, Wisma Kosgoro, 53, Jl. M.H. Thamrin, Jakarta, Tel: 325008.

The Chase Manhattan Bank NA, Chase Plaza Building 5th floor, Jl. Jend. Sudirman Kav-21, Jakarta, Tel: 5782213.

The Hongkong & Shanghai BC, Wisma Metropolitan II, Jl. Jend. Sudirman Kav-51, Jakarta, Tel: 5780054/6, 5780075/85.

HEALTH

Yellow fever vaccination is required if you arrive within 6 days of leaving or passing through an infected area. It is also advisable to be vaccinated against cholera, typhoid and paratyphoid.

A traveller runs mimimal risk of contracting a major disease on Java, but diarrhoea will almost certainly be a problem unless you are coming from a nearby Asian country. This type of stomach upset, a reaction to new food and unfamiliar, though not necessarily malignant, bacteria, is best cured by a diet of hot tea and a little patience. Otherwise, problems can be prevented by a daily dose of Doxycycline, an antibiotic used to prevent "traveller diarrhoea". Obtain this from your doctor at home. If diarrhoea persists for more than a few days, and is accompanied by serious cramps, see a physician.

All water, including well water, municipal water and water used for making ice, MUST be made safe before consumption. Bringing water to a rolling boil for 10 minutes is an effective method. Iodine (Globoline) and chlorine (Halazone) may also be used to make water potable.

All fruit should be carefully peeled before eaten and no raw vegetables should be eaten except in obviously clean and well-kept restaurants.

Last but not least, protect yourself against the sun. Tanning oils and creams are expensive in Indonesia, so bring your own.

Good doctors and hospitals are easily available in Jakarta and other major towns, but medical services may be hard to obtain in rural and provincial areas.

You are advised to carry with you any prescription medicine that you may have to take regularly, and to refer to the hotel desk for the address of the best doctor in town.

In Jakarta, first class hotels have resident doctors, and a number of western style clinics offer excellent services.

British Medical Scheme, Setiabudi Bldg., Jl. Rasuna Said, **SOS**, Jl. Prapanca.
Pertamina Hospitals, Jl. Kyai Maja, Kebayoran Baru, and Pondok Indah.

In Yogyakarta:
Panti Rapih Indonesia (S1, Cikditiro 30)

WHAT TO WEAR

Java is a tropical country with a very warm climate: bring light, informal clothes, but keep in mind that excessively scant shorts and singlets make you conspicuous and may reduce your chances of being accepted.

A *batik* shirt with long sleeves is considered "formal dress" in Indonesia. To participate in palace ceremonies and official gatherings, you may be asked to wear a full Javanese costume, which means a *batik* skirt and assorted accessories. Unless you can manage to do this with style, which is difficult, you will be a figure of fun. Refuse to comply with requests that diminish your dignity, and remember that western good manners are nothing to be ashamed of, even when they do not match those of the locals.

If you are going to the mountains or the woods, you may come across chilly nights at any time. Bring sweaters and, if you have space, a sleeping bag. Carrying your own bedding is a simple way to sleep comfortably in many seedy *losmen*s that cannot be avoided.

GETTING ACQUAINTED

CLIMATE

The best time to visit Java is probably during the months of July, August, September which are the driest. There are no definite seasons in Indonesia except for a loose distinction between dry and wet months. Humidity is very high throughout the year (75% average), and no month is absolutely dry.

The wet season spans from November to April, but West Java is considerably wetter than East Java, where serious drought is not uncommon. The peak of the rainy season is usually December, January and February (300 mm of rain in Jakarta). Violent thunderstorms occur, but there are no true hurricanes. Rain usually falls heavily for a few hours, but seldom for a whole day.

Travelling during the rainy season may be hazardous as roads are very slippery, and mountain or secondary roads are treacherous. During downpours visibility is almost zero, and accidents are frequent.

Although the temperature varies only slightly during the year (average min. 22°C, average max. 29°C), it decreases sensibly with the altitude; evenings in the mountains are definitely chilly. The North Coast is usually hotter than the Southern part of the island, which enjoys a constant breeze from the sea.

TIME ZONES

The Indonesian Archipelago is spread over three time zones. Western Indonesia standard time is GMT plus 7 hours. Somehow solar time and official time do not always coincide, and days seem to be exceedingly short. Wake up early if you want to get things done.

BUSINESS HOURS

Business offices are usually open from 8 a.m. to 4 p.m. or 9 a.m. to 5 p.m., with a long break for lunch. Some offices work half day on Saturday.

Government office hours are from 8 a.m. to 3 p.m. from Monday through Thursday, from 8 a.m. to 11 a.m. on Friday, and from 8 a.m. to 2 p.m. on Saturday.

Banks are open from 8 a.m. to 3 p.m. from Monday through Friday, and 8 a.m. to 1 p.m. on Saturday.

Business hours for shops vary from town to town, and are quite erratic. It's not unusual to find anything you need late at night, while afternoons and early morning are often quite dead. A long siesta from 1 p.m. to 5 p.m. is not uncommon.

Culture Plus

COURTESIES

The people of Java combine natural friendliness with an exceptional degree of courtesy. Although different ethnic groups within Java have their own customs, the basic aim is to make life harmonious and pleasant for everybody. Naturally, foreigners are not expected to be aware of the many subtleties of etiquette, but a general knowledge of local manners will help make your stay more comfortable.

Generally, Indonesians dislike being conspicuous and are basically conformist at heart. To be different is embarrasing. It is essential to avoid shaming people (making them *malu*), particularly in front of others. No matter how hot or tired or frustrated you get, try not to shout or show anger.

Since the Javanese dislike saying unpleasant things to another person, they avoid doing so directly and will often say what they think the listener wants to hear; an outright "no" is seldom heard (be prepared for "perhaps" or "maybe next week").

More often than not, this attitude results in some confusion, as many things are said just for the sake of politeness. An invitation to join a table, for example, or to visit a home for dinner may have been proferred without actually expecting you to show up. In such cases in better to double-check before making a visit.

Similarly, appointments may be made with the sole intent to avoid displeasure, and the person will never show up, or if he does it may be 3 hours late. The Javanese call their notion of time *"Jam Karet,"* literally "rubber time."

There are a number of odd taboos that puzzle the foreigner: One of these involves the use of a red pen or pencil, which implies that the writer is angry with recipient of the note. Avoid doing this at all cost.

The majority of people in Java are Muslim (at least nominally), and certain Islamic customs are widely observed. The major ones relate to the left hand, which is used for private bodily cleansing and is therefore unclean. Giving or receiving anything with the left hand is strictly avoided (you may notice Javanese clasping their right forearm with their left hand as they give you food or money). When you eat without a spoon (for example, when tackling fried chicken) use only the right hand.

Thére are other courtesies regarding eating and drinking. When given food or drink, never start until actually asked to do so. Most people like their tea or coffee much cooler than Westerners, so you may have to watch your drink get progressively cooler until your host says *"silakan minum"* (please drink). Don't empty your glass completely unless you want a refill; leave a small amount in the bottom. When eating, help yourself to only a small portion of food initially, and take more when invited.

Once you have entered somebody's house, you should not leave until they have served some sort of refreshment, however simple this may be; otherwise you will shame your host. It may take hours to boil water over charcoal, and the reason for your visit may be a simple enquiry. If you are in a rush, avoid going to people's homes, because the exercise may occupy the better part of your day.

You may want to compensate people who have been helpful to you with an amount of money. This should always be placed in an envelope and left under a fruit basket, a teapot, or one those plastic centerpieces that figure prominently in Javanese homes. If you are giving a tip, pass it over with your hand closed. (and do not forget to use the right one!)

Negotiations of any kind are better done through an intermediary, whether you want to buy an object, rent a room or a car, or simply invite a girl to the disco. This way you give the other person a chance to refuse without being impolite, and you stand a better chance of discovering what he really wants.

Although it is sometimes hard to remember, pointing with your finger (especially at people) is considered ill-mannered, so use your thumb with your fingers tucked lightly underneath. If you're beckoning someone, don't rake the air with a crooked finger – it's more acceptable to use a downward wave of the hand. Putting your hand or hands on your hips is interpreted as showing defiance or arrogance, and this social gaffe is compounded if you stand with your legs akimbo, gun-slinger style.

When sitting, legs and feet should be tucked away. Shoes are often removed when entering a house, but this rule is not strict: observe what the people in the house do and do the same.

Beggars and parking attendants will spring up from nowhere, even in the middle of a forest or a deserted beach. They do not expect that you know the complex rules of Javanese politeness, but they will never leave unless you give them some money, however little.

Except in proper shops, you will rarely get change for the money you hand over. Be prepared to round off the figure to the next 500 rupiah, or have ready plenty of small coins.

When visiting a monument, it is customary to place a small donation in the guest book. Caretakers are usually not paid, or are underpaid, and tipping may be their only income.

Unlike in many other Muslim countries, foreigners are usually welcome to visit mosques and other places of worship, with a few exceptions like the royal tombs of Imogiri. Remove your shoes and keep some cash ready for a donation.

To sum up, the three rules of thumb in Java are: be as inconspicuous as you can, take nearly every "yes" for a "no", and keep plenty of coins in your pocket.

COMMUNICATIONS

TELEPHONE & POSTAL SERVICES

Phone calls remain one of the main causes of complaint for residents and foreigners throughout Java, including the capital. In Jakarta, local calls are difficult to make, and if you are calling a busy office (such as that of your airline to reconfirm your ticket), you may waste a full morning trying to get through. Inter-city calls are also very difficult.

Hotels throughout the archipelago are known to inflate the cost of inter-city and international phone calls, and to cheat about the length of your calls. The problem is compounded by the fact that lines are often bad, and you get cut off easily, so you are charged several times for the same call. Keep track of the length of the conversation, and fight your case at the cashier's counter.

Normally, it is quicker to walk to the post office than to wait for the hotel operator to place the call for you unless the hotel has IDD service, which is expensive, surcharged and subject to cheating.

A recent improvement is the installation of cardphones, which seem to work much better than regular phones. Unfortunately, their number is still limited. Fax machines are becoming popular, but obviously suffer from the same problems. The express mail seems to deliver correspondence and small parcels quite rapidly, but regular mail is unreliable.

In any case, when travelling through Java, be prepared to be cut out from your family, your office and the rest of the world even if you can afford five-star hotels.

Courier services are the most reliable system for important mail, but they are more expensive than in the Bangkok-Hong Kong-Singapore business triangle. Even reputable couriers will try to surcharge small pieces of correspondence on the excuse that they contain dutiable items. All in all, if you have

a trustworthy homing pigeon, take it to Java with you.

EMERGENCIES

SECURITY

Chances that you will be assaulted or robbed in Java are far less than in Rome or New York. Pickpockets, however, are very active on buses and trains and if you are staying in cheap *losmens* you had better carry your valuable with you all the time. Passports are still a very desirable item and should not be left unattended.

GETTING AROUND

DOMESTIC TRAVEL

By far the quickest and easiest way to get around the island is to fly. You can go from Jakarta to Yogyakarta, for example, in only half an hour as opposed to the 10 or even 12 hours if you take the bus or train. Air tickets are invariably two or three times the price of a first-class train ticket and as much as 10 times more than the bus.

Travel between major cities in Java is comfortably accomplished by airplane. The national carrier is Garuda Indonesia, which has a subsidiary called Merpati. Domestic routes are progressively being turned over to Merpati, but at present the process is not complete and many major internal flights are still operated by Garuda. The standard of service, however, is not different.

The problem with both is that it is practically impossible to get a confirmed booking out of a different city than the one you are in; the same applies to international flights. The problem is compounded by the difficulty in making internal calls; the only solution is to make a program before you start your journey, reconfirm all flights as soon as you can, and stick to your original plan.

Should you succeed in making a booking by phone, when you arrive at the airport you may discover that you have no seat. In any case, try to obtain written proof of your reconfirmation, the name of the employee who made it, and the computer code. If you find yourself without a seat at the airport, try your luck with a little tip, handled discreetly, Javanese style.

GARUDA DOMESTIC OFFICES

Head Office: 13 Jl. Merdeka Selatan, Jakarta, Tel: 3801901, 3806276 or 3806558;
Jakarta: Wisma Dharmala Sakti (sales), Jl. Jend. Sudirman 31, Tel: 588797, 588519 or 5701292;
Hotel Indonesia: Jl. M.H. Thamrin, Tel: 3100568-70;
Borobudur Inter-Cont'l Hotel: Jl. Lapangan Banteng Selatan, Tel: 360048 or 359901;
BDN Building: Jl. M.H. Thamrin 5, Tel: 334425, 334429, 334434 or 334430.
Semarang: Jl. Gajah Mada 11, Tel: 20178, 20910 or 23317.
Solo: Kusuma Sahid Prince Hotel, Jl. Suryopranoto 22, Tel: 6846, 4238 or 2105.
Surabaya: Jl. Jend Sudirman 70, Tel: 42383 or 470621.
Yogyakarta: Jl. Mataram 60X, Tel: (0274) 62664
Bandung: Jl. Asia Afrika 73, Tel: 56986, 51496, 50444 or 439774.

MERPATI DOMESTIC OFFICES

Head Office: Jl. Angkasa 2 Jakarta, Indonesia, Tel: 413608, 417404, Telex: 49154 Merpati IA.
Bandung: Jl. Veteran No. 46, Tel: 57474, 437893 or 439742.
Semarang: Jl. Gajah Mada 58D, Tel: 23027 or 23028.
Surabaya: Jl. Urip Sumoharjo No. 68, Tel: 40773, 40648 or 45870, Telex: 34362 MNA SUB IA.
Yogyakarta: Jl. Sudirman 9-11, Tel: 4272.

BOURAQ OFFICES

Head Office: 1-3, Jl. Angkasa Jakarta 10720, Tel: 6295364, 6295388, 6595326 or 6595398, Telex: 41247 BO JKT IA, Cable: BOURAQ P.O. Box: 2965 JKT.
Bandung: Jl. Cihampelas 27, Tel: (022) 437896 or 438795.
Jakarta: Jl. Angkasa No 1-3, Tel: (021) 6295150, 6595179 or 6595195.
Semarang: Jl. Gajah Mada 61D, Tel: (024) 23065
Solo: Nata Thur Jl. Gajah Mada 86, Tel: (0271) 4376.

PUBLIC TRANSPORT

Inter-city trains: They are quite comfortable, if a bit slow. First-class carriages have air-conditioning and a dining car that serves passable meals (generally a set dinner of rice, chicken and pickles with tea).

Though the train equipment is imported from Germany, the service is certainly not. Javanese trains are often late – sometimes many hours late as only a single track connects many major cities, so if one train is held up, they are all late.

Inter-city buses: Generally faster and more punctual than trains. They are also considerably cheaper. Most Indonesians travel this way, and you can go across Java for as little as US$10! Long-distance express buses operate at night, leaving major cities at either end of the island in the late afternoon, stopping to pick up and discharge passengers in Central Java in the middle of the night, and arriving at the other end of the island early in the morning. Seats are narrow – six across in a bus that in West would only seat four across. Major routes are served by 'VIP' night buses, which offer air-conditioning, videos and an on-board toilet. Bus drivers drive like maniacs, at breakneck speed with little concern for safety. Accidents are not uncommon. Definitely not a method of travel for the weak at heart.

Express Mini-buses ("colt"): Smaller than buses, seem safer as they are slower and carry 12–14 passengers. They are more comfortable than the intercity buses, and slightly more expensive.

PRIVATE TRANSPORT

Private rented car: You still cannot rent a car in Java without a driver (as you can in Bali), but a chauffeur is not an extravagance here. Automobiles are heavily taxed and expensive, and the price of renting one reflects that – US$50 a day is common. However, there are beat-up taxis and older cars which can be rented for as little as US$20 a day with a driver.

Rented mini-bus ("colt"): The most comfortable and practical way to go. These can be rented for US$30 per day including a driver. For trips out of town or across the island you need only pay for the driver's food and lodging (about US$10 a day), and you may have to buy some or all of the petrol. Still, with a group of four or five people you can go from Jakarta all the way to Yogyakarta via Bandung and the North Coast in a week for about US$300 about the same cost as flying. Arrange for such a rental through your hotel in Yogyakarta or Jakarta. This may take some negotiation. Be sure that the agreement is all worked out clearly in advance, including the amount you will give the driver every day for food and lodging (tips are not expected, though of course they would be appreciated). You may have difficulty finding a driver who speaks some English, so expect to pay a premium for this. Count on one extra day's rental fee and a full tank of gas for the driver to get home.

293

FOOD DIGEST

RESTAURANTS

You can have good food in Indonesia but not everywhere. If you do not like spicy food, Chinese restaurants are the best bet, but they are available only in large towns, when you are on the road you may have to have very simple Indonesian food, which is usually plain rice, a warm beer or a sweet bottled drink, and, if you are lucky, a bony chicken. If you enjoy soupy curries, you may be able to feed yourself more often.

Europeans, who have a long culinary tradition and a definite taste, are less appreciative of exotic food than, say, Americans or Australians. They invariably get tired very soon of the coconut oil taste that dominates any Indonesian dish, and repair to hotel coffee shops to have some long-for Western food. They are likely to be disappointed, as the coconut taste, present in butter as well, will reappear on their spaghetti and they will have to pay dearly for it this time.

Surprisingly, refrigerators are still a luxury even in restaurants that boast a satellite dish on their roof and an "es batu", a piece of ice made of impure water, may appear in your glass. This is dangerous, and is better to have a warm beer than an amoebic infection. Remember that 90 percent of the local population have intestinal parasites.

Streets stalls are good places to take in the local atmosphere and meet amusing people. However, they are not always clean, and the safest way to join the local crowd is to have a glass of tea, some peanuts and a pack of cigarettes.

In most restaurants, the waiter will make a brief appearance and drop on the table an Indonesian menu, a pen and a slip of paper.

You are expected to write your order by yourself, and you had better learn the names of basic ingredients so soon so you can.

In Padang restaurants, that serve a variety of spicy Sumatran curries, a selection of precooked dishes is brought to the table as soon as you take a seat, and you pay only for what you eat.

JAVANESE FOOD

Centuries of contact with other great civilisations have left their mark on the varied cuisine of Indonesia, Indian and Arab traders brought not only merchandise, Hinduism and Islam, but new spices such ginger, cardamom and turmeric. Later the Chinese and (to a lesser extent) the Dutch added their own distinctive touch to the cooking pot. The result is a happy blend of each culinary tradition.

Spices abound in Javanese cooking, and are usually partnered by coconut milk (made by squeezing the grated flesh of the nut) which adds a rich flavour and creamy texture to dishes containing intriguing tropical vegetables, poultry, meat and fish. Happily for the unaccustomed foreign palate, Javanese cooks are light-handed with both spices and chillies (unlike their Sumatran counterparts). They are fond of using sugar as well as fragrant roots and leaves, and the result is food which is both subtle and sophisticated.

The basis of an Indonesian meal is rice (the word for rice and meal is the same: nasi). Each person helps himself to a heap of steaming white rice and then to a little of the three of four dishes of vegetables or meat (known as lauk) which are placed in the centre of the table for all to share. Indonesians do not swamp their plates with food on the first round, but help themselves to a little more of their fancy as the meal progresses. A side dish or sambal, made with red-hot chillies ground with dried shrimp paste and other seasonings such as lime juice, should be approached with caution, but gives a delicious edge to food as you grow used to it (if you ever scorch your mouth or throat with chillies don't rush for the nearest glass of water to quench the flames: water aggravates the problem, and cold beer or other fizzy drinks are even worse; the quickest relief comes from plain boiled rice, bread, cucumber or a banana). Common side dishes are tempe, a protein-rich savoury cake of fermented soya beans, and small crisp cookies (rempeyek) made of peanuts.

The Dutch word rijsttafel (rice table) is sometimes associated with Indonesian food. The name was originally given to gargantuan banquets of rice and countless dishes of vegetables and meats accompanied by savoury offerings such as krupuk (fried prawn or fish crisps), acar (cucumber pickles), sliced banana, peanuts, chillies, and anything else capable of adding fragrance and flavour to the whole mountainous spread. Full-scale extravaganzas are seldom witnessed these days, although a few hotels make a modest attempt at imitation, and all of the individual dishes of the old rijsttafel can still be found and enjoyed.

National favourites include gado-gado, a lightly cooked vegetable salad which includes beansprouts, cabbage and potatoes covered with a rich peanut sauce; Padang food from Central Sumatra is robust and fiery (the beef rendang and otak or brains are particularly good); sate, sometimes regarded as Indonesia's national dish, is a tempting assortment of meat, chicken or seafood grilled on skewers over a charcoal fire and served with a spicy sauce.

A taste, substantial soup known as soto is found everywhere. Try soto Madura, a rich coconut-milk soup delicately spiced and chock full of noodles, chicken, beansprouts and other vegetables, or *soto Bandung* made from tripe.

Chinese influenced noodle dishes such as *mie goreng* (fried wheat-flour noodles) and *bakmi* (rice-flour noodles, either fried or in soup) are also common. *Capcai* (previously *tjap tjai*) is very popular and tastes much better than its Western name 'chop suey' would suggest.

Javanese vegetables dishes are excellent. The slightly sour *sayur asam* (especially around Jakarta) is well worth trying. Other Jakarta specialities are *martabak* (an Indian stuffed pancake) and *gulai kambing*, a thin mutton curry with a taste of turmeric.

Central Javanese delicacies include *gudeg*, made from young jackfruit cooked in coconut milk, and *ayam goreng* (fried chicken). The variation known around Yogya as *Bok Berek*, is superb: the chicken is simmered in spiced coconut milk before being fried.

You will, of course, find *nasi goreng* (fried rice) everywhere; topped with a fried egg, it is often the best bet when everything else looks suspicious. *Nasi rames*, white rice served with a small helping of savoury meat and vegetables can be good, when served in clean places.

Like all Indonesians, the Javanese are very fond of snacks. Wherever you go, you'll find someone selling sticky cakes, crunchy peanut biscuits, strange salted nuts and lentils, steamed sweetmeats wrapped in banana leaf, and a host of other extraordinary goodies. Although ice-creams and other iced confections are sold in most places, it's wise to avoid those sold by street vendors.

The tropical fruits of Indonesia are excellent: pineapples, bananas (ranging from tiny fingersized *pisang mas* up to the footlong *pisang raja*), papayas and mangoes are joined by even more unusual seasonal fruits. Some of the most outstanding are *rambutan* (hairy red skins enclosing sweet white meat), *mangosteen* (purplish black skins with a very sweet juicy white fruit inside) and *jeruk Bali* (pomelos). The huge spikey *durian* has (to most people) a revolting rotten smell, but its buttery-rich fruit is adored by local people and a few adventurous visitors.

DRINKING NOTES

Most familiar Western drinks are available in Java, though some of them take on new dimension. Javanese tea is usually very fragrant, and similar to Chinese tea in flavour. Served hot or cold, *manis* (with sugar) or *tawar* (without), it is safer than water. Javanese coffee is a delight to real coffee lovers, being served almost Turkish-style with a few grounds floating around (known as *kopi tobruk*). Locally manufactured beer (Anker and Bintang) is similar to European lager beer. It's moderately priced and available everywhere, but as it is seldom kept chilled, you may be faced with the choice of

warm beer, beer *pakai es* (with ice) or no beer at all.

Fresh fruit juices are popular. *Air jeruk*, as orange juice is called, is served either hot or cold: be sure to specify what you want. There are also juices made from pineapple, apple and other common fruits. Westerners accustomed to regarding avocado as a vegetable will probably be amazed at the *alpokat* drink, but it's worth trying: avocado, rum or coffee essence, palm sugar and tinned milk are blended to make a thick and rich liquid.

Cordials are known as *stroop*: among the best are *zirzak*, made from soursop and *markisa*, made from passionfruit. *Es kopyor* is a favourite concoction of rose syrup, ice and scoops of jelly-like flesh from the inside of the *kopyor* coconut. *Es campur*, a mixture of shaved ice with fruits and jelly (also known as *cendol*) *es tape* and *dawet santen* are all absolutely delicious.

PHOTOGRAPHY

PHOTOGRAPHY, FILM & PROCESSING

Java offers some of the most spectacular landscapes in the world and whether you are a serious photographer or you simply want to bring back some souvenirs, a camera is a must.

The splendid landscapes of Java are, however, more elusive than its people, who are camera-friendly and love to have their picture taken. The great volcanos are usually enshrouded in clouds, and the only chances to see them are at the very break of dawn. If you are serious about photography, be prepared to some very early morning calls.

Because of the heat, most activities take place early in the morning or late in the night. The nice afternoon light usually coincides with siesta time, and is better used to photograph temples and monuments than for people.

Standard equipment should include wide angles and short and medium tele. Long tele lenses (over 200 mm) are seldom useful, because of the haze and or excessive humidity. Landscapes, when they are visible, call for a moderate wide angle rather than tele lenses.

A flash will be useful, as most cultural performances are either in closed spaces or held at night. You may also want to try very high speed film for a more natural effect. Shadow plays are not photographed with a flash, a mistake frequently made by beginners who are then confronted with the picture of a white piece of canvas.

Interesting details of temples, carved out of black volcanic stone, are often in deep shadow and are impossible to reproduce without the help of a tripod and a flash held separately from the camera (possibly diffused by a reflector). A tripod will also be useful for a number of scenic pictures, that must be taken when the sunlight is still too dim. Forests and gardens are usually quite dark, and nature lovers should make good use of rainy days and a tripod.

Bring your own supply of film, which in Indonesia is expensive and often not fresh. Camera equipment is also expensive, although Jakarta and Surabaya have well equipped stores.

For developing slides, as well as photographic supply, the best shop is **Jakarta Photo**. Quick service photo shops to develop color prints are now widespread and cheap, but the quality may be disappointing. If you think you have invaluable material exposed on film, it may be safer to develop it back home or in Singapore.

LANGUAGE

Indonesia's motto, *Bhinneka Tunggal Ika* (Unity in Diversity) is seen in its most driving, potent form in the work of language. Although there are over 250 distinct languages and dialects spoken in the archipelago, the one national tongue, *Bahasa Indonesia*, will take you from the northernmost tip of Sumatra through Java and across the string of islands to Irian Jaya. *Bahasa Indonesia* is both an old and new language. It is based on Malay, which has been the *lingua franca* throughout much of Southeast Asia for centuries, but it has changed rapidly in the past few decades to meet the needs of a modern nation.

Even though there are four major languages spoken on Java (including Betawi, the local dialect proudly spoken by many Jakartans) almost all residents of Java speak *Bahasa Indonesia*. *Bahasa Indonesia* is both an old and new language. It is based on Malay, which has been the *lingua franca* throughout much of South East Asia for centuries, but it has changed rapidly in the past few decades to meet the needs of a modern nation.

Although formal Indonesian is a complex language demanding serious study, the construction of basic Indonesian sentences is relatively easy. A compact and cheap book, *How to Master the Indonesian Language* by Almatseier, is widely available in Indonesia and should prove invaluable in helping you say what you want to say. Indonesian is written in the Roman alphabet and, unlike some Asian languages, is not tonal.

Indonesians always use their language to show respect when addressing others, especially when a younger person speaks to his elders. The custom is to address an elder man as *bapak* or *pak* (father) and an elder woman as *ibu* (mother), and even in the case of slightly younger people who are obviously VIPs, this form of address is suitable and correct. *Bung* (in West Java) and *mas* (in Central and East Java) roughly translate as "brother" and are used with equals, people your own age whom you don't know all that well, and with hotel clerks, taxi drivers, tour guides and waiters (it's friendly, and a few notches above "buddy" or "mate"); *nyonya* is polite when speaking with a married woman, *nona* with an unmarried woman.

Listed below are a few general guidelines on the pronunciation of *Bahasa Indonesia* which, with minor exceptions, is written phonetically with much the same sound values as Italian. The pre-1972 spellings, where applicable, are in brackets. The best way to acquire the correct pronunciation is of course, to listen to the way Indonesians speak. Once you start to use the language you will find that most people are eager to help and to understand you.

a short as in 'father'
(*apa* = what, *ada* = there is)

ai rather like the 'i' in 'mine'
(*kain* = material, *sampai* = to arrive)

k hard at the beginning of a word as in 'king', hardly audible at the end of a word.
(*kamus* = dictionary, *cantik* = beautiful)

kh (*ch*) slightly aspirated as in 'khan' or the Scottish 'ch' in 'loch'
(*khusus* = special, *khabar* = news)

ng as in 'singer', never as in 'danger' or 'Ringo'
(*bunga* = flower, *penginapan* = cheap hotel)

ngg like the 'ng' in 'Ringo'
(*minggu* = week, *tinggi* = high)

r always rolled
(*rokok* = cigarette, *pertama* = first)

u (*oe*) as in 'full', never as in 'bucket'
(*umum* = public, *belum* = not yet)

y (*j*) as in 'you'
(*saya* = I or me, *kaya* = rich)

c (*tj*) like the 'ch' in 'church'
(*candi* = temple, *kacang* = nut)

e 1. often unstressed as the barely sounded 'e' in 'open'
(*berapa*, sounded like *b'rapa* = how much?)
2. sometimes stressed, sounding somewhere between the 'e' in 'bed' and 'a' in 'bad'
(*boleh* = may, *lebar* = wide)

g hard as in 'golf', never as in 'ginger'
(*guntur* = thunder, *bagus* = very good)

h generally lightly aspirated
(*hitam* = black, *lihat* = to see)

i either short as in 'pin' or a longer sound like 'ee' in 'meet'
(*minta* = to ask for, *ibu* = mother)

j (*dj*) as in 'John'
(*jalan* = road or street, *jahit* = to sew)

Two minor points about spelling. Despite the new rules you will find many instances where people's names continue to be spelled with the old 'oe' rather than the current 'u', some may change, but most stick to their birthright, including the President whose name is Soeharto and only rarely used by the press as Suharto. Less important are the subtle distinctions in Central Java between two forms of 'o' and the liquid sounds of 'l' or 'r'; the niceties are of interest only to experts in phonetics, but in practical terms it means that the city of Solo may also appear as Sala, and that the Siva temple at Prambanan may be written (in its popular form) as Lara Janggrang, Loro Jonggrong or Roro Jonggrang...and they are all correct.

GREETINGS & CIVILITIES

thank you (very much)	*terima kasih (banyak)*
please	*silahkan*
good morning	*selamat pagi*
good day (roughly 11 to 3 p.m.)	*selamat siang*
good afternoon, evening	*selamat sore, malam*
goodbye (to person going)	*selamat jalan*
goodbye (to person staying)	*selamat tinggal*
I'm sorry	*ma'af*
welcome	*selamat datang*
please come in	*silahkan masuk*
Please sit down	*silahkan duduk*
what is your name?	*siapa nama saudara?*
my name is...	*nama saya...*
where do you come from?	*saudara datang dari mana? or dari mana?*
I come from...	*saya datang dari...*

PRONOUNS & FORMS OF ADDRESS

you (singular)	*kamu* (to children), *saudara, anda*
he, she	*dia*
we	*kami* (not including the listener)
we	*kita* (including the listener)
you (plural)	*saudara-saudara, anda*
they	*mereka*
Mr	*Tuan/'Pak/Mas/'Bung*
Mrs	*Nyonya/Ibu*
Miss	*Nona*
I	*saya*

DIRECTIONS & TRANSPORT

left	*kiri*
right	*kanan*
straight	*terus*
near	*dekat*
far	*jauh*
from	*dari*
to	*ke*
inside	*didalam*
outside of	*diluar*
between	*antara*
under	*dibawah*
here	*disini*
there	*disana*
in front of	*didepan, dimuka*
at the back	*dibelakang*
next to	*disebelah*
to ascend	*naik*
to descend	*turun*
pedicab	*becak*
car	*mobil*
bus	*bis*
train	*kereta-api*
aeroplane	*kapal terbang*
ship	*kapal laut*
bicycle	*sepeda*
motor cycle	*sepeda motor*
where do you want to go?	*mau kemana?*
I want to go...	*saya mahu ke...*
stop here	*berhenti disini, stop disini*
I'll be back in five minutes	*aya akan kembali lima menit*
turn right	*belok kekanan*
how many kilometres?	*berapa kilometer jauhnya?*
slowly, slow down	*pelan-pelan/perlahan-perlahan*

IMPORTANT PLACES

hotel	*hotel, penginapan, losmen*
shop	*toko*
train station	*stasium kereta-api*
airport	*lapangan terbang*
cinema	*bioskop*
bookshop	*toko buku*
petrol station	*pompa bensin*
bank	*bank*
post office	*kantor pos*
swimming pool	*tempat pemandian, kolam renang*
Immigration Dept.	*Departemen Immigrasi*
tourist office	*kantor parawisata*
embassy	*kedutaan besar*

SPENDING THE NIGHT

room	*kamar*
bed	*tempat tidur*
bedroom	*kamar tidur*
bathroom	*kamar mandi*
toilet	*kamar kecil*
towel	*handuk*
bedsheet	*seprei*
pillow	*bantal*
water	*air*
soap	*sabun*
fan	*kipas angin*
to bathe	*mandi*
hot water	*air panas*
cold water	*air dingin*
to wash	*cuci*
to iron	*gosok*
clothes	*pakaian*
shirt	*kemeja*
trousers	*celana*
How much for one night?	*Berapa harganya satu malam?*
Please wash these clothes	*Tolong cuci pakaian-pakaian ini*

EATING

restaurant	*restoran, rumah makan*
dining room	*kamar makan*
food	*makanan*
drink	*minuman*
breakfast	*makan pagi*
lunch	*makan siang*
dinner	*makan malam*
boiled water	*air putih, air matang*
iced water	*air es*
ice	*es*
tea	*teh*
coffee	*kopi*
cordial	*stroop*
beer	*bir*
fresh orange juice	*air jeruk*
milk	*susu*
bread	*roti*
butter	*mentega*
rice	*nasi*
noodles	*mie, bihun, bakmie*
soup	*soto*
chicken	*ayam*
beef	*daging (sapi)*
pork	*babi, daging babi*
lamb	*domba*
goat, mutton	*kambing*
liver	*hati*
brains	*otak*
fish	*ikan*
prawns	*udang*
vegetables	*sayur*
fruit	*buah*
banana	*pisang*

pineapple	*nanas*
coconut	*kelapa*
mango	*mangga*
egg	*telur*
soft-boiled egg	*telur setengah matang*
fried egg	*telur mata sapi*
dumpling (small)	*pangsit*
dumpling (large)	*bakpao*
sugar	*gula*
salt	*garam*
pepper	*merica, lada*
soya sauce	*kecap*
vinegar	*cuka*
sweet	*manis*
sour	*asam*
bitter	*pahit*
without sugar	*tawar*
hot (temperature)	*panas*
hot (spicy)	*pedis, pedas*
fried	*goreng*
served in stock	*godok*
sauce	*kuah, saus*
cup	*cangkir*
plate	*piring*
glass	*gelas*
spoon	*senduk*
knife	*pisau*
fork	*garpu*

SHOPPING

shop	*toko*
money	*uang*
change (of money)	*uang kembali*
to buy	*beli*
price	*harga*
expensive	*mahal*
cheap	*murah*
fixed price	*harga pas*
How much is it?	*Berapa?/ Berapa harganya?*
It is too expensive.	*Itu terlalu mahal.*
Do you have a cheaper one?	*Adakah yang lebih murah?*
Can you reduce the price?	*Bisa saudara kurangkan harganya?*
What is this?	*Apa ini?*
I'll take it.	*Saya akan ambil ini.*
I don't want it.	*Saya tidak mau.*
I'll come back later.	*Saya akan kembali nanti.*

TIME

day	*hari*
night	*malam*
today	*hari ini*
morning (to about 10.30 a.m.)	*pagi*
noon (broadly 10.30 a.m. to 3 p.m.)	*siang*
evening (3 to 8 p.m.)	*sore*
now	*sekarang*
just now	*baru saja*
soon, presently	*nanti*

always	*selalu*
before	*dahulu, dulu*
when (= the time that)	*waktu*
when? (interrogative)	*kapan?*
tomorrow	*besok*
yesterday	*kemarin*
minute	*menit*
hour	*jam*
week	*minggu*
month	*bulan*
year	*tahun*
past (the hour)	*liwat*
to (before the hour)	*kurang*
What is the time?	*Jam berapa sekarang?*
It is ten past eight.	*Jam delapan liwat sepuluh.*

NUMBERS

one	*satu*
two	*dua*
three	*tiga*
four	*empat*
five	*lima*
six	*enam*
seven	*tujuh*
eight	*delapan*
nine	*sembilan*
ten	*sepuluh*
eleven	*sebelas*
twelve	*duabelas*
thirteen	*tigabelas*
fourteen	*empatbelas*
fifteen	*limabelas*
sixteen	*enambelas*
seventeen	*tujuhbelas*
eighteen	*delapanbelas*
nineteen	*sembilanbelas*
twenty	*duapuluh*
twenty-one	*duapuluh satu*
thirty	*tigapuluh*
forty	*empatpuluh*
fifty-eight	*limapuluh delapan*
one hundred	*seratus*
two hundred and sixty-three	*duaratus enampuluh tiga*
one thousand	*seribu*

DAYS OF THE WEEK

Sunday	*Hari Minggu*
Monday	*Hari Senin/Senen*
Tuesday	*Hari Selasa*
Wednesday	*Hari Rabu*
Thursday	*Hari Kamis*
Friday	*Hari Jum'at/Juma'at*
Saturday	*Hari Sabtu*

HANDY WORDS & PHRASES

yes	*ya/ia*
no	*tidak, tak* (also *'nggak'*)
(that's) correct	*betul*
(that's wrong)	*salah*
much, many	*banyak*
very much	*banyak sekali*
and	*dan*
but	*tetapi, tapi*
if	*jika, kalau*
with	*dengan*
this	*ini*
that	*itu*
like this	*begini*
like that	*begitu*
similar to	*seperti*
here	*sini, disini*
very nice	*bagus*
more	*lebih*
less	*kurang*
because	*karena*
perhaps	*barangkali, mungkin*
about (approximately)	*kira-kira*
then	*kemudian, lalu*
good, alright	*baik*

SOME VERBS

There are several verbal prefixes such as *me, mem, men-, meng-,* and *ber-.* They can be confusing. You will be understood if you just use the root of the verb.

bring	*bawa*
carry	*angkat*
take	*ambil*
give	*kasi, beri*
buy	*beli*
sell	*jual*
ask/ask for	*tanya/minta*
see	*lihat*
try	*coba*
look for	*cari*
wash	*cuci*
want	*mau*
can (permission)	*boleh*
can (possible, though commonly signifying permission as well)	*bisa*
speak	*bicara*
tell/say	*bilang/berkata*
I don't understand.	*Saya tidak mengerti.*
I don't speak Indonesian.	*Saya tidak bisa bicara Bahasa Indonesia.*
I speak only a little Indonesian	*Saya bisa bicara sedikit saja Bahasa Indonesia.*
Please speak slowly.	*Tolong bicara pelan-pelan.*

INTERROGATIVES

who	*siapa*
what	*apa*
when	*kapan*
where (location)	*dimana*
where (direction)	*kemana*
why	*kenapa, mengapa*
how	*bagaimana*
how much, how many	*berapa*
which, which one	*yang mana*

A few more nouns:

cigarette/clove cigarette	*rokok/kretek*
matches	*korek api*
train (railway)	*kereta-api*
house	*rumah*
paper	*kertas*
newspaper	*surat khabar, koran*
hair	*rambut*
map	*peta*
place	*tempat*
stamp (postage)	*prangko, perangko*
electricity	*listrik*
foreigner	*orang asing*
tourist	*turis, wisatawan*

USEFUL ADJECTIVES

big	*besar*
small	*kecil*
young	*muda*
old (person)	*tua*
old (thing)	*lama*
new	*baru*
beautiful	*cantik*
good	*baik*
no good	*tidak baik*
hot	*panas*
cold	*dingin*
delicious	*enak*
clean	*bersih*
dirty	*kotor*
red	*merah*
white	*putih*
blue	*biru*
black	*hitam*
green	*hijau*
yellow	*kuning*
gold	*mas*
silver	*perak*

UNDERSTANDING SIGNS

Many Indonesian words have been borrowed from other languages, and quickly reveal their meanings: *sekolah, universitas, mobil, bis, akademi, sektor, proklamas* and *polisi*. Other important signs leave you guessing; the following short list may help you.

buka, dibuka	open
tutup, ditutup	closed

masuk	entrance
keluar	exit
jangan pegang	don't touch
dilarang merokok	no smoking
tolak	push
tarik	pull
pintu	gate
loket	ticket window
keterangan	information
umum	public
rumah sakit	hospital
apotik	pharmacy
karcis	ticket
wisma	house (institutional sense)
pusat	central
kota	city
daerah	district
kebun binatang	zoo
pasar	market
gereja	church
lapangan golf	golf course
bea dan cukai	customs

FILLING IN FORMS

Forms are an unavoidable part of travel. Within Indonesia few forms carry translations into other languages, so here with a few key words and phrases to help you out.

nama	name
alamat	address
alamat lengkap	full address
laki-laki, perempuan	male, female
umur	age
tanggal (tgl.)	date
jam	time
berangkat	departure
kawin	marital status
agama	religion
kebangsaan	nationality
pekerjaan	profession
surat keterangan	identification (passport, etc.)
pembesar yang memberikan	issued by
maksud kunjungan	purpose of visit
tanda tangan	signature

Further Reading

LITERATURE

Conrad, Joseph. *Victory*. Part of this novel is set in Surabaya and the book helped to create the city's romantic allure.

Kartini, Raden Adjeng. *Letters of a Javanese Princess*. One of the earliest Indonesian literary masterpieces, this book played an important role in the battle for civil rights in the Dutch colonies. For the contemporary reader, the most fascinating aspect is the portrayal of Javanese court life at the turn of the century.

Kcoh, C.S. *The Year of Living Dangerously*. The popular film starring Sigourney Weaver captured only one side of this complex novel where adventure and romance blend with politics. The stage is the last turbulent years of Sukarno's dictatorship, and the drama offers a deep insight into the way of thinking of the Javanese.

Lubis, Mochtar. *Twilight in Djakarta*. The best novel of the leading Indonesian contemporary writer, imprisoned by Sukarno for his political views, vividly portrays the plights of the poor in the darkest hours of this giant Third World city.

Multatuli. *Mas Havelaar*, or *the Coffee Auctions of the Dutch Trading Company*. The book (1860) which made the Dutch aware of the injustice of their colonial administration. Available in English from Penguin.

Scidmore, E.R. *Java: The Garden of the East*. A late 19th century travel book, written by an American woman with a keen interest in plant life and an eye for the social blunders of the Dutch elite.

ARTS & CRAFTS

Bernet Kempers, A.J. *Ancient Indonesian Art*. Photographs and description of all Javanese temples, compiled in 1959 by the head of Archaeological Service.

Brandon, James. *On Thrones of Gold: Three Javanese shadow plays*. Translation of three popular *wayang kulit* stories.

Dumarcay, Jacques. *The Temples of Java*. A succinct summary of the evolution of Javanese temple architecture.

Eliott, Inger McCabe. *Batik: Fabled cloth of Java*. The ultimate book on *batik*, with splendid photos by Brian Brake.

Fontein, Jan. *The Sculpture of Indonesia*. The catalogue of the exhibition of the Festival of Indonesia in USA (1990–91) lavishly illustrated and produced.

Gittinger, Mattiabelle. *Splendid Symbols: Textiles and traditions in Indonesia*, an overview of the textiles of the Archipelago.

Holt, Clair. *Art in Indonesia: continuities and change*. The standard work on Javanese art (1967), now almost impossible to find.

Jessup, Helen. *Court Arts of Indonesia*. The companion volume to *The sculpture of Indonesia* prepared for the USA exhibition, presents the best of the rich artistic traditions of the royal courts.

Lee Chor Lin: *Batik, Creating An Identity*. Splendid catalogue of the 1992 exhibition of Indonesian *batiks* at the Museum of Singapore.

Miksic, John. *Borobudur, Golden Tales of the Buddhas*. The most readable analysis of a very complex monument, which has otherwise been the subject of an incredibly esoteric literature.

Miksic, John. *Old Javanese Gold*. Detailed description of an ancient Javanese jewellery collection.

Rodgers, Susan. *Power and Gold*. Jewellery from Java and other islands of the archipelago, as well as the Philippines and Malaysia; the beautifully illustrated catalogue of an exhibition at the Barbies-Mueller Museum in Geneva.

Various authors and photographers. *Borobudur, Prayer in Stone*. Impressive collection of stunning photographs and old documents, but with rather confusing text by De Casparis, Dumarcay and others.

HISTORY

Boxer, C.R. *The Dutch Seaborn Empire, 1600–1800*. The classic work of the history of colonialism in Indonesia.

Raffles, Thomas Stamford. *The History of Java*. A monumental work covering every aspect of Javanese culture, history, and geography, written by the governor of Java and founder of Singapore in 1817. Easily available (Oxford University Press).

Ricklefs, M.C. *A History of Modern Indonesia* a short overview of Indonesian history, from the 13th century to the present.

Legge, J.D. *Sukarno: A Political Biography*. A good introduction to contemporary history, with flashes into Javanese life.

McDonald, Hamish. *Suharto's Indonesia*. The most recent history of Indonesia, told through the life of President Suharto. His Javanese background plays an important part.

SOCIOLOGY & RELIGION

Anderson, B.R. *Mythology and the Tolerance of the Javanese*. (Cornell University Press, New York, 1965) A classic study on Javanese behaviour, seen through the characters of the shadow play. An indispensable tool for any sociological study, is now made outdated by the profound changes of the last decade.

Geertz, Clifford. *The Religion of Java*. The other "classic" of American anthropology of Java, written in 1960. This interpretation of Javanese society as a non-muslim entity is becoming rapidly outdated in view of the recent strong revival of Islam in the Far East.

Koentjaraningrat. *Javanese Culture*. Although researched in 1970, this recently published volume is more subtle in its interpretation than Geerts' and survives better the recent developments. It is also more easily available (Oxford University Press).

GEOGRAPHY & NATURAL HISTORY

Wallace, A.R. *The Malay Archipelago*. The travel diary of the famous English naturalist, contains a vivid description of Java before the demographic explosion: among description of tigers, rhinos, jungles, the author presents his revolutionary theory about the dispersal of fauna and flora through the archipelago.

Veevers-Carter, W. *Land Mammals of Indonesia*. Zoological dates for all Indonesian mammals.

Atmowiloto, A. and others. *Indonesia from the Air*. A picture book that presents a visual summary of Indonesia's and Java's geographical features.

USEFUL ADDRESSES

INDONESIA TOURIST PROMOTION OFFICES OVERSEAS

Asean and Hongkong: Indonesia Tourist Promotion Office, 10, Collyer Quay, 15-07, Ocean Building, Singapore 0104, Tel: 5342837 or 5341795, Telex: RS 35731 INTOUR, Fax: 5334287.

Australia: Public Relations Agency Garuda Indonesia Office, 4, Bligh Street, P.O. Box 3836, Sydney 2000, Tel: 232-6044, Telex: 22576, Fax: 2332828.

Europe: Indonesia Tourist Promotion Office, Wiessenhuttenplatz 17, Frankfurt am Main, Tel: (069) 2336778, Tel: 04 189186 ITPOD, Cable: INDOTOUR, Frankfurt am Main, West Germany, Fax: (069) 230840.

North America: Indonesia Tourist Promotion Office, 3457 Wilshire Boulevard, Los Angeles, CA

90010 U.S.A., Tel: (231) 387-2078, Telex: 182192 INDOTOUR LAX, Fax: (213) 3804876.

GOVERNMENT TOURIST OFFICES

The Directorate General of Tourism (DGT) is located in Jakarta and administratively is under the Department of Tourism, Post and Telecommunications which has offices in all main tourist destination areas. The Offices are known as KANWIL DEPPARPOSTEL or Regional Office of Tourism, Post and Telecommunications. Each of the 27 provinces of Indonesia also has its own tourist office which can be identified by the abbreviation DIPARDA (provincial tourist service) or BAPPARDA (provincial tourist agency). All of these offices can offer assistance and information about their areas.

Art of Tourism, Post and Telecommunication, 36, Jl. Kebon Sirih, Tel: 372305, 349142, 340172, Telex: 45157 MPPTEL IA, Fax: 375409.

Directorate General of Tourism, 81, Jl. Kramat Raya, P.O. Box. 409, Tel: 3103117, Telex: 61525 INTOUR IA, Cable: INTO JAKARTA, Fax: 3101146.

JAKARTA

Kanwill V Depparpostel DKI Jakarta, Jl. K.H. Abdurrohim, Kuningan Barat, Jakarta 12710, Tel: 511742/816, 510968.

Diparda DKI Jakarata, Jl. Abdurrohim, Kuningan Barat, Jakarta 12710, Tel: 511070, 511738, 511369.

CENTRAL JAVA

Kanwill VII Depparpostel Jawa Tengah, Jl. K.H. Achmad Dahlan No. 2, Semarang 50241, Tel: (024) 311169, 318021.

Diparda Tk. I Jawa Tengah, Gedung PPDI, Jl. Veteran 1-A, Semarang 50133, Tel: (024) 24146.

YOGYAKARTA

Kanwil VIII Depparpostel D.I. Yogyakarta, Jl. Adisucipto km 7-8, P.O. Box 003, 87899, Yogyakarta, Tel: (0274) 5150.

Diparda D.I. Yogyakarta, Jl. Malioboro 14, Yogyakarta 55271, Tel: (024) 3543, 2812.

WEST JAVA

Kanwil VI Depparpostel Jawa Timur, Jl. K.H. Penghulu Hasan Mustafa, Bandung 40263, Tel: (022) 72355, 75412.

Diparda Tk. I Jawa Barat, Jl. Cipaganti 151-153, Tel: (022) 81490, 56202.

INDONESIAN DIPLOMATIC & CONSULAR MISSIONS ABROAD

Australia: Indonesian Embassy, 8, Darwin Avenue Yarralumia, Canberra Australia ACT 2600, Tel: (062) 733222, Telex: 62525-62537, Fax: 062-733748, Cable: Indonesia Canberra.

Austria: Indonesian Embassy, Gustav Tschenmakgasse 5-7, 1180-Wien-Austria, Tel: (0222) 342533, 342534, 342535, 316663, Telex: 115578 INDON IA, Cable: Indonesia Wina.

Belgium, Luxembourg & E.E.C: Indonesian Embassy, Avenue de Tarvueren 294, 1150 Brussel Belgium, Tel: (02) 7715060, 7711776, 7712014, Telex: 21200 INDON B, Fax: NA (A) 7712291, Cable: Indonesia Brussel.

Brunei Darussalam: Indonesian Embassy, EDR. 4303 Lot 4498 KG. Sungai Hanching Baru, Simpang 528, Jl. Muara, P.O. Box: 3013 Bandar Sri Begawan, Tel: 30180, 30445, Telex: No. BU 2654 INDO BRU, Fax: 30646, Cable: Indonesia BSB

Canada: Indonesian Embassy, 287, Maclaren Street, P.O. Box: 430 Terminal "A" KIN 8V5, Ottawa, Ontario, Canada K2P OL9, Tel: (613) 236-7403, 7404, 136-7405, Telex: (053) 3119 INDONESIA OTT, Fax: (613) 5632858, Cable: INDONESIA CANADA.

Denmark: Indonesian Embassy, Rehj Alle 1, 2900 Hellerup Denmark, Tel: (01) 624422, 624539, 624184, Telex: 16274 INDON DK, Cable: PER-WAKIN COPENHAGEN.

Finland: Indonesian Embassy, 37, Berikinkatu, 00810 Helsinki Finland, Tel: 6947744, Cable: INDONESIA HELSINKI.

France: Indonesian Embassy, 47-49 Rue Contambert, 75116 Paris France, Tel: 45030760, 45041373, Telex: 648031, 648056.

Germany: Indonesian Embassy, Bernkasteler Strasse 2, 5300 Bern 2 (Federal Republic of Germany), Tel: 0228-328990, Cable: INDONESIA BONN.

Great Britain & Ireland: Indonesia Embassy, 157 Edgware Road London W2 2 HR UK, Tel: 01-499-7661, Cable: INDONESIA LONDON.

India: Indonesian Embassy, 50 A, Chanakyapuri – New Delhi 110021 (India), Tel: 602348, 602352, 602354, Telex: (031) 65709 KBRI IN, Cable: INDONESIA NEW DELHI.

Italy and Malta: Indonesian Embassy, Via Compania 53, 00187-Rome (Italy), Tel: 4759251/3, Telex: 610317 INDORO I, 622183 INDORO I.

Japan: Indonesian Embassy, 2-9 Higashi Gotanda 5 Chome, Shinagawa-ku Tokyo-Japan, Tel: 441-4201/9, Cable: INDONESIA TOKYO, Telex: J 22920.

Republic of Korea: Indonesian Embassy, 55, Yoido-Dong, Young-Deong Po-Ku, Seoul (Republic of Korea), Tel: 7835675, 7635676, 7835677.

Malaysia: Indonesian Embassy, Jl. Tun Razak No. 233, P.O. Box: 10889, 50400 Kuala Lumpur (Malaysia), Tel: 9842011, 9841354, 9841228, Cable: INDONESIA KUALA LUMPUR.

New Zealand, Fiji & West Samoa: Indonesian Embassy, 70, Glen Road, Kelburn, Wellington (New Zealand), P.O. Box: 3542, Tel: 758695/6/7/9, Telex: 3892 & 30251, Cable: PERWAKILAN WELLINGTON.

Netherlands: Indonesian Embassy, 8, Tobias Asserlaan, 5517, KC'S Gravenhage, Tel: 070-469796, Fax: (070) 643331, Cable: INDONESIA DEN HAAG.

Norway: Indonesian Embassy, Gt. 8, Inkognito, 0258 Oslo 2, Norway, Tel: (02) 441121, Telex: 72683 INDO PN, Cable: INDONESIA OSLO.

Pakistan: Indonesian Embassy, Diplomatic Enclave Ramna 5/4 Islamabad-Pakistan, P.O. Box: 1019, Tel: 820266 PABX, 824977 (81121-94), Telex: 5679 INDON PK, Cable: ISLAMABAD (Pakistan).

Papua New Guinea: Indonesian Embassy, 12/140, Sir Jhon Guisc Drive Waigani, P.O. Box: 7165 Baroko, N.C.D. Port Moresby, Papua New Guinea, Tel: 253116/18, 253544, Telex: 22164-23311, Cable: INDONESIA PORT MORESBY.

Philippines: Indonesian Embassy Building, 185, Salcedo Street, Legaspi Village, Makati, Metro Manila, P.O. Box: 372 MCC, Makati, Metro Manila (Philippines), Tel: 85-50-61/68, Cable: INDONESIA MANILA.

Singapore: Indonesian Embassy, 7, Chatsworth Road Singapore 1024, Tel: 7377422, Cable: INDONESIA SINGAPORE.

Russia: Indonesian Embassy, 12, Novokuznetskaya Ulitsa Moskouw, Tel: 2319549, 2319550, 2316320, Cable: INDONESIA MOSCOW, Telex: 413444 INAB SU.

Spain: Indonesian Embassy, 65, Calle de Agestia, 28043 Madrid Espana, Tel: 4130849, 4130594, 4130294, Cable: PERWAKILAN MADRID.

Sri Lanka & Maldives: Indonesian Embassy; 1, Police Park, Colombo 5, Sri Lanka, Tel: 580113, 580194, Telex: 21223 KBRI CE

Sweden: Indonesian Embassy, 47/V Strandvagen 11456, Stockholm (Sweden), Tel: 6635470/75, Cable: INDONESIA STOCKHOLM, Telex: 19371 INDON S.

Switzerland: Indonesian Embassy, 51, Elfenauweg, P.O. Box: 270. 3006 Bern (Switzerland), Tel: (031) 440983/85, Telex: 911525 INDO CH, Cable: INDONESIA BERN.

Turkey: Indonesian Embassy, Cankaya, Abdullah Cavdet Sokak 10, P.K.C 42 Cankaya 065552 Ankara, Turkey, Tel: (4) 1382190 (4 lines), Telex: (067) 43250 INDO TR, Cable: INDONESIA ANKARA.

United Nations Organization: Indonesian Permanent Mission to The United Nations, 16 Rue Saint Jean, 1203 Geneva, P.O. Box: 2271 CH 1211, Geneva 2, Switzerland, Tel: 453350, 453357, 453358/59, Cable: PERWAKILAN GENEVA.

United States of America: Indonesian Embassy, 2020 Massachusets Avenue N.W., Washington D.C. 20036 (USA), Tel: (202) 775-5200, 775-5207, Cable: INDONESIA WASHINGTON.

Thailand: Indonesian Embassy, 600-602 Petchburi Road, Bangkok, Thailand, P.O. Box: 3013, Tel: 252-3135/40, 2523177/8, Cable: INDONESIA BANGKOK.

Yugoslavia & Greece: Indonesian Embassy, Bulever Oktoberske Revolucije 18, 11040 Beograd, Yugoslavia, P.O. Box: 559, Tel: 663344, Telex: 11129 INDO YU & 11990 INDO YU, Cable: INDONESIA BEOGRAD.

CONSULATES

Adelaide: Indonesian Consulate, 3rd floor Waish Bld, 44 Gawler Place, Adelaide, S.A. 5000, Tel: 08-2236535.

Athens, Yunani: Indonesian Consulate, 11-13 Skyrou Street Athens 811, Greece, Tel: 9914082.

Antwerp, Belgium: Indonesian Consulate General, Suikerul 5 Bus No. 9, 2000 Antwerpen, Belgium, Tel: 031/322130.

Barcelona, Spain: Indonesian Embassy, Rambia Estudios 119, Apartado 18, Barcelona-2, Spain, Tel: 3171900, 3184130.

Berlin, Germany: Indonesian Consulate, Rudeloffweg 1000 Berlin 33, Tel: (030) 8135076/77/78/79, Telex: 183010 RIBER D, Cable: PER-WAKILAN BERLIN BARAT.

Bombay, India: Indonesia Consulate, 19, Altamount Road, Cumballa Hill, Bombay, 400 026 India, Tel: 368678, 381051, Telex: 75854 KRIB IN, Cable: INDONESIA BOMBAY.

Bremen, Germany: Indonesian Consulate, Damhof 26, d-2800 Bremen 1, Federal Republic of Germany, Tel: (0421) 3322224.

Calcutta, India: Indonesian Consulate, Raj Kamal Bhaven, 128 Rash Bahari Avenue, Calcutta, India, Tel: 460297.

Chicago, U.S.A: Indonesian Consulate, Two Illinois Center, 233 North Michigan Ave, Suite 1422 Chicago, Illinois 60601 USA, Tel: (312) 9380101, Fax: (312) 938-3148, Telex: 210222 INAC UR, Cable: INDONESIA CHICAGO.

Charleroi, Belgium: Indonesian Consulate, Boulevard de Tirou, 11 Bte 7, 6000 Charleroi, Belgium, Tel: 071/310050.

Darwin, Australia: Indonesian Consulate, 22, Coronation Drive, Stuart Park, P.O. Box: 1953, Darwin N.T. 0801, Australia, Tel: (089) 819352, Cable: INDONESIA DARWIN.

Davao, Philippines: Indonesian Consulate General, Ecoland Subdivision, P.O. Box: 156, Martina, Davao City Philippines, Tel: 78486-89 (PLDT), Telex: 24882 KJD PH-INTERNATIONAL, Cable: INDONESIA DAVAO.

Duesseldorf, Germany: Indonesian Consulate General, Berliner Alle 2, Post Fach 9140, Duesseldorf, Federal Republic of Germany, Tel: (0211) 353081.

Fukuoka, Japan: Indonesian Consulate, Kyuden Bldg. 1-82, Watanabe-Dori-Chome, Chou-Ku, Fukuoko-Shi, Fukuoda Japan, Tel: (092) 761-3031.

Genoa, Italy: Indonesian Consulate, Via Fiesche No. 319 Genoa, Italy, Tel: 268322.

Hamburg, Germany: Indonesian Consulate General, Bebelallee 15, 2000 Hamburg 60, Federal Republic of Germany, Tel: (040) 512071, 512072, 512073, Telex: 212906 RIHAMB D, Cable: PERWAKILAN HAMBURG.

Hannover, Germany: Indonesia Consulate, Gerog Platz 1, d-3000 Hannover, Federal Republic of Germany, Tel: (0511) 10 32 150.

Helsinki, Finland: Indonesian Consulate General, Papeerinkerays Oy, Aielsanterinkatu 48 B, 00100 Helsinki 10, Finland, Tel: 17 70 15, 17 59 75.

Hongkong: Indonesian Consulate General, 127-129 Leighton Road, (6-8 Koswick, St. Entrance), Tel: HK (5) 8904421-8, Telex: 802-73270 INDON HK, Cable: INDONESIA HONGKONG.

Houston, U.S.A: Indonesian Consulate General, 5633 Richmond Avenue Houston, Texas 77057, Tel: (713) 785-1691, Cable: INDONESIA HOUSTON.

Honolulu, Hawaii, U.S.A: Indonesia Consulate, Pri Tower 733 Bishop Street, P.O. Box: 3379 Honolulu, Hawaii 96842, U.S.A Tel: (808) 524-4300.

Karachi, Pakistan: Indonesia Consulate, E/1-5, Clifton Karachi-6, Pakistan, Tel: 531938, 530944, 530932, Telex: 23367 INSIA PK, Cable: PERWAKILAN KARACHI.

Kiel, Germany: Indonesia Consulate, Sophienblatt 33 D.2300 Kiel, Federal Republic of Germany, Tel: (0431) 6032010.

Kota Kinabalu, Sabah, Malaysia: Indonesian Consulate General, Jl. Coastral, Karamunsing, P.O. Box: 11595, 88817 Kota Kinabalu, Sabah, Malaysia, Tel: 54100, 54245, 55110 53571, Telex: 80039 ANSWER BACK : KRIKK MA 80039, Cable: PERWAKILAN KOTA KINABALU.

Kobe, Japan: Indonesian Consulate General, Kato Building 3rd floor, 76-1, Kyomachi, Chuo-ku Kobe 650, Tel: (078) 321-1656, Fax: (078) 392-0792, Telex: 5624166, INDKOB J, Cable: PERWAKILAN KOBE.

Los Angeles, U.S.A: Indonesian Consulate General, 3457 Wilshire Boulevard, Los Angeles, CA, 90010, U.S.A, Tel: 213/385, 5126-8, Telex: 674415, Cable: INDONESIA LOS ANGELES.

Luxembourg: Indonesian Consulate, 15, Gote d Eich Luxembourg, G.D. Luxembourg, Tel: 00352/471591.

Marseille, France: Indonesian Consulate, 25, Boulevard Carmagnole, 13008 – Marseille, France, Tel: 9171 35 35, Telex: 430744 INDOMAR, Cable: INDOMAS.

Melbourne, Australia: Indonesian Consulate, 3rd floor, 52 Albert Road, South Melbourne, Victoria 3205, Australia, Tel: (03) 690-7811, Telex: Krimel AA 35223, Cable: PERWAKILAN MELBOURNE

MonteVideo, Uruguay: Indonesian Consulate, Avenida Brasil 3074, Piso – 6 Montevideo, Uruguay, Tel: 78-2043.

Munich, Germany: Indonesian Consulate, Widermayer Strasse 24 d-8000 Muenchen 22, Federal Republic of Germany, Tel: (089) 294609.

Napoli, Italy: Indonesian Consulate, Via S. Pasquale No. 55 Napoli, Italy, Tel: 400143.

New York, U.S.A: Indonesian Consulate General, 5, East 68th Street, New York, N.Y. 10021 U.S.A, Tel: (212) 879-0600, Telex: 12-7652 (PERWAKILAN NYK), Fax: (212) 570-6206, Cable: PERWAKILAN NEW YORK.

Penang, Malaysia: Indonesian Consulate, 467 Jl. Burma, P.O. Box. 502, 10350 Pulau Pinang, Malaysia, Tel: (04) 25162, 25163 & 374956, Telex: NA. 40656, Cable: PERWAKILAN PENANG.

Perth, Australia: Indonesian Consulate, 133 St. George's Terrace Perth, WA 6000, Australia, Tel: 219821.

San Francisco, U.S.A: Indonesian Consulate, 1111 Columbus Avenue San Francisco, CA, 94133, Tel: (415) 474-9571, Telex: 278187 KRIS OR, Cable: INDONESIA SAN FRANCISCO.

Stuttgart, Germany: Indonesian Consulate General, Lenzhalie 65 d-7000 Stuttgart 1, Federal Republic of Germany, Tel: (0711) 22 37 29, Telex: 723985.

Sydney, Australia: Indonesian Consulate General, 236-238 Marcubra Road, Marcubra N.S.W. 2035, Sydney Australia, Tel: (02) 3449933, Telex: KJRI SD AA 27366, Cable: PERWAKILAN SYDNEY.

Sapporo, Japan: Indonesian Consulate, 883-3 Chome 4-jo, Miyayanomori, Chuo-ku, Sapporo Shi's Sapporo, Japan, Tel: (011) 251-6002 (day), (011) 643-4531 (night).

Trieste, Italy: Indonesian Consulate, Via di campo Marzia No. 4, Trieste, Italy, Tel: 765601, 765602.

Toronto, Canada: Indonesian Consulate, 425 University Avenue 9th floor, Toronto Ontario M5G 1T6 Canada, Tel: (416) 5916481, 5916462, Fax: (416) 5916613, Cable: INDONESIA TORONTO.

Vancouver, Canada: Indonesian Consulate, 1455 West Georgia Street, 2nd floor, Vancouver, B.C. Canada V6G 2T3, Tel: (604) 682-8855, Fax: (604) 662-8396, Telex: 04-508353 INDONESIA VCR.

INTERNATIONAL AIRLINES IN JAKARTA

On Line

Cathay Pacific: Borobudur Inter-Continental, Jl. Lapangan Banteng Selatan, Tel: 3806664, 3700108 Ext. 76087

China Airlines: Duta Merlin Jl. Gajah Mada, Tel: 354448/354449/353195.

Garuda Indonesia: Danareksa Building, 11th, 13, Jl. Merdeka Selatan, Tel: 3801901.

Japan Airlines: Mid Plaza Jl. Jend. Sudirman, Tel: 5703883/5703189.

KLM Royal Dutch Airlines: Plaza Indonesia Jl. M.H. Thamrin, Tel: 320708/320053.

Korean Airlines: Ground floor, Wisma Metropolitain II, Jl. Jend Sudirman, Tel: 5780236/257/258/262.

Lufthansa: Panin Centre Bldg Jl. Jend. Sudirman, Tel: 710247-251.

Malaysia Airlines: Hotel Indonesia Jl. M.H. Thamrin, Tel: 320909.

Philippines Airlines: Hotel Borobudur Inter-Continental, Jl. Lapangan Banteng Selatan, Tel: 3805555/ 370333.

Qantas: BDN Building Jl. M.H. Thamrin, Tel: 327707/326707.

Royal Brunei Airlines: GSA: Duta Cardindo, 33-B, Jl. Hasyim Ashari, Tel: 373741/367853.

Saudia: Ground floor, Wisma Bumi Putera, 75, Jl. Jend. Sudirman, Tel: 5780873/5780615/5780628.

Singapore Airlines: Ground floor, Chase Plaza, Jl. Jend Sudirman, Tel: 584040-1/5704204-4213/ 5704403-4423.

Swiss Air: Hotel Borobudur Inter-Continental, Jl. Lapangan Banteng Selatan, Tel: 373608.

Thai International: BDN Building, Jl. M.H. Thamrin, Tel: 320607.

UTA: 9th floor, Summitmas Tower, 61, Jl Jend. Sudirman, Tel: 5202263/5202262.

Off Line

Air India: Hotel Sari Pasific Jl. M.H. Thamrin, Tel: 325534/325470.

British Airways: 10th floor, Wisma Metropolitan I, Jl. Jend. Sudirman, Tel: 5782460 (4 lines).

Sabena: Hotel Borobudur Inter-Continental, Jl. Lapangan Banteng Selatan, Tel: 371915/372039.

S.A.S: S. Wijoyo Centre 57, Jl. Jenderal Sudirman, Tel: 584110.

General Sales Agents

Air Canada/Air New Zealand/Finnair: PT. Aviamas Megabuana, Ground floor, Chase Plaza, Jl. Jend. Sudirman Kav. 21, Tel: 588185, 588195, 588550.

Alitalia: Amaran International Courier, Ground floor, Wisma Metropolitan II, Jl. Jend. Sudirman, Tel: 5781710.

American Airlines: PT. Aerojasa Perikasa, BDN Building 5, Jl. M.H. Thamrin, Tel: 325600, 325728, 325792.

Canadian Pacific: Iwata Tours and Travel, Wisma Kosgoro, 5th floor 53, Jl. M.H. Thamrin, Tel: 324742, 336521, 336397.

Continental Airlines/Eastern Airlines: PT. Golden Air Transport, Ground Floor BDN Annex Building, 5, Jl. M.H. Thamrin, Tel: 334417, 334418.

Delta Airlines: Tirta, Jakarta Jati Ltd, Hotel Indonesia, Jl. M.H. Thamrin, Tel: 320008 Ext. 149.

Hawaiian Airlines/Royal Brunel Airlines: PT. Delta Cardindo, Hotel Indonesia, Bali Arcade 8, Jl. M.H. Thamrin, Tel: 327214, 327265.

Northwest Orient: PT. Belco, Oriental Building, Jl. M.H. Thamrin, Tel: 320558, 326439.

Pakistan International Airlines: PT. Belco, Oriental Building, Jl. M.H. Thamrin, Tel: 357542, 345278.

Trans World Airlines: PT. Ayuberga, P.P. Building, Jl. M.H. Thamrin, Tel: 321979, 326810.

United Airlines: PT. Samudra Indonesia Dirgantara, Hotel Borobudur Inter-Continental, Jl. Lapangan Banteng Selatan, Tel: 361707.

There are many "musts" in Jakarta, but be forewarned about trying to do too much. Two major sights or areas of the city a day are enough. Take a siesta or a swim in between to recover from the heat. Get an early start in the cool morning hours, do your errands and sightseeing, then get in out of the noonday sun before venturing out again in the late afternoon and early evening when the weather has cooled off and the crowds are thinner.

GETTING THERE

JAKARTA

There are five major train stations, one airport and three inter-city bus terminals in Jakarta. When making arrangements to leave the city, be sure to ask the name of the one you will be using.

Air: All Jakarta flights now operate to and from the international airport at Cengkareng, 20 km (12 miles) to the west of the city. An expressway links **Cengkareng** to the city's western edge, but from here heavy traffic can mean it will take about an hour to reach the central hotel districts.

Sea: All ocean-going vessels berth at **Tanjung Priok Harbour**, 10 km (6 miles) to the north-east of the city. Tanjung Priok is about half an hour and US$6 from the city centre by cab.

Train: There are five major train stations in Jakarta, but only two serve the First Class inter-city trains. **Kota Station** in the north of the city is the gateway for Central and East Java, whereas **Gambir Station** on the eastern side of Medan Merdeka serves trains bound for Bogor and Bandung.

Train tickets should be purchased one day in advance from **Carnation Travel Agency**, corner of Jl. Kebon Sirih and Jl. Menteng Raya (Jl. Menteng Raya 24, Jakarta Pusat, Tel: 344027, 356728 or else on the morning of your departure from the station ticket window. Allow 1 hour to reach the Kota Station during business hours, because of the heavy traffic in that part of town. Most trains depart in the afternoon, although the Parahiangan trains to Bandung depart four times daily.

Gambir Station, Jl. Merdeka Timur, Tel: 342777, 352981.
Jakarta Kota Station, Jl. Station 1, Tel: 679194.

Bus: There are three bus terminals for buses operating to the west, the south, and the east of Jakarta. Buses to Sumatra and Java's west coast operate from **Grogol Terminal** (Tel: 592274) on the western edge of Jakarta. Those to Bandung, Bogor and other points south operate from **Cililitan terminal** (Tel: 803554) just beyond the old Halim Airport. Those to Central and East Java operate from **Pulo Gadung Terminal** (Tel: 4893742) where Jl. Bekasi Timur Raya meets Jl. Perintis Kemerdekaan. All buses terminals are connected by local city buses to the city centre. By cab they are not more than US$4 from the city centre. Inter-city buses also pick up passengers at their offices in the city, so if you know the address and don't mind getting there early and waiting on the bus as they collect passengers, you can save the trip out to the terminal.

Mini-buses/inter-city taxis: Best way to get to nearby cities like Bogor, Bandung or Cirebon. They will pick you up and deliver you directly to your destination, about same fare as the train and slightly more than an air-conditioned bus. They do not operate directly to more distant destinations. Ask your hotel to book seats for you a day or more in advance.

"4848" Inter-city taxis, Jl. Prapatan 34, Tel: 348048, 364488.
Media, Jl. Johan 15, Tel: 343643.
Metro, Jl. Kopi 2C, Tel: 674585/674000.
Parahyangan, Jl. R.H. Wahid Hasyim 13, Tel: 336155, 325539, 333434.

GETTING AROUND

At Jakarta's centre lies **Medan Merdeka** (Freedom Square), a vast parade ground crisscrossed by broad ceremonial boulevards, with the National Monument towering in its midst. Going north, the major artery is Jl. Gajah Mada/Jl. Hayam Wuruk, two one-way roads with a canal separating them. This is the older, commercial area of town, horribly congested throughout much of the day and practically deserted at night. At the north end of this artery lies the old colonial city and the old harbour, now both major tourist sights. To the east along the coast are Ancol, a sprawling entertainment complex, and Tanjung Priok, the port.

The "main street" of Jakarta is now **Jl. Thamrin/Jl. Jend. Sudirman**, which connects Medan Merdeka (the central square) with Kebayoran Baru (the satellite suburb). Many international hotels, office buildings, theatres, restaurants and nightclubs are on this street. To the east of Jl. Thamrin lie the older colonial residential areas of **Menteng, Cikini** and **Gondangdia**, with their luxurious mansions and tidy, tree-shaded streets. **Jl. Imam Bonjol/Jl. Diponegoro** is "Embassy Row", lined with many of the finest mansions in Jakarta and worth a quick drive or walkthrough. Many shops, boutiques and restaurants are in this area, as is TIM, the arts centre of Jakarta.

JAVA TRAIN TIMETABLE

1. JAKARTA - SURABAYA

TRAIN	ROUTE	DEPARTURE	ARRIVE
Gaya Baru Malam Selatan	Jakarta (Gambir) - Yogyakarta - Surabaya	12.15	04.30
BIMA 2	Jakarta - (Kota) - Yogyakarta - Semarang	15.30	05.43
MUTIARA 2 Utara	Jakarta (Kota) - Semarang - Surabaya	16.30	04.24
Gaya Baru Malam Utara	Jakarta (Ps. Senen) - Semarang - Surabaya	18.05	06.25

2. JAKARTA - SEMARANG

TRAIN	ROUTE	DEPARTURE	ARRIVE
Fajar Utama	Jakarta (Ps. Senen) Cirebon - Semarang	08.00	15.15
Senja Utama	Jakarta (Ps. Senen) Cirebon - Semarang	20.00	03.15
Senja Ekonomi	Jakarta (Ps. Senen) Cirebon - Semarang	12.15	04.30

3. JAKARTA - YOGYAKARTA - SOLO/SURAKARTA

TRAIN	ROUTE	DEPARTURE	ARRIVE
Senja Utama	Jakarta (Gambir) - Cirebon - Yogyakarta - Solo	13.15	03.30 (Yogya)
Senja Utama	Jakarta (Gambir) - Yogyakarta - Solo - Cirebon	17.50	04.27 (Yogya)
Senja Utama (Yogyakarta)	Jakarta (Gambir) - Cirebon - Yogyakarta	19.30	04.43 (Yogya)
Fajar Utama (Yogyakarta)	Jakarta (Gambir) - Cirebon	07.00	15.27 (Yogya)
Senja Ekonomi (Solo)	Jakarta (Tanah Abang) - Cirebon - Yogyakarta	21.10	09.05 (Solo)
Senja Ekonomi (Yogyakarta)	Jakarta (Gambir) - Cirebon - Yogyakarta	20.15	- 05.51 (Yogya)

4. JAKARTA - BANDUNG

TRAIN	ROUTE	DEPARTURE	ARRIVE
Parahyangan 2	Jakarta (Kota) - Bandung	05.30	08.33
Parahyangan 4	Jakarta (Kota) - Bandung	09.20	12.33
Parahyangan 6	Jakarta (Kota) - Bandung	11.20	14.33
Parahyangan 8	Jakarta (Kota) - Bandung	13.20	16.33
Parahyangan 10	Jakarta (Kota) - Bandung	15.20	18.33
Parahyangan 12	Jakarta (Gambir) - Bandung	16.50	20.33
Parahyangan 14	Jakarta (Gambir) - Bandung	18.55	21.47
Parahyangan 16	Jakarta (Gambir) - Bandung	20.40	23.33

5. JAKARTA - CIREBON

TRAIN	ROUTE	DEPARTURE	ARRIVE
Cirebon Express 2	Jakarta - Cirebon	10.00	13.16
Cirebon Express 4	Jakarta - Cirebon	15.35	18.51
Gunung Jati 2	Jakarta - Cirebon	07.00	10.52

Taxis: By far the most practical way of getting around the city and fares are reasonable. The flag down fare is currently Rp 600 or about US30¢ for the first km (0.6 miles) and Rp 20 for each subsequent 100 metres. It costs about US$2 to US$5 for most cross-town journeys. Cabs are available at any hotel and easily hailed on major roads. President and Bluebird are the largest and generally the most reliable companies. Radio cabs may be summoned by phone. Be sure the meter is on when you get in, and that it stays on for the entire journey. Some cabbies will try and take you for a ride. It is a good idea to rent a cab by the hour if you intend making a lot of stops. Tipping is not customary, but drivers rarely have change, so carry some with you and even then be prepared to round off to the nearest Rp 500 (US50¢).

Rental Cars: Available with drivers from Avis and Hertz or from any major hotel. Hourly or daily rates are available within the city; trips out of town are charged on a round-trip basis according to a fixed schedule. For example, a trip to Bogor and back will cost roughly US$25 for a total distance of almost 160 km (100 miles) and an elapsed time of between 3 and 4 hours.

Avis Car Rental, Jl. Diponegoro 25, Tel: 331974, 332900.
Bluebird Taxi, Jl. H.O.S. Cokroaminoto No. 107, Tel: 325607, 333461, 333485.
Hertz Car Rental, Jl. Teuku Cik Ditiro 11E, Tel: 332610, 332739.
Multi Sri, Jl. Diponegoro No. 25, Tel: 334495.
National Car Rental, Jl. M.H. Thamrin No. 10, Kartika Plaza Hotel, Tel: 333423.

City Buses: Cheap (Rp 100 fixed fare), but often crowded and sometimes dangerous as they do not stop completely when picking up and discharging passengers. You must also beware of pickpockets, especially during peak hours. Your hotel staff can advise you which buses to take, and a bus map is sometimes available from the **Tourist Information Centre** in the Jakarta Theatre Building on Jl. Thamrin.

WHERE TO STAY

ACCOMMODATION

Jakarta has come a long way since the 1960s, when the only international-class hotel in town was the Hotel Indonesia, built by the Japanese as a war reparation. Of the older, pre-war establishments, only the Transaera and the Royal remain, but neither is truly "colonial" in ambience.

HOTELS

Luxury Class
(Above US$125 per night)

Jakarta now has five five-star hotels. Two have extensive grounds and sports facilities: the **Borobudur Intercontinental** and the **Jakarta Hilton**. In addition to Olympic-size swimming pools, tennis courts, squash courts, health clubs, jogging tracks and spacious gardens, they also boast dancing discos and a full complement of European and Asian restaurants. The other hotels in the same category, the **Mandarin,** the **Hyatt,** and the **Sahid Jaya** are newer "city" hotels-providing central locations and emphasising superior service and excellent food.

Borobudur Intercontinental (1172 rooms), Jl. Lapangan Banteng Selatan, P.O. Box 329, Jakarta, Tel: 3805555/370333, Fax: 359741.
Grand Hyatt, Jl. M.H. Thamrin, KAV 28, Jakarta, Tel: 335551.
Hyatt Aryaduta (340 rooms), Jl. Prapatan 44-46, P.O. Box 3287, Jakarta, Tel: 376008, Fax: 349836.
Jakarta Hilton International (664 rooms), Jl. Jend. Gatot Subroto, P.O. Box 3315, Jakarta, Tel: 583051, 587991, Fax: 583991.
Jakarta Mandarin (467 rooms), Jl. M.H. Thamrin, P.O. Box 3392, Jakarta, Tel: 321307.
Le Meridien Jakarta, Jl. Jend. Sudirman, Tel: 588250, Fax: 588252.
Sahid Jaya Hotel (514 rooms), Jl. Jend. Sudirman 86, P.O. Box 41, Jakarta, Tel: 587031, 581376.

First Class
(US$75 to US$125 per night)

There are another half-dozen or so first-class hotels in town. The **Sari Pacific** is centrally located and has a popular coffee shop and deli. The **Horison** has a restaurant specialising in seafood and the best croissants in town. The **President Hotel** is Japanese operated with several Japanese restaurants. And the venerable **Hotel Indonesia** has a supper club with nightly floor shows and a swimming pool garden open to the public (US$4 admission).

Horison Hotel (350 rooms), Jl. Pantai Indah, Taman Impian Jaya Ancol, P.O. Box 3340, Jakarta, Tel: 680008, Fax: 684004.

Hotel Indonesia (611 rooms), Jl. M.H. Thamrin, P.O. Box 54, Jakarta, Tel: 320008, 322008, Fax: 321508.

Jayakarta Tower (310 rooms), Jl. Hayam Wuruk 126, Jakarta, Tel: 624408, Fax: 6496760.

Kartika Chandra (146 rooms), Jl. Jend. Gatot Subroto, Jakarta, Tel: 511008, Fax: 5204238.

President Hotel (354 rooms), Jl. M.H. Thamrin 59, Tel: 320508, Fax: 333631.

Sari Pacific Hotel (500 rooms), Jl. M.H. Thamrin 6, P.O. Box 3128, Jakarta, Tel: 323707, Fax: 323650.

Intermediate
(US$35 to US$80 per night)

At the upper end of the moderate price range, the most centrally located hotel is the **Sabang Metropolitan** (about US$35 and up for a double), convenient for business and shopping. The three **Menteng** Hotels (I, II and Grand) in Cikini are popular with businessmen paying their own way. The once-sleazy **Marco Polo** has now been upgraded, and has the best breakfast value in town.

In Kebayoran Baru, you may opt to stay at the **Kemang** or the **Kebayoran Inn**, both popular with frequent visitors for their reasonable prices and quiet, residential surroundings. Or try the **Interhouse**, centrally located by Kebayoran's shopping district, Blok M.

Garden Hotel (116 rooms), Jl. Kemang Raya, P.O. Box 41, Kebayoran Baru, Jakarta, Tel: 715808.

Interhouse Hotel (130 rooms), Jl. Melawai Raya 18-20, P.O. Box 128, Kebayoran Baru, Jakarta, Tel: 716408.

Kartika Plaza (331 rooms), Jl. M.H. Thamrin 10, P.O. Box 2081, Jakarta, Tel: 321008, Fax: 322547.

Kebayoran Inn (61 rooms), Jl. Senayan 57, Kebayoran Baru, Jakarta, Tel: 716208.

Kemang Hotel (100 rooms), Jl. Kemang Raya, P.O. Box 163, Kebayoran Baru, Jakarta, Tel: 793208.

Marco Polo Hotel (181 rooms), Jl. Teuku Cik Ditiro 19, Jakarta, Tel: 375208.

Menteng I (71 rooms), Jl. Gondangdia Lama, Jakarta, Tel: 352508.

Menteng II (70 rooms), Jl. Cikini Raya 105, Jakarta, Tel: 325543.

Orchid Palace (85 rooms), Jl. Letjend. S. Parman, Slipi, P.O. Box 2791, Jakarta, Tel: 593115, 596911, Fax: 599584.

Putri Duyung Cottages (111 cottages), Taman Impian Jaya Ancol, Jakarta, Tel: 680611, 680108.

Sabang Metropolitan (157 rooms), Jl. H. Agus Salim 11, P.O. Box 2725, Jakarta, Tel: 354031, 357621, Fax: 3711083.

Transaera Hotel (50 rooms), Jl. Merdeka Timur 16, P.O. Box 3380, Jakarta, Tel: 351373, 359336, 357621.

Wisata International (165 rooms), Jl. M.H. Thamrin, P.O. Box 2457, Jakarta, Tel: 320308, 320408.

Budget
(Under US$20 per night)

True budget travellers almost invariably stay at Jl. Jaksa No. 5 (**Wisma Delima**) or one of the other homestays on that street. In the US$3 to US$5 a night class, the **Borneo Hostel** around the corner and the **Pondok Soedibyo** are perhaps cleaner. The nearby **Bali International** costs more at US$10. At the **Royal** a double room with fan and breakfast costs US$18, and for a bit more you can get an air-conditioned room at the **Srivijaya**.

Bali International (31 rooms), Jl. K.H. Wahid Hasyim 116, Tel: 334967, 325067.

Borneo Hostel, Jl. Kebun Sirih Barat Dalam 35, Jakarta, Tel: 320095.

Pondok Soedibyo, Jl. Kebon Sirih 23, Jakarta.

Royal Hotel (60 rooms), Jl. Juanda 14, Jakarta, Tel: 348894, 357068.

Srivijaya Hotel (106 rooms), Jl. Veteran 1, Jakarta, Tel: 370409.

Wisma Delima, Jl. Jaksa 5.

Wisma Esther, Jl. Matraman Raya 113.

FOOD DIGEST

Dining in Jakarta can be a delightful experience, though restaurant meals are expensive here by Indonesian standards and the food is highly uneven in quality. Locals seek out obscure roadside stalls (*warung*) for a special *soto* or *sate* but many visitors are hit with a stomach bug and this can ruin a week or more of your stay. It is possible to eat a meal for US$2 and truly excellent Indonesian or Chinese food can be had for US$5 a head. With the exception of Western-style food and service, a meal at the best restaurants will rarely cost more than US$10 per person, all inclusive. Seafood of any sort is excellent so don't leave Jakarta without sampling some.

WHERE TO EAT

Indonesian Food: Indonesian food is of course the traveller's first choice in Jakarta, particularly as one may indulge in gastronomic island hopping on consecutive nights.

Beginning with the northern tip of Sumatra, try the Acehnese restaurant, **Sinar Medan**, conveniently located on Jl. Sabang. Acehnese food is displayed and served cold on many small plates, in the same way as Padang food, but some say it is more delicately spiced, with a wider range of flavours.

The best Padang food is found at **Roda** and **Sari Bundo**. Here, as in all Padang restaurants, between 10 and 15 spicy dishes are placed in front of you and you pay only for what you eat. For slightly more atmosphere and a view (and at higher prices), try **The Pepper Pot**.

Javanese cuisine may be divided into four categories: Sundanese (West Javanese), Central Javanese, East Javanese and Madurese cooking. For an excellent Sundanese meal of grilled carp (*ikan mas bakar*), grilled chicken (*ayam bakar*), prawns (*udang pancet*), barbequed squid (*cumicumi bakar*) and a raw vegetable salad with shrimp paste chili sauce (*lalap/sambal cobek*), try the popular **Sari Kuring**. This is, incidentally, one of the best seafood places in town, and serves a deliciously cooling cucumber and lime-juice drink.

The Central Javanese delicacies are fried chicken and *gudeg*. Javanese chickens are farmyard chickens, allowed to run free in the village. As a result they are full of flavour but very tough in comparison with factory feed chickens in the West. The Javanese boil their chickens first in a concoction of rich spices and coconut cream for several hours, before deep frying them for about a minute at very high temperatures to crisp the outer coating.

The two famous fried chicken places in Jakarta are both in Kebayoran: **Ayam Bulungan** and **Ayam Goreng Nyonya Suharti**.

Gudeg is the speciality of Yogyakarta, consisting of young jackfruit boiled in coconut cream and spices, served with buffalo hide boiled in chili sauce, chicken pieces, egg and gray. The best *gudeg* is to be had at a branch of the Yogya restaurant, **Bu Tjitro's**.

East Java and Madura are known for their soups and their·*sate*. For *soto madura* (spicy chicken broth with noodles or rice), the best place is **Pondok Jawa Timur**. For chicken or mutton *sate* (barbequed meat skewers), the **Senayan Satay House** has a near monopoly on the Jakarta Scene, with its three convenient locations.

For street food in hygenic surroundings, the basement of **Sarinah Pasaraya** in Blok M has stalls serving food from throughout the archipelago, with European and Japanese thrown in.

For the visitor's convenience here follows a list of restaurants and even stalls, where they can dine and take their time.

Ayam Bulungan, Jl. Bulungan No. 64, Tel: 772005.
Ayam Goreng Monas, Jl. Silang Monas, Tel: 363756.
Ayam Goreng Pemuda, Jl. Tomang Raya 32.
Ayam Goreng Ratu, Jl. Hayam Wuruk No. 81, Tel: 6292163.
Ayam Goreng Mbok Berek, Jl. Prof .Supomo No. 2.
Ayam Goreng Mardun, Jl. Mangga Besar VIII/78C, Tel: 6290229.
Athitya Loka, Satriamandala Museum, Jl. Jend. Gatot Subroto, Tel: 516102.
Gudeg Bu Tjitro, Jl. Cikajang No. 80, Tel: 713202.
Handayani, Jl. Abdul Muis No. 35E, Tel: 373614.
Jawa Tengah, Jl. Pemuda, Tel: 884197.
Jawa Timur, Jl. Jend. A. Yani No. 67, Tel: 884197.
Kadipolo, Jl. Panglima Polim Raya, Tel: 710739.
Lembur Kuring, Jl. Asia Afrika, Senayan.
Lingkung Lembur, Jl. Jend. A. Yani No. 2.
Natrabu, Jl. H. Agus Salim No. 9A, Tel: 371709.
Oasis, Jl. Raden Saleh No. 47, Tel: 327818.
Pujasera I, Jl. Mangga Besar 65, Tel: 6592445.
Pujasera II, Gedung Depnaker, Jl, Gatot Subroto.
Regina's, Jl. Melawai Raya 71, Tel: 732813.
Rice Bowl, Wisma Nusantara Building 30th Fl., Jl. M.H. Thamrin, Tel: 337813.
Salero Bagindo, Jl. Panglima Polim 107, Tel: 772713, 733571; Jl. Kebon Sirih 79, Tel: 3103047.
Sari Kuring, Jl. Silang Monas Timur 88, Tel: 352972, 362203/4; Jl. Matraman Raya No. 69, Tel: 881968; Jl. Batuceper 55 A, Tel: 341542.
Sari Madu, Jl. Paglima Polim IX, Tel: 7390447, 774772.
Senayan Satay House, Jl. Kebon Sirih 31A, Tel: 326239; Jl. Pakubuwono VI/6, Tel: 715821; Jl. Tanah Abang 11/76, Tel: 347270; Jl. H.O.S. Cokroaminoto No.78, Tel: 344248.

Seafood: Seafood was formerly eaten either at Tanjung Priok, near the harbour, or on Jl. Pecenongan at streetside stalls. Although these places are still popular, the prices have risen so that it is just as cheap, and far more pleasant, to eat seafood in a good restaurant. The most famous one is **Yun Njan**, formerly of Tanjung Priok. The atmosphere here is somewhat plastic and busy, but the plates of steamed, grilled or fried crab, fish, prawns and squid are unfailingly fresh. Another good place nearby is the **Sanur** which also has a full menu of Chinese delicacies. The **Sari Kuring** mentioned above and located next to Yun Njan, also has excellent seafood. More pricey but excellent Chinese seafood can be had at the **Mina Restaurant** in the Sahid Jaya Hotel. The **Horison Hotel** in Ancol also has a charming seafood restaurant, right by the sea.

SEAFOOD RESTAURANTS

Perahu Bugis, Horison Hotel, Ancol, Tel: 680008.
Mina restaurant, Sahid Jaya Hotel, Jl. Jend. Sudirman 86, Tel: 584151, 583981.
Sanur, Jl. Ir. H. Juanda III/No. 31.

Sari Kuring, Jl. Batu Ceper No. 55A, Tel: 341542.
Yun Njan, Jl. Batu Ceper 69, Tel: 364063, 364434.

Chinese Food: The Chinese food served in Jakarta cannot compare to that in Singapore, Hong Kong or Taiwan, but it's very popular and compares favourably to Chinese food in the West. The premier banquet houses are the Cahaya Kota and the Istana Naga. For northern Chinese/Mongolian cuisine, try the Barbeque Restaurant in Blok M, Kebayoran.

While visiting the Chinatown/Kota area, or in fact for a light lunch anywhere, it is de rigeur to sample a bowl of Chinese noodles with chopped pickled vegetables and beefballs (mee bakso). The largest noodle house in Chinatown is Bakmie Gajah Mada.

CHINESE RESTAURANTS

Angke Restaurant, Jl. Mangga Besar No. 32, Tel: 6297254.
Bakmie Gajah Mada, Jl. Gajah Mada No. 92, Tel: 6294689; Jl. Melawai VI/25, Tel: 773975.
Bakso Super, Jl. Gajah Mada, (Gajah Mada Plaza Lt. 1).
Bakmie Naga, Jl. Melawai IV/43, Jl. Matraman Raya.
Bakmie Summer Palace, Jl. Cikini Raya 60B, Tel: 321653, 321654, 321657.
Blue Ocean, Jl. Hayam Wuruk 5, Tel: 366650.
Brilliant Palace, Jl. Ir. H. Juanda No. 17, Tel: 360813, 360679.
Cahaya Kota, Jl. K.H. Wahid Hasyim 9, Tel: 353015, 342436.
Chopstick, Jl. Persahabatan Timur No. l.
Fajar, Golden Truly Supermarket, Jl. Suryopranoto No. 8A, Tel: 356609, 356660.
Flamingo, Hai Lai Building, 2nd Fl., Ancol, Tel: 680028, 683227.
Furama, Jl. Hayam Wuruk 72, Tel: 632599, 636372.
Dragon Gate, Jl. Ir. H. Juanda No. 19, Tel: 360813, 360619.
Istana Naga, Jl. Jend. Gatot Subroto, Tel: 511809.
Jade Garden, Jl. Blora No. 5 Tel: 334928, 333084.
Jumbo, Jl. Hayam Wuruk No. 100, Tel: 6391081.
Moon Palace, Jl. Melawai VIII/15A, Tel: 711765.
Oriental, Jl. Hayam Wuruk 120, Tel: 6293340.
Palace, Gajah Mada Plaza, Jl. Gajah Mada 1926, Tel: 357725.
Paramount, Jl. Blora No. 35, Jl. Teuku Cik Ditiro, Tel: 353111.
President Restaurant, Jl. Gajah Mada 186, Tel: 6290008, 6290246.
Sim Yan, Gajah Mada Plaza, Jl. Gajah Mada 1926, Tel: 353655.
Sky Room Permai, Duta Merlin, Jl. Gajah Mada 305, Tel: 372225.
Summer Palace, Tedja Buana Building, 7th Fl., Jl. Menteng Raya 29, Tel: 332989, 332970.
Ratu Bahari, Jl. Batuceper No. 59, Tel: 370918.
Nelayan, Hai Lai Building, Ancol.
Kingdom, Taman Impian Jaya Ancol, Tel: 681778.

European Food: European Food is available in every first class hotel, but is seldom good. For a night out, try the magnificent Oasis Restaurant, a turn-of-the-century mansion turned eatery. Specialities of the house include a flaming sword shishkebab and the traditional Dutch colonial rijsttafel ("rice table") consisting of 20 Indonesian dishes served by 16 attractive young ladies. Rijsttafel is also the speciality of the Club Noordwijk, which has a tempo doeloe ("olden times") atmosphere in a somewhat less regal setting. Both establishments provide nightly musical entertainment. A less expensive place for Indische colonial food and atmosphere is the Arts and Curios Restaurant and Art Shop, located near TIM, the performing arts centre of Jakarta.

For French cuisine with a local touch, many residents are devotees of Rima Melati's Le Petit Bistro, although the Mandarin and the Hyatt Hotels also boast fine French eateries replete with both traditional and nouvelle cuisines. The Coffee Shop in the Sari Pacific Hotel is the popular place for breakfast and brunch, as it serves the best breads and croissants in Jakarta, prepared by a French pastry chef. For an evening steak, you can try one of the many Ponderosa,chain restaurants. Of course, all hotels have coffee shops for breakfast, lunch and a late night snack Hotel Indonesia's Ramayana Coffee Shop is a popular place.

EUROPEAN RESTAURANTS

Arts & Curios, Jl. Kebon Binatang III/8A, Tel: 8322879.
Cafe Expresso, Jl. Kemang Raya 3A, Tel: 797754.
Casablanca, Kuningan Palza, Jl. H.R. Rasuna Said Kuningan, Tel: 514800, 5781175.
Club Noerdwijk, Jl. Ir. H. Juanda 5A, Tel: 353909.
East West Barbeque, Lina Building, 6th Fl., Jl. H.R. Rasuna Said Kuningan, Tel: 582283, 587731 ext. 205.
Front Page, Jl. Merdeka Selatan (Wisma Antara Building), Tel: 348045.
Gandy Steak House, Jl. Gajah Mada 82A, Tel: 622127; Jl. Melawai VIII/2, Tel: 774337; Jl. H.O.S. Cokroaminoto, Tel: 333292.
Kallista Restaurant & Lounge, Jl. Panglima Polim Raya 35, Tel: 714696, 773056.
La Bodega, Jl. Terogong Raya, Cilandak, Tel: 767798.
Le Bistro, Jl. K.H. Wahid Hasyim 75, Tel: 364272.
Le Fonda, Jl. Ir. H. Juanda 4B, Tel: 365390.
Melawai Barbeque, Jl. Melawai Raya No. 7.
Memories, Wisma Indocement, Gr. Fl., Jl. Jend. Sudirman, Tel: 5781008.
Oasis, Jl. Raden Saleh 47, Tel: 326397, 327818.
Orleans, Jl. Adityawarman 67, Tel: 715695.
Pete's Club, Gunung Sewu Building, Jl. Jend. Gatot Subroto, Tel: 515478.
Pinocchio, Wisma Metropolitan I, Top Fl., Jl. Jend. Sudirman, Tel: 514736.
Pizza Hut, Jakarta Theatre Building, Jl. M.H.

Thamrin 9, Tel: 352064, 342049; Pondok Indah, Jl. Lapangan Hijau 3, Tel: 764028; Jl. Jend. Haryono, Tebet, Tel: 826096.

Pizzaria, Hilton Hotel, Jl. Jend. Gatot Subroto, Tel: 583051.

Ponderosa (Steak House), Wisma Antara, Jl. Merdeka Selatan. Tel: 348045, 342398; S. Widojo Centre, Jl. Jend. Sudirman, Tel: 583823, 587731 ext. 205, 251; Centre Point Building, Jl. Jend. Gatot Subroto, Tel: 5780480, 5780202 ext. 1001, 1002; Arthaloka Building, Jl. Jend. Sudirman, Tel: 583280.

Raffles Tavern, Ratu Plaza, 3rd Fl., Jl. Jend. Sudirman, Tel: 711894.

Shakey's Pizza, Jl. Bulungan 8, Kebayoran Baru, Tel: 770288.

The Black Angus, Jl. H.O.S. Cokroaminoto 86A, Tel: 331551.

The Club Room, Mandarin Hotel, Jl. M.H. Thamrin, Tel: 359141.

The George & Dragon, Jl. Teluk Betung 32, Tel: 325625.

The Green Pub, Jakarta Theatre Building, Jl. M.H. Thamrin 9, Tel: 359332; Setiabudi Building, Jl. H.R. Rasuna Said Kuningan, Tel: 356559.

The Palm Beach, Prince Centre Building, Jl. Jend. Sudirman, Tel: 586683.

The Swiss Inn, Arthakoka Building, Jl. Jend. Sudirman 2, Tel: 583280.

The Thistle Bar & Restaurant, Wisma Metropolitan, 18th Fl., Jl. Jend. Sudirman, Tel: 584736.

Toba Rotisserie, Borobudur Intercontinental Hotel, Tel: 5781659.

Other Asian Fare: Finally, there are a handful of Japanese, Korean, Indian and Thai restaurants. The big Japanese chains are well represented here, with the **Ginza Benkay** (President Hotel) and the **Jakarta Okoh** (Horison Hotel) and the **Keio** (Borobudur Intercontinental) all having branches with imported food, furnishing, cooks and prices. One small Japanese establishment stands out from the rest by virtue of the fact that it is the oldest in Jakarta and serves locally caught and grown delicacies at reasonable prices: the **Kikugawa**, located in a converted house near TIM. The several Korean restaurants in town, all owned by Koreans, are reasonably good.

KOREAN RESTAURANTS

Arirang, Jl. Gereja Theresia 1, Tel: 3100151.

Daewon, Jl. Sunan Kalijaga No. 65, Tel: 713266, 717097.

Korean Garden, Jl. Teluk Betung 33, Tel: 322544.

Korean International, Jl. Melawai VI/No. 3 (Blok M), Kebayoran, Tel: 713776.

Korean Tower, BBD Plaza, Jl. Imam Bonjol, Tel: 330311, 330312.

New Korean House, Kuningan Plaza North Tower, Jl. Rasuna Said, Tel: 513800.

Seoul House, Jl. Teluk Betung 38, Tel: 321817.

JAPANESE RESTAURANTS

Asuka, Central Plaza Building, Jl. Jend. Sudirman, Tel: 511608, 511978.

Chikuyo Tei, Summitmas Tower, Gr. Fl., Jl. Jend. Sudirman, Tel: 588220.

Furusatu, Sari Pacific Hotel, Jl. M.H. Thamrin, Tel: 323707.

Ginza Benkay, President Hotel, Jl. M.H. Thamrin, Tel: 320508.

Jakarta New Hama, 4th Fl., Ratu Plaza, Jl. Jend. Sudirman, Tel: 711895, 711333.

Jakarta Nippon Kan, Jakarta Hilton, Tel: 586111 ext. 627, 628.

Jakarta Okoh, Horison Hotel, Tel: 680008 ext. 111, 129.

Kasuga, Prince Centre, Jl. Jend. Sudirman 34, Tel: 586097.

Keio, Borobudur Intercontinental, Jl. Lepangan Banteng Selatan, Tel: 370108.

Kikugawa, Jl. Kebon Binatang III/No. 3, Tel: 341808.

Kobe, Dewan Press Building, Jl. Kebon Sirih, Tel: 352030.

Mitsuyo, Jl. Raden Saleh 44.

Ogayawa, Prince Centre Building, Jl. Jend. Sudirman 304, Tel: 584885, 586706.

Sagano, Jl. Mahakam 1/2, Tel: 772864.

Shima, 17th Fl., Hyatt Aryaduta Hotel, Jl Prapatan 44/48, Tel: 376008.

Shogun, Jl. Gajah Mada 77, Tel: 637799, 626841.

Takano, Jl. Cikini Raya 58C, Tel: 337550.

Tokyo Garden, LIPPO Life Building, Jl. H.R. Rasuna Said, Kuningan, Tel: 517828, 517069.

Yakiniku Daidomon, BBD Plaza, 30th Fl., Jl. Imam Bonjol, Tel: 320775, 320779.

Yamato, Panin Bank Centre, Jl. Jend. Sudirman, Tel: 712703, 710757.

Yamazato, Hotel Indonesia, Jl. M.H. Thamrin, Tel: 323875.

THAI RESTAURANTS

D'jit Pochana, Kehutanan Building, Gr. Fl., Jl. Jend. Gatot Subroto, Tel: 581784, 583034.

VIETNAMESE RESTAURANTS

Paregu, Jl. Sunan Kalijaga 64, Tel: 774894, 772191; Jl. H. Agus Salim 22, Tel: 337713.

SHOPPING

WHAT TO BUY

Jakarta is not known as a shopper's paradise – imported goods are heavily taxed and domestic manufactures can only rarely compete in quality, though they are cheap. The good buys are limited mainly to two categories: handicrafts and antiques.

"Batik": Batik Keris, with a showroom on Jln Cokroaminoto, has the largest selection of *batik* in Jakarta, particularly yard goods and inexpensive *kain*. Another big Solo-based *batik* maker, **Danar Hadi**, specialises in finer tulis work fabric and ready-made shirts and dresses. The **Government Batik Cooperative (GKBI)**, is rather disappointing – a place to get medium-grade Central Javanese *batik*. Connoisseurs will want to stop in at the shop of designer **Iwan Tirta**. For *batik* paintings, Yogya-based **Amri** is the best known artist. Smaller, quality boutiques selling a range of clothes and fabrics include **Srikandi** and several of the shops on Jl. Palatehan I (Blok M, Kebayoran). You may also want to see *batik* being produced at one of the factories in the Palmerah area. Try Berdikari or Hayadi.

Amri Gallery, Jl. Utan Kayu 66E.
Batik Berdikari, Jl. Masjid Pal VII, Palmerah Barat, Tel: 323663, 324579.
Batik Hajadi, Jl. Palmerah Utara 46, Tel: 540656, 540584.
Batik Mira, Jl. M.P.R. Raya 22, Tel: 761138.
Batik Semar, Jl. Tomang Raya 54, Tel: 593514.
Batik Wijaya, Jl. H. Agus Salim, Tel: 337891.
Danar Hadi, Jl. Raden Saleh 1A, Tel: 342390, 343712.
GKBI, Indonesian Government *Batik* Cooperative, Jl. Jend. Sudirman 28, Tel: 581022.
Hayadi, Jl. Pelmerah Utara 46, Tel: 5480584.
Iwan Tirta, Jl. Panarukan 25, Tel: 333122.
Jl. Kemang Raya Kay. 1, Kebayoran Baru, Jakarta Selatan. Tel: (021) 7998249.
Keris Gallery, 2nd Floor, Jl. HOS Cokroaminoto 87-89 Menteng, Jakarta Pusat, Tel: (021) 326993, 334516.
Ratu Plaza, Ground Floor, Jl. Jend. Sudirman, Jakarta. Tel: (021)711579.
Royal Batik Shop, Jl. Palatehan I/41, Tel: 773599.
Semar, Jl. Tomang Raya 54, Tel: 593514; Jl. Hang Lekir II, Tel: 771849, Sarinah Department Store 4th

Fl., Jl. M.H. Thamrin.
Sidomukti, Jl. Prof. Dr. Saharjo, Tel: 8291271.
Soekarno-Hatta Airport, Waiting Room Terminal A, Jakarta, Tel: (021) 5507092.
Srikandi, Jl. Melawai VI/6A, Tel: 736604; Jl. Cikini Raya 90, Tel: 354446.

Handicrafts: These are produced outside of Jakarta (with the exception of cane furniture and some *batik*). Nevertheless all are available in the city, and short of going to the original producer, you cannot get them cheaper elsewhere. The first stop for handicrafts of every description is the **Handicraft Centre** in the Sarinah Pasaraya Department Store in Kebayoran. Here you can get everything from baskets to cane chairs to leather sandals. Then for paintings, carvings, *wayang* puppets and other "art" items, spend an afternoon or evening at the **Art Market** (Pasar Seni) in Ancol, where you can observe crafts-men at work and chat with them.

Many of the antique and art shops at Jl. Kebon Sirih Timur Dalam, Jl. Majapahit and Jl. Paletehan (Kebayoran) also sell handicrafts. A few shops, such as the **Irian Art and Gift Shop** specialise in tribal handicrafts and primitive art.

Antiques and Curios: These are available throughout the city, but especially on **Jl. Kebon Sirih Timur Dalam**, where there are several tiny shops with names like **Bali**, **Bima**, **Djody** and **Nasrun**-all stocked with old furniture, weavings, masks, puppets and porcelains. Nearby **Johan Art** has one of the largest collections of old Chinese porcelains; they will refund your money if you are not satisfied with your purchase, a rarity in Jakarta. Farther down Jl. Wahid Hasyim is a shop specialising in pewter ware: **The Banka Tin Shop**. Several other shops are on Jl. H. Agus Salim (Jl. Sabang). All the above are within walking distance of Sarinah or the Sari Pacific Hotel. There are concentrations of antique and art shops in three other areas of the city: The **antique market** on Jl. Surabaya, near Embassy Row (Jl. Diponegoro) consists of about 20 stalls. Porcelains, puppets, tiles, brass and silver bric-a-brac-much of it new but made to look old-spill forth onto the sidewalk. Nearby, two homes house a cache of antique Dutch furniture: **Alex Papadimitriou's**, and the **Srirupa Shop**.

A new row of chic boutiques, galleries and studios catering to the foreign community and wealthy Jakartans is located in Kebayoran on **Jl. Palatehan I** (Djelita, Maison Young, Urip, Pura, Pigura, Royal, Tony's and Oet's).

Alex Papidimitriou (antiques), Jl. Pasuruan 3.
Arjuna Craft Shop, Jl. Majapahit 16 A, Tel: 344251.
Bali Art & Curio, Jl. Kebon Sirih Timur Dalam 42.
Bandung Art Shop, Jl. Pasar Baru 15, Tel: 360524.
Banka Tin Shop, Jl. K.H. Wahid Hasyim 178.
Bima Arts & Curios, Jl. Kebon Sirih Timur Dalam 257.

Djelita Art Shop, Jl. Palatehan I/37, Tel: 770347.
Djodi Art & Curio, Jl. Kebon Sirih Timur 22, Tel: 347730.
Garuda NV, Jl. Majapahit 12, Tel: 342712.
Hadiprana Gallery, Jl. Falatehan I/38, Tel: 771023.
Indonesian Bazaar, Jakarta Hilton Hotel, Jl. Jend. Gatot Subroto, Tel: 587981.
Irian Art and Gift Shop, Jl. Pasar Baru 16A, Tel: 343422.
Jakarta Handicraft Centre, Jl. Pekalongan 12A, Tel: 338157.
Johan Art Curio, Jl. H. Agus Salim 59A, Tel: 336023.
King's Gallery, Jl. H. Agus Salim 35, Tel: 323316; Jl. K.H. Hasyim Ashari 36, Tel: 345602.
Lee Cheong, Jl. Majapahit 32.
Lindungan Store, Jl. H. Agus Salim 48, Tel: 342819.
Lucky Art Shop, Jl. Ciputat Raya 2 Tel: 742774.
Made Handicraft, Jl. Pegangsaan Timur 2.
Magasin L'Art, Jl. Cikini Raya 71.
Majapahit Arts & Curios, Jl. Melawai III/4, Blok M, Kebayoran Baru, Tel: 715879.
Naini's Fine Arts, Jl. Palatehan I/20, Kebayoran Baru.
Pigura Art & Gift Shop, Jl. Palatehan I/41, Kebayoran Baru, Tel: 771143.
Pura Art Shop, Jl. Falatehan I-43, Tel: 773173.
Ramayana, Jl. Ir. H. Juanda 14A.
Srirupa Shop, Jl. Pekalongan 16.
Tony's Gallery, Jl. Palatehan I/31, Kebayoran Baru.
Urip Store, Jl. Palatehan I/40, Kebayoran Baru.

Jewellery: Many jewellery shops in Jakarta design and produce their own gold and silver work here. Prices are higher than in Kota Gede (Yogyakarta) and Bali, but the quality and designs are vastly superior-especially if you are interested in Indonesian gems: Borneo diamonds, purple amethyst, natural pearls and the West Javanese black opal. This can also be a good place to buy chains, filigree and *repousse* work. Labour is cheap and workmanship can be good. Check the papers for the current cost of gold and silver per gramme before shopping, so you know exactly how much you are paying for workmanship and design. Most of the quality shops are in the hotels:

Ana Gold, Gajah Mada Plaza I/F-39, Jl. Gajah Mada, Tel: 341437.
Christian Diamond Jewellery, Ratu Plaza G35-36, Jl. Jend. Sudirman, Tel: 711819.
Dinasty Collection, Ratu Plaza G8B, Jl. Jend. Sudirman, Tel: 711815.
F. Spiro Jewellers, Jakarta Hilton Hotel, Tel: 587441 ext. 618.
Jay's Jewellery, Shopping Arcade, Mandarin Oriental Hotel, Jl. M.H. Thamrin, Tel: 321397 ext. 2781.
Joyce Spiro Jewellery, Shopping Arcade, Hotel Sari Pacific, Jl. M.H. Thamrin, Tel: 323707.
Judith Tumbelaka, Jl. H. Agus Salim 94, Tel: 348252.
Kevin's Jewellery, Jakarta Hilton Hotel.
Linda Spiro Jewellery, Shopping Arcade, Borobudur Intercontinental, Jl. Lapangan Banteng Selatan, Tel: 370198.
Olislaeger Jewellers, Jl. Ir. H. Juanda II, Tel: 341850.
Pelangi Jewellery, Jakarta Hilton Hotel, Tel: 587981.
Pelangi Opal & Jewellery Centre, Jl. R.S. Fatmawati 42, Cilandak, Tel: 7601523.
SCL Jewellery, Gajah Mada Plaza I/F45, Jl. Gajah Mada, Tel: 346452.
Sesotya, Sahid Jaya Hotel.
Sri Sadono, Hotel Indonesia.

Indonesian Paintings: These are generally of three types: traditional, modern and poster kitsch. For works of serious artists, go to the **Duta Fine Arts Gallery** in Kemang.

Several artists also maintain their own galleries. One example is **Adam Lay's**. Check the English language press for exhibitions of Indonesian art at TIM and in the foreign embassy cultural centres. Traditional Balinese and other paintings can be found in the shops selling antiques and curios. The best place to see kitsch is **Taman Suropati** in Embassy Row. The **Art Market** in Ancol also has several shops where you may watch artists at work and commission a portrait. Quick portraits can be ordered from the sidewalk artists in front of the General Post Office on Jl. Veteran.

Adam's Gallery, Sari Pacific Shopping Arcade.
Duta Fine Arts Gallery on Jl Kemang Utara 63.
Harris Art Gallery, Jl. Cipete 41, Kebayoran Baru, Tel: 766860.
Oet's Gallery, Jl. Palatehan I/33, Kebayoran Baru.

SHOPPING AREAS

Shopping Centres: Visit the shopping streets and big shopping centres in Jakarta, just to see what is available and to indulge in some people-watching. This is best done in the early evening when it is cool. The two best places are **Pasar Baru** ("New Market") and the more fashionable **Blok M** in Kebayoran. A visit to one of the air-conditioned shopping plazas like **Gajah Mada Plaza** and **Ratu Plaza** can also be a cool way to escape the noonday sun.

Aldiron Plaza, Jl. Melawai, Kebayoran Baru.
Duta Merlin Shopping Centre, Jl. Gajah Mada.
Gajah Mada Plaza, Jl. Gajah Mada.
Glodok Plaza, Jl. Pinangsia.
Glodok Shopping Centre, in the middle of Jakarta's Chinatown.
Hayam Wuruk Plaza, Jl. Hayam Wuruk, Pasar Senen, located at Jl. Pasar Senen, provides all kinds of textiles, electric fixtures, ready made dress, etc.

Jalan Sabang, along Jl. H. Agus Salim.
Matahari Department Store, Ratu Plaza Shopping Centre, 3rd Fl., Blok M Shopping Area, Jl. Melawai IV; Pasar Senen Shopping Area, 1st Fl.; Pasar Baru Shopping Area; Jatinegara Shopping Area.
Pasar Baru, several square blocks of shops, where everything and anything can be bought.
Pasar Tanah Abang, not far from Sarinah Department Store, this shopping centre provides all kinds of textiles and batiks.
Ramayana Department Store, Pasar Senen Shopping Area, 2nd Fl., Tel: 353677; Blok M Shopping Area, Jl. Melawai IV/27, Tel: 772595, 772191; Jl. H. Agus Salim No. 22, Tel: 337713.
Ratu Plaza, Jl. Jend. Sudirman, Senayan, one of the newer and brighter air-conditioned shopping malls, with a supermarket, bookstore, many electronics goods shops, restaurants and a cinema.
Sarinah Department Store, Jl. M.H. Thamrin No.11, Tel: 327425
Sarinah Jaya Shopping Centre, Jl. Iskandarsyah II/2, Tel: 730171.
Tomang Plaza at Jl. Kyai Tapa.

NIGHTLIFE

Unlike most other Indonesian cities, Jakarta rages on into the night. This is perhaps one more reason to have a nap in the afternoon, so that you can get out on the town in the evening, when a cool breeze blows in from the sea.

Cultural Events: For culture in any form, the first place to check is Taman Ismail Marzuki (TIM), the cultural and performing arts centre of Jakarta. TIM hosts an eclectic variety of Indonesian dance performances, wayang kulit and wayang orang, singing groups, poetry readings, modern and traditional theatre productions, as well as performances of ballet, modern dance, and classical and jazz music by visiting artistes. Check at your hotel or in the English-language press for details.

"Wayang Orang": If you are not planning to visit Central Java, then you will perhaps want to attend the popular Javanese wayang orang performances at Baharata Theatre, Jl. Pasar Senen 15. The audience is almost entirely Javanese and are generally very appreciative-often more so than in Yogya and Solo these days, where there is rarely a good turnout and tourists often outnumber the locals. This in itself is

a good reason to see wayang orang in Jakarta. Performances nightly between 8 p.m. and 11 p.m.

Night Shopping: Visit the Art Market (Pasar Seni) at Ancol, where three or four nights a week there are live, open-air performances, and one may walk leisurely about the pavilions inspecting the handicrafts and paintings for sale. Chat with the artists and then sit down at one of the sidewalk cafes for a tasty bowl of soup, a hamburger or a plate of noodles. Ancol is about 10 km (6 miles) or US$3 by taxi from the centre of town. Ask at your hotel or the Tourist Information Office for programme details.

Hotel Performances: Regularly scheduled performances put on by the big hotels and foreign embassies. The Hilton and the Borobudur are, culturally speaking, the most active hotels. The French, British, Dutch, American, Australian and German embassies all maintain cultural centres with scheduled exhibitions, tours films and lectures. Call them up to find out the details.

Radio Live Shows: Rounding out the cultural scene, the Jakarta station of Radio Republik Indonesia (RRI) broadcasts live from their studios on Jl. Medan Merdeka Barat, with traditional music from all over Indonesia, classical concerts and wayang performances. Ask your hotel to phone RRI for details and ticket availability. Several restaurants also have live music, notably the Oasis restaurant with its band of strolling Batak players (see list of eating places). And on Sundays, Taman Mini to the south of Jakarta comes alive with traditional drama and music from any of Indonesia's 27 provinces. Also on Sunday morning, at the Wayang Museum, there is a brief puppet performance from 10 a.m. to noon.

Movies: With the new agreements between the Indonesia film distribution monopoly and American distributors, many good movies are showing up in Jakarta's theaters. All "21" chain theatres are new, with good sound and comfortable seats.

Discos, Bars and Pubs: Western style nocturnal amusements also abound in Jakarta. The disco craze hit the city a decade ago and is here to stay. Every weekend, wealthy youngsters in designer clothes pack the fashionable clubs. Two swank hotel establishments have ruled the scene for some time now: Sari Pacific's Pitstop and the Oriental Club at the Hilton. The cover is steep (about US$10 to US$15 per person), as are the drinks, but for this clientele it doesn't matter-transported to a fantasy world of plush carpeting, flashing lights and pounding rhythms, they are busy getting their money's worth. No sandals, blue jeans or T-shirts allowed, naturally.
Expatriates looking for a looser (and less expensive) atmosphere in which to unbend generally end up at Tanamur, Jl. Tanah Abang Timur 14, South-

east Asia's oldest disco and the one Jakarta club that attracts all levels of society. The **Bali International**, Jl. K.H. Wahid Hasyim 116, has a disco which attracts the young foreign travellers from nearby Jl. Jaksa and the local long-haired motorcycle crowd.

For a drink and a sing-a-long, it's over to the lively **Jaya Pub** piano bar on Jl. Thamrin or the larger **Pete's Place** on Jl Gatot Subroto. Other popular expatriate watering holes include the **Hotmen Bar** (Menteng Hotel), and some clubs along Jl Paletehan in Blok M. The **Green Pub** in the Jakarta Theatre has passable country/rock or jazz bands nightly.

The Mandarin and Hyatt hotel bars have regularly scheduled jazz nights, and the Hotel Indonesia has a supper club, the **Nirwana Room**, with Australian and European entertainers. And finally for a truly bizarre night out, try one of the Chinese cabarets on Jl. Gajah Mada/Hayam Wuruk: Blue Ocean, Sky Room, Paramount, Tropicana. They serve up Chinese banquets and Taiwanese singers for the sugar daddy *cukong* crowd.

NIGHTCLUBS

Shamrock, Jl. Pantai Indah, Taman Impian Jaya Ancol, Tel: 683005.
Sea Side, Taman Impian Jaya Ancol, Tel: 681512.
New Flamingo, Taman Impian Jaya Ancol, Tel: 683227.
Blue Ocean, Jl. Hayam Wuruk 5 Tel: 366650, 361194.
Marcopolo, Jl. Cik Ditiro, Tel: 326679.
Blue Moon, Jl. Gajah Mada 37, Tel: 6394008.
L.C.C., Jl. Silang Monas, Tel: 353525.
The Grand Palace, Jl. Gajah Mada, 19-26, Tel: 354203.
Nirwana Supper Club, Hotel Indonesia, Jl. M.H. Thamrin, Tel: 320008, 322008.

DISCOTHEQUES & PUBS

Ebony, Kuningan Plaza, Jl. H.R. Rasuna Said, Tel: 513700.
Executive Club Le Mirage, Hotel Said Jaya, Tel: 687031.
Green Pub Rest & Bar, Jakarta Theatre Building, Tel: 359332.
Hotmen Bar Diskotik, Hotel Menteng, Tel: 325208.
Jaya Pub, Jaya Building, Jl. M.H. Thamrin 12, Tel: 327508.
Manhattan Disco, Jl. Pantai Indah, Copacobana Building Ancol.
New Oriental Diskotik, Hotel Hilton, Tel: 83051.
Permata, Bakrie Building, Jl. H.R. Rasuna Said.
Pink Panther, Hotel Bali Intercontinental, Tel: 334967.
Pitstop Diskotik, Hotel Sari Pacific, Tel: 323707.
Stardust, Jayakarta Tower Hotel, Tel: 6294408.
Tanamur, Jl. Tanah Abang Timur No. 14, Tel: 353947.
2001 Executive Club, Garden Hotel, Tel: 795808.

GETTING THERE
THOUSAND ISLANDS

Motorboat launches may be hired to all the islands from the Jaya Ancol Marina, located within the vast Ancol "Dreamland" amusement park on Jakarta's north-eastern shore. Pulau Onrust and the other islands closest in to the mainland are only 20 to 30 minutes away, making this an easy and relaxing day trip "escape" from the city to the beach. Pulau Rambut is about an hour away from Ancol. The boat out to Pulau Puteri or Pulau Melinjo, takes 3 hours and costs US$50 per person round trip. The developers of this resort, Pulau Seribu Paradise, also provide an air charter service from Kemayoran Airport, for US$120 per person round trip.

A regular morning ferry leaves from Sanggar Bahari pier at Tanjung Priok harbour at 8 a.m. for several of the closer islands (Onrust, etc.), returning in the afternoon. For the farther islands, such as Pulau Puteri, Pulau Genteng and Opak Bersar, boats leave from the Kartika Bahari pier.

HOTELS

Pulau Putri: Pt. Pulau Seribu Paradise, Jl. KH. Wahid Hasyim 69, Jakarata 100829, Tel: (021) 348533, 324039, Fax: (021) 344039.
Pulau Pelangi: Pt. Pulau Seribu Paradise, Jl. KH. Wahid Hasyim 69, Jakarata 100829, Tel: (021) 348533, 324039, Fax: (021) 344039.
Pulau Perak: Pt. Pulau Seribu Paradise, Jl. KH. Wahid Hasyim 69, Jakarata 100829, Tel: (021) 348533, 324039, Fax: (021) 344039.
Pulau Melintang: Pt. Pulau Seribu Paradise, Jl. KH. Wahid Hasyim 69, Jakarata 100829, Tel: (021) 348533, 324039, Fax: (021) 344039.
Pulau Petondan: Jl. M.H. Thamrin, Jakarata pusat, Tel: 320807, 320982.
Pulau Papa Theo: Jl. M.H. Thamrin, Jakarata pusat, Tel: 320807, 320982.
Pulau Bidadari: Pt. Seabreeze, Marina Ancol Reservation, Tel: 680048, 683173, 683996.
Pulau Ayer: Pt. Sarotama Bumi Perkasa, Jl. Ir. H. Juanda 111/6, Jakarata 10120, Tel: 342031, 370708, 683996.
Pulau Kotok: Kalpataru Resort, Duta Merlin Shopping Arcade, Tel: 362948.
Pulau Sepa: Thousand Island Resort and Diving Centre, Jl. Kalibesar Barat, Tel: 678828, 679885.

Pulau Pantara (Pulau Hantu): Pt. Pantara Wisata Jaya, Room 6/7 Hotel Borobudur Int, Jl. Lapangan Banteng Selatan Direct line, Jakarta, Tel: 370108 Ext. 76085, 76086.

Pulau Rambut: P.H.P.A. Dinas Kehutanan, DKI Jakarata Jl. Rasuna Said, Kuningan, Tel: 5201422.

Pulau Bokor: P.H.P.A Dinas Kehutanan, DKI Jakarata Jl. Rasuna Said, Kuningan, Tel: 5201422.

GETTING THERE

BANTEN & THE WEST COAST

To visit the ruins at Banten, which are some distance from the main road, hire a car or taxi. A round-trip Jakarta-Banten excursion by car will cost US$50.

A taxi or rental car to the west coast beaches at Anyer or Carita will take about 4 hours and cost about US$60. A chartered minibus ("colt") will cost less, about US$30, and carry more people (ask someone in your hotel in Jakarta to arrange this for you). In either case you can make the detour to Banten along the way though this should be negotiated as part of the fare in advance.

Inter-city buses run hourly from Jakarta's Grogol Terminal to the port of Labuan on the west coast (about 5 hours) via the inland route through Serang and Pandeglang (fare about US$2), and from here you can catch a "colt" going north along the coastal road to the beach areas for just a few hundred rupiah (about US20 – 50¢, depending on your destination). Or you can take the slow, local train from Tanah Abang Station in Jakarta to Cilegon, and from here catch a "colt" on the main road going south. Remember that if you intend to visit the National Park at Ujung Kulon, you must first get your permit and make arrangements through the PPA head offices in Bogor (Department of Nature Conservation-see Ujung Kulon below).

Alternatively, phone the Jakarta booking office of any west coast hotel to make all the arrangements for you. They will be happy to arrange transportation (generally at a slightly higher cost than if you do it yourself), if you plan to stay at the hotel (see accommodation below). Private tours to Ujung Kulon, Krakatau and the west coast can also be arranged. Contact travel agents in Jakarta for details (try Vayatour, Jl. Batu Tulis 38, Jakarta, Tel: 3800202.)

WHERE TO STAY

ACCOMMODATION

Serang is a fairly small town with only a few *losmen* for more comfortable accommodation continue on to Cilegón, Merak or to the west coast beaches.

The **Krakatau Guest-house** is open to the general public air-conditioned motel-style bungalows renting for about US$20, a bit seedy now but quite inexpensive. The **Merak Beach Motel**, located right on the water just next to the Merak Bakauhuni ferry terminal at the far northwestern tip of the island, is clean and reasonable at US$25 to US$30 a night for an air-conditioned room (tax and service included).

The most comfortable place on the west coast beaches to the south is the **Anyer Beach Motel**. Tidy little concrete bungalows set in a grove by a broad, secluded beach for US$30 on up to US$80 a night for a suite (plus 21 percent tax and service).

Farther south around the village of Carita are two somewhat more rustic seaside establishments: the **Selat Sunda Wisata Cottages**, a small resort with several air-conditioned bungalows by the shore (US$35 per night), and the larger **Carita Krakatau Beach Hotel** US$36 per night, plus 21 percent tax and service.

Anyer Beach Motel (30 rooms), Jl. Raya Karang Bolong, Anyer, Serang Banten, Jakarta, Tel: 367594, 367838 ext. Anyer 196, 197, 198. Reservations: Gedung Patra, Jl. Jend. Gatot Subroto, Kav. 32-34, Jakarta, Tel: 510322.

Carita Krakatau Beach Hotel (150 rooms), Carita, Labuan, Pandeglang, West Java, Jakarta. Office: Wisata, Jl. M.H. Thamrin, P.O. Box 2457, Tel: 320408.

Guest-house Krakatau Steel, Kompleks P.T. Krakatau Steel, Kota Baja, Cilegon, Banten, West Java.

Merak Beach Hotel (30 rooms), Jl. Raya Merak, Banten, West Java, Tel: 15, Jakarta Tel: 367838, ext. Merak 164.

Selat Sunda Wisata Cottage, Cibenda, Carita Beach, Labuan, Banten, West Java. Jakarta Office: Jl. Panglima Polim Raya 21, Kebayoran Baru, Tel: 714683.

GETTING THERE

KRAKATAU

Boats may be chartered to the four uninhabited islands of the Krakatau group from Labuan. Cost is anywhere from US$60 for a small fishing craft, and up to US$200 for a motorised fibreglass launch that carries up to 10 people. Arrangements can be made through any of the hotels listed above, or at the port. Bring along lunch and refreshments, as it is hot and there is no fresh water out there. The boat trip takes about 5 hours each way, so get an early start in order to have some time to explore the islands.

Most visitors land at the eastern side of Anak Krakatau and then climb up from here to the top of the first ridge for a view into the smoking crater and across to the other three islands: Sertung to the west, Small Krakatau to the east and Big Krakatau to the south. Not recommended during the rainy season, November to March, when the seas are rough.

UJUNG KULON NATIONAL PARK

A. Hoogerwerf's authoritative book on Ujung Kulon's floral and faunal species is recommended. It is available from the publisher, E. J. Brill in Leiden. The Directorate-General of Tourism in Jakarta also publishes a very informative brochure about Ujung Kulon, and Vayatour (Jl. Batu Tulis 38, Jakarta, Tel: 365008, 377339) offers a deluxe 3-day deep-sea fishing tour to the park for US$375 per person, all-inclusive.

The first step is to get a permit at the head offices of the PPA (Department of Nature Conservation) at Jl. Juanda No. 9 in Bogor, just to the left of the Botanical Gardens (Kebon Raya) – an hour south of Jakarta by car or bus (see "Bogor" below). Bring your passport along and get there in the morning (they are open daily Mon. to Sat. from 8 a.m. to noon). There are forms to fill out and a small fee to pay. Ask them to call the PPA office in Labuan while you are there, to reserve space in a guest bungalow within the park for the dates of your intended visit.

It is important to equip yourself well for the trip. The bungalows in the park do provide bedding and cooking utensils, even a cook, but you must bring your own food. A mosquito net (available for only US$3 from any housegoods shop) and repellent are a must, you may also want to bring along your own sheets, a first aid kit and some camping supplies (if you intend to make the two-day hike around the south and west coasts). Many basic provisions, such as canned foods, bottled drinks and rice can be purchased in shops in Labuan, but you may want to bring your supplies from Jakarta.

Once in Labuan (to get there, see "Banten and the West Coast"), check in at the PPA office to show them your permit and to make arrangements for a boat and a bungalow. It is a good idea to confirm all fees in advance, including payments for services provided by park staff (such as cooks and guides), and use of park equipment, such as motorboats. The government launch may be available to take you into the park, otherwise the PPA officers will help you charter a local fishing craft. Cost is about US$100 each way be sure that you make an appointment for the boat to pick you up at a specified time and day, and if you want to detour on the way back via Krakatau for a look at the volcano, this should be negotiated in advance. If you arrive at Labuan early enough, then it may be possible to embark immediately for Ujung Kulon, otherwise spend the night at one of the hotels in nearby Carita Beach just a short distance to the north.

The park's guest bungalows are situated on two small islands. **Handeleum Island** is somewhat closer (5 hours from Labuan) and has one older, two-storey bungalow that sleeps eight. **Peucang Island** (7 hours from Labuan) has two newer cabins, sleeping a total of 16 people with a comfortable lounge area. Both islands are populated by monitor lizards, wild deer and long-tailed macaques and are worth exploring in their own right. The bungalows have resident staff and small motor boats that may usually be hired to cross over the straits and motor upriver, though you may have to supply the gasoline (inquire at the PPA office about this before leaving, and purchase a few 5-litre jerry cans in Labuan if necessary).

GETTING THERE

GETTING THERE

BOGOR

Most Jakarta taxis will take you to Bogor and back for US$25, waiting while you spend a couple of hours in the Botanical Gardens. For a more leisurely visit, rent a car or "colt" mini-bus for the entire day.

Buses leave for Bogor very frequently from Jakarta's Cililitan Terminal (in the south of the city). Express buses marked "Jl. Tol Jagorawi-Bogor" are the fastest (1 hour) and cheapest (US60¢), dropping you at the Ciawi terminal just above the town to the south. From here, mini-buses circulate into Bogor, going right by the Kebun Raya entrance. Fare is Rp 100.

The **Jabotabek** (Jakarta-Bogor-Tanggerang-Bekasi) commuter train is a slower but cheaper way to get there. Board the train at Gambir, Pegangsaan or Mangarai stations in Jakarta.

ACCOMMODATION & RESTAURANTS

Wisma Pangrango, 23 Jl. Pangrango, Tel: 28670
Wisma Miram, 5, Jl. Mandalawangi, Tel: 23520
The best restaurant in town is **Bogor Permai**, 20, Jl. Sudirman.

PUNCAK & CIBODAS

A rental car or taxi up to Puncak Pass or Cipanas will cost up to US$50 and take 2 hours from Jakarta. Inter-city taxis like "4848" bound for Bandung also take this route and cost about US$6 per person (see Jakarta above for listings). Buses cost only about US$1.20 from Jakarta's Cililitan Terminal or US60¢ from the Ciawi Terminal outside Bogor.

ACCOMMODATION

There are many good hotels around Puncak and Cipanas, including one that perches dramatically on the edge of the steep mountain slope just below the pass. For a group of people or a longer stay, private holiday bungalows may be rented for anywhere from US$20 to US$100 per night. Just walk around and inquire at houses that look promising. Most of them are vacant during the week. Budget travellers can stay at the new youth hostel just below the Cibodas Botanical Gardens for US$2 a night.

Bukit Indah (41 rooms), Jl. Raya 116, Ciloto, Cianjur, Tel: (0263) 49.
Bukit Ray (92 rooms), Jl. Raya 219, Cipanas, Cianjur, Tel: (0255) 2605.
Evergreen (101 rooms), Jl. Raya, Puncak, Tugu, Bogor, Tel: (0251) 4075.
Puncak Pass Hotel (45 rooms), Jl. Raya Puncak, Sindanglaya, Cianjur, Tel: (0255) 2503, (0255) 2504.
Sanggabuana (29 rooms), Jl. Raya 4-6, Cipanas, Cianjur, Tel: 2227, 2696.
Sindanglaya (22 rooms), Jl. Raya 43, Pasekon, Cianjur, Tel: 2116.
Tunas Kembang (66 rooms), Jl. Raya , Cipanas SDL, Cianjur, Tel: 2719.
USSU International (180 rooms), Jl. Raya, Cisarua, Bogor, 4499 Gadog.
Wisma Remaja Youth Hostel, Kebon Raya Cibodas, Pacet, Cianjur.

GETTING THERE

PELABUHAN RATU

The roads to Pebabuhan Ratu are excellent. Pelabuhan Ratu can be reached in only 4 hours from Jakarta by car. A taxi or rental car will charge up to US$60 to take you there, and you should arrange to have them pick you up for the return journey. To get there by bus, hop on one bound for Sukabumi from either Jakarta's Cililitan Terminal or the Ciawi Terminal south of Bogor and then alight at the intersection at Cibadak. From here, "colts" will take you down to Pelabuhan Ratu.

ACCOMMODATION

One hotel, called **Bayu Amrta,** rents small rooms perched on a cliff overlooking the sea for US$10 a night and has bungalows sleeping up to six people for only US$20. The place is in need of repairs, but the beach is beautiful and they serve very good seafood. Another place called **Karangsari** across the road is about the same price and slightly cleaner but without the view. Even the first-class **Samudra Beach Hotel** is not exorbitant considering the facilities, at US$35 per night for a standard double room (plus 21 percent tax and service).They keep a room here for Loro Kidal, the goddess of the South Sea. Closer in to town, the **Pondok Dewata** offers small air-conditioned bungalows by the sea for US$23 and larger ones (with two bedrooms and four beds) for US$45, all inclusive.

Bayu Amrta (12 rooms), Pelabuhan Ratu, Sukabumi
Karangsari, Pelabuhan Ratu, Sukabumi.
Pondok Dewata Seaside Cottage (14 rooms), Pelabuhan Ratu, Sukabumi, Tel: 22. In Jakarta, Tel: 772426 for reservations.
Samudra Beach Hotel (106 rooms), Sangkawayana, Pelabuhan Ratu, Sukabumi, Tel: 23. In Jakarta, make reservations through the Hotel Indonesia, Tel: 322008 ext. 171.

GETTING THERE

BANDUNG

Bouraq, Merpati and Garuda operate frequent flights to Bandung From Jakarta, but it's so close and the mountain scenery is so spectacular that it seems a pity to fly. Most Indonesians take the bus or train. The Parahiangan Express takes just over 3 hours from Jakarta to Bandung and costs about US$6 first class, US$4.50 second class. There are five trains daily, leaving from Jakarta's Gambir Station at 5.30 a.m., 10.15 a.m., 1.30 pm 3.15 p.m. and 6.45 p.m., with a similar return schedule.

The next quickest way is by shared inter-city taxi ("4848" and its equivalents see "Jakarta" for listings), a ride of 4 hours (generally in a huge Holden with six other people) costing about the same as the train (but delivering you to your doorstep). The express bus is a bit slower, because of the stops but cheaper, about US$3.50 for an air-conditioned express, even less for a local. Bandung-bound buses leave from Jakarta's Cililitan Terminal at the south of the city.

GETTING AROUND

There are a few cruising metered cabs. For excursions outside of the city, a minibus is the best bet, about US$30 per day including gas and driver, a bit more or less depending on the destination. Ask at your hotel or the Tourist Information Kiosk how to travel around the city by bus.

WHERE TO STAY

ACCOMMODATION

Bandung has several international class hotels: the **Santika**, the **Panghegar**, the **Grand Preanger** and the **Sheraton Inn**. The **Savoy Homann** is of a similar standard and very charming.

Many of Bandung's hotels fall into the intermediate category. Several small guest-houses are in old Dutch mansions, including the **Soeti** and **Kwik's**.

For a bit more money, Cisitu's newer **Sangkuriang Guest-house** (US$30 a night plus 21 percent tax and service) is very pleasant located in a residential neighbourhood just above the ITB university campus. The **Hotel Istana** is clean and reasonably priced at US$25 a night for a double (plus 21 percent), with an excellent restaurant. The **Hotel Trio** has spotlessly clean rooms, excellent service, a sumptuous breakfast, free transportation to and from the airport or train station, and free coffee and tea all for US$30 but is usually fully booked.

There are few good *losmens* for the budget traveller. The cheap hotels around the train station are rather dingy. The **Wisma Gelanggang** youth hostel is not too bad at US$1.50 a night for a dorm bed. For about US$12 you can get a decent room at the **Hotel Dago** or **Hotel Lugina.**

First Class (above US$60-US$100 a night)
Grand Hotel Preanger (63 rooms), Jl. Asia-Afrika 81, P.O. Box 124, Bandung, Tel: 430682-3.
Istana Hotel (34 rooms), Jl. Lembang 22-24, Bandung, Tel: 57240, 58240.
Kumala Panghegar (65 rooms), Jl. Asia-Afrika 140, P.O. Box 507, Bandung, Tel: 430351.
New Naripan (200 rooms), Jl. Naripan 31-33, Bandung, Tel: 511667, 59383.
Panghegar Hotel (123 rooms), Jl. Merdeka 2, P.O. Box 506, Bandung, Tel: 432295-7.
Patra Jasa Motel (33 rooms), Jl. Ir. H. Juanda 132, Bandung, Tel: 81644, 82590.
Savoy Homann (100 rooms), Jl. Asia-Afrika 112, P.O. Box 9, Bandung, Tel: 430082, 430987.
Sheraton Inn (111 rooms), Jl. Juanda 390, Tel: 210303.

Intermediate (US$15-US$30 a night)
Arjuna Plaza Hotel (30 rooms), Jl. Ciumbuleuit 128, P.O. Box 171, Bandung, Tel: 81328, 84742.
Braga Hotel (68 rooms), Jl. Braga 8, Tel: 51685.

Cisitu's International Sankuriang Guest-house (44 rooms), Jl. Cisitu (Jl. Sangkuriang) 45 B, Bandung, Tel: 82420, 82285-6, 84707.
Trio (89 rooms), Jl. Gardujati 55-61, Bandung, Tel: 58056, 61505-9.

Budget (under US$15 a night)
Brawijaya, Jl. Pungkur 28, Bandung, Tel: 50673.
Dago, Jl. Ir. H. Juanda 21, Bandung, Tel: 58696.
Gania Plaza, Jl. Bungsu 30, Bandung, Tel: 56557.
International, Jl. Veteran 32, Bandung.
Melati Baru, Jl. Kebonjati 24, Bandung, Tel: 56409.
Sahara, Jl. Otto Iskandardinata 3, Bandung, Tel: 51684.
Wisma Gelanggang Generasi Muda (100 beds), Jl. Merdeka 64, Bandung, Tel: 50155.

FOOD DIGEST

WHERE TO EAT

Tizi's (Jl. Hegarmanak 14), high up near ITB just off Jl. Ir. H. Juanda is managed by the wife of a former Indonesian ambassador to Germany and has an open-air garden dining area, with German specialities and excellent breads and pastries. The **Sukarasa** (Jl. Tamblong 52, Tel: 56968) is a more formal and expensive establishment with a French-style menu. Many Westerners also patronise **The Coffee Shop** opposite the Kumala Panghegar Hotel on Jl. Asia-Afrika. The Sidewalk Café in the Savoy Homann has a 50s diner atmosphere.

The **Braga Permai**, in the middle of Jl. Braga (no. 58, Tel: 50519) is a popular sidewalk café serving ice-cream, pastries, yoghurt, sandwiches and rice dishes. And no visit to Bandung is complete without a visit to the **Dago Teahouse.** Turn left at the top of Jl. Ir. H. Juanda and follow a narrow winding road through the Christian university campus to the teahouse parking lot at the very end, for a lovely vista of the city.

Another of Bandung's treats is **Babakan Siliwangi**, an open-air Sundanese restaurant set amid acres of green rice paddies and large fish-ponds, below the ITB campus (Jl. Siliwangi 7, Tel: 81394). They serve all the traditional Sundanese delicacies: grilled carp (*ikan mas bakar*); barbequed chicken in sweet soya (*ayam panggang*); fish with coconut and spices wrapped in banana leaves (*ikan mas pepes*) and sour vegetable soup (*sayur asem*). Other good Sundanese restaurants are **Bale Kambang**, Jl. Bungur 2, and **Ponyo** on Jl. Malabar.

The best-known Chinese restaurants are the **Queen** (Jl. Dalem Kaum 53 A, near the *alun alun*), the **Tjoan Kie** (Jl. Jend. Sudirman 46), and the **Trio Restaurant** (Jl. Gardujati 55-61, in the Hotel Trio).

SHOPPING

Bandung is a good place to buy baskets and mats (woven in nearby Tasikmalaya, an hour to the east past Garut on the Yogya highway), bamboo *angklung* instruments, *wayang golek* puppets (old and new, though most old-looking puppets are "antiqued" by hanging them over the kitchen stove). High-quality ceramics (including many imitations of Chinese antiques) are produced in the nearby village of Plered (to the north, past Lembang) and sold in Bandung. You can have good leather shoes made in many shoe stores. They will copy your favourite pair for a fraction of what you would pay at home. And the city also has many talented young artists. The biggest souvenir shops are located on Jl. Braga, there are also many bookstores here.

For *wayang golek* puppets, try E. Sukatma Muda. For a set of *angklung* instruments, go out to Pak Udjo's Saung Angklung on the eastern edge of town. They make the instruments here and they have frequent afternoon performances.

If you are interested in ceramics, visit the Balai Penelitian Keramik (Ceramic Research Office), Jl. A. Yani 390, in the mornings, where you can observe the whole process and also buy the finished products. There is a Textile Institute in the same complex.

THE PARAHYANGAN

The Tangkuban Prahu volcano, the Ciater hot springs, Lembang and the waterfall at Maribaya are all less than an hour to the north of Bandung and easily reached by renting a car or "colt" for a day. If you have the time, you might even want to stay at one of the hotels in these hills. The luxurious **Panorama Panghegar**, located between Lembang and Tangkuban Prahu offers horse-riding, tennis courts and a large swimming pool in a delightfully scenic location (60 rooms, make reservations through Hotel Panghegar, Bandung).

The highlands to the south of Bandung are even more spectacular, and anyone really seriously inter-ested in exploring them should get a copy of *Bandung and Beyond* by Richard and Shila Bennett, available for US$7 from Bandung Man (Jl. Cihampelas 120). This little booklet has very detailed instructions on how to get to a wide variety of mountain destina-tions, and descriptions of what you can see there.

GETTING THERE

YOGYAKARTA

A majority of foreign visitors to Yogya arrive by air. **Merpati** has several daily flights from Jakarta's Soekarno-Hatta International Airport, and in fact it is often possible to bypass Jakarta completely and hopping on the first plane to Yogyakarta upon arrival from overseas.

The first-class **Bima Express** train that plies the Jakarata-Yogyakarta-Surabaya route nightly in ei-ther direction is Java's finest featuring comfortable air-conditioned sleeper cars with small three mat-tress bunk compartments. The schedule is less than ideal, nonetheless. The Bima leaves' Jakarta Kota Station at 4 p.m. and arrives in Yogya 10 hours later, which means that your sleep is interrupted and you travel by night. At US$25 one way, it's about half the price of an air-ticket. The second class **Senja Utama** and **Senja Yogya** trains from Jakarta cost much less (only US$8) but they are slower and not air-conditioned. The Fajar leaves Gambir at dawn with one "executive class" air-conditioned car, equipped with airline-style seats. The Fajar arrives in Yogya late afternoon, making a fine relaxing day of gazing at ricefields and volcanoes.

Inter-city buses always travel at night. The Jakarta-Yogyakarta trip takes about 9 hours and is less than US$10. From Bandung it's 6 hours and about US$6. The more expensive Mercedes buses are air-conditioned.

From Semarang or Solo or other nearby cities, it's better to take a mini-bus, with runs all day. Costs only US$1.20 from Solo, US$2.50 from Semarang.

GETTING ACQUAINTED

GETTING AROUND

Yogya's main street is **Jl. Malioboro**, which runs north-south from the front steps of the **"kraton"** or palace all the way up to the Tugu monument that stands in the middle of the intersection with Jl. Jend. Sudirman and Jl. Diponegoro. From the map, you'll see that Malioboro's northern half is called Jl. Mangkubumi, while its southern end is known as Jl. A. Yani. A rail line bisects this main street, and the train station is located here. The new inter-city bus terminal is in the south-eastern corner of the city, on Jl. Veteran, though you can buy tickets and board most express buses on Jl. Sosrowijayan, just off Malioboro. The "colt" offices in Yogyakarta are on Jl. Diponegoro just left of the Tugu monument.

Jl. Pasar Kembang is a small street lined with inexpensive hotels and shops once Yogya's red-light district, but now "cleaned up" and taken over by budget travellers. **Jl. Sosrowijayan**, the next small street to the south also has budget hotels, as do several of the lanes connecting these two streets.

The more fashionable suburbs of Yogyakarta are located to the east of Jl. Malioboro/Mangkubumi, across the river. From here, it is about a mile north to the campus of **Gajah Mada University**. Farther down is **Jl. Solo**, which has become a busy shopping area lined with stores, restaurants and hotels on both sides almost a second Malioboro and a good place to shop for photo accessories or other necessities not available on the latter. The **Ambarrukmo Palace Hotel** and the **Adisucipto Airport** are located several miles out of town to the east along this road.

Taxis and Mini-Buses: Meter taxis are now available for trips around town. Hire taxis and mini-buses are expensive in Yogya because of the tourist demand. Drivers have come up with fixed fares, though a few will accept less after bargaining. Some will demand more so be sure you fix the fare before getting in.

Most hotels, including the budget guest-houses on Jl. Prawirotaman, will meet you at the airport or train station with transportation if you inform them before arrival.

From the airport, the standard fare into town is now US$5 (if you don't have much luggage, you can just walk out of the airport to the highway and flag down a passing mini-bus heading into the city which is to the left as you come out for only Rp 200 or about US20¢). For trips around the city, taxis now charge US$3.50 per hour (with a 2-hour minimum). Out of town trips have been worked out according to the following, rather arbitrary schedule:

Borobudur (round trip) 84 km (52 miles) US$20
Prambanan (round trip) 32 km (20 miles) US$15
Parangtritis (round trip) 56 km (35 miles) US$20
Surakarta (round trip) 130 km (81 miles) US$30
Dieng Plateau (round trip) 180 km (112 miles) US$50
Surabaya (one way) 327 km (202 miles) US$100
Bandung (one way) 425 km (264 miles) US$125
Jakarta (one way) 600 km (372 miles) US$ 160
Bali (one way) 720 km (447 miles) US$190

Arrange for taxis (up to 4 persons) or mini-buses (up to 8 persons) through any hotel or travel agent or through the Tourist Information Office on Jl. Malioboro, or by going to the taxi stand to the east of the G.P.O. on Jl. Senopati (where you may be able to get a cheaper rate for one of the older cars).

Pedicabs: Pedicabs or *becaks* are convenient for short distances in town. Yogyakartans use them for their daily transportation, and some tourists have taken to "chartering" one to tour around in. The problem is that *becak* drivers have gotten wise to the fact that tourists have a lot of money, don't know the fares and don't understand how to bargain. As a result, they sometimes try to charge outrageous amounts, and often won't come down to a reasonable price even if you do know the fares. Bargaining for *becak* rides is something of an art anyway, and this makes it doubly difficult for foreigners to use them. The key to good bargaining is to smile and joke about how high the first offer is, then to walk away once you have stated your final price. If it is reasonable, he will usually accept and call you back.

A few of the drivers who hang around Malioboro and the *kraton* speak some English, and several enterprising young English-speaking guides have taken up *becak* driving in order to solicit tourists for guided tours of the city. Not a bad way to go, provided that you don't pay more than a few dollars for a morning or afternoon tour. (A reasonable fare is Rp 10,000 per hour). Many of them just want to take you shopping, though, so they can get a commission. Again, be sure to settle the fare in advance.

City-buses: Within the city, orange-coloured Mercedes city-buses circulate all day along eight fixed routes until 8 p.m. In addition, there is a whole fleet of smaller pick-up **micro-buses** that are perhaps more convenient, because they travel in smaller circuits. Fare is fixed at Rp 150 regardless of distance. A few of the more useful routes are:

• A **counter-clockwise circuit** (Campus) serves the north-eastern quadrant of town, going down Malioboro, east on Senopati and Sultan Agung, up Jl. Dr. Sutomo to Jl. Jend. Sudirman and by the university in a small detour along Jl. Cik Ditiro, then down Mangkubumi/Malioboro again. Useful for getting to the university, ASTI and Jl. Solo.

• A **clockwise circuit**, meanwhile, goes up the western side of town along Jl. Bhayangkara to Diponegoro and then comes down Mangkubumi/Malioboro and turns west on Jl. K.H. Ahmad Dahlan.

• From Malioboro down to the *kraton* or Taman Sari, you want the **Ngasem** line, that travels down around the *alun-alun* to Jl. Ngasem. To get down to the south-eastern corner of town from Malioboro, take **Pojok Beteng.**

• To get out to Borobudur or Prambanan or Parangtritis via public transportation is not difficult. You simply have to study the map and ask for some advice where to get on and off the buses or mini-buses. Most people are very helpful, and if you can just pronounce the names of the places properly, they will indicate where to get off or where to change buses even if they speak no English. Check with someone at your hotel or with the Tourist Information Office to be sure of the route and method of transport for each destination.

Andong: Lastly, you can hire an **andong** or **dokar** pony cart for trips into the country along scenic back roads a very nice and slow way to get out to Kota Gede or even to Imogiri or Parangtritis. Not recommended on major highways, however. To Kota Gede, pay about Rp 500 each way; Rp 2,000 to Imogiri or Parangtritis (count on at least 2 hours each way). Dokars generally wait to the east of the post office, along Jl. Senopati, or on side roads at edge of town; villagers still use them to get to and from the city.

TOURS/TRAVEL AGENTS

Certainly the easiest way to see the city is by guided tour, though it can be grating to go on a large bus tour with people you don't know. For your own private tour, hire a car (US$20 to US$30 a day) and arrange for a guide (US$10 to US$20 a day) from one of the travel agencies below (or through the Tourist Information Office). Agencies like **Intan Pelangi** organise daily bus tours of the city (including a *wayang* performance, Taman Sari, the *kraton* and a *batik* factory), Borobudur, Dieng and Prambanan for as little as US$7 per person. Call them or check with the Tourist Information Office or your hotel for the latest schedules.

TOUR OPERATORS & TRAVEL AGENCIES

Intan Pelangi, 18, Jl. Malioboro, Yogyakarta, Tel: 5173, 3272.

Intrastour, 177, Jl. Malioboro, Yogyakarta, Tel: 3189, 86972.

Jatayu Mulya Utama, Ambarrukmo Palace Hotel, Jl. Adisucipto-Yogyakarta, Yogyakarta, Tel: 88488 ext. 134.

Natrabu, Ambarrukmo Palace Hotel, Jl. Adisucipto, Yogyakarta, Tel: 88488 ext. 705.

Nitour, 71, Jl. K.H. Ahmnad Dahlan, Yogyakarta, Tel: 3165, 3450.

Pacto, Ambarrukmo Palace Hotel, Jl. Adisucipto 57, Yogyakarta, Tel: 2740.

Royal Holiday, Ambarrukmo Palace Hotel, Jl. Adisucipto, Yogyakarta, Tel: 88488 ext. 709.

Satriavi, Ambarrukmo Palace Hotel, Jl. Adisucipto, Yogyakarta, Tel: 88488 ext. 742.

Sri Rama, Ambarrukmo Palace Hotel, Jl. Adisucipto, Yogyakarta, Tel: 88488.

Tourista, Puro Pakualam, Sewandanan, Yogyakarta, Tel: 2221, 5498, 88117.

Vayatour, Ambarrukmo Palace Hotel, Jl. Adisucipto, Yogyakarta Tel: 88488 ext. 121.

Vista Express, Garuda Hotel, Jl. Malioboro 72, Yogyakarta, Tel: 2114, 88196.

WHERE TO STAY

⊙ ACCOMMODATION

Yogya has a room for everyone, from the US$350 a night Presidential Suite at the Ambarrukmo to the dollar a night closets at the "Home Sweet Homestay" on Gang Sosrowijayan I. There is even one agency, Indraloka, that will place you in the home of an English or Dutch-speaking family where you share home-cooked meals and enjoy the warm hospitality of the Javanese.

HOTELS

First Class (US$35 and up a night)

The 4-star **Ambarrukmo Palace Hotel**, built by the Japanese in the early 1960s, is the oldest international-class luxury hotel in Yogya, with rooms going for US$65 on up (plus 21 percent tax and service). It is situated some miles to the east of town near the airport upon the grounds of the old royal *pesanggrahan* or rest house once used to entertain visiting dignitaries to the court. Some of the old buildings are still standing, including the elegant *pendapa* and the *dalem agung* ceremonial chambers.

The old **Hotel Garuda** (US$35 to US$50 a night) right on Malioboro has just added a second seven-storey extension. Their spacious colonial suites (huge rooms and bathrooms, with high ceilings and an outer sitting-room/balcony looking out onto a central courtyard) are *the* places to stay in Yogya. The hotel has quite a history, as it housed several government ministries during the Indonesian revolution (1946–49).

The **Hotel Santika** on Jl Sudirman is the newest addition to Yogya's upmarket hotels, with rooms with small balconies going for US$70. The hotel also boasts a good pool and fitness facilities.

The newer **Mutiara Hotel** down the street is just 10 minutes' walk from the *kraton* and the museum. Prices are about the same as the Garuda. Motel-style "cottage" hotels include the **Sahid Garden**, nice and thoroughly Javanese. Owned by an aristocratic Surakartan family (from US$45 plus 21 percent tax and service). ·

It's hard to beat the **Puri Artha's** friendly service and well-manicured surroundings (US$35 a night). The nearby **Sri Manganti** and the **Sriwedari** (opposite the Ambarrukmo) are about the same price.· All of these hotels have pools and quiet gardens, but none is within walking distance of Malioboro, so you'll have to think about transport.

Ambarrukmo Palace Hotel (265 rooms), Jl. Adisucipto, P.O. Box 10, Yogyakarta, Tel: 88488, 88984.

Hotel Garuda (120 rooms), Jl. Malioboro 72, Yogyakarta, Tel: 2113-4.

Mutiara Hotel (140 rooms), Jl. Malioboro 18, P.O. Box 87, Yogyakarta, Tel: 3272, 4530-1.

Puri Artha (59 rooms), Jl. Cendrawasih 9, Yogyakarta, Tel: 5934-5.

Sriwedari (70 rooms), Jl. Adisucipto, P.O. Box 93, Yogyakarta, Tel: 3599, 5341-61.

Sri Manganti (46 rooms), Jl. Urip Sumoharjo, P.O. Box 46, Yogyakarta, Tel: 2881.

Sahid Garden (48 rooms), Jl. Babarsari, Yogyakarta, Tel: 3697.

Intermediate (US$15–US$35 a night)

The above-mentioned **Indraloka Homestay Service**, founded and run by Mrs. B. Moerdiyono, currently costs US$21 a night for a double (plus 21 percent tax and service) including breakfast. Home-cooked lunch or dinner is an additional US$6. The families are mostly headed by Dutch educated professionals (doctors and university lecturers), and the rooms have all the western amenities and a fan. Mrs. Moerdiyono also arranges tours through Java to Bali, using her network of homestays in other cities. Write to her for details. (See address below under "Indraloka".)

Other choices depend on where you want to be and how much you want to pay. The **Arjuna Plaza** and the **New Batik Palace hotels** are centrally located on Jl. Mangkubumi (US$25 to US$30 for a double, plus 21 percent). The **Gajah Mada Guesthouse**, with air-conditioned doubles for US$24 is a quiet place located on campus in the north of town. Mrs. Sardjito, the widow of Gajah Mada University's first rector also rents rooms at her elegant home on Jl. Cik Ditiro, opposite the Indraloka office.

Many other small hotels and guesthouses cluster along **Jl. Prawirotaman** in the south of Yogya. A few of these have air-conditioned rooms in the US$15 to US$25 range (plus 21 percent), including breakfast. Try the **Airlangga** or the **Duta**.

Airlangga (30 rooms), Jl. Prawirotaman 4, Yogyakarta, Tel: 3344.

Arjuna Plaza (24 rooms), Jl. Mangkubumi 48, Yogyakarta, Tel: 3036.

Batik Palance Hotel (24 rooms), Jl. Pasar Kembang 29, P.O. Box 115, Yogyakarta, Tel: 2149.

Duta Guest-house (15 rooms), Jl. Prawirotaman 20, Yogyakarta, Tel: 5219.

Gajah Mada Guest-house (20 rooms), Jl. Bulaksumur, Kampus Universitas Gajah Mada, Yogyakarta, Tel: 88461, 88688 ext. 625.

Indraloka Homestay (40 rooms), Jl. Cik Ditiro 14, Yogyakarta, Tel: 0274, 3614.

Koba Cottages (48 rooms), Jl. Babarsari I, Tambakbayan Baru, Yogyakarta, Tel: 3697.

New Batik Palace Hotel (22 rooms), Jl. Mangkubumi 436, Yogyakarta, Tel: 2149.

Wisma LPP, Jl. Demangan Baru 8, Yogyakarta, Tel: 88380.

Budget (under US$15 a night)

The guest-houses along **Jl. Prawirotaman** are all converted homes, generally quiet, clean and comfortable. Cheapest rate available here for a double is US$7.50, including tax, service and breakfast; but most are in the US$10-to-US$12 a night range. Some also have air-conditioned doubles for only US$15 a night.

The many small hotels around **Jl. Pasar Kembang** (also on Jl. Sosrowijayan and down the small lanes in between), are substantially cheaper and more central, but this is not a pleasant area. Many places here have rooms for US$3 to US$5 and even less. Try the **Kota** down at the end of Jl. Pasar Kembang which is very clean.

Asia Afrika, Jl. Pasar Kembang 25, Yogyakarta, Tel: 4489.

Agung Guest-house, Jl. Prawirotaman 68, Yogyakarta, Tel: 2715.

Aziatic Hotel, Jl. Sosrowijayan 6, Yogyakarta.

Kota Hotel, Jl. Gandekan Lor 79, Yogyakarta.

Pura Jenggala Guest-house, Jl. Cendrawasih 2, Yogyakarta, Tel: 2238, 88509.

Ratna Hotel, Jl. Pasar Kembang 17 A, Yogyakarta, Tel: 2654.

Rose Guest-house, Jl. Prawirotaman 22, Yogyakarta, Tel: 2715.

Srivijaya Guest-house, Jl. Prawirotaman 7, Yogyakarta, Tel: 2387.

FOOD DIGEST

WHERE TO EAT

The pilgrimage point for fried chicken lovers from all over Java (and all over the world) is **Nyonya Suharti's** (also known as Ayam Goreng "Mbok Berek," after the women who invented this famous fried chicken recipe), located 7 km (4 miles) to the east of Yogya on the road to the airport (a short distance beyond the Ambarrukmo on the same side). Nyonya Suharti's chicken is first boiled and coated in spices and coconut, then fried crisp and served with a sweet chilli sauce and rice. Excellent when accompanied by pungent petai beans and raw cabbage. Indonesians patronise the place in droves,

and you can see Jakartans in the airport lounge clutching their take-away boxes of the special chicken for friends and family back home.

Nasi padang fanatics also rave about the fare at **Sina Budi Restaurant**, at Jl. Mangkbumi 41, about 500 metres north of the railway tracks on the left (opposite the cinema). Mutton's brain opor, beef *rendang* and *gulai ayam* (chicken curry) await you at a moment's notice. Be sure to ask for their spicy potato chips (*kentang goreng*) Sinar Budi's answer to the barbeque flavoured variety in the West.

The Yogya speciality is *gudeg* a combination plate consisting of rice with boiled young jackfruit (*nangka muda*), a piece of chicken, egg, coconut cream gravy and spicy sauce with boiled buffalo hide (*sambal kulit*). **Juminten** at Jl. Asem Gede 22, Kranggan 69, just north of Jl. Diponegoro, is known for its *gudeg*. The other *gudeg* restaurant is **Bu Citro's**, just opposite the entrance to the airport out on Jl. Adisucipto (a good place to eat while waiting for a flight). Most restaurants in Yogya also serve the dish, and there is excellent *gudeg* just north of Taman Sari on the eastern side of Jl. Ngasem. **Pesta Perak** (Jl. Tentara Raykat Mataram 8) is popular with tour groups and offers an Indonesian buffet.

Western food is now readily available in Yogya, and not just in the large hotels. The **Legian Garden Restaurant** on a terrace looking on to Jl. Malioboro serves excellent steaks, chops, sauteed fish, avocado seafood cocktails, yoghurt and corn, and crab soup as well as Indonesian dishes. Everything is very reasonable, the beer is cold and the vegetables are not overcooked. Enter via a well-marked doorway around the corner from Jl. Malioboro-Jl. Perwakilan 9 (Tel: 87985). The Legian Garden now has a branch, called **The Rose,** on the southern side of Jl. Solo the same menu and prices but more atmosphere. For more money, the **Gita Buana** offers air-conditioning and low lighting at two locations: Jl. Diponegoro 52 A and out at Jl. Adisucipto 169 by the Ambarrukmo hotel. The **French Grill** in the Arjuna Plaza Hotel (Jl. Mangkubuni 48) is also good, and they have puppet and dance performances every other night.

Many other on both sides of Jl. Malioboro cater to the young tourist crowd, offering a standard **Kuta Beach** menu of fruit drinks, yoghurt, sandwiches, vegetarian plates, desserts, ice cream and other western dishes, in addition to a full range of Chinese and Indonesian meals.

The most popular hang-out with the budget crowd (because it is the cheapest), is Superman's known to foreigners as **Superman's** on Gang Sosrowijayan I, a narrow lane parallel to Malioboro between Jl. Pasar Kembang and Jl. Sosrowijayan.

Another favourite hang-out, with better food, is **Mama's Gado-Gado** on Jl. Pasar Kembang behind the train station. Mama holds court nightly with the aplomb of an Italian pasta queen. Papa is occasionally there too, tending his songbirds and collecting the bread. Local foreign residents like to pop in for a *nasi campur*, a fruit salad and a cold beer. Breakfast is also served: French toast, banana pancakes with honey, fresh fruit juices and coffee with fresh milk.

There several good restaurants along Prawirotaman. **Hanuman's Forest** does a Yogya version of dinner theatre with a short *wayang kulit* performance accompanying the Western-style meals.

There are several fine Chinese restaurants in town. The old standby and the favourite of the local Chinese community is the **Tiong San**, at Jl. Gandekan 29, a block west of Malioboro. **Moro Senang**, Jl. Solo 55 (on the north side next to Miroto's Supermarket), is also very good. The best seafood, and probably also the best Chinese food, is to be had at **Sintawang**, several doors north of Jl. Diponegoro at Jl. Magelang 9, on the west side of the street.

SHOPPING

Yogyakarta is commonly said to be a shopper's paradise, but when you come right down to it, most of the stuff sold here is pretty tacky. Nevertheless it is all extremely cheap, and for this reason alone tourists seem to buy it. Concentrate on getting a few quality items that you will enjoy and use.

BATIK

Most tours take you to one of the factories around **Jl. Tirtodipuran** in the south of Yogya, to see the *batik* process and to shop in the showroom, but they don't sell much *tulis* work here – most of the *batik* is made by the quicker copper-stamp (*batik* cap) method. They do have good yard-goods, including some that are on heavier cotton, to be used for curtains and upholstery.

Batik Gurda, Jl. Parangtritis 77 B, Yogyakarta, Tel: 5474.

Batik Plentong, Jl. Tirtodipuran 28, Yogyakarta, Tel: 2777.

Rara Djonggrang, Jl. Tirtodipuran 6 A, Yogyakarta, Tel: 2209.

Sumiharjo, Jl. Mandkuyudan 15A, Yogyakarta, Tel: 3061.

Surya Kencana, Jl. Ngadinegaran M.D. VII/98, Yogyakarta, Tel: 3798.

Tjokrosoeharto, Jl. Panembahan 58, Yogyakarta, Tel: 3208.

Winotosastro, Jl. Tirtodipuran 34, Yogyakarta, Tel: 2218.

For high-quality traditional Javanese *batik* tulis, try **Toko Terang Bulan** at Jl. A. Yani 76, next to the central market. The prices here are fixed and reasonable. They have one of the best selections in Central Java.

Otherwise, you should seek out one of the boutiques of the better-known *batik* artists in town. Most of them produce both *batik* paintings and yard goods; many of them also teach one week *batik* minicourses. Some of the better known names are **Kuswadji**, **Amri**, **Sapto Hudoyo** and **Bambang Oetoro**. Within the **Taman Sari** *batik* painters complex, the best place is **Gallery Lod**, on the western edge of the kampung.

Direx Gallery, Jl Solo

Agus, Jl. Taman Siswa Mg, III/102, Yogyakarta.

Amri Gallery, Jl. Gampingan 67, Yogyakarta, Tel: 5135.

Bagong Kussudiardjo, Jl. Singasaren 9, off Jl. Wates, Yogyakarta.

Bambang Oetoro, Jl. Taman Siswa 55, Yogyakarta, Tel: 2147.

Gallery Lod, Taman Sari, Yogyakarta.

Kuswadji K., Jl. Alun-Alun Utara, Pojok Barat Daya, Yogyakarta, Tel: 4995.

Sapto Hudoyo, Jl. Solo 9 km, Maguwo, Yogyakarta, Tel: 87443.

SILVER

Kota Gede, to the south-east of Yogya, almost a suburb of the city now, is the centre of the silver industry. There are two major workshops, **M.D. Silver** and **Tom's Silver**, and a number of minor ones where (buying or not) you can pass an intriguing half hour watching the hammering, beating, heating, cleaning and polishing of the precious metal. Deft fingers create spider-web filigree; anvils clang till your ears ring; gentle hammer-blows tap out elegant repousse work.

Do not be constrained to buy only what is on display. Any workshop will produce pieces to your specifications. All that is needed is a drawing or a specimen to copy. In most workshops, prices are calculated strictly according to the weight and grade of the silver used (generally either 80 percent or sterling, 92.5 percent), except for certain exceptional or truly original designs (almost non-existent here because they all copy one another). A good place in Kota Gede, is at the home and workshop of **Tan Jam An** in Yogya (just north of the Tugu monument on the right-hand side).

M.D. Silver, Jl. Keboan, Kota Gede, Yogyakarta, Tel: 2063.

Sri Moeljo's Silver, Jl. Mentri Supeno UH XII/I. Yogyakarta, Tel: 88042.

Tan Jam An, Jl. Mas Sangaji 2, Yogyakarta.

Tjokrosoeharto, Jl. Panembahan 58, Yogyakarta, Tel: 3208.

Tom's Silver, Jl. Kota Gede 3-1 A, Kota Gede, Yogyakarta, Tel: 3070, 2818.

LEATHER GOODS

Yogya's buff-coloured hand-tooled suitcases, overnight bags, briefcases, pocketbooks, sandals, belts and money pouches produced from buffalo hide are slowly improving in quality, but one of the problems is that the tanning process employed here is still very crude, so they are unable to produce finer, softer grades of leather. Another problem is the finishing flimsy brass or tin clasps and hinges, and poor stitching.

There are many shops on Malioboro, one of the better ones being **Toko Setia**. For a bit better quality, though, try **Kusuma** just off Malioboro, or **Moeljosoehardjo's** near Taman Sari.

One notable exception is **Yamin's** shop in the Ambarrukmo Arcade. Most of Yamin's output goes overseas, but his shop stocks a selection of his popular "Yogya Gucci" pieces.

Buffalo hide is also the starting point for making **"wayang kulit" puppets**, though the thin, translucent *kulit* used to make them is not tanned at all and should properly be called "parchment." For the best quality puppets, try **Ledgar** and **Swasthigita**.

Aris Handicraft, Jl. Kauman 14, Yogyakarta.
B.S. Store, Jl. Ngasem 10, Yogyakarta.
Budi Murni, Jl. Muja-muju 21, Yogyakarta.
Kusuma, Jl. Kauman 50, Yogyakarta.
Ledjar, Jl. Mataram DN I/370, Yogyakarta.
Moeljosoehardjo's, Jl. Taman Sari 37 B, Yogyakarta, Tel: 2873.
Swasthigita, Jl. Ngadinegaran MD 7/50, Yogyakarta, Tel: 4346.
Toko Setia, Jl. Malioboro 79, Yogyakarta; Jl. Malioboro 165, Yogyakarta.

ANTIQUES & CURIOS

Hunting grounds include the many shops that line Jl. Tirtodipuran and some on Jl. Malioboro. Try also the streets to the south and west of the *kraton* and the handful of small shops near the Ambarrukmo Palace Hotel. Most of the *batik* galleries listed above also sell antiques. **Ardianto** sells top quality antiques, also the art gallery on Jl. Pramuka.

Among the things that may catch your eye are carved and gilded chests for herbal medicines, or a pair of polychrome *loro blunyo*, seated wedding figures that were traditionally kept in the ceremonial chamber of an aristocratic Javanese home. A handful of 18th-century copper coins with the Dutch East Indies trading company's (VOC) insignia can be fashioned into interesting decorations; and all sorts of elaborately carved old Dutch and Chinese teakwood furniture is available; roofed and walled wedding beds; gilded panels; marble-top tables; wicker chairs; massive chests and delicate vanities. Then there are *naga*-wreathed stands for *gamelan* instruments, bronze statuettes of Durga, Nandi, Siva, Ganesa, Agastya, Buddha and innumerable bodhisattvas, crude *wayang klitik* figures and antique blue-and-white Ming

porcelains from Annam and China. Many of these things are cheaper and more readily available in Solo (see below).

Antiques Art Shop, Jl. Kota Gede, Yogyakarta.
Ardianto, Jl. Pejaksan 21, Yogyakarta.
Arjuna Art Shop, Jl. Solo 110, Yogyakarta.
Asmopawiro, Jl. Letjend. Haryono 20, Yogyakarta.
Edi Store, Jl. Malioboro 13A, Yogyakarta, Tel: 2997.
Ganeda Art Shop, Jl. Abdul Rahman 69, Yogyakarta.
Hastirin Store, Jl. Malioboro 99, Yogyakarta.
Jul Shop, Jl. Mangkubumi 29, Yogyakarta, Tel: 2157.
Ken Dedes, Jl. Sultan Agung, Yogyakarta.
La Gallerie, Jl. Kota Gede, Kota Gede, Yogyakarta.
Mahadewa Art Shop, Jl. Taman Garuda, Yogyakarta.
Pusaka Art Shop, Jl. Taman Garuda 22, Yogyakarta.
Seni Jaya Art Shop, Jl. Taman Garuda 11, Yogyakarta.
Sidomukti Art Shop, Jl. Taman Kampung III/103 A, Yogyakarta.
The Ancient Arts, Jl. Tirtodipuran 30, Yogyakarta.

PAINTING

Works by **Affandi**, Indonesia's "grand old man" are now sold exclusively through the **Direx Gallery**, across the road from the late artist's large studio-cum-gallery overlooking the river on Jl. Solo, close to the Ambarrukmo Palace Hotel. In 1973, Affandi acquired the status of "painter laureate" when his egg-shaped concrete dome received the blessing of the government as a permanent private museum (the first of its kind in Indonesia), though unfortunately for the collector, most of his earlier and finer work is not for sale. The works of other artists, including his daughter **Kartika**, are also displayed.

A few meters toward town, a sign indicates the turnoff to **Nyoman Gunarsa's** gallery on Jl Wulung. Besides this transplanted Balinese painter's expressionist works, the gallery also showcases the best of Yogya's contemporary art.

The **Cementi Modern Art Gallery** on Jl. Ngadisuyan near the *alun-alun kidul* has a rotating selection of works by newer artists.

To find out where the up-and-coming generation is moving in painting, sculpture and handicrafts, pay a visit to Yogya's **Academy of Fine Arts (ASRI)** on Jl. Gampingan. This is considered one of the top art academies in the country.

MASKS & WOODEN PUPPETS

For the finest work, made by one of the few remaining craftsmen who still carves for the actors and *dalang*, rather than for casual visitors, visit **Pak Warno Waskito**, a shy, gentle old man who's been playing his craft for more than 50 years. He never went to school, and is self-taught.

To reach Pak Warno's secluded hideaway, take the Bantul road south from Yogya, turn right at the

7.6-km marker, walk about 300 metres, turn left, and stop at the first house on your right. Signposts will guide you.

POTTERY

On your way back to Yogya from Pak Warno turn left at the 6.5-km post (a sugar cane trolley track crosses the road at this point) and follow the side-road for about 1 km. If you've admired the jauntily coloured "piggy banks" in the form of elephants, roosters, mythical beasts and mounted cavalry which can be found in Yogya, especially around Pasar Ngasem, **Kasongan** is where you can see them being modelled by hand, fired in an open blaze of roots and palm leaves, and then painted with a verve and panache that's almost Mexican in feeling. Almost every household you come to will have a potter. You can have items made to order. Allow up to a week or 10 days.

PERFORMANCES IN YOGYA

There are basically two types of performances: those that are put on especially for tourists and those that are put on for the Javanese.

Tourist performances are not necessarily any less authentic or in any way inferior (as some people insist), even though they are frequently shortened or excerpted versions of the originals, adapted for the benefit of foreign audiences.

What they do lack, of course, is a Javanese audience, and as the audience is as much a part of the performances as the players (especially in Java), you should try if at all possible to catch a village or *kampung* shadow play or dance drama. Being here at the right time to see one is just a matter of luck. Check with the **Tourist Information Office** (Jl. Malioboro 16) and travel agencies for up-to-date information.

GETTING THERE

DIENG PLATEAU

A taxi or mini-bus seating any number from one to eight persons may be chartered to Dieng for only US$45 (for a one day return trip see Yogya: "Getting Around"). Public inter-city buses and mini-buses operate from Yogya to Wonosobo (from the terminal on Jl. Veteran in Yogyakarta and the "colt" offices on Jl. Diponegoro). From here you can get a local "colt" up to Dieng. Intan Pelangi (see Yogya: "Tours/Travel Agents") offers a day-long guided bus tour to Dieng and Borobudur for only US$12 per person. Check with your hotel or directly with the travel agencies for schedules. Check also with the Tourist Information Office, Jl. Malioboro 14, for other tours.

WHERE TO STAY

ACCOMMODATION

Assuming you are travelling to Dieng on your own, there are several small *losmen* and a restaurant facing right onto the central plain and temples, where you can spend the night for only a few dollars. Be sure to bring some warm clothing. Better accommodation is available in the town of Wonosobo, though there is no first-class hotel.

Bhima, Jl. A. Yani 5, Wonosobo.
Jawa Tengah, Jl. A. Yani 45, Wonosobo
Merdeka, Jl. Sindoro 2, Wonosobo
Nirwana, Jl. Tanggung 18, Wonosobo

GETTING THERE

SURAKARTA (SOLO)

The easiest way, from Yogya, is to book a seat on an express "colt" at one of the travel offices on Jl. Diponegoro just west of the Tugu monument for US$1.20. They leave all day at half-hour intervals and will drop you anywhere in Solo. You can also flag down a bus or mini-bus heading east on Yogya's Jl. Jend. Sudirman or Jl. Solo and get to Solo for about half the price, but it takes a lot longer and it is usually very crowded.

The other alternative is to rent your own taxi or mini-bus from Yogya with up to seven other people for US$17.50 one-way, US$22.50 round trip (returning on the same day). Solo also has its own airport, with two or three flights operating daily to and from Jakarta and Surabaya. And all trains stopping at Yogya also stop here.

GETTING AROUND

Almost everything is within walking distance. Otherwise take a pedicab (*becak*). See Yogya: "Getting Around" for tips on bargaining for *becaks*. The fares here are essentially the same, and you normally pay no more than Rp 500 to go about a mile in the centre of town. With some practice you may be able to get rides for Rp 200.

ORIENTATION

Solo's main street is **Jl. Slamet Riyadi**, a broad boulevard which runs east-west and is a continuation of the highway into town from Yogya. At its eastern end stands a Tugu monument, just in front of the northern gates leading into the *alun-alun* (town square) and the *kraton* precincts. The General Post Office, government buildings, banks, the telephone office and the central market (Pasar Gede) are all nearby. Most hotels, restaurants and shops are also within walking distance, on or near Jl. Slamet Riyadi, and the interesting areas of town to explore on foot are mostly centred around the two palaces- the **Kasusuhunan** and the **Mangkunegaren**. **Jl. Secoyudan** is the main shopping street and runs parallel to Salmet Riyadi. The travel offices are in between these two streets, on **Jl. Yos Sudarso**, and this is where you book and board an express "colt" back to Yogya. Most inter-city bus companies have offices and representatives along Jl. Veteran in the south of the city, as well as at the **bus terminal** near the city "bypass" (Jl. Parman/Tendean/Haryono) in the north.

WHERE TO STAY

ACCOMMODATION

First Class (US$30 and up a night)
The best hotel in town is the **Kusuma Sahid Prince**, with very comfortable doubles ranging from US$24 on up to US$200 a night for an "Indraloka Suite" (plus 21 percent tax and service). They have a good sized swimming pool, that can be used by outsiders for US$1.50. The **Mangkunegaran Palace Hotel** is just nearby (same price, US$24 and above). Two other hotels in the same category, the **Cakra** and the **Solo Inn**, are similarly priced and quite adequate, but being on busy Jl. Slamet Riyadi are not as spacious or as quiet (without pools). The **Sahid Sala** is a bit older and slightly less expensive (US$20 for an air-conditioned double, plus 21 percent).

Cakra Hotel (57 rooms), Jl. Slamet Riyadi 171, Solo, Tel: 35847, 35086.
Solo Inn (32 rooms), Jl. Slamet Riyadi 318, Solo, Tel: 36077.
Kusuma Sahid Prince Hotel (100 rooms), Jl. Asrama 22, Solo, Tel: 37022, 36356.
Mangkunegaran Palace Hotel (48 rooms), Jl. Istana Mangkunegaran, Solo, Tel: 35683, 35811.
Sahid Sala (40 rooms), Jl. Gajah Mada 104, Solo, Tel: 35889.

Intermediate & Budget
(under US$20 a night)
Your best bet in the intermediate range is the **Ramayana Guest-house**, with several rooms ranging in price from US$12 up to US$22 for a large room with a fan, including breakfast. Very clean and

airy, but a bit far from town. Several other guest-houses nearby, like the **Sarangan** and the **Putri Ayu** in the same price category, are only slightly less comfortable.

The **Indah Jaya** near the train station gives you good value: air-conditioning, carpeting, colour T.V. and breakfast for as little as US$15.50 a night (plus 21 percent). The **Hotel Trio** is a centrally located Chinese-run establishment right opposite Pasar Gede with small, clean rooms in the back for US$10. They also have several large older rooms in the front that sleep three or four for the same price. The newly remodelled **Mawar Melati** has rooms with a fan and private bath for only US$38, as well as some cheaper rooms for US$3.

Budget travellers invariably stay at **Mawardi's** (also known as "**The Westerners**") in Kemlayan for US$1.50. The *becak* drivers all know the place. If they are full, try the Mawar Melati, the **Kota** or the **Central**, all nearby.

Central Hotel, Jl. K.H. Ahmad Dahlan, Solo, Tel: 32842.
Dana Hotel, Jl. Slamet Riyadi 232, Solo, Tel: 33890-1.
Indah Jaya, Jl. Srambatan 13, Solo, Tel: 37445.
Kota Hotel, Jl. Slamet Riyadi 113, Tel: 32841.
Mawar Melati, Jl. Imam Bonjol 44, Solo, Tel: 36434.
Mawardi's, Jl. Kemlayan Kidul 11, Solo.
Ramayana Guest-house, Jl. Dr. Wahidin 15, Solo, Tel: 32814.
Seribu Hotel, Jl. Marconi 28 A, Solo, Tel: 3525.
Trio Hotel, Jl. Urip Sumoharjo 33, Solo, Tel: 32847.

FOOD DIGEST

WHERE TO EAT

The overall best Javanese restaurant, by general consent, is the **Sari**, on the south side of Jl. Slamet Riyadi (No. 351), but it's about 3 km (2 miles) from the centre of town. The specialities here are *nasi liwet* (a Solonese speciality rice cooked in coconut cream with garnishes), fried chicken and various types of *pepes* (prawns, mushrooms or fish wrapped in a banana leaf with spices and steamed or grilled). Closer to town, the original **Timlo Solo**, Jl. Urip Sumoharjo 106, is also very good. They have excellent daily specials, but also the standard

Javanese fried chicken, *pecel* (boiled vegetables with peanuts sauce), *nasi gudeg* (the Yogyanese speciality) and *nasi kuning* (rice cooked in turmeric), with *tahu*, *tempe* and coconut. For the best Javanese-style fried chicken in town, try the new **Tojoyo** at Jl. Kepunton Kulon 77. That's all they serve and it goes fast (open only 6 p.m. to 9 p.m.).

The best Chinese restaurant is the **Orient**, Jl. Slamet Riyadi 341 A (several doors down from the Sari). Here you can order a beef hotplate, sweet and sour pork or fish (a whole gurame), corn and crab (or shark's fin) soup, Chinese broccoli with black beans (*kailan tausi*), and their speciality: boiled chicken with garlic, onion and ginger sauce (*ayam rebus*). The **Centrum** at Jl. Kratonan 151 is much more central and also very good. Let the manager order for you. They are famous for their crab rolls (*sosis kepiting*), prawns stir-fried in butter (*udang goreng mentegar*), fish with salted vegetables (*ikan sayur asin*) and fried crab claws (*kepit kepiting*).

For the best chicken and mutton sate in town, go over to the **Ramayana** at Jl. Ronggowarsito 2 (one block in front of the Kusuma Sahid Hotel). They also have excellent Chinese dishes such as fried spinach (*kangkong*) and deep-fried pigeon (*burung dara goreng*).

A convenient spot for a light lunch is the **Segar Ayem** restaurant on Jl. Secoyudan opposite Pasar Klewer (the central *batik* market), within walking distance of the *kraton*. Excellent iced fruit drinks here, with some simple Javanese dishes like *gado-gado*, *pecel* and *nasi rames*.

Another nearby luncheon spot, good for Chinese noodles of many types as well as iced fruit juices and cold beer, is **Bakso Taman Sari** on Jl. Jend. Gatot Subroto (42C) between Secoyudan and Slamet Riyadi. Another good place for Chinese noodles is **Miroso**, Jl. Imam Bonjol 10. The best *nasi padang* place is **Andalas**, on Jl. Ronggowarsito opposite and a bit to the east of the Mankunegaran Palace Hotel entrance.

Finally, you should sample the sweet coconut cream cakes sold from little carts all along Jl. Slamet Riyadi at night a local speciality called *serabi*.

SHOPPING

"Batik": Solo is known as *"Batik* City" and the three largest producers are all based here: **Batik Keris**, **Batik Semar** and **Batik Danar Hadi**. Visit their showrooms. Danar Hadi has many better quality *kain* and *batik* shirts in the US$10 to US$20 and up range. Semar aims at the mass-market, with printed *batik* dresses and shirts selling for as little as US$2. Keris is in between. For the best in Solonese *tulis* work, visit Ibu Bei Siswosugiarto (**Sidomulyo** is her label) in the south of town, where most pieces cost between US$40 and US$120. **K.R.T. Hardjonegoro**, one of Java's best-known *batik* designers also lives and has his factory here, but generally sells only through outlets in Jakarta. You might try his home though. Have a look also at the thousands of pieces for sale in **Pasar Klewer**, and wander the side streets nearby, behind the Grand Mosque, where there are several quality producers.

Batik Danar Hadi, Jl. Dr. Rajiman.
Batik Keris, Jl. Yos. Sudarso 37, Solo.
Batik Semar (factory showroom), Jl. Pasar Nongko 132, Solo.
Batik Semar (branch), Jl. Slamet Riyadi 76, Solo.
K.R.T. Hardjonegoro, Jl. Kratonan 101, Solo.
Sidomulyo (Ibu Bei Siswosugiarto), Jl. Dawung Wetan R.T. 53/54, Solo.

Antiques: Visit the **Pasar Triwindu** market first, to get an idea what is available. Many of the vendors and dealers here also have caches of antique furniture and other valuable items at home, or they can guide you around to some of the refinishing workshops in town. No obligation to buy if you go with them, though you should pay for the *becak*. But then visit the established antique shopfronts on Slamet Riyadi and Urip Sumarharjo, where all sorts of treasures are sitting gathering dust. They are a bit more reputable and less likely to sell you fakes. But still beware and bargain hard!

Eka Hartono, Jl. Dawung Tengah 11/38, Solo.
Mertojo "Sing Pellet", Jl. Kepatihan 31, Solo.
Mirah Delima, Jl. Kemasan RT XI, Solo.
Parto Art, Jl. Slamet Riyadi 103, Solo.
Singo Widodo, Jl. Urip Sumoharjo 117, Solo.
Trisno Batik & Art Shop, Jl. Bayangkara 2, Solo.

"Keris": To buy an antique *keris* dagger, visit Pak Suranto Atmosaputro, an English lecturer at the university, at his home just down a narrow alley across from the RRI radio studios on Jl. Kestalan III/21).

"Wayang" Puppets: The acknowledged centre for *wayang kulit* production in Java is the village of **Manyaran**, about 35 km (21 miles) to the south and west of Solo (take a "colt" first to Wonogiri and then change for Manyaran). Here the village head, **Pak Sukar Hadiprayitno** organises the village craftsmen and sells their wares at quite reasonable fixed prices. Smaller figures cost about US$10 to US$15 while large gunungan go for US$50 (US$100 with gold leaf). Visit his home in Kampung Kepuhsari, Manyaran.

You can also pay a visit to the workshop of **Pak Parto** in Pajang Kampung Sogaten, RT 27, RK IV) just to the west of Solo (travel out of town on the main highway for about 4 km/2.5 miles and turn left onto a dirt road just after the bridge and ask for directions).

"Gamelan": To buy a complete *gamelan* orchestra, a single instrument or just to observe these bronze metallophones being cast and forged as they have been in Indonesia for thousands of years, using hand-operated bellows, teak-wood charcoal and primitive tools, visit the *gamelan* assembly of **Pak Tentrem Sarwanto**. His family have been suppliers of instruments to the court for many generations. Located in the southeast of town: Jl. Ngepung RT 2/RK I, Semanggi, Solo.

THE PERFORMING ARTS

Taman Sriwedari on Jl. Slamet Riyadi boasts the most accomplished *wayang orang* troupe in Java.

The Taman Hiburan Bale Kambang amusement park complex, located in the north-west of the city, houses two theatres. One, the popular Sri Mulat comedy theatre, presents an ordinary fare of slapstick routines such as "Big, Bad Dracula" and "The Commercial Gigolo" nightly.

The other offers more serious **Ketoprak** folk dramas, enactments of historical tales and legends. There are also several open-air restaurants and billiards hall in the park, as well as a video hall. Shows begin nightly at 8 p.m. except Sundays (when there is a matinee beginning at 10 a.m.).

GETTING THERE

SURABAYA

Convenient air services connects Surabaya with almost all cities in Indonesia and with a **Merpati** shuttle every other hour to and from Jakarta (about US$90 one-way). Many flights heading for the northern and eastern islands also make a stopover here.

A good number of trans-Javan express trains and buses terminate or originate in Surabaya, with many immediate onward connections.

GETTING AROUND

Metered cabs are abundant in this city of more than 3 million. Private hire cars may be rented by the hour at any hotel and at the airport. The fare from the airport to the city is US$5.

City buses and mini-buses (*bemo*) circulate throughout the city, converging on the **Joyoboyo Bus Terminal** in front of the zoo. The important lines to know are those that travel north-south between here and the old section of town through the central hotel district: Jembatan Merah ("Red Bridge") Tunjungan-Joyoboyo and Jembatan Merah-Diponegoro-Joyoboyo. Fare is Rp 100. Ask at your hotel for details about other lines.

ORIENTATION

Jl. Tunjungan/Basuki Rachmat is generally regarded as the main street, running north-south, and parallel to the river.

There are three train stations: **Pasar Turi**, **Semut** (also known as **Kota**) and **Gubeng**. The last is the closest to the hotel districts, if you have a choice where to alight. The **Joyoboyo Bus Terminal** is in the south of the city, just opposite the Surabaya Zoo,

about 2 km (1 mile) south of Jl. Tunjungan. **Juanda Airport** is 15 km (9 miles) farther south, on the road to Malang and Tretes. (So if you are going straight to the mountains, you need not enter the city.) Intercity bus company offices (like **Elteha**) are around Jl. Basuki Rachmat on side-lanes like Embong Sawo.

The **Tourist Information Office** at Jl. Pemuda 118 has brochures and a "Calendar of Events" with dates for events like the fortnightly bull races on Madura (August/September) and the Ramayana Ballet performances at Pandaan (June to November).

WHERE TO STAY

ACCOMMODATION

First Class

Hyatt Regency Surabaya (US$75 a night on up, plus 21 percent tax and service) is the only five-star luxury hotel. The **Simpang**, at the corner of Jl. Tunjungan and Jl. Pemuda, costs US$64 a night (plus 21 percent). The **Mirama** and the **Ramayana** just to the south are in US$50 to US$60 range (plus 21 percent), and the **Elmi** and the **Garden**, also in the same area, have rooms for a bit less.

The older **Majapahit Hotel** on Jl. Tunjungan (formerly the "Oranje" built in 1910) is something of a historical monument. It is the site of the famous "flag incident" that sparked off the revolutionary battle for Surabaya. Air-conditioned rooms for US$40, non-air-conditioned ones for US$24, plus 21 percent).

Elmi Hotel (140 rooms), Jl. Panglima Sudirman 42-44, Surabaya, Tel: 515615.
Garden Palace (200 rooms), Jl. Yos Sudarso 11, Surabaya, Tel: 470001.
Garden Surabaya Hotel (100 rooms), Jl. Pemuda 21, Surabaya, Tel: 470000-9.
Hyatt Bumi Surabaya (269 rooms), Jl. Basuki Rachmat 124-128, Surabaya, Tel: 511234.
Majapahit Hotel (106 rooms), Jl. Tunjungan 65, P.O. Box 199, Surabaya, Tel: 43351-5.
Mirama Hotel (105 rooms), Jl. Raya Darmo 72-74, P.O. Box 232, Surabaya, Tel: 69501-9.
New Grand Park (101 rooms), Jl. Samudra 3-5, Surabaya, Tel: 331515.
Patra Jasa Motel (63 rooms), Jl. Gunung Sari, Surabaya, Tel: 68681-3.
Simpang Hotel (128 rooms), Jl. Pemuda 1-3, P.O. Box 36, Surabaya, Tel: 42150-9.

Intermediate & Budget
(under US$35 a night)

No guest-houses here. Budget travellers always stay at the **Bamboe Denn/Transito Inn**, with dorm beds for US$1, singles for US$2 and doubles for US$3. They have lots of travel information here to help you get around and they serve cheap breakfasts and snacks. For a bit more (US$6 to US$8) try **Wisma Ganeca** near Gubeng Station.

Bamboe Denn/Transito Inn, Jl. Pemuda 19, Surabaya, Tel: 40333.
Cendana Hotel (23 rooms), Jl. K.B.P.M. Duryat 6, Surabaya, Tel: 42251-2.
Lasmana Hotel (54 rooms), Jl. Bintoro 16, Surabaya, Tel: 67152.
Olympic Hotel (22 rooms), Jl. Urip Sumoharjo 65-67, Surabaya, Tel: 43215-6.
Pregolan Hotel (25 rooms), Jl. Pregolan Bunder 11-15, Surabaya, Tel: 41251-2.
Ramayana Hotel (100 rooms), Jl. Basuki Rachmat 67-69, Surabaya, Tel: 46321-9.
Royal Hotel, Jl. Panglima Sudirman 68, Surabaya, Tel: 43547-8.
Sarkies Hotel (51 rooms), Jl. Embong Malang 7-11, Surabaya, Tel: 44514, 43080, 40494, 40167.
Wisma Ganeca, Jl. Sumatra 34. A, Surabaya.

FOOD DIGEST

Surabaya is well known for its Chinese food. The **Bima Garden** (Jl. Pahlawan 102) specialises in Hong Kong style *tim sum*. The best-known banquet houses are located along the river: the **Mandarin** (Jl. Genteng Kali 93) and the **Phoenix** (Jl. Genteng Kali 15). Try also the **Hoover** in the Wijaya Shopping Centre (2nd floor), and the **Oriental**, Jl. T.A.I.S. Nasution 37. For something less pricey, go to Chinatown: **Kiet Wan Kie** at Jl. Kembang Jepun 51 and a small hole-in-the-wall opposite the New Grand Park Hotel on Jl. Samudra (excellent fish here).

For seafood, try the **Satellite Garden** down on Jl. Raya Kupang Baru 17.

The best-known Indonesian restaurant is **Bibi & Baba** right on Jl. Tunjungan 76. **Taman Sari Indah** (Jl. Taman Apsari 5), just opposite the Joko Dolog statue next to the Post Office is also very clean and good serving *pepes* and *sate*.

Most travel agents will arrange a private tour of the area for any number of people, via rented taxi or mini-bus with a guide. **Turi Express** organises excursions to Bromo and East Java's temples. The **Tourist Information Office** (Jl. Darmokali 35) will also arrange special bull races and trance dances.

SHOPPING

It is said you can buy cameras, tape recorders and portable electronic items here as cheaply as in Singapore. Try the shopping centre on Jl. Tunjungan or the new Wijaya Shopping Centre.

There is a whole string of antique and curio shops around the Hyatt on Jl. Basuki Rachmat. Also on Jl. Tunjungan (**Kundadas** at No. 97 and **Sarinah** at No. 7). Several more are located down on Jl. Raya Darmo (**Rochim** at No. 27 and **Bangun** at No. 5).

For *batik* and hand-woven cotton textiles, the area around the Sunan Ampel mosque in the middle of the Arab quarter is best.

NIGHTLIFE

ENTERTAINMENT

Javanese *wayang orang*, *ludruk* and *ketoprak* folk dramas are performed nightly at two theatres in the **People's Amusement Park** (Taman Hiburan Rakyat) on Jl. Kusuma Bangsa. There is also a hysterically funny Sri Mulat slapstick comedy troupe here featuring a whole gang of transvestites. Shows start at about 8 p.m. Tickets are cheap.

From June to November there are fortnightly (first and third Saturdays of each month) Sendratari classical Javanese dance-drama performances at the huge open-air **Candra Wilwatikta** amphitheatre in Pandaan, 45 km (28 miles) south of Surabaya on the Malang road. The Tourist Information Office can arrange an East Javanese *kuda kepang* "hobbyhorse" trance dance performance if you notify them three days in advance. Regular bull races are now held monthly in the new stadium at **Bangkalan** just across the straits of Madura. Check with the Tourist Information Office for dates.

GETTING THERE

TRETES

Tretes is only an hour south of Surabaya by very good roads. The turn-off is at Pandan and from here it's about 20 km (12 miles) up the hill to this large resort. Only about US$20 by taxi or rental mini-bus. Otherwise catch any bus or mini-bus from Surabaya headed in the direction of Malang (south) and get off at the intersection in Pandaan (fare will be only Rp 200 to 300). From here "colts" go up to Tretes (Rp 200).

WHERE TO STAY

ACCOMMODATION

The best hotel is the **Natour Bath**, with doubles starting at US$45 a night (plus 21 percent). It has a spring-fed swimming pool. The **Digahaya Indah** also has a large pool, and rooms for about US$20. You can also rent an entire bungalow for only US$20 with two or more bedrooms, and a very deluxe house could be had for US$50 a night. Walk around Tretes and inquire, most bungalows are for rent during the week.

Dirgahaya Indah (12 rooms), Jl. Ijen 5, Tretes, Tel: (0343) 81932.
Natour Bath Hotel (50 rooms), Jl. Pesanggrahan AO 2, Tretes, Tel: (0343) 81161, 81776-8.
Pelita, Jl. Wilis 19-21, Tel: (0343) 81802.
Tanjung Plaza (62 rooms), Jl. Wilis 7, Tretes,

Tel: (0343) 81102, 81173.
Tretes Raya, Jl. Malabar 166, Tretes, Tel: (0343) 81902.

MALANG

Unlike many Javanese towns which lie dead straight along a dreary, shuttered, down-at-heel main street, Malang sweeps and winds over gentle ridges and gullies along the banks of the Brantas River, with unexpected views and quiet back-streets that beg to be explored. It hasn't experienced the explosive growth of other large Javanese cities, and it remains a small, quiet town.

GETTING THERE

Although there are local 3rd-class trains running along the old tracks from Surabaya to Malang, the express "colt" taking the highway is quicker and more comfortable, and costs just US$2, it delivers you to your doorstep in Malang. Ask your hotel in Surabaya to book a seat for you. Buses also leave regularly from Surabaya's Joyoboyo bus terminal and the fare is only about US$1.

WHERE TO STAY

ACCOMMODATION

The small (36 rooms), stylish **Tugu Park Hotel** is regarded as one of the best hotels in Indonesia, and certainly is *the* place to stay in Malang. Javanese, Dutch and Chinese antiques adorn all areas of the hotel, which is close to the town centre. The colonial-style **YMCA** has huge, spotlessly clean rooms with hot water and a fan for only US$14 (including tax, service and breakfast). For a bit more, the **Splendid Inn** is very pleasant: a spacious guest-house with gardens. Air-conditioned rooms are US$20 to US$25 (including tax, service and breakfast). The old **Pelangi** facing on the town square has many large rooms for US$10 to US$18 and some cheaper ones at the back for only US$7 (including tax and service). Budget travellers stay at the **Bamboe Denn** for US$2 and can stay for free if they attend some English classes at the language school.

Tugu Park Hotel, Jl. Tugu 3, Malang, Tel: 63894, Fax: 62747.
Bamboe Denn/Transito Inn, Jl. Semeru 35, Malang, Tel: 24859.
Pelangi Hotel (74 rooms), Jl. Merdeka Selatan 3, Malang, Tel: 2004.
Santoso, Jl. H. Agus Salim 24, Malang, Tel: 23889.
Splendid Inn (23 rooms), Jl. Majapahit 2-4, Malang, Tel: 23860.
YMCA, Jl. Basuki Rachmat 68-76, Malang, Tel: 23605.

FOOD DIGEST

There's good Padang food opposite the **YMCA** at the **Minang Jaya** (Jl. Basuki Rachmat 22). Nearby is **Toko Oen's**, an old favourite which serves Dutch food like *wienerschnitsel*, *broodjes* and *uitsmijters*. For steaks and ice creams, try the new **La Vanda** ice cream parlour at Jl. Semeru 49. For Chinese food, try the **New Hongkong**, Jl. Arif Rahman Hakim.

SHOPPING

There are many antique and curio stores on Jl. Basuki Rachmat. Also try the antique section of the **Pasar Besar** market, on the second floor at the back left-hand corner. This can be a great place to buy old Dutch glasses, trays and silverware.

Just above Malang, 23 km to the west, is the hill town of **Batu** with its neighbouring colonial resort, **Selecta**. Several motels with swimming pools have been built around here, notably the large **Songgoriti** complex located on the main road some distance past

Batu. The older Dutch bungalow resort at Selecta is still very well kept, with huge suites available for only US$15.

Asida (65 rooms), Jl. Panglima Sudirman 99, Batu, Malang, Tel: 22988.
Batu Hotel, Jl. Hasanuddin 4, Batu, Malang.
Libra Bungalows, Jl. Konto 4, Batu, Malang, Tel: 64.
Palem (38 rooms), Jl Trunojoyo 26, Batu, Malang, Tel: 91917.
Palem Sari (22 rooms), Jl. Raya Punten, Batu, Malang, Tel: 92219, 91219.
Purnama (95 rooms), Jl. Raya Selecta, Batu, Malang, Tel: 92700-09.
Santoso II, Jl. Tulungrejo, Batu, Malang.
Selecta Hotel & Pool, Jl. Tulungrejo, Batu, Malang.
Songgoriti Hotel, Jl. Songgoriti, Batu, Malang.

GETTING THERE

THE NORTH COAST

CIREBON

Cirebon is about 4 hours (260 km/160 miles) overland from Jakarta, only 3 hours by road from Bandung. There is a small airport with two weekly flights from Jakarta, but trains and mini-buses are generally more convenient.

There are two air-conditioned first class trains operating on the Jakarta-Cirebon coastal route. On these, however, you must pay for a further destination just to occupy the seat as far as Cirebon. The Bima Express leaves Jakarta's Kota Station daily at 4 p.m. and arrives in Cirebon at about 8 p.m., costing US$25 one-way (the fare to Yogya). The Mutiara Utara leaves from Kota Station at 4.30 p.m. and arrives in Cirebon at 6.45 p.m., costing US$17.50 one-way (the fare to Semarang).

Two non-air-conditioned second class trains also serve Cirebon. The Gunung Jati makes two daily runs, leaving from Jakarta's Pasar Senen Station at 7 a.m. and again at 2.27 p.m. and arriving about 5 hours later. Tickets are US$4 one-way. The evening Senja Utama also departs from Jakarta's Gambir Station at 6.15 p.m. and arrives in Cirebon at 9.50 p.m. Tickets are US$7.50 each way (the fare to Yogya).

A more convenient way to go is by nine-seater "colt" mini-bus. They will fetch you in Jakarta and deliver you to your hotel in Cirebon, approximately 4 hours later. Departures are hourly 6 a.m. to 4 p.m. daily; the fare is only about US$6 each way. Some companies offer air-conditioned buses; ask your hotel to book a seat for you one or more days in advance of departure (try **Libra Express**). Mini-buses also operate Bandung-Cirebon, and on from Cirebon to Semarang via Pekalongan. You have to change in Semarang to get to or from Yogya.

Numerous eastward-bound inter-city buses leave Jakarta in the late afternoon (between 3 p.m. and 5 p.m.) from Pulo Gadung Terminal, arriving in Cirebon 4 hours later. The fare is about US$3 one-way. From Bandung's Cicaheum Terminal, buses to Cirebon generally depart in the early evening (between 6 p.m. and 8 p.m.) and arrive 2 hours later. Fare is about US$1.50.

GETTING AROUND

Everything in town is pretty much within walking distance. You can also take a pedicab (*becak*) almost anywhere for Rp 300. For trips out to Gua Sunyaragi, Trusmi and Gunung Jati, you can rent a car or "colt" from your hotel (between US$20 and US$25 per day) or simply catch one of the local mini-buses headed in that direction.

WHERE TO STAY

ACCOMMODATION

The most modern hotels in town are the Bentani and the Patrajasa. The palladian facade of the Grand Hotel is there to deceive travellers looking for a nostalgic atmosphere. The rooms are depressing and the bathrooms primitive.

First Class (over US$30 a night)
Bentani, Jl. Siliwangi 6, Tel: 23246.
Patrajasa, Jl. Tujparev 11, Tel: 29402.

Intermediate
Grand Hotel, Jl. Siliwangi 110
Cirebon Plaza Hotel, Jl. Kartini 48
Kharisma, Jl. Kartini 48

Budget
Asia, Jl. Kalibaru Selatan 15.
Priangan, Jl. Siliwangi 108.

FOOD DIGEST

Cirebon is famous for its seafood (the city's name means "shrimp river"), and the best seafood restaurant in town is **Maxim's** (Jl. Bahagia 45-7, Tel: 2679, 3185), just a short walk back along the road next to the Thay Kak Sie Chinese temple. Giant steamed crabs and prawns here are fresh and cheap. They also serve tasty Chinese food.

For spicy Padang food, there's **Sinar Budi** (Jl. Karang Getas 20, Tel: 3846) not far from the Grand Hotel, where they also serve good fresh fruit drinks.

SHOPPING

To get the best *batik*, visit **Ibu Masina's** studio in Trusmi, 12 km (7 miles) to the west of Cirebon just off the Bandung road (a small sign marking the narrow lane in Weru, turn off to the right from the main highway; it's about 1 km to the showroom and workshop). For Cirebonese *topeng* masks, visit **Pak Kandeg** at Suranenggala Lor village about 5 km (3 miles) north of Cirebon on the road to Gunung Jati. *Topeng* masks and paintings on glass incorporating Arabic calligraphy are also produced in Palimanan and Gegesik villages, north-west of Cirebon. They are also interesting villages for all sorts of local dance and theatre traditions, including the *sintren* trance ritual.

PEKALONGAN

Pekalongan is between 3 and 4 hours from Cirebon by bus or "colt". Two hours from Semarang. The best way to get around town is to walk or take a *becak*.

WHERE TO STAY

ACCOMMODATION

Intermediate
Istana Hotel (48 rooms), Jl. Gajah Mada 23-25, Pekalongan, Tel: 61581.
Nirwana Hotel (63 rooms), Jl. Dr. Wahidin 11, Pekalongan, Tel: 41691, 41446.

Budget
Gajah Mada, Jl. Gajah Mada 11A, Pekalongan.
Hayam Wuruk (56 rooms), Jl. Hayam Wuruk 152-158, Pekalongan, Tel: 41823, 21405.
Ramayana, Jl. Gajah Mada 9, Pekalongan, Tel: 21043.

FOOD DIGEST

DINING

Your best bet here is Chinese food at the **Remaja** (Jl. Dr. Cipto 20, Tel: 21019), or the **Serba Ada** (Jl. Hayam Wuruk 125). For breads, ice cream and snacks, try the **Purimas** bakery on Jl. Hayam Wuruk. There is also a cafeteria next to the *alun-alun*. **Bunani** (Jl. Tirto, 2 km out of town) offers a wide selection of seafood.

SHOPPING

BUYING BATIK

Besides the several shops on Jl. Hayam Wuruk and Jl. Hasanuddin where fabrics is sold, seek out individual *batik* makers.

Tobal Batik at Jl. Teratai 24, Klego, (Tel: 61885) specialises in export clothing. Many of the *batik* sundresses and shirts you see in boutiques in California and Australia are drawn, dyed and sewn here. While they produce to order for wholesale customers and do not normally sell individual pieces, they often have overstocks of certain items that they are happy to sell to casual visitors.

Ahmad Yahya (Jl. Pesindon 221, Tel: 41413 enter the small lane near the bridge on Jl. Hayam Wuruk, next to the Sederhana Restaurant). His fabrics have been selling in New York for many years, and have been used to decorate Jackie Onassis' bathroom and Farrah Fawcett's bedroom.

Achmad Said at Jl. Bandung 53 is another producer well known to foreigners, producing bold, brightly coloured cap fabrics under the "Zaky" label.

Salim Alaydras (Jl. H. Agus Salim 31, Tel: 41175) produces and sells some floral piece goods and has antique fabrics for sale.

For higher-quality, hand-drawn tulis work, visit **Jane Hendromartono** at Jl. Blimbing 36 (Tel: 1003). Her superb work is in the permanent collection of the Textile Museum in Washington D.C. as well as in many private collections around the world. She generally has a variety of original *sarung* and *kain* pieces ranging in price from US$25 up to US$100, as well as some Chinese altar cloths done in *batik* and several types of less-expensive *batik* cap.

Perhaps Pekalongan's most famous *batik* artist is **Oey Soe Tjoen**, who bought over and continued many of the designs of the great Eliza Van Zuylen, an Indo-Dutch woman whose rare *batik*, produced in the 1920s and 1930s, now fetch thousands of dollars from avid collectors in Holland and New York. Oey Soe Tjoen's wife and son now continue the business at their home and workshop in Kedungwuni, 9 km to the south of Pekalongan (Jl. Raya 104, Kedungwuni, located just about 200 metres before the police station on the left).

GETTING THERE

SEMARANG

From Jakarta, take the Mutiara Utara air-conditioned express train (leaves Kota Station at 4.30 p.m., reaches Semarang at 1.15 a.m., US$17.50), or catch a Merpati shuttle from Soekarno-Hatta Airport 8 daily flights, no advance bookings. Mandala also has daily flights from Jakarta, and Bouraq links Semarang with Kalimantan and Sulawesi.

To get here directly from Bandung, you have to take the bus, but from Cirebon, Pekalongan, Yogya or Solo, you can travel by more comfortable and convenient inter-city "colt" instead.

WHERE TO STAY

ACCOMMODATION

Semarang's best hotel is the **Graha Santika** in midtown, US$70. The **Patra Jasa** is located up on a hill in Candi Baru overlooking the city (US$35 to US$60 for a double, plus 21 percent tax and service). The **Candi Baru Hotel**, closer to the city but still in the hills, has spacious rooms with a view for less money (US$17 to US$28 for a double; US$40 for a suite), and in the same area, the **Green Guest-house** is a bargain at US$14 to US$18 for an air-conditioned double with breakfast (tax and service included).

Down in the centre of town, the best hotel is the **Metro Grand Park** (doubles are US$35 to US$45 plus 21 percent). The old Dutch hostelry, the **Dibya Puri**, is just across a busy intersection from here only US$25 for an air-conditioned double, with breakfast (tax and service included), but the place is looking (and smelling) a bit wilted these day. The **Queen Hotel** around the corner on Jl. Gajah Mada is a newer place and about the same price.

Budget travellers can check out some of the hotels on Jl. Imam Bonjol around the train station, like the **Dewa Asia**, the **Tanjung** and the **Singapore**, all with rooms in the US$5 to US$10 range. The **Nam Yon Hotel**, right in the middle of the Chinatown district, also has clean rooms for as little as US$4.50 a night.

WHERE TO STAY

FOOD DIGEST

HOTELS

First Class (US$50 and up a night)
Metro Grand Park (83 rooms), Jl. H. Agus Salim 2-4, Semarang, Tel: 27371-9.
Patra Jasa Hotel (147 rooms), Jl. Sisingamangaraja, P.O. Box 8, Semarang, Tel: 314441-7.
Siranda Hotel (60 rooms), Jl. Diponegoro 1, Semarang, Tel: 313271-5.
Sky Garden Motel (82 rooms), Jl. Setiabudi, Grogol, Semarang, Tel: 312733.

Intermediate (US$25-US$35 a night)
Candi Baru (23 rooms), Jl. Rinjani 21, Semarang, Tel: 315272.
Candi Indah (32 rooms), Jl. Dr. Wahidin 122, Semarang, Tel: 312515.
Dibya Puri Hotel (62 rooms), Jl. Pemuda 11, P.O. Box 562, Semarang, Tel: 27821.
Green Guest-house (20 rooms), Jl. Kesambi 7, Candi Baru, Semarang, Tel: 312528, 312787.
Merbaru Hotel (46 rooms), Jl. Pemuda 122, Semarang, Tel: 27491.
Queen Hotel (26 rooms), Jl. Gajah Mada 44, Semarang, Tel: 97603.
Telomoyo Hotel (73 rooms), Jl. Gajah Mada 138, Semarang, Tel: 20926, 25436.

Budget (under US$15 a night)
Grand (25 rooms), Jl. Plampitan 39, Semarang, Tel: 21729.
Islam (23 rooms), Jl. Pemuda 8, Smarang, Tel: 20538.
Dewa Asia (21 rooms), Jl. Imam Bonjol l, Semarang, Tel: 22547.
Nam Yon/Nendrayakti (41 rooms), Jl. Gang Pinggir 68, Semarang, Tel: 22538.
Rama Losmen (16 rooms), Jl. Plampitan 37, Semarang, Tel: 288951.
Singapore (27 rooms), Jl. Iman Bonjol 12, Semarang, Tel: 23757.
Tanjung (15 rooms), Jl. Tanjung 9-11, Semarang, Tel: 22612.

This town is famous for its Chinese food. The best Chinese restaurant is probably **Pringgading** (Jl. Pringgading 54, Tel: 288973, 27219, 27364), though the **Gajah Mada** (Jl. Gajah Mada 43, Tel: 23753) is a bit more centrally located. Also on Jl. Gajah Mada is a complex of open-air eateries known as the **Kompleks Warna Sari**, containing a wide assortment of Chinese and Indonesian restaurants. There are also many Chinese restaurants in Chinatown on **Gang Lombok**, just beside the Thay Kak Sie temple, all of them quite good.

At night, food stalls set up along both sides of Jl. **Depok** just off of Jl. Gajah Mada. This is a great place to get inexpensive seafood grilled prawns and steamed crabs, as well as barbequed chicken and a variety of other dishes.

For Sundanese grilled fish and chicken, try **Lembur Kuring** on Jl. Gajah Mada, or for sate go over to **Sate Ponorogo** (Jl. Gajah Mada 107, Tel: 20637).

The most notable restaurant in town, though, is **Toko Oen** (Jl. Pemuda 52, Tel: 21683) a holdover from colonial times, with Dutch items like *Paprika Schnitzel* and *Uitsmijter Roastbeef* and *Biefstuk Compleet* on the menu. They also have an exotic assortment of ice creams *Vruchten Sorbet*, *Cassata* and Oen's *Symphoni* as well as cakes, cookies and Chinese dishes.

CULTURE PLUS

Semarang residents are avid theatre goers, and this city boasts not one but three venues to watch nightly performances of the popular *wayang orang* and *ketoprak* There are more troupes here than in any other Javanese city!

Ngesti Pandowo, Jl. Pemuda 116.
Sri Wanito, Jl. Dr. Dipto.
Wahyu Budoyo, Kompleks Tegal Wareng, Jl. Sriwijaya.

DEMAK

To visit any of the towns east of Semarang – **Demak**, which is famous for its 16th-century mosque; **Kudus** with its old carved teakwood houses, its strange old mosque with a Hindu-Javanese minaret and its *kretek* cigarette industry; **Jepara** with its wood-working industry and **Rembang** and **Lasem** with their beautiful Chinese temples (*klenteng*) – just book a seat on a "colt" mini-bus from the Semarang central terminal on the corner of Jl. M.T. Haryono and Jl. H. Agus Salim, or alternatively you can take an eastward-bound bus at the Terminal Bis across the street.

WHERE TO STAY

ACCOMMODATION

None of these places has a first-class hotel, but the **Notosari** in Kudus is still pleasant. If you're visiting Rembang and Lasem, book a room in the **Pati**. There is also a Pesanggrahan or government resthouse in Colo, 6 km (3.5 miles) above Kudus on the slopes of Mt. Muria.

Air Mancur, Jl. Pemuda 70, Kudus.
Anna, Jl. Jend. Sudirman 36, Pati.

Duta Wisata, Jl. Sunan Muria 194, Kudus.
Kurnia, Jl. Tondonegoro 12, Pati.
Menno Jaya Inn, Jl. Diponegoro 40/B, Jepara, Tel: 143.
Mulia, Jl. Kol. Sunandar 17, Pati, Tel: 2118.
Notosari, Jl. Kepodang 17, Kudus, Tel: 21245.
Pati, Jl. Jend. Sudirman 60, Pati.
Pesanggrahan Colo/Gunung Muria, Jl. Sunan Muria, Colo, Kudus, Tel: 557 Kudus.

BANDUNGAN

The trip from Semarang to Yogyakarta is a delightful 2-hour ride which will take you over the mountains across the narrow "waist" of Java. If you have the time, spend a night halfway in the mountain resort of **Bandungan**, to see the Gedung Songo temples about 10 km (6 miles) from here. Try to get up to the temples in the early morning. They are spectacular at sunrise. There are hot springs at the end of the trail beyond the temples, so bring along your swimsuit and a towel.

GETTING THERE

Turn right at the sign in the middle of Ambarawa (or get off the bus here and wait for a mini-bus going up the hill). Bandungan is 7 km (4 miles) above Ambarawa.

WHERE TO STAY

ACCOMMODATION

There are many hotels in Bandungan at the top of the road. The **Wina** and the **Gaya** are the biggest. None are expensive – US$20 a night, with many rooms for less than US$10. The best place is the **Rawa Pening Hotel**; turn left at the top of the hill and continue out of Bandungan town for about 1 km. You will see an old colonial mansion with bungalows above it on your right. You can get a bungalow here for US$20 to US$25 a night, a double room for US$12.

ON THE WAY TO BALI

The following excursions can be made en route to Bali, or as side-trips from Bali.

Bromo: Best approach is by the 20-km road which winds up from the north coast highway at Tongas, just west of Probolinggo, through Sukapura to **Ngadisari**. Lots of "colts" make this journey and you can board one at the Tongas turnoff (fare to Ngadisari is about US30¢). From here, a cobble-stone road covers the last 3 km (2 miles) up to **Cemara Lawang** on the lip of the caldera, but special permission must be sought from the police in Ngadisari to use this road (if you have your own vehicle). Otherwise, all public transport stops at the Ngadisari parking lot and you have to walk or rent a pony for the final, steep climb. Try to get up there before sunset. It takes about 5 hours to reach the caldera's rim from Surabaya, a bit less from Tretes.

The **Bromo Permai Hotel** at Cemara Lawang sleeps 30 and usually has space available. Call the booking office in Probolinggo (Jl. Panglima Sudirman 237-242, Tel: 21510, 21983) for reservations, especially during the peak tourist seasons. The rooms are very basic, costing only US$4 to US$10 a night for a double, many without private bath. The hotel restaurant is quite adequate, serving coffee, tea, beer, eggs, toast and a few rice dishes. Temperatures can drop below freezing at night because of the altitude. The hotel supplies you with a thin blanket, but bring along extra covers and several layers of warm clothing.

Hire a pony to make the 2-hour trek down into the caldera and across the famous "Sand Sea" to the base of Bromo. From here, a flight of steps leads up to the rim of this volcano-within-a-volcano so that you can peer down into Bromo's steaming, sulphurous pit. The horsemen like to get you up at 3 a.m. and ride you across to Bromo for the sunrise, so that they get home by 9 a.m. while it is still cool, but this is a miserable cold and windy journey in pitch blackness. The view of the sunrise is better from the caldera's rim anyway, just near the hotel. So watch it from here, have breakfast, and then go down to Bromo (bring some water along, because it does get hot). The horse ride normally costs US$3 to US$5 round trip.

It is also possible to continue on from Bromo across the Sand Sea in a southerly direction to the village of **Rano Pani** (about 20 km away) and then to **Rano Kumbolo** (another 12 km away) for the climb up Mt. Semeru, Java's highest mountain (3,676 metres/12,500 feet). You'd better be well prepared for this, though, both physically and with good camping gear. There are three beautiful lakes nestling in this highland massif, amid grassy meadows and pine forests. From Rano Pani you can descend to the west via **Ngadas** and **Gubug Klakah**, from where there is a road leading down through Tumpang to Malang.

Banyuwangi: This is the capital of eastern Java's Banyuwangi regency, just 7 km (4 miles) south of the Java-Bali ferry terminal at Ketapang-the jumping-off point for visits to Ijen, Meru Betiri (Sukamade) and the Blambangan Peninsula. There are many inexpensive hotels in and around Banyuwangi, including the two-star Manyar located by the ferry in Ketapang (see listing below). You can also stay up at the hill resort of **Kaliklatak**, 15 km (9 miles) west of Banyuwangi's (see below).

Banyuwangi's **Tourist Information Office** at Jl. Diponegoro 2 (Tel: 41761) is very helpful in advising you how to reach the places mentioned below, and the **Nitour** office at Jl. Raya 43 C will arrange guided tours to fit different budgets.

Manyar Hotel (50 rooms), Jl. Situbondo, Ketapang, Banyuwangi Hotel (20 rooms), Jl. Dr. Wahidin 10, Banyuwangi, Tel: 41178.

Wisma Blambangan (18 rooms), Jl. Dr. Wahidin 4, Banyuwangi, Tel: 21598.

Ijen Plateau: The focal point for a visit here is the spectacular blue-green lake inside of the **Ijen Crater**, west and north of Banyuwangi. By the lake are many steaming fumeroles where labourers collect bright-yellow sulphur and then carry 60-kg loads of it in baskets along a steep trail to a processing plant at **Jambu**, 17 km (10.5 miles) down the mountain. It's about a 7-hour hike each way, though horses can be rented for the climb in Jambu, and if you have a sleeping bag you can stay overnight at the volcanology station at **Ungkup-Ungkup**, about an hour below the crater (it gets very cold).

Banyuwangi Selatan Reserve: The main attraction here is the huge rollers, measuring between 10 and 30 feet, that come crashing onto the western shore of the narrow Blambangan Peninsula from May to July. At **Plengkung**, surfers have constructed a few crude huts here to be able to take advantage of what is said to be one of the best surfing spots in the world.

This "surfer's camp" can be reached in three ways. The first is to charter a launch directly from Bali, which is expensive (about US$100 each way).

The second way is to go by road to the fishing village of **Grajagan** on the southern coast opposite Plengkung, and then charter a fishing boat from here for the crossing of Grajagan Bay. Grajagan is 52 km (32 miles) from Banyuwangi and can be reached by *bemo*, via Benculuk and Purwoharjo.

The third and most difficult route is to travel by motorcycle or jeep directly into the reserve as far as **Pancur**, and then to cover the last 10 km (6 miles) to the camp on foot. Pancur is 60 km from Banyuwangi, reached via Muncar and Tegallimo.

Meru Betiri Reserve: This is the most exciting nature reserve on Java, second only perhaps to Ujung Kulon. Access is via **Pesanggaran**, a village 68 km (42 miles) west and south of Banyuwangi (turn off to the south at Genteng, 35 km (22 miles) west of Banyuwangi). From Pesanggaran a 24-km (15-mile) rutted track leads west into the reserve over rickety bridges and across several river fords. At **Rajegwesi** there is a small guest-house that sleeps up to six (make prior arrangements at the PPA office in Banyuwangi).

From Rajegwesi, it is 11 km (7 miles) further to the **Sukamade Baru** coffee estate, which has a more comfortable guest-house that sleeps 30. The guest-house is several kilometres inland from **Pantai Penyu** ("Turtle Beach"), which should be visited at night to see the huge 200-kg female green and leatherback turtles laying their eggs.

ART/PHOTO CREDITS

INDEX

N & O

P

Q & R

S

T

A
B
D
E
F
G
H
I
J
a
b
c
d
e
f
g
h
i

k
l

INSIGHT GUIDES

COLORSET NUMBERS

You'll find the colorset number on the spine of each Insight Guide.